PRAISE FOR *THE HOUR OF S*

"This moving memoir vividly portrays aspects of Palestinian life rarely encountered by the English reader: childhood under occupation in Jerusalem's Muslim Quarter, the hidden world of Arab security prisoners in Israeli jails, and the stories of Palestinians struggling to transform their oppressive reality through dialogue, nonviolence and cultivation of a shared vision of the future with Israeli Jews. Sami Al Jundi's story, with its triumphs and tragedy, should be required reading for those who ask, 'Where are the Palestinian peace activists?'"

—Mohammed Abu-Nimer, Professor of International Peace and Conflict Resolution at the American University and Director
ititute

"This book is the most auth
ordeal that I have ever read.
deep understanding of the I
of Palestinian and Israeli societies."

il
in a
ric

—Akiva Eldar, chief political columnist, *Ha'aretz,* and co-author of *Lords of the Land*

"Both nuanced and realistic, its soaring prose is to be savored by everyone who wonders whether enduring peace can be built. This is a true story, missed by the media."

—Mary Elizabeth King, author of *A Quiet Revolution*

"In fiercely compelli
rowing and redempt
and historical silenc
Hour of Sunlight. Th
soldiers and militant
and Palestinians and
masterly, the story ri
—Car

da
he
ts,
lis

r of
our

"I expected this book to be illuminating, but I didn't know it would be so enthralling. Co-authors Sami Al Jundi and Jen Marlowe offer a beautifully written, insightful account of Al Jundi's childhood as a Palestinian in Jerusalem, his teenage radicalization, his years in Israeli prisons, and his later embrace of nonviolence. *The Hour of Sunlight* is a refreshingly frank and utterly gripping chronicle of Al Jundi's personal journey that also grapples with the broader social and political developments that make his story so vital."

—Joanne Mariner, Director of Human Rights Watch's
Terrorism and Counterterrorism Program

"This is a fascinating, beautiful, unforgettable memoir. After the romance of insurrection and the school of long years in prison, Sami Al Jundi embarked on perhaps the most revolutionary path of all: a courageous confrontation with the deepest prejudices of both his own Palestinian society and that of Israel, challenging both peoples to recognize the equal humanity of the other. In so doing, he shows us the path to a resolution of this seemingly endless conflict."

—Roane Carey, editor of *The Other Israel* and *The New Intifada*

"*The Hour of Sunlight* fills an important void in our understanding of entrenched international conflicts by detailing the rare process whereby an extraordinary person develops deep empathy and compassion for an enemy, and then goes one step further to work on the ground to advance peace. The book demonstrates the thinking and leadership qualities that are necessary to resolve the Arab-Israeli conflict."

—Peter Weinberger, United States Institute of Peace

The Hour of Sunlight

ALSO BY JEN MARLOWE

Darfur Diaries (with Adam Shapiro and Aisha Bain)

The Hour of Sunlight

One Palestinian's Journey
from Prisoner to Peacemaker

SAMI AL JUNDI
AND JEN MARLOWE

NATION
BOOKS
New York

17⁰⁰
4/11

Published by Nation Books,
A Member of the Perseus Books Group
116 East 16th Street, 8th Floor
New York, NY 10003

Excerpt from "On This Earth" by Mahmoud Darwish, from the collection *Unfortunately, It Was
Paradise,* reprinted by permission of the University of California Press. Excerpt from the poem
"Identity Card" by Mahmoud Darwish kindly granted by its English translator, Dr. John Asfour.

Designed by Jeff Williams

Library of Congress Cataloging-in-Publication Data
Jundi, Sami al, 1962–
    The hour of sunlight : one palestinian's journey from prisoner to peacemaker / by Sami Al Jundi
and Jen Marlowe.
        p. cm.
    Includes bibliographical references.
    ISBN 978-1-56858-448-5 (alk. paper)
    1. Jundi, Sami al, 1962– . 2. Palestinian Arabs—Israel—Biography. 3. Prisoners—Israel—
Biography. 4. Pacifists—Biography. 5. Arab-Israeli conflict—Influence. I. Marlowe, Jen. II. Title.

DS113.7.J86 2010
956.9405'4—dc22
[B]
                                                                            2010029340I

E-book ISBN 978-1-56858-631-1

10 9 8 7 6 5 4 3 2 1

This book is dedicated to those we have loved and lost:

To Sami's mother, Myassar Al Jundi, known as Um Samir by most, called *Yamma* by Sami and his siblings, and to the people of Zakariyya, known by her true name—Yusra.

To Sami's brother Azzam Al Jundi, who always reminded us to laugh, especially at ourselves.

To Alma Rous Lazarus, who we never met, but whose loss we feel deeply.

To our friend Aseel Asleh, in whose memory we pledge to continue our struggle for peace with justice.

This book is also dedicated to the children in our own lives whom we love deeply: Nasser, Asala, Yazan, Mera, Emil, Renée, Alex, and Maya. We hope you will have a chance to meet someday. Your future is why this book was written.

Al Jundi kids enjoying a snowy day in Jerusalem circa 1972. Order from left to right: Sami, Samir, Riyyad, Azzam, Samira. *Courtesy of Sami Al Jundi.*

We have on this earth what makes life worth living:
the final days of September, a woman keeping her apricots ripe
after forty, the hour of sunlight in prison, a cloud reflecting
a swarm of creatures, the people's applause for those who
face death with a smile, a tyrant's fear of songs.

Mahmoud Darwish, from "On This Earth"
Translated by Carolyn Forché and Munir Akash

CONTENTS

AUTHORS' NOTE

The Hour of Sunlight is Sami Al Jundi's life story. Dialogue and details have been reconstructed; however, the memoir expresses with full honesty the essence of Sami's life experiences. In chapters where the events were lived jointly by the authors, both authors' memories and experiences are intertwined. We recognize that memory can be like mercury; difficult to pin down.

Some names have been changed, either because they could not be recalled, to protect someone's privacy/identity, or because of a request from the person being written about. In some cases, composite characters were created, as the number of different people to identify and remember would have been difficult for a reader. This is particularly true during the chapters dealing with Sami's ten years in Israeli prison, but is also true in other instances. For example, a few of Sami's earlier childhood stories occurred with various friends; these stories have been all attributed to Sami's two closest friends. Some aspects of Sami's life we have not revealed in this book, in order to protect those he cares about.

We have retained the use of many Arabic words, whenever it felt appropriate to the tone of the narrative. The first time an Arabic word is encountered in the text, there is a footnote defining it. If the word is used again, it is defined in the glossary. The transliteration of the Arabic words is based on colloquial Palestinian Arabic and does not follow standard literary Arabic transliteration. This choice was made to facilitate understanding for a general readership.

How to name places is always contentious, as the politics of naming has much to do with the politics of control over those locations. For example, the city where Sami was born is called *Al Quds* in Arabic, *Yerushalayim* in

Hebrew, and *Jerusalem* in English. Generally, we named places the way Sami speaks about them—in Arabic. There are, however, some exceptions to that. Because certain English place-names contain resonance for English-speaking readers, such as *Jerusalem, Hebron,* and *Nazareth,* we chose to keep those names (and a few others) in English, rather than using the Arabic *Al Quds, Al-Khalil,* and *Nasra.* Occasionally, the Hebrew name of a city or town is also used. We made this choice when Sami was referring to the location in the context of it being the home of an Israeli friend. This is by no means meant to abdicate the Palestinian connection or claim to any place, but is rather an effort to respect how the person mentioned in the passage calls his or her home.

Sami Al Jundi
Jen Marlowe

INTRODUCTION

SAMI AL JUNDI WALKS THROUGH the cobblestone streets of the Old City in Jerusalem, greeting passersby.

"Sami! How are you?" an elderly man says in Arabic, shaking his hand vigorously.

"He was my cell mate in Asqalan prison," Sami tells me after the man continues on his way. "He taught a course about world revolutions."

"*Habibna! Salaam!*" Sami calls out warmly to another man across the road buying falafel. "That one is in my poetry writing group. We are meeting tomorrow night at the Palestinian National Theatre."

Sami's cell phone rings as we move inside the coffee shop to work on the chapter about his blind mother's childhood, fleeing from her village as a little girl during the war of 1948.

"Yoel! Shalom!" Sami greets the caller in Hebrew and then covers the mouthpiece of the phone and whispers to me apologetically, "Sorry, Jen, this is my old friend Yoel who was in my Israeli-Palestinian dialogue group. . . . He is inviting us to lunch at his home this Shabbat. . . ."

I have never known anyone like Sami Al Jundi.

I first met Sami in June 2000, when I began working at the Seeds of Peace Center for Coexistence in Jerusalem. Sami and Ned Lazarus had cofounded the Seeds of Peace Middle East follow-up program in 1996. They picked me up at the Jerusalem Central Bus Station in Al Buraq—Sami's battered blue Ford Transit that had been their primary source of bringing Israeli and Palestinian youth together for the past four years.

We went straight to work that afternoon, organizing a dizzying array of activities for the summer program. It was two months before the Camp David final status talks of the Oslo Accords would fail, and less than four months before the Second Intifada would erupt. But sitting with Sami, Ned, and the rest of the staff at the Seeds of Peace Center for Coexistence, working out program plans, I had no idea how precarious the peace process actually was, or how all we were doing would soon be rendered impossible.

As I watched Sami coordinate logistics and transportation, dispatching his brothers all over the country to bring Israeli and Palestinian youth to the Center to work together on art, drama, and photography projects, I certainly did not yet realize what an extraordinary human being my new colleague was. I got some inkling of it from the hours I spent driving with Sami in the Ford Transit. But it was only starting in 2007, when Sami and I first began work on this book, recording in detail his earliest memories, discussing in depth his beliefs and passions, that I gained a full appreciation for my friend and his inspiring journey of perseverance and personal transformation.

Perhaps the most extraordinary thing about Sami is his unshakeable belief that not only is it possible for Israelis and Palestinians to live together on this land, but that both peoples would benefit from the presence of and relationship with the other. Sami passionately believes that the only way forward is to work jointly, Israelis and Palestinians together, to end the occupation and all forms of violence. Basil Liddell Hart, British military historian and general, wrote that the best way to vanquish your enemy is to disarm him. The most effective way to disarm your enemy, according to Sami, is to turn your enemy into your friend.

During his decade in Israeli prison, Sami found a book about Mahatma Gandhi. He read an anecdote about a Hindu man who murdered a Muslim baby and came to Gandhi repentant, expecting to burn in hell. The punishment Gandhi issued? The Hindu man must adopt a Muslim orphan and raise him as his own for twenty years, providing him with an Islamic education. Twenty years . . . It took twenty years to build a life, Sami reflected, but only seconds to destroy one. The foundation of Sami's vision for the future rests on one basic premise: it is better for all of our children if every child's needs and rights are secured. The solution is not nearly as complicated as everyone claims: a full end to the occupation, and full normalization of relations. Palestinians will experience independence with dignity and honor and Israelis will experience security. Sami's life work has been to build the people who are ready to take this step. He knows from years of experience that it is hard, painful work. But the alternative is far more agonizing.

There will be those who vehemently disagree with Sami, either with his view about the interconnection between humankind (which he calls "the human being circle") or with his suggestion for a solution to the conflict (one confederation, with equal rights for all people). There will be those who object to his description of the brutality he experienced at the hands of Israeli security officials, and others who will be made uncomfortable by his description of the violence and hypocrisy he witnessed at the hands of fellow Palestinians. Sami makes no attempt to soften any piece of his life story or worldview. He is not hesitant to state that which may not be politically expedient. Sami tells his story with honesty, humor, pain, and, ultimately, compassion for all Palestinians and Israelis.

"I am ready to live with my family in a small tent, if it means that everyone else has their own tent," Sami said to me once. "It will be better than prison."

Sami's ultimate dream is for his children, together with the children of his many Israeli friends, to be able to play together in the sunlight every hour that it shines. May this book assist, in some small way, in the realization of that goal.

Jen Marlowe
Seattle, 2010

CHAPTER ONE

❧

THE SUN WAS JUST BEGINNING TO RISE, but I was already sweating. It was going to be a hot day, even for August. One by one, the ten workers climbed into my blue Ford Transit, greeting me warmly. Wassef handed me a bunch of juicy grapes.

"These grapes are from today?" I asked with appreciation.

"I cut them from the vine just half an hour ago," Wassef replied as I began to drive away. He reached over and touched my shoulder. "You know, Sami, you deserve better! Stop the car!"

"Why?"

"Just stop the car!"

I did, confused. Wassef slid open the door and jumped out. He leapt over a low stone wall and returned with a bunch of grapes still perspiring with dew. He held them up. "You will eat grapes from the moment, not from the morning!"

"Did you just take someone's grapes?"

He laughed. "Don't worry. These belong to my brother, Karim. He'll be thrilled to have given you grapes." *Karim* means generous. His brother had been aptly named.

The drive from Halhoul to the city of Asqalan began. I had spent more than four years of my life in Asqalan but had not seen anything outside of the prison walls. My passengers saw very little of the city as well, aside from the stones they lifted and the concrete they mixed. Abu Hussein tore a chunk of the round *taboun** bread for everyone, still warm from his wife's clay oven. "It's from your sister, Um Hussein," he said as he handed me a piece. I knew

---

*Flatbread.

Um Hussein must have risen before dawn to mix the flour and knead the dough in order to bake it before the morning prayers. Issa passed around a bottle of cold water. I popped in a cassette of the Egyptian singer Sheikh Imam. They called him "Sheikh" out of respect because he was old and blind and had been a scholar of Qur'an in his youth. His music wasn't religious, however, but political. Sheikh Imam sang about revolution and love for ordinary people and the simple life. We sang along, all of us eating grapes from the moment.

The Israeli checkpoint was half a mile ahead of us. I shut off the music as tension seeped into the van. I veered my Transit off the road, joining a line of old, dilapidated cars and vans heading west, creeping around rocks and trees on a path in the Hebron hills that scarcely existed, all of them filled with Palestinians going to work inside the Green Line,* none of whom had permits from the Israeli army to be there. We bounced and jolted our way over rocks and bushes past Nuba and Beit Ulla villages in order to bypass the checkpoint. It was illegal, according to Israeli law, and it was dangerous, but what choice did we have? We had the right to work to feed our families. Military jeeps regularly patrolled the area. If we were stopped, my Transit would be taken to the checkpoint. The workers would be forced to squat in the punishing sun all day with their hands on top of their heads, released in the evening to return home dehydrated, humiliated, and without the day's wages. As a Jerusalem resident, I would not be detained; however, I would be fined hundreds of shekels. But it was difficult for the patrolling jeeps to catch us. In 1995, there were multiple routes through the mountains and we knew them all.

My Transit crawled forward. The mountain way met the road just past Kharas village. We drew a collective sigh of relief as I guided the van back onto the asphalt. We had safely crossed the Green Line and were back on the main road to Asqalan. We joked and sang once more, consuming the remainder of the warm bread and fresh grapes.

The rocky landscape covered with olive trees became fields of grass, groves of fruit trees, and one bizarre orchard of enormous satellite dishes, fenced off with chain link and topped with barbed wire. The Ford Transit sailed along, heading west toward the Mediterranean. I scarcely had to steer. My van knew the way.

---

* The Green Line refers to the 1949 armistice lines demarcating the border between Israel and the West Bank.

Through the grape orchard, I could make out the minaret of the old Zakariyya mosque rising above the houses. The hills on the other side of the road, also part of Zakariyya's rich, fertile land, were covered with pine trees. This was my mother's village.

A large rope lay ahead in the road. Suddenly it began twisting and turning. It was a snake, crossing from the forest to the grapevines. Wassef stood up and shouted excitedly, "Get the snake, Sami! Run him over! Aim at his head; we can smash him! *Yallah,* * Sami, quickly!" Everyone pressed toward the front of the van, their heads and hands filling the reflection in the rearview mirror.

My eyes flicked to the tree-covered hill where the snake had come from. In 1948, my mother was a little girl huddled under those trees with her brothers and her granny, peering through the grapevines to the homes they had just fled, afraid for their lives. I slammed on the brakes of the Transit, jolting the excited workers. The snake slithered past the front tires, which had been but an inch away from crushing its head.

My passengers slumped back into their seats in disappointment. "It's just a snake, Sami. Why won't you run over it?"

I watched the snake languidly continue toward the grapevines.

"There are three reasons why I didn't kill this snake. Maybe he is exactly like us, leaving his home early in the morning in order to feed his family."

"And the second reason, Sami?"

"This is my mother's village. The nature in this area—the trees, the rocks, this snake—is almost all that remains. This snake may have been a witness to what happened in 1948. He is a connection to the people of Zakariyya, one of the only souls still protecting this village. If someone kills this snake, it won't be me."

I then told my passengers everything that I myself had only recently learned.

I have always known that my mother was from Zakariyya and my father was from Deir Yassin. Zakariyya is an ancient village; it can be spotted on a mosaic map dating back to Roman rule, when it was called Caper Zacharia. I heard stories about life in Zakariyya regularly when we visited my mother's relatives in Dheisheh refugee camp in Bethlehem. The memories of their homes were still fresh and their descriptions vivid. I could almost smell the

---

* "Let's go!" or "Come on!" in Arabic.

lemon trees in their yards. But when the stories turned to the *Nakba*,* their voices grew dim and their eyes glazed over. I never pressed for details. In prison, I had studied maps of historic Palestine, learning the names and locations of the more than four hundred destroyed villages.** I had identified Zakariyya on the map then, later seeing Zekharya on an Israeli road map. Like so many of our places, the Israelis had Hebraized the original Arabic name. Zekharya was now an Israeli *moshav*.***

A few years after I was released from prison, I began transporting workers from Halhoul to Asqalan. I drove past Zakariyya daily, but I never entered. My instinct told me I would not be welcome. But one day, after I dropped the workers off in Asqalan, my curiosity won over my trepidation. I had to know what it felt like to step on the land of my native village.

I steered the Transit off the main road. How could I explain what I was doing there should I be asked? It would not be wise to tell the current residents that I had roots in this village. But I did not want to be treated as a visitor merely passing through.

I located the mosque easily, though it was deep inside the *moshav*. A house from the original village was next to it that I guessed had once belonged to my extended family, the Adawis. It appeared that an Israeli family was now living in the house. I parked the Transit next to the chain-link fence surrounding the abandoned mosque and shut off the engine. The mosque was in a state of decay; stones were missing from the base of the minaret as if someone had taken a large, jagged bite out of it. According to the legend I had often heard from the old people in Dheisheh, the Israelis had tried unsuccessfully to topple the minaret, using bulldozers. A Palestinian was brought to drive the bulldozer for the final attempt. In the middle of the operation, his arm became paralyzed. He jumped out of the bulldozer and ran away. So the minaret remained, damaged, but standing tall and proud. I placed my hand on its warm stones. This mosque, one of the only remaining original buildings, was Zakariyya. The old Zakariyya. The real Zakariyya.

I brooded for the rest of the drive. Many Palestinians had remained in their villages inside the Green Line after 1948. Why had the people of Zakariyya fled from the tranquility of the old mosque?

---

*"Catastrophe"; used to describe the 1948 war.

**The exact number of destroyed villages varies according to source.

***An Israeli community; similar to a village.

My mother knew immediately that something was wrong when I arrived home that night. She took her fingers off the large Braille book she had been reading and placed them on my face, deciphering my mood.

"You are angry, Sami. What is wrong?"

"I went to Zakariyya today."

"Ahhh, did you, my son?" She removed her fingers from my cheeks and pressed them together. "How was it there?"

My anger boiled over. "How could you have left that beautiful village? Tell me!"

"*Ya* Sami, I wasn't more than thirteen years old, just a small girl!"

"Damn your father then, and all his generation!"

My mother was shocked. "No, no, my son! You mustn't say that! Your grandfather was a hero. And he is a *shaheed*.* The British killed him in 1939, long before the *Nakba*."

A *shaheed*? From the British? I had not known that. My temper eased. I sank down on the couch next to my mother. "How was he killed? What happened to Zakariyya?" I suddenly realized that I knew almost nothing of the personal history of the woman who had raised my eight brothers and sisters and me. "What is your story, *Yamma*?"**

My mother closed her book. She turned to face me on the couch. Running her fingertips over my face one more time to satisfy herself that I was no longer angry, she took my hands in hers and began talking.

"My mother and father went from Zakariyya to Yaffa before I was born so that my father, Ahmad Adawi, could find work. He got a job in the harbor. I was born in Yaffa in 1934. When I was nine months old, my mother was pregnant with my little brother, your uncle Mustafa. One day, she had a craving for *taboun* bread. Our neighbor had a clay *taboun* oven outside her home and baked the flatbread daily. My mother lifted me in her arms to go ask them for a piece of *taboun*. The neighbor woman held me as my mother satisfied her craving. 'Look at this precious little girl with such gorgeous green eyes!' the neighbor exclaimed. 'What a perfect little baby!' She turned to my mother. 'May God give you a son with beautiful, perfect eyes like your baby girl's!' My mother took me home, and almost immediately I began to rub and scratch my eyes. My mother did everything she could to soothe them, but nothing worked. I scratched them even more vigorously as the hours

*Martyr.

**"Mom," or "Mama."

passed and my eyes soon became very red. The next day, my parents brought me to Jerusalem to see the famous eye doctor, Dr. Ticco.

"Dr. Ticco examined me right away, but my eyes were so red, he could not even see inside them. He was angry at my parents. 'Did you wait until the baby lost her sight before you brought her to me?'

"'The irritation did not begin until yesterday afternoon!' my mother explained.

"Dr. Ticco put down his examination tools. 'It is too late for me to do anything. One eye is already gone. The second one will follow shortly. I am very sorry.' Dr. Ticco's prediction came true. Within a week, I was fully blind. My mother felt sure it was connected to the neighbor woman's effusive praise. Her baby daughter had become a victim of the evil eye.

"I lived in Yaffa with my mother, my little brother Mustafa, and my baby brother Mousa. My father was deeply involved with the Arab Revolt resisting British colonialism and Jewish immigration to Palestine. It began with a general strike in 1936. Fighting intensified in 1937. My father returned to Zakariyya and became a field commander in the area.

"One morning, early in 1939, my father was getting ready to leave home. 'What should I prepare for your lunch?' his mother, my granny, asked him.

"'Would you cook *waraq dawali*?* I'm longing to eat *waraq dawali.*'

"My granny spent all day preparing the meal. She picked dozens of grape leaves off the vine and boiled them. She mixed rice with minced lamb meat, placing a small ball of the mixture in the center of each leaf, wrapping it snugly, and layered the leaves in a large pot with tomato slices and garlic. She simmered it all together in water.

"Lunchtime came and went and my father was not home. Granny removed the pot from the fire so the food would not dry out. He still did not return. She sat outside the home, watching anxiously for him to appear. The grape leaves remained untouched. As the shadows began to lengthen, she saw several young men approach the house. Even from a distance, she could tell her son was not with them.

"'*Um Ahmad*,** they said when they arrived, lowering their heads in respect, 'we have very bad news for you.' They told her about the attack the Palestinian fighters had launched from the mountain against British military vehicles in the valley below. My father led the charge. He was shot in the

---

*Stuffed grape leaves.

**"Mother of Ahmad." In Arabic, parents are usually called "Mother of . . ." or "Father (Abu) of . . ." the firstborn son.

heart. The fighters aborted the attack and rushed to save their commander. It was too late. He died in the battlefield. 'Abu Mustafa was very brave and noble,' they told Granny. 'Allah *yerhamo*.'*

"My father's comrades had to bury his body in the village quickly before the British came to look for it. If the British found the grave, they would know the identity of the *shaheed*. They would punish our family as revenge, beating our men and jailing or killing our youth. Perhaps they would remove my father's remains, fearing that his grave would become a symbol of the revolution against them. Every night for three nights, the British came and searched for my father's body. And every night for three nights, my father's comrades moved his remains to a new spot. On the fourth night, my father's friends buried him in a small cavernous opening under the doorway of his uncle's house. They planted a fig tree to conceal the opening. They told no one he was there until long after the British stopped searching. The fig tree grew on top of my father, giving fruit.

"I was only five years old. Mustafa was three and Mousa was a baby. My father had been in Zakariyya most of my life. I scarcely knew him. My mother, a young woman of only twenty-two years, went to her family so they could find another husband for her. My father's brothers came and took Mousa, Mustafa, and me from Yaffa back to Zakariyya. My granny took care of us from that point on.

"My mother soon remarried, someone also from Zakariyya. We saw her regularly, but because she was starting a new family with her new husband, we continued to stay with Granny.

"Granny was very, very kind. She took special care of me. When she bathed me in the evenings, she spoke to me in a voice full of love. 'Look at this pretty little girl,' she said as she scrubbed me clean. 'Just like a beautiful doll!'

"Life in the village was wonderful and simple. People were connected to each other, sharing the social life and the resources. The Adawi family had plentiful land, so neighbors with less would plant fruit and vegetables on our fields, giving us some of their yield as payment. We ate what we planted, supplemented by lamb or chicken that we raised. We cooked on a wood stove. We ate *maqlubeh*,** *mjadarah*,*** bread with olive oil, and *za'atar*.‡ We ate

---

*"God have mercy on him"; said when someone has died.

**Palestinian specialty made with chicken, rice, and fried vegetables such as cauliflower or eggplant; literally means "upside down" because of how it is served.

***Palestinian dish made with rice, lentils, and fried onion.

‡Dried, wild thyme.

wild *khubezzeh** that we collected. But not *waraq dawali*. My granny never prepared it again.

"My little brothers went to the village school with the other boys and girls, but the school had no ability to teach a blind girl, so I stayed at home and helped my granny. I was a very good help to her. If the eye of the gas lamp became clogged, Granny gave me the needle to open it. It astonished everybody that I could do this better than anyone with working eyes. Afterward, I would thread the needle and help my granny sew!

"After school, Mustafa and Mousa made a ball from rolled-up sheets and played soccer with the other boys. Or they built stone towers and had a contest to see who could knock them down from the farthest distance. The girls played with me. We chased each other in circles as one girl sat in the middle. Usually they let me sit in the middle. In the harvest season, we all picked olives.

"I was thirteen years old in 1948. The fighting had not yet come to Zakariyya, but we heard stories of what was happening all over Palestine. People who fled from other villages took shelter with us. We shared our food with them. They were very grateful. 'I hope God will let you remain here always,' they would say. But God did not allow this.

"Egyptian soldiers were defending our area, but they couldn't really be called an army. Just a few soldiers with an officer stationed at the monastery in Beit Jamal, about a mile and a half from Zakariyya. Beit Jamal fell very quickly to the Jewish militias.

"Late one night in October I heard an airplane fly overhead, circling many times. In the morning, the village was abuzz. Everyone was talking about the Jews.** My younger brother Mustafa ran into our house. 'Look at this!' he shouted in excitement. He handed my granny a small piece of paper, which she passed to Mousa and then to me. I stroked the front and the back, but I could not see what was on it.

"'They dropped these from the plane,' Mustafa told me. 'Hundreds of them! The papers are warning us to leave the village, or they will do to us what they did to the people in Deir Yassin!'

---

*A wild leaf, similar to spinach, and a good source of nutrition for the poor.

**Before 1948 the term *Jews* meant either Jewish residents and immigrants of the British Mandate of Palestine or members of one of the pre–Israeli state paramilitary organizations, such as Haganah, which became the IDF forces in 1948. Since 1948, the terms *Jews* and *Israelis* often have been used interchangeably.

"A chill went up my spine. We knew about the massacre in Deir Yassin. Over one hundred villagers had been killed there by Jewish paramilitary groups six months earlier, on April 9. Granny told us to stay in the house and went to talk to other adults in the village. She returned just as a shrieking whistle pierced the air, followed by an explosion. Fear and worry vibrated from Granny's entire body. She began to put bread and fruit and cheese inside a basket.

"'Let's go, children!' she called out to us. 'Mustafa, take this.' She handed him a jug of water. 'Yusra, you hold on to Mousa's hand.'

"'Are we going on a picnic, Granny?'

"'Yes, a picnic. Now come!'

"I was excited to go on a picnic. But as we walked with other villagers, there were more explosions around us. I could taste the people's fear. Granny held the basket of food, Mustafa carried the jug of water, and I clutched onto the hand of my little Mousa.

"'Where are we going?'

"'With everyone.'

"'But where is everyone going?'

"'Wherever we can go. What can we do? We have no way to protect ourselves in the village if they come like they did in Deir Yassin.'

"We walked through the olive trees and continued until the village and the explosions were far behind us and a steep hill was in front of us. Children, young women, old people—everyone began climbing the hill. Most of the young men stayed behind to try and guard the village. We struggled to the top. Everybody began settling under the pine trees. Granny found one for us to rest under.

"'I can see the minaret of our mosque,' Mustafa said to me. 'It's far, but I can still see it.'

"We sat for one, two, three hours, waiting to see what would happen. Granny opened the basket and gave each of us a small serving of bread, cheese, and fruit. She passed the jug of water to each of us.

"'Just one small sip of water each,' she instructed.

"'But Granny, I'm very thirsty!' I said.

"'I know, my child, but we must make it last,' she said. We sat for another hour as mortars coming from the direction of Beit Jamal exploded on Zakariyya. The shelling was intensifying. An old woman sitting under the tree behind us began wailing. 'My son! My son is still in the village!' Mousa shook with each explosion. I held him tightly on my lap, trying to control my own trembling.

"The shelling continued nonstop. Many women who had sons or husbands in the village were crying. Prayers coming from the mouths of the old people surrounded me. I held on to Mousa without speaking. The sun grew low in the sky and cold began to seep into my bones.

"'Surely we won't be spending the night here, with no blankets?' I said to my granny.

"'What shall we do? We don't have anywhere else to go,' Granny answered. 'If we wait long enough, perhaps the Jews will finish their shelling and we can go back home.'

"The night grew darker and colder. We huddled against each other for warmth. Little Mousa buried his face in my lap, trying to muffle the sound of his sobs, *ya maskeen.** I did my best to comfort him, stroking his hair and back. Morning finally came and with it the warmth of the rising sun. But just as Granny was dividing the last of the provisions, a terrifying rumor began to circulate, passed from tree to tree. Jewish soldiers had captured three men, a woman, and a small boy from Zakariyya. They took them to Beit Jamal. After holding them there for several hours, they slit the throats of the three men and then let the woman and the child go.**

"We could stay no longer. There were no belongings to gather this time. We didn't even have the food and water to carry anymore. We all walked southeast toward Hebron, hungry, thirsty, and exhausted. I was nearly stumbling with fatigue when we reached the area of Beit Ulla and Nuba villages."

I jumped a little as the names pricked my brain. Beit Ulla. Nuba. This was the exact area of the mountain path I navigated every day to bypass the checkpoint! My mother did not notice my reaction. She continued her story.

"We were too exhausted to go farther. We collapsed shivering under the trees. We remained there for a week, not knowing where to go or what to do. Believe me, *ya* Sami, I cannot imagine how we survived. No food, no shelter. After a week we continued walking and reached a village called Sa'ir, just next to Hebron. Granny gathered Mustafa, Mousa, and me under a fig tree. A woman came out of a nearby house. I thought she was going to offer us something to eat and a place to lay our heads. Instead she shouted at us, 'Get out of here! Move!'

---

*"Poor thing."

**The surviving woman (Adeeba) and the small boy (Fayez) are still alive as of 2010 and live in Ramallah.

"My granny began to cry. She had been so strong when it came to walking, having no food, nothing to protect us from the cold. But being treated so rudely . . . this was more than she could bear.

"My granny's cousin, Uncle Ahmad, found us squatting under the tree. 'What do you think about returning to the village?' he asked her.

"'How can we go back?' Granny responded.

"'We've been wandering for almost two weeks now, moving from this spot to that spot. We have no food. We are sleeping under trees. What other option do we have? I am old and my wife is old. You are with little children. The Jews will see we are helpless. They won't kill us. Let's go back.'

"My granny lightly touched our faces. 'All right,' she said to Uncle Ahmad. 'We'll go back.'

"In the morning, we began walking once again. Uncle Ahmad and his wife, Baddo, were on their donkey, my granny and the rest of us on foot. We walked until evening, when we reached the village of Kharas."

"Kharas," I interjected, nodding. "Kharas is where the mountain way meets the road."

My mother clapped her hands together, not noticing the interruption. "Uncle Ahmad reached the first house in the village. He pleaded with the owner, 'Please, let us sleep with you tonight. First thing in the morning, we will continue on our way.'

"The man looked at us, a collection of old people and small children. 'You are welcome to stay here,' he told us. 'Come inside the house. Sit with me.' We did. He was a very good man—he brought us food. We were so very hungry!"

My mother paused for a moment with a smile. "He brought us bread, olives, yogurt. This was what he had. We ate . . . and we ate . . . and we ate. We ate until we were satisfied. The man gave us a small room to sleep in. He did not have mattresses or blankets for us, but the room was warm and dry. I fell asleep almost before I lay down. Granny woke us in the morning. 'It's time to go,' Granny said and we began walking again. In the afternoon, we reached the trees we had hid under when we first left the village. We sat under the same trees again. The grown-ups decided that we should wait until evening. They didn't want the Jews to see us when we entered the village.

"After the sun set, we resumed walking. We made our way through the fields. It was harvest time, and the soil in the fields had been plowed upside down. The earth was full of bumps and holes. I would walk and fall, get up to take a few more steps, trip, and fall again. Thorns pierced my hands and my face. But it was better to walk and fall down than to be in plain view on the road. We were afraid of the soldiers.

"We arrived to the village late in the night and everyone went to his own home. I had never been so happy to reach any place in my life. In the morning, my granny told Mustafa and me to go and inform the *mukhtar** that we were back.

"We found him outside his house, surveying the skies to see if there were any planes in sight. 'Uncle,' I said to him, 'we returned last night and we want to stay.'

"He nodded. Many others had also returned. 'Tell your granny to put a white sheet on the roof.'

"As Granny was hanging the sheet, I felt a warm tongue lick my hand. It was our neighbor's dog. They had fled and, unlike us, had not returned.

"'Please, Granny, can I keep it?' I begged. Granny agreed. The little dog became my best friend. He led me all over the village. He was my eyes.

"My mother and her new family were gone. I did not know where she was. I missed her terribly. One month passed, then two months. The winter was harsh that year, covering Zakariyya with snow. I had never felt or tasted snow before. Three months passed. Then four. Jewish soldiers came regularly to the village. I was afraid of them and afraid of their guns, but they never spoke to me.

"After a year, bandits began to arrive in Zakariyya in the middle of the night. They burst into people's homes with sticks and clubs and began beating the young men. Night after night they returned, threatening people that soon worse would come. No one knew who these attackers were. They looked Arab and spoke Arabic. There were Arabs who worked with the Jews. But they could have also been Jews who came from Arab countries. We never found out for certain who sent them, but everyone felt they were connected to the Jewish paramilitary organizations. The entire village was scared.

"After several nights, the Jewish military commander for the area arrived. He gave the *mukhtar* a few old guns. 'You can guard the village with these weapons,' he said. The *mukhtar* assigned Muhammed Jaber, his son, and two of his nephews to stand guard that night at the southern entrance of the village.

---

*The head of a village or local community.

"The next morning I went to walk with my little dog. Everyone in the village was talking about what had happened the night before. Muhammed Jaber and his son and nephews had been shot and killed by Jewish soldiers while they were standing guard! I quickly turned with my dog to go back home and inform Granny.

"A deafening gunshot ripped through the air as I approached our garden. The rope that was tied to my little dog went limp. I knelt down and felt for him. I felt blood, hot and sticky. My little dog was dead. Using my hands to feel the way, I ran inside our home. 'They killed him, Granny!' I cried. 'The soldiers shot my dog right in front of me!'

"Granny got very nervous. 'Thank God that they didn't kill you, child!'

"'It doesn't matter if they killed me or not . . . they killed my dog!' I was so sad that I almost forgot to tell Granny the other news. 'They also killed the watchmen.'

"This made Granny's voice sharp. 'What?'

"I told her what I had heard. But I did not fully understand. Why had they given us weapons to protect ourselves and then killed the ones with the weapons? Granny seemed more worried about the guards than about my poor little dog.

"Jewish soldiers came to the village that night and the next night. I was scared when I heard them patrolling outside my home. After three nights, they called everyone to meet at the school. 'You have to leave the village,' the soldiers told us once we had gathered. 'We are not able to protect you here anymore. Go, prepare your clothes, and then return here to wait until we come.'

"We quickly gathered whatever we could carry and went back to the school. We waited under the trees the entire night. At 8 o'clock the following morning, an army truck arrived and a Jewish soldier told us to get on. They were taking us to Ramle, they said.*

"The truck dropped us off at Nabi Saleh, the big tower in the center of Ramle. Each family was given a tent by the Red Cross to set up around the tower. The Red Cross told us we must stay inside the tents until they were certain that we did not have any diseases or lice. Every day for a week a Red Cross doctor came to examine us. The doctor did not find anything dirty or

*According to Israeli historian Benny Morris, an Israeli Interior Ministry representative pushed to expel the residents of Zakariyya, arguing in March 1949, "In the village there are many good houses, and it is possible to accommodate in them several hundred new immigrants." In January 1950, Israeli upper leadership decided to depopulate Zakariyya.

unwell, so at the end of the week, we were permitted to move from the tents. We found a small cinder-block room with a corrugated-iron sheet roof. There was no electricity and no running water. We had to pay rent, but people from Zakariyya earned a bit of money by working on local farms. Granny could not do heavy farm work, and we were all too young, but relatives helped us.

"One day, Granny and I were investigating the shops in Nabi Saleh to search for the lowest prices for rice, flour, and lentils.

"'Um Ahmad, is that you?' I heard a man say in broken Arabic. 'My name is Mordechai. We met many years ago. I used to work at the port in Yaffa with your son Ahmad.'

"'Yes, Mordechai, I remember meeting you! This is Ahmad's daughter, Yusra.'

"'What a beautiful girl you are, Yusra! And how is my friend Ahmad? It has been so many years since we have seen each other!'

"'You didn't know? He was killed nearly ten years ago, Allah *yerhamo*. By the British.'

"Mordechai spent many minutes cursing the British for having killed my father. And when he learned about our situation, he took pity on us.

"'I have a small shop, just down this road,' he said to my granny. 'Anything you need, you get it from me.'

"We always went to Mordechai's store after that. He refused to take much money from us. We lived like this for over six months until my granny decided it would be better for us in the West Bank, which had been under Jordanian control since the 1949 armistice agreements.* There was an Israeli truck coming from Majdal and Asqalan to take people to the Hebron area. The truck stopped in Ramle to pick us up. We made our way east, stopping here and there to squeeze in other families. By nighttime the truck reached the outskirts of Daharia, in the south Hebron area. The truck stopped next to a Jordanian military base. We were unloaded there and the truck drove away.

"The men from Majdal began explaining to the Jordanian soldiers where we had come from and asked them to let us enter Daharia.

"'You must wait here until our commander comes and tells us what to do with you,' the Jordanian soldiers answered.

*The 1949 armistice agreements officially ended the 1948 war. The border established from these agreements became known as the Green Line.

"There was nowhere to go except under trees. It was cold. Some of the men from Majdal had blankets. They draped them over the branches to make a small shelter that we could all huddle under. I had spent too many nights of my life shivering under trees. I bit my knuckles to try and keep myself from crying but tears came anyway. I finally fell asleep leaning against my granny. I woke in the morning hungry. But there was nothing. We waited all day and another night for the commander to come. Finally, the next morning, the men from Majdal began arguing with the Jordanian soldiers.

"'Just let a few of us go into Daharia to find provisions! Do you think these women and children can go a third day without food?' The soldiers agreed to let two men enter Daharia. A few hours later the men came back with three sacks full of bread, olives, yogurt, cheese.

"'The people in Daharia are very good,' the men told us as they distributed the items to the hungry families. 'We went to the mosque and told them our situation, and they immediately began collecting food for us.'

"Finally, after two more days, the Jordanians brought a bus and took us to Hebron. They put us under a big tent. Doctors gave us injections. After two nights, Jordanian officials arrived.

"'Does anyone here have relatives in the West Bank?' they asked.

"'I have people in Al Arroub camp,' Granny said.

"The officials made some marks on a clipboard. 'Fine. We'll take you to Arroub,' he told us.

"The next day we were in Al Arroub refugee camp, reuniting with many of our people. They welcomed us, made us food, and invited us to stay in their tents until we received our own. The situation in Arroub camp was very hard, but there was one bright light. My mother was there. She clung to us tightly and covered our faces with kisses.

"We had been in Arroub camp for less than two weeks when my granny heard about a veterinarian in the camp. Although he was a doctor for animals, Granny thought it was a good chance to have someone examine my eyes."

My mother laughed at the memory. "Poor Granny, she was still trying to find a way to fix my eyes. The veterinarian told her to see Dr. Allenby, an American doctor at the clinic in Arroub. 'Doctor, please,' she begged him, 'is there anything you can do for my precious girl?' Dr. Allenby examined my eyes, realizing very quickly that there was no hope for restoring my sight. But he had another hope to offer. 'There is a special school in Bethlehem for blind girls,' he told Granny. 'Your granddaughter can study there, sponsored by the Catholic Church. She will get a good education. She will be with other children like her.'

"Granny consulted our relatives in Arroub and they all agreed. Dr. Allenby could take me to the school in Bethlehem. The very next day the arrangements were made. I went to Bethlehem to study. Though it was difficult to be separated from my family, I was so glad to finally have my chance to go to school! I loved learning Arabic, English, reading and writing Braille. I was the most clever of all the pupils!

"Granny, Mustafa, Mousa, and my mother moved from Arroub to Dheisheh refugee camp in Bethlehem, where many people from Zakariyya had gone. Dheisheh camp was much closer to my school than Arroub had been. I could see my family for all the festivals and special occasions. But I was afraid to sleep in their tent. The tent made strange and scary noises at night, as the canvas was buffeted by the wind. I preferred sleeping in the dormitories of the school. The other girls and I would imagine our futures; what we would do, whom we would marry, where we would live. I hoped that someday I would live in Jerusalem.

"I studied for eight years! Dr. Allenby came to see me when I was in the twelfth grade. He wanted to send me to America to continue my studies. I refused. 'I will not leave the country that I was born in,' I told him. He tried to persuade me. 'It's not forever, Yusra! You can study there and then come back!' 'No. I don't want to go. I will stay here all my life, until I die. I cannot leave my home, Dr. Allenby. The war is not over yet.'

"Around that time, a young man named Saber Al Jundi started inquiring after me. He was from Deir Yassin, but his family had fled to the Old City of Jerusalem in 1948. Saber attended the school for blind boys in Ramallah and his classmate knew me from Dheisheh camp. He asked my mother for permission to marry me. My mother came to me and asked if I will agree. At first I refused. I did not want to get married.

"'Think carefully, Yusra,' my mother said. 'You will not stay at school forever.'

"I thought very much about her words. I had refused to go to America because I wanted to stay in my country. If I married Saber Al Jundi, I could stay here. I would even live in my dream city of Jerusalem! In the end, I agreed to marry your father. I was twenty-two years old. And *al hamduli'llah*,* I have lived all my life since then in Jerusalem." My mother patted my hands. "That's it. *Bikaffee*."** She stood up. It was time to prepare the evening meal.

*"Praise be to God."

**"Enough."

I sat there a few moments longer, thinking about her story. From now on I would have compassion for my mother's family and for all the people of Zakariyya. They were all victims of the *Nakba*. Even more than that, I was proud of my mother: she had struggled to survive; she had worked hard to get an education. She had refused to leave her homeland.

We were nearing Asqalan by the time I finished the story. The Transit was quiet, everyone deep in their own thoughts.

Wassef finally broke the reverie. "What's the third reason you didn't kill the snake, Sami?"

I grinned. "Because this snake was going toward the grapevines. Maybe it loves grapes fresh from the moment just like we do!"

Early the next morning, the workers piled into the Transit again, singing, laughing, and enjoying grapes, freshly baked *taboun* bread, and water. As we neared Zakariyya, Abu Hussein tapped me on my shoulder.

"Do you think we'll see the snake again?" he asked.

We slowed to a crawl as we passed the area, heads craning in all directions. The snake was nowhere to be seen.

"I miss our snake," Issa would say with a sigh each morning when our quest to spot him went unfulfilled yet again. "I love that snake."

The workers I transported had hands as hard as the stones they built with, but their hearts were like butterflies.

CHAPTER TWO

⁂

MY FIRST STEPS ARE A HAZY DREAM. Warm, shadowy images of family surrounding me in our home in the Old City of Jerusalem. My grandfather and uncles are among them, clapping and calling, "Sami! Walk here!" Everyone cheers as I teeter on wobbly legs. When I fall, the strength of the hands that lift me up and the warmth of the arms that embrace me are definitely my grandmother's and aunties'.

There were five stone steps leading from the road to the iron gate of our house. The gate opened up to a small stone courtyard. The house was divided between my family and Abu Zuheir's family. Abu Zuheir was blind like my parents, and his wife, Um Zuheir, had only one functioning eye. Their son Zuheir was my age. When my grandparents and uncles came to visit, we all sat together in the courtyard. The adults talked and drank sweet tea with sage, my uncles slipping candies to my big brother Samir, Zuheir, and me. Samir and I played among their ankles and knees. One beautiful day my uncles brought us a wooden rocking horse. They pulled us around the courtyard on it. "More! More!" I laughed and shouted.

*Sidi** carried and fed me long after I could walk and eat for myself. I was secure and happy high in his sturdy arms. His moustache tickled my face when he kissed me. *Sidi* fed me better than anyone else. The red beans with tomato sauce that I took from his spoon were warm in my belly. I opened my mouth for more, and more again.

"Look how Sami loves those beans!" the others exclaimed. *Sidi* never had a shortage of beans to feed me. He loved feeding me beans.

*Arabic for "Grandpa."

When my walking grew stable, I was permitted to navigate the cobblestone alleys to my grandparents' house. I never got lost. Everyone was happy to see me there. Samir, baby Azzam, and I were the only grandchildren.

I watched as my uncles Zaki and Is'haq prepared their very peculiar breakfast. They broke pieces of bread into their bowls, smeared them with sheep lard, sprinkled sugar on them, and poured hot tea over the whole concoction. They dug into it with their spoons with great gusto, smacking their lips after each bite.

"Try it, Sami!" Uncle Is'haq encouraged me.

I was skeptical. "What is it?"

"It's called *fateet shay!*" Uncle Zaki offered me a bite. I hesitantly took it. It was delicious. From then on, I ate only *fateet shay* for breakfast, just like my uncles.

My mother did not approve of this diet. "The boy should be eating olive oil and *za'atar* with his bread!" she protested. "Please, Sami, won't you eat olive oil and *za'atar*? It's very healthy!" So, to make my mom happy, I did. I poured olive oil and *za'atar* in my bowl with the bread, sugar, lard, and tea and ate it all mixed together.

Fateet shay tasted best when I ate it off my Uncle Zaki's special spoon. It was square and made from white stainless steel. I had to eat stealthily if my big brother was around. Samir had declared himself the only one who could use Uncle Zaki's things. I could touch Uncle Is'haq's possessions, but Uncle Zaki's belongings were Samir's domain.

My mother's brother frequently visited us from Dheisheh refugee camp. Uncle Mustafa was a member of the Jordanian police. I wanted the entire neighborhood to see him walking into our home in his smartly pressed uniform with shiny buttons. I wanted them to know that he belonged to us. Uncle Mustafa let me touch his gleaming buttons and wear his police cap.

I was happy when my father's sister came to visit from Hebron. Aunt Fatmeh did not have any children of her own, so she showered us with affection, cradling me in her arms like a baby, even when I was already a big boy. Aunt Fatmeh had two gold teeth inside her mouth. They fascinated me. I always tried to make Aunt Fatmeh laugh just so I could get a glimpse of those beautiful, shining teeth. Luckily, it was easy to make Aunt Fatmeh laugh.

I was not as fond of her husband, Abdel Jaber. He worked in trade and he sometimes accompanied Aunt Fatmeh to Jerusalem so he could check on shops where he had business. In the daytime, Abdel Jaber collected the money he was owed. In the evenings, he counted his money over and over again, stacking the coins into piles repeatedly.

"Look at how much money he has!" I whispered to my mom in the next room.

"Shh . . . *uskut,** *ya* Sami! His money is his business!"

"Okay, okay, but why does he need all that money? He doesn't even have any kids!"

My mother shushed me again.

Samir and I sat close to Abdel Jaber as he stacked and restacked his money. Maybe tonight he would give us a coin. Our father had taught us to never, ever ask anyone for money. If an uncle offered us a shilling, it was permitted to accept it. But we must never ask like a beggar. So we sat at Abdel Jaber's feet and waited patiently. But he never gave us one coin. Instead, my father slipped us a few piasters. Samir and I scampered out to the street to buy candies.

"Think about how many sweets we could buy from even one of Abdel Jaber's big coins!" I said, sucking loudly on my strawberry candy.

"Who is Abdel Jaber? Don't you mean *Abu Camouneh?*"** Samir joked back.

I woke up one morning and ran to my grandfather's home as usual. The house was filled with many people I had never seen before. My grandmother and aunties were crying. No one had to tell me my grandfather was gone. I just knew it. It was an abscess in his stomach, Uncle Is'haq told me. I had no idea what an abscess was. All I knew was that *Sidi*'s moustache would no longer tickle me and he would no longer feed me beans.

When I was four years old my father pulled me to his side.

"You're getting to be such a big boy now, *ya* Sami."

I stood up as straight as I could, to demonstrate just how tall I really was.

"You are registered to begin kindergarten tomorrow. Do you want to go to school?"

Samir went to school every morning. I always peeked enviously at the colored pencils inside his bag, but I was not allowed to touch them. Yes. I wanted to go to school too.

In the morning, my mother handed me a folded garment. "Your school uniform," she told me. I inspected it. It was a white and red shirt. I liked those

---

*Arabic for "be quiet!" or "shut your mouth!"

**Literally translated: "father of the cumin seed." Used to signify someone so stingy that he clutches a small cumin seed in his fist; tightfisted.

colors. My mom held it over my head as I poked my arms through and wriggled my head into the neck opening. Only then did the horror strike. This was not a shirt at all! It was a dress!

"Get this off of me! Get this off of me!" I shouted and frantically tried to pull it off.

"*Ya* Sami, all the kindergarten students have to wear this! Don't you want to go to school?" In my writhing, I had managed to tangle myself in the sleeves. I desperately tried to extricate myself.

"I want to go to school, but not with a dress! This is for girls! I don't want to be a girl!"

I cried every morning as my mother forced the red and white dress over my head. Once inside the classroom, I didn't mind. All the boys and girls were dressed the same. But the way to and from school was awful. Kids pointed at me and chanted, "Sami is a girl! Sami is a girl!"

In the afternoons, Samir and I changed out of our school clothes and took lunch to my father at the Arab Blind Organization and Workshop. Samir carefully balanced the tins of hot food and I carried the bread.

My father's colleagues recognized us by our footsteps. "Sami! Samir! *Ahlan wa sahlan!*"* they called out as we entered the workshop. The big radio was on softly in the background. Samir raised the volume once, just slightly.

"Don't fill our ears with the music!" came the gentle reprimand. "We want to see what's going on around us!"

It was fun to watch them make broom handles and stools. I liked playing in the curly wood shavings. I especially loved working the big scale. I placed the one-kilo and two-kilo weights on both arms, trying to make it balance.

When there was a delivery of fresh wood in the courtyard, I always volunteered to organize it, stacking it in piles according to type. If I was not sure which tree a piece of wood came from, I only had to bring it inside. One of the workers would sniff it. "This is from a lemon tree," he would tell me decisively. Or, "It's pine."

After leaving the workshop, Samir played soccer with his friends. Sometimes they used socks rolled in a ball. Other times they got a cast-off soccer ball from the nearby plastics workshop. I tried to join them, but Samir and his friends pushed me away. "Go home! You're too small!" they said.

---

*"Welcome!" in Arabic.

I played my own game of soccer with Zuheir in our courtyard. My ball of socks was smaller than Samir's. My little brother Azzam tried to play with us. Sometimes we let him, but most of the time we told him to go away. He could play with Siham, Zuheir's little sister. They were the same age.

My mom darned and patched our clothes, keeping them impeccably clean. I loved to watch her hang the freshly laundered items onto the clothesline on our roof, even though my father warned me many times that it was dangerous up there.

"Stay far from the edge, Sami," my mom told me as we climbed up the steps.

"I will, *Yamma*."

I went straight for the edge and leaned over it, tempting fate. Fate won. I tumbled, my forehead smacking the stone courtyard six feet below. Before I felt any pain, I heard my mother shouting for help. Our neighbor came rushing over.

"Take him to the hospital! Hurry, please!"

The neighbor scooped me in his arms. Only then I saw the blood. I was covered in it. I began crying. The neighbor ran with me in his arms. "Take me to my father! Take me to my father!" I shouted hysterically, squirming in his arms. The neighbor seemed to know where my father worked. He was getting close to the street. I relaxed in his arms. I would soon be with my father and that meant I would be okay. But the neighbor ran right past the Arab Blind Organization. I began to scream again. "No! No! My father is here! Take me to my father!"

The neighbor stopped running only when he arrived at the local hospital, housed in the Austrian Hospice. Strange people surrounded me. One of them set me on a cot with white sheets and held my arms down to keep me from thrashing. Another mopped the blood off my face. A third began stitching my forehead back together with needle and thread. I continued to cry and scream for my father. Just as the doctors and nurses were wrapping my head in an enormous white bandage, I heard the tapping of my father's cane. I stopped crying immediately. Samir was with him.

"Wow, look at all that blood," Samir said. He seemed suitably impressed.

My father lifted me off the bed to carry me home. He couldn't use his cane since both his arms were holding me. Samir led us by my father's elbow through the Old City streets.

"How did you manage to fall, eh?" my father scolded me. "I told you a million times not to go up on that roof!" But I was not scared. The bandage on my head ensured that I would not be tasting his switch. And he sounded more worried than angry. I let my throbbing head fall against his chest, safe and secure, as his scolding washed over me like warm water.

My head throbbed painfully. I could not go out to play. I could only lie down. Usually my parents kicked me out of their bed when I tried to climb in with them in the small hours of the morning. But now their bed was turned over to me. My uncles all visited and gave me candies. I even ate from Uncle Zaki's spoon right in front of Samir.

After a week, I was able to play again with my friends in the neighborhood, though I had to be careful not to play roughly. The bandage still covered the upper portion of my head. "Hey, here comes Sheikh Sami!" Zuheir called out, as if the bandage was a turban. I was not a sheikh.* I wished he would stop calling me that.

If I played too hard and my head started aching again, I would go inside. Then my mom let me help her bake bread. She put a can of water on the fire, dipping her finger in it to determine when it was warm enough. She measured flour with one cup and water with another, mixing them together in a big round aluminum pan. She added exactly the right amount of yeast and then immersed her hands past her wrists into the dough, kneading, kneading, kneading. Her hands were white from the flour. I stroked one. It was silky soft. The touch of my finger on her hand made her smile. "Sami, *habibi,*** get me another half cup of water."

I helped my mother break the mound of dough into symmetrical pieces— smaller ones for us kids—and she rolled them out with a wooden rolling pin. She laid the flattened round dough back onto the pan. Samir put a piece of cloth on his head. My mother helped him place the pan on his head so he could walk to the bakery to bake the bread in its oven.

Next: preparing the lentils. My mother poured the dry lentils into another aluminum pan. The small yellow beans covered the bottom of the pan. She sifted through them, her fingers constantly moving, always feeling, removing any small stone or piece of wood they encountered. When the lentils were picked clean, she poured water on them, stirring them once more to pluck out any remaining impurity, and then poured the lentils into a strainer. She repeated the same process with the rice. My mother had eyes in her fingers.

---

*Literally meaning "elder," is used to signify someone wise or a scholar of Islam.

**Arabic for "my beloved" for a male; *habibti* is the female equivalent.

۞

THE ADULTS BEGAN TO LISTEN to the radio more and more. They spoke about things that were far away and had nothing to do with my life. I preferred to strategize about how to get my hands on a strawberry candy. Sometimes they talked about the other side of Jerusalem, where they said the Jews were. As far as I was concerned, the other side of Jerusalem was farther than the end of the earth. But in the spring of 1967, rumors were passed from kid to kid about the Jews who lived there. One rumor fascinated me in particular: the Jews had tails, just like cats! I wished I could see one for myself.

On June 5, 1967, I was in the courtyard, playing with the treasured Monkey that Uncle Zaki had given me for my fifth birthday. When I wound it up, it marched and banged cymbals together, making a fantastic sound. Azzam was trying to catch Monkey as it marched and clanged merrily. But I pushed my little brother out of the way. He was only four years old, way too little to be playing with my Monkey! He couldn't even wind him up!

Suddenly, explosions erupted. "*Ya* Allah!"* my mother cried, running out of the house into the courtyard, holding my baby brother Riyyad. "They're shooting! Get inside right away, boys!" My two-year-old sister, Samira, sat on the floor wailing as my mother started frantically throwing baby clothes into a small case. Samir and my father burst into the house.

"The war has begun!" my father shouted. "The Jews are shelling!"

My father grabbed a small bag of lentils and thrust it at me. "Carry this!" Samir took a bag of rice with one hand and grabbed onto Samira with the other. Azzam held the case of baby clothes and led my mother, who was cradling Riyyad to her chest. My father managed to grab a few thin blankets and I helped guide him by his elbow.

"Hurry! Hurry!" my father called to us as we pushed our way out the gate and onto the street, joining a line of people already streaming from their homes, each one carrying bundles and sacks. The gunfire and explosions sounded louder outside the protection of our own gate. Our neighbors pushed past us, breathing fast. The only time I had seen grown-ups frightened like this was when I had fallen off the roof. Adults were not usually afraid for no reason.

---

*Arabic for "My God!" *Allah* alone is Arabic for God.

"This way, this way!" a man on the street called out to us. He led us through an alley and down a flight of stone steps to underground stables. "Bring the children here. They'll be safe!" he shouted to my parents. My mother entered but immediately recoiled from the stench of fresh donkey feces. "It's filthy in here! No! Better to die outside than to suffocate here!"

We went back out to the street. The sounds of exploding ordnance continued.

"The Old City is just yards away from the front!" a man yelled as he led his family past us. I didn't know what "the front" was, but the panic in his voice convinced me that it was dangerous. We followed the other people on the street, shuddering with each explosion until we came to the bakery. I knew this place. This was where my mother sent Samir to bake her dough into fresh bread.

Samir hustled us down the stairs. It took my eyes a moment to adjust from the bright sunlight to the dark, underground, cavelike room. The room, about thirty by fifteen feet in size, was already packed with people who were crying and shouting, "*Ya* Allah, save us all!" The muffled sound of shelling from mortars and gunfire could still be heard. I stood in the doorway, frozen with shock and fear. Samir led us to a small area that had not yet been occupied. More people poured in behind us from the street. Was the entire neighborhood heading here?

We huddled together on the bakery floor. My father touched all our heads to make sure we were accounted for. Suddenly I remembered Monkey. He would still be out there, marching and banging his cymbals in the courtyard. I tried very hard not to cry. I understood that tears over a toy would not be acceptable right now, not when the grown-ups were so afraid.

Just then I heard Abu Zuheir yell to Um Zuheir, "Where is Siham?"

Um Zuheir shouted back, "You brought her!"

"What are you talking about, woman? You were supposed to bring her!" Abu Zuheir suddenly became very silent. "She's under the bed."

"What?"

"When the shelling started, I told her to hide under the bed. She's probably still there! I have to go and get her!"

An explosion detonated. Um Zuheir grew frantic. "You can't go alone! You won't be able to see if a soldier is coming with his gun!"

"She's only three years old. We can't leave her there!"

My father placed his hand on Samir's head. "Samir will go with you, Abu Zuheir." Samir twisted his neck sharply to face our father. Before he could utter a word of protest, I felt my father's strong hand on my head as well. "Sami will go too."

Samir was already taking Abu Zuheir's elbow. I did not want to appear more frightened than Samir. I took his other hand.

"Don't be afraid, boys," Abu Zuheir said. "It's just one hundred yards to the house. Nothing can happen in a hundred yards."

We are safe with Abu Zuheir, I told myself. *He's strong and tall.* Abu Zuheir had a big, thick walking stick unlike my father's narrow cane. If soldiers tried to shoot us, he would beat them with that stick and they would run away. I tried not to notice that Abu Zuheir's arm was shaking. Instead, I counted our steps.

The streets were entirely deserted. Aside from bursts of ammunition and occasional distant explosions, the silence was eerie. "Abu Zuheir, where are the cats?" I asked.

"Eh, what's that?"

"All the cats in the streets. They're gone."

"*Wallah,** I don't know, Sheikh Sami. Perhaps they found their own safe place."

The doors to all the houses were wide open, including ours. We entered the courtyard. The house was still, as if its soul was gone.

Abu Zuheir went straight inside his room and got down on his hands and knees. "Siham!" he called under the bed. His voice trembled. "Are you there?"

I heard a mewing sound. Had the neighborhood cats taken refuge under Abu Zuheir's bed?

"Sami, go and get her out."

I crawled under the bed. Siham was curled up in the corner, next to a big yellow can. "Come on, Siham, we have to go." She was too frightened to speak, much less move. She squeaked again like a small kitten. I took her hand and half-coaxed, half-pulled her out. Abu Zuheir gathered her in his arms and Samir and I led them back to the bakery. Um Zuheir snatched her daughter out of her father's arms and embraced the little girl tightly to her chest. "I was alone!" Siham reproached her mother over and over. "You left me alone!"

The women were assembling the foodstuffs they had managed to carry, pooling together lentils, rice, beans, and tea. The bakery had some dry black

---

*Arabic for "By God."

bread. My mother returned to the family after the provisions had been organized.

"No one brought milk," she said, shaking her head sadly. "The children will have to do without milk." Samira and Azzam were leaning against her as she cradled baby Riyyad in her arms. "The baby will drink my milk, but the other little ones . . ." She stroked Samira's dark hair. "What a pity for them."

The can under the bed next to Siham. There had been a picture on the yellow label of a woman smiling brightly, holding a cup of white, frothy liquid.

"There's milk at Abu Zuheir's house," I said. "There's a big can of powdered milk."

Abu Zuheir sat up straight. "The boy is right! I bought the can just a few days ago." He stood up. "Okay, Sheikh Sami. Let's go back one more time: you, Samir, and me. Together we'll bring the milk."

I couldn't object; after all, I had mentioned the can in the first place. My only protest was to mutter quietly, "I'm not a sheikh. I'm just a kid."

"Thank you, Sami, Samir." My mother kissed our cheeks, my father patted our heads, and Samir and I took hold of Abu Zuheir's elbow, slowly leading him out of the bakery again. The shooting and explosions did not frighten me now. We would be heroes twice in one day. We arrived at the house and I crawled under the bed to pull out the can of milk. I handed it to Abu Zuheir proudly.

"Okay, boys. Let's return to the others." Abu Zuheir took the can of milk in his left hand and Samir and I held his right, guiding him back over the cobblestone street to the bakery. We were almost there when a loud explosion rocked the entire area. Small stones from nearby houses rained down around us. A large piece of tile from someone's floor fell from the sky and shattered right next to me. I froze in terror.

"The milk! The milk!" Abu Zuheir shouted. I looked. He was still holding the can, but the lid had been blown off from the force of the explosion. "Sheikh Sami, find the cover, quickly!"

Every ounce of my body was pulled toward my mother and father as if by gravity. We had to get to the bakery and not venture out again, not for any little girl under a bed, not for any amount of powdered milk.

"I'm going straight back to the bakery. If you want to find the cover, find it alone!"

Abu Zuheir did his best to keep the powdered milk from spilling as Samir and I guided him as fast as he could move to the bakery, through the door, and down the stairs.

"Milk!" I announced when we entered the room, breathing hard. Samir grabbed the can from Abu Zuheir and held it up triumphantly.

"But no cover," Abu Zuheir added ruefully.

The adults made tea on the bakery oven as evening began to fall. Four children together had to share one cup of tea. But Samir and I were heroes that evening. We each got our very own cup of tea, with a heaping spoonful of powdered milk stirred in. I sipped mine slowly and with a loud slurping noise, making sure everyone remembered who had been brave enough to rescue Siham and to rescue the milk. It was only then that I realized—on both trips I had forgotten to rescue Monkey.

Time in the bakery was endless. It was stiflingly hot. Every inch of the soot-stained floor was packed with people. The air was close, making it difficult to breathe. The odor from the hundred or so bodies crowded together began to grow. There was only one toilet and it was never free. Samir, Azzam, Samira, and I squatted over a plastic bucket.

There was a big transistor radio. When it was turned on, everyone was silent. Sometimes the news made the adults cheer. Other times it drove them to pray to Allah to save us all. The feelings would change as often as the stations were switched.

The Israeli planes are dropping like flies, the Egyptian station Sawt al Arab* announced. *Be hungry, sharks*, the announcer Ahmad Said warned. *We will throw the Jews to the sea!*

But the next station reported that the Zionist army was advancing and ours was losing ground and soldiers. The news made the adults fret more and more with each passing hour.

The boredom was overwhelming. There was no space to play or even walk around. There was nothing to do but sleep. We had only a thin blanket between us and the filthy stone floor, but my mother's soft body cushioned our sleep. I lay on my mom for hours and hours, imagining battles raging over our heads. The adults were irritable and sad. If Samira cried, or if Samir, Azzam, and I tried to joke or wrestle with each other, they shouted at us to be quiet and not to move. I tried very hard to sit quietly, but hunger got the best of me. For two long days we had eaten only dry black bread, dipping it into a shared cup of tea, sucking on small pieces in order to make it last as long as possible.

"I want my *fateet shay!*" I complained loudly with tears.

My mother tried to soothe me. "Sami, we're lucky to have this tea and bread. There are people who have nothing at all."

---

*Voice of the Arabs.

"There are lentils and beans and rice here!" Samir said, pointing to the small food stock the women had organized.

"We don't know how long we will be here, *habibi*," my mother tried to explain. "We have to make the food stretch as long as possible."

Azzam joined in my protest of tears and my mom pulled him into her lap, next to baby Riyyad. "We'll be home soon. You'll be able to eat as much good food as you like."

That night the women prepared lentils over a small fire. They served them only to the kids. We ate a few bites each. But now a quarter of our communal stock of lentils was gone. I realized the gravity of the situation. I did not cry about being hungry again.

On June 7, the third day, the shooting was directly above our heads. I heard snatches of conversation around me: the Jordanian soldiers were now fighting the Jews inside the Old City itself! With each spurt of gunfire, Azzam buried his face in my mother's lap. His whole body shook.

"We're safe here. Nothing can hurt us," my father reassured us. But I could tell that even he was not fully convinced.

By afternoon, it was silent and still overhead. A few hours later, a man I had never seen before ducked into the entrance of the bakery. "It's over," he said in a tight voice. "We lost Jerusalem." What did he mean? We waited for him to continue. He ran out the door.

"It can't be true," Abu Zuheir muttered quietly. We sat mutely for a few more moments when someone else burst in. "Go quickly! To your homes, everyone! Raise something white on top of your house!"

We stood up in a daze and followed the stream of our neighbors shuffling slowly out of the bakery. The smell of explosives lingered in the air. I blinked in the unfamiliar bright sunlight. I stretched my leg muscles and gulped the fresh, cold air, imagining the heaps of food my mother would now prepare for us at home. But it was hard to feel happy when everyone around me was still so sad and anxious. We walked back to our houses wordlessly.

A voice shouted over a megaphone, repeating the instructions that everyone should put a white cloth on top of his house for his own safety. I could not understand why hanging a white cloth would keep us safe or why these orders were further upsetting the adults.

Abu Zuheir was frantic to find something white to hang.

"Samir, find a white sheet or blanket . . . ," my father started to instruct, but Abu Zuheir interrupted him nervously.

"We don't have time for the boy to search!"

Abu Zuheir went quickly inside his house and emerged waving the long, white underpants that he always wore underneath his *qumbaz*.* "Here, my underpants!" he shouted. "This is what we'll hang!"

My father laughed. "You're going to hang your underpants on our house for the Jews to see? This is better than Samir looking for a white sheet?"

Abu Zuheir smiled out of the corner of his mouth. "I don't care if all the world sees my underpants. I care only about our safety! How can blind ones like us verify if the sheet is white or blue or yellow? My underpants I am sure of—they are as white as yogurt!"

My mother tied Abu Zuheir's underpants securely onto a broom handle. Abu Zuheir scrambled up the iron gate with surprising agility for a man who could not see. He wedged the broomstick with the underpants flag between the stones at the top of the gate.

Abu Zuheir nimbly climbed back down. The laughter quickly melted into concern. "What's next?" my mother asked no one in particular. "Will they let us live here in peace, or will they kill us like in Deir Yassin?"

The two families lingered together in the courtyard a few more moments.

"An old man's underpants," Abu Zuheir muttered with a sigh before going inside. "*Ya* Allah, what have things come to?"

The next morning, young Zuheir ran up to our room. "The Jews are coming to count us!" he announced. "They're two houses down right now."

My mother was agitated. "Counting?"

My father tried to calm her. "It will be okay. The fighting is over. Just answer the questions that they ask."

We gathered in the courtyard when the Jews arrived. Two of them were dressed in soldiers' uniforms. They entered our house.

"What are they doing?" I whispered to Samir.

"Probably looking for guns," Samir whispered back.

One man remained with us in the courtyard. He was tall and was wearing khaki pants and shirt. He had a floppy hat with a brim.

"How many people live in this house?" Floppy Hat asked my father in Arabic.

"We are two families here," my father answered.

---

*A traditional Palestinian robe worn by men.

Floppy Hat started with our family. "Name and birth date?" he asked my father and then my mother. He jotted it down in his notebook.

"Why are you writing all this?" my mother asked nervously.

"So we can issue identity cards for you," he answered, as he began recording the names and ages of the children.

As Floppy Hat was writing Samira's birth date, he turned to my father. "What is your son doing?"

My father sensed immediately that I was not next to the rest of the family. "Sami! Get over here!"

I had been behind Floppy Hat, trying to examine his bottom. I crept back to my father red-faced.

"What were you doing?" Samir whispered to me.

"I wanted to see his tail!" I whispered back.

"What did it look like?"

"I don't know. I couldn't find it!"

When Floppy Hat turned around to count Abu Zuheir's family, Samir and I craned our necks, but we could see nothing resembling a tail.

"Maybe he tucked it inside his pants?" I whispered to Samir hopefully.

"But then we would see some bulge!" Samir pointed out.

Perhaps there was something the matter with this Jew, I told myself. But when the soldiers came out of the home, we saw no sign of a tail on them either. I was bitterly disappointed.

⚉

FLOPPY HAT and the soldiers came back the next day with Israeli-issued ID cards for my mother and father. My father's card: Saber Al Jundi, #20, my mother's: Myassar Al Jundi, #21. The names and numbers of the kids were listed on their cards: Samir Al Jundi, #22, Sami Saber Al Jundi, #23. I wanted to dash to my grandmother's home to show everyone my parents' new cards. Did they get cards also? What number was Uncle Zaki? What about Uncle Is'haq? But my father stopped me. "I don't want you running around the streets at this time," he told me. "And anyway . . . your uncles and aunties are not there."

I was stunned. Not there? Where could they possibly be? Did they die in the war? I buried my face in my mother's dress, crying. "Shh, no, Sami, they're not dead. They left Jerusalem when the fighting began," she said, trying to comfort me. "Your father thinks they're in Amman, but he's not sure." I did not know where Amman was, but if it was too far for me to eat from my Uncle Zaki's spoon, then they might as well be dead.

Soldiers entered our courtyard again the following morning. Floppy Hat was not with them. They spoke to my father in English, a language that I did not understand. My father's voice was strained in response, high and tense. The soldiers left. My father began cursing them in a loud voice. My mother ran out in alarm. "Saber, what? What happened?"

"They said we have to leave the home. The Al Sharaf Quarter of the Old City will be only for the Jews now."

My mother sank down onto a chair. "Leave our home? And go where?"

My father started pacing back and forth across the small courtyard. "We can go to Amman. There are buses at Damascus Gate* that will take anyone who wants to Amman. It will be safer for us there."

My mother shook her head vehemently. "I will not!"

"We can find my brothers . . ."

"No! Even if we die under the feet of the Jews, I am not leaving my city. The children and I will die here!"

"Myassar, be reasonable . . ."

"I refused once to leave my country and go to America. How can I leave now? I want to die under these stones. If you want to go to Amman, go alone! I will stay here. The war is not over yet."

I had never seen my parents argue like that before. Samir, Azzam, and I crouched in the corner of the courtyard, trying to be quiet as cats so they would not tell us to go inside.

"I don't want to go to Amman," Samir whispered to me. "I don't have any friends there."

Amman was a strange, faraway place. But if Uncle Is'haq and Uncle Zaki were there, maybe it wouldn't be so bad.

Finally my father grabbed his cane and stormed out of the courtyard.

"Do you think he went to Amman without us?" I asked Samir quietly. Azzam began to cry.

An hour later my father returned, looking exhausted. "It's settled," he said to my mother. "We can stay at the Arab Blind Organization. Our family and Abu Zuheir's. The director said we can use the top floor until we find something more permanent."

Samir and my parents went back and forth multiple times from our house to the Arab Blind Organization, each time carrying what their arms could hold. Azzam and I guided our mother and father. Neighbors helped us carry

*One of the entrances/exits to the Old City.

some of the bigger items. Some of those neighbors spoke about taking the bus to Amman. Others said they would seek refuge in Shu'afat refugee camp, north of Jerusalem. But everyone had to leave the Al Sharaf Quarter. Soldiers with guns came every day for the rest of the week to remind us of the urgency of our departure. Each time they came, my mom erupted into fresh tears. I no longer cared if they had tails or not. I hated them. They were making us leave our home. They were making my mother cry.

Um Zuheir and my mother organized the big room on the second floor that the eleven of us would now be sharing. They put two large cupboards in the middle and hung a sheet from either end so that there would be a bit of privacy between the families. But it was easy to push aside the sheet and move from one half of the room to the other. It was fun being in the big room all together. My brothers, sister, and I played with Zuheir and Siham. At night, when the blind workers went home, Samir, Zuheir, and I could explore the entire downstairs.

The Helen Keller Foundation made a donation of clothes to the organization. We were invited to take what we needed. The kids pawed eagerly through the big cardboard box, pulling out shirts and trousers to see the sizes and colors. In the bottom of the box was a beautiful bright red and yellow necktie. Zuheir and I grabbed it at the exact same moment.

"It's mine!" Zuheir shouted, yanking it away from me.

"No, it's not, it's mine! Get your hands off it!" I yelled, snatching it back.

The tug of war continued until we were both in tears. Our fathers took the tie away and consulted in the corner about how to resolve our conflict. Zuheir and I pouted on separate sides of the room as we waited for the verdict. Finally, Abu Zuheir called us together. "Well, boys, we decided to cut the tie and give you each half of it. Will you be satisfied then?"

I eyed Zuheir suspiciously to make sure he was not receiving some hidden benefit from this deal. Zuheir eyed me back. We both nodded. It was fair. Abu Zuheir fetched a large pair of scissors from downstairs and the surgery on the necktie was executed swiftly. Zuheir and I each clutched our half happily, friends once more.

One month slipped into two and then three.

"It's time for us to find a real home," Abu Zuheir said one night with his shoulders stooped and head bowed.

I didn't want to. It was fun living in the big room all together. But more than that, I knew it meant abandoning the chance of going back to our house. My memories of the house were already growing shadowy and dim.

Now these memories would stay in shadows. But there was no hope, my mother tried to explain to me gently. Our home, our entire neighborhood, had been demolished by the Israelis, who were building new houses and calling the area the Jewish Quarter.

Every evening after work, my father and Abu Zuheir went out to search. They came back one night smiling. "We found two rooms in a house in the Old City. In the Assa'diya neighborhood, near Herod's Gate.* We can move in right away." The Assa'diya neighborhood was in the Muslim Quarter. I hoped the Jewish soldiers would leave us alone there.

The next afternoon, we took our first armloads to the new house. I inspected it carefully. There was a small courtyard, smaller than the one in our old house. There were four rooms; Abu Zuheir's family got the small downstairs one and we got the large room upstairs. The remaining rooms were inhabited by two other families. There were two small kitchens for the four families to share.

The seven of us settled quickly into our big room upstairs. I cautiously began to explore the outside. I did not know the nooks and crannies of the streets like the old neighborhood. There were many kids my age but I did not want to play with them. It would be disloyal to my old friends. There were gun-toting Israeli soldiers wandering everywhere, talking in a language I could not understand.

One day, Zuheir pulled me out of the house by my sleeve. "I have to show you something amazing, Sami!" Zuheir took off running through the narrow alleyways with me at his heels. We arrived at an opening leading down to a large chamber.

"This is it!" Zuheir said proudly, pointing. "A candy factory right in our neighborhood!"

I stared at Zuheir wide-eyed and stuck my head inside the doorway to get a better look.

The mouthwatering fragrance of strawberry filled my nostrils. I could not believe my luck. The vats turned and mixed the sticky rose-red sugary substance as I watched and drooled.

The discovery of the candy factory helped compensate for the bathroom problem. There was one Turkish-style toilet for the four families to share. If I did not wake up very early to relieve myself, Abu Mustafa from downstairs would get in first. That was a disaster. He would be in there for half an hour, smoking his cigarette. I willed Abu Mustafa to finish before Um Jalal came. It would be disrespectful for a five-year-old to dart into the bathroom ahead of an adult.

---

*One of the entrances/exits to the old city.

There was no running water in the house; in fact, there was no running water in any of the houses in the new neighborhood. There was an ancient well in the courtyard, but the water Samir and I hoisted up was murky gray with a filmy substance on top; my mother warned us not to drink it or even wash with it. Two or three times a week my father and I had to fetch water from a central water tap. My father filled two twenty-liter metal cans, paid the municipal waterman, and carried the cans back to the house. It was my job to lead my father. I was impressed by the colorful language spilling out of his mouth every time we embarked on this task. He cursed the Israelis, the Jordanians, the occupation—everything and everyone under the sun. We had to make four or five trips to the tap in order to fill our 50-liter *ziir** and 120-liter petrol drum. I played a game with myself: looking only at their receptacles, could I figure out who was in line ahead of us? Our old neighbor Abu Fakhri always filled one large yellow plastic jerry can. Abu Manar had four tin buckets.

My mother poured all the water into the *ziir* and petrol drum and then organized it in different pots for different needs. We were careful not to move any pot of water that she placed, whether in the kitchen or outside the bathroom door. When she needed it, she would know exactly where to find it.

Fridays were bath day. First thing in the morning, my mother filled an iron bucket with water from the *ziir*. She heated the water on a burner, feeling with her hands until the temperature was right. She called us one by one: Samir, Sami, Azzam, Samira, Riyyad. One at a time, we sat in the middle of a tin pan with water one inch deep. Three times she washed every inch of our bodies with a scratchy cotton cloth and a block of soap made in Nablus. Three times she scrubbed our hair and faces, pouring fresh water over us to rinse the suds away. I liked being immersed in the warm water. I enjoyed the feel of my mother's strong hands scrubbing me all over, one, two, three times. Azzam hated it. He wriggled and squirmed.

"I want to be dirty!" Azzam protested.

"No child of mine will be dirty!" My mother held him down firmly and lathered his hair. "No one will say that my children aren't clean."

After each bath, she poured the dirty water into another can, which we used to flush the toilet or clean the courtyard floor.

Every month we received rations from UNRWA:** flour, milk, margarine, sardines, lentils, sugar, rice. The flour bags served a double function. My mother scrubbed the empty sacks, hanging them on the roof to dry. The next

*A large ceramic vase.

**United Nations Relief and Works Agency for Palestine Refugees.

day she used Um Mustafa's sewing machine. She returned with underwear for my brothers, sister, and me. Azzam and I compared the labels on our butts.

"You've got a gift from UNRWA!" Azzam laughed, slapping me on my behind.

"What about you? Your underwear is courtesy of USAID!"* I returned the slap.

I knew if I could see the underwear of all forty boys in my first-grade classroom, they would also be gifts from UNRWA or USAID.

I loved school. Mr. Walid, our teacher, wrote Arabic letters in thick, black ink on colorful squares of paper. He held each square up, telling us the name of the letter and the sound it made. We repeated after him. My chest puffed with pride when I announced to my mother, "I learned how to write *alif* today!"

"Wonderful, Sami!" She patted my hand gently. "Maybe tomorrow you'll learn *ba!*"

Before long, Mr. Walid held up three letters next to each other. I sounded them out slowly, *ba, nun, ta*. That spelled *bint*!** An actual word! I nearly jumped out of my seat in surprise. I couldn't wait to tell my mom that night. I was the first student at my desk the following morning, eager for Mr. Walid to hold up more letters in new and exciting combinations.

On holidays, we visited my mother's family in Dheisheh refugee camp. Everyone from Zakariyya came to welcome us. "*Ahlan wa sahlan, Yusra!*" They hugged and kissed my mother and then turned to us kids. "*Ibn Yusra!*"*** they said as they covered me with hugs and kisses. "We are very happy to see you!"

The kids in the camp absorbed us easily into their games. We ran and played with them, climbing the big hills and enjoying the open space and fresh air. Our cousins taught us how to make cars out of sardine cans and brown wire, which we drove through cities that we constructed from stones. We spent the night together in one of Uncle Mustafa's two rooms, or on the porch under the trellis covered with grapevines.

---

*U.S. Agency for International Development.

**Arabic for "girl."

***Arabic for "Son of Yusra."

In the morning, nearly everyone from Zakariyya and their children would come to see us off. "Goodbye, Yusra!" they called as we got on the bus heading back to Jerusalem. "*Ibn* Yusra, promise you'll visit us again soon!"

"Why do they call you Yusra?" I asked my mom after one visit. "Your name is Myassar!" Myassar was what my father always called her; that was the name on the identity card that Floppy Hat had issued.

"Ohhh . . ." My mother clapped her hands together. "When I first started studying at the school for the blind, there were three other girls in my class named Yusra. The principal came to our class one day and said she needed to speak to Yusra. She got four of us. She looked at us all and said, 'I'm sorry about this, but we can't have four Yusras in one class. I will write four names down on slips of paper and each of you will choose your new name.' My paper told me that my new name was Myassar." She laughed at the memory. "This is why I love to go to Dheisheh camp. The people from Zakariyya still know I am Yusra."

Our relatives in Dheisheh were not our only family. The Palestinian blind community in Jerusalem was family to us as well. Christian and Muslim blind families broke the Ramadan fast and celebrated Christmas together.

"Where is Azzam? Where is Samira?" our blind uncles and aunts asked at every celebration. We shook their hands and permitted them to see us properly. "Sami, you're getting bigger!" they said as their fingers traveled over my face and head, exploring my features gently. "Your hair is healthy, like silk," they said, rubbing a few strands through their fingers. "Nice eyes . . . good sturdy nose . . . your skin is getting rough. Stay out of the sun. It will make you dark!" If we saw one of them in the road, they made use of our eyes. Being escorted by Samir, Azzam, Samira, or me was quicker than navigating with a walking stick.

After a few years, Abu Zuheir's family left the small room downstairs. They were moving to another area of Jerusalem. We expanded into their room. I was sad to see them go, but it was nice to have more space, especially since my mom kept bringing more babies. Twins had been born the previous year, but my parents, with red and swollen eyes, buried them both the following day. A year later a baby boy called Mazin arrived. He mostly slept and cried. But everyone else seemed thrilled when he joined us, and later a girl called Hanadi. My Uncle Mustafa from Dheisheh and Aunt Fatmeh from Hebron came to visit. New babies had some advantages—the rest of us got chocolates as a congratulation. Plus, the more babies that arrived, the more birthdays we would celebrate. My mother baked big, gorgeous birthday cakes that melted in our mouths. She always sent plates over to the neighbors.

"Sami, you have a birthday coming up, don't you?" Abu Fakhri asked me weeks in advance of my ninth birthday.

I grinned. "Looking forward to your slice of cake?"

Abu Fakhri winked at me and leaned forward on his cane. "Do you think it will be chocolate or orange this time?"

My mother cooked with as much skill as she baked. When she heard us enter the courtyard after school, she put down the book she had been reading to greet us and to prepare a hot lunch. I examined her book as she cooked, closing my eyes and feeling the Braille letters to try to decipher some words.

"Sami, Samir, Azzam, Samira, Riyyad, lunch is ready!" She placed the food in front of us. Sometimes I ate it cheerfully. Other times I was angry. "Lentils again? Why do you always cook lentils and beans?" I wanted chicken or meat.

My mother never got upset at my temper tantrums. "This is what we have, son. We'll have something better to eat soon, I promise you. We'll eat *maqlubeh* on Friday."

I never felt poor. Nobody around us had more than we did. *Poor* was a word my parents used to describe Um Sa'eed.

Um Sa'eed lived in a one-room dwelling. Azzam and I tried to guess her age as she sat on her stoop, selling candies and needle and thread.

"I think she's eighty-five," I whispered to Azzam.

"You're wrong," Azzam whispered back. "She's got to be over one hundred!"

Um Sa'eed was an Arab Gypsy whose husband had died; she was alone. Her eyes were very dark. She could barely open them. She wrapped her hair in a white scarf but I could always spot some escaped strands, red from henna. She had tattoos on her hands and around her mouth. She wore a dark dress with equally dark embroidery across the chest.

"Buy from Um Sa'eed," my parents told us when they gave us a few lira to purchase treats. So we did. If she wasn't on her steps, Azzam and I entered her room.

"Good afternoon, *Hajeh** Um Sa'eed," I said. The windowless room was dark, dank, and musty, like a cave. Clutter was everywhere. Smoke burned my eyes from the small wood fire smoldering in a tin can.

---

*Usually used to refer to someone who has completed the pilgrimage to Mecca, *Hajeh* (female) or *Haj* (male) can also be used to show respect to an elder.

Azzam held out a small coin and requested quietly, "Some candies, please."

Um Sa'eed silently wrapped a few strawberry candies in paper and pressed the parcel into Azzam's hands, plucking the coin from his fingers. As we turned to leave, her raspy voice implored us, "Come again, boys."

Poverty did not separate my family from my neighbors, but something else did. I wanted to punch the stupid kids who teased me about my parents' disability. "Even if your mom and dad have the best eyes in the world, their minds and hearts are smaller than a cumin seed!" I wanted to shout at them. I bristled when the shopkeeper referred to me as "the blind folks' son." But I had to control my reactions, especially if my father was with me. If I said or did anything disrespectful to an adult, even in defense of my family, I would feel the sting of my father's switch the moment we got home.

Azzam was the brother who felt the switch most often. He left the house each morning with the rest of us, carrying his books and heading toward school. In the afternoons he returned with all of us as well. But in between, he was often caught and punished for playing near the mosque with other kids who skipped school.

More important than avoiding my father's switch was getting his approval. Some evenings he came home with a small gift. "This is for doing well on your exam," he would say as he handed me the candies. Or, "I saw your teacher today and he said you are a great boy. Keep it up." It was hard for him to tell us in words that he loved us. He found other ways.

Chores were passed from brother to brother. Initially Samir took the small wheelbarrow every week in the winter to the petrol station outside of Lions' Gate* and filled our two-gallon jerry can with kerosene for our heater. When I was big enough to push the wheelbarrow, the job was passed down to me. It was a bitterly cold task. I returned home shivering and with numb fingers from the wheelbarrow's metal handles. After a few winters, fetching the kerosene became Azzam's chore.

Samira, and later Hanadi, helped my mother. On Fridays, *maqlubeh* day, Samira removed the inside bits of the chicken. These were always fed to the cats, more populous in the Old City than people. Azzam, Mazin, and I liked to sneak up on the cats when they were busy consuming the chicken bits and try to hit them without being scratched.

---

*Another of the entrances/exits to the Old City.

"*Haraam!*"* my mother scolded us when the yowl of a cat told her what her sons were up to. "It's wrong to hit the cats!"

A low wall separated Abu Fakhri's courtyard from ours. Our beloved old neighbor was our favorite victim. Abu Fakhri was eating dinner in his courtyard one evening. A large cat was snoozing on the wall separating our homes. Azzam crept to the wall silently and in one fluid motion pushed the cat into Abu Fakhri's courtyard. There was a clatter of plates, tortured yowling, and frightened screams of "Cat! Cat!" It must have landed right on his dinner table! Azzam, Riyyad, and I ran inside the house, covering our mouths to muffle our laughter.

In the summers, my brothers and I played soccer on the street with other kids from the neighborhood. From time to time, the ball would smash into someone's window, shattering the glass. We fled in every direction. After the window's owner had finished cleaning up the glass, cursing the idiot kids who made life so difficult, we slowly, stealthily crept back to the neighborhood.

Our play sometimes got us in trouble. An old man on the street slapped me hard across the neck. I darted into my house, showing Aunt Fatmeh my red, smarting neck and telling her in full detail the grave injustice that had just been visited upon me. Aunt Fatmeh was ready to wage war. We went in search of my attacker.

"There, that's him!" I pointed out the old man, who hadn't gone more than a few yards.

Aunt Fatmeh strode to him without hesitation, and before he could utter a word, she had her slipper in her hand and was pounding him with it, shouting, "If you ever touch Sami again, *ya haj,* I will beat you twice as hard!" I watched gleefully as the astonished old man tried to defend himself against Aunt Fatmeh's Slipper of Vengeance. I did not bother mentioning to Aunt Fatmeh the reason the old man had slapped me: I had punched his grandson in the stomach during a scuffle while playing soccer.

In the winters, we divided the downstairs room down the middle, transforming it into a battlefield. Azzam and I were together, taking cover behind a table, and Samir and Riyyad were the other team, building their fort from chairs. Sometimes we let Mazin watch. We stockpiled orange and lemon peels as ammunition and used rubber bands for slingshots. Shoes made excellent grenades. The game always dissolved, however, when it came time to choose who would be Jews and who would be Arabs. We all wanted to be the

---

*Arabic for "forbidden" in a religious sense, used to mean "not right!" or "have mercy!"

Arabs. The shoe grenades and lemon-rind bullets were usually launched in the struggle to determine the teams. If things ever got too loud or violent, my father put an end to it swiftly. "Quiet down there!" he shouted, banging his cane on the floor above our heads. "I don't want to hear another peep out of you!" We turned to a calm game of dominoes, but my father's orders of silence were never upheld for very long. Dominoes somehow induced Samir to dare Azzam to climb on the roof and cluck like a chicken at the top of his lungs.

School cut severely into my playing time. In 1972, fifth grade, we began to learn Hebrew. Our teacher's name was Avital. She was the first Israeli I met who was not a soldier. Avital was not so different from us. Her clothes were shabby, though clean and neatly patched, just like ours. She always greeted us cheerfully and with a warm smile. But we didn't want to learn Hebrew. And we definitely did not want to learn it from an Israeli woman. The class began tormenting Avital. Every time she entered the classroom, we started chanting, "Avital! Avital!" pounding our hands in rhythm on the desks. Avital never yelled or disciplined us like any other teacher would have. I watched her face one day as we were pounding and shouting. She looked as if she was trying not to cry. I stopped banging and clasped my hands together stiffly on top of my desk. I wanted Avital to see that I was no longer supporting this behavior against her. When my classmates eventually calmed down, Avital was an excellent teacher. But the kids jumped at the slightest excuse to torment her again. Avital left after two months. Her replacement was a Palestinian man from inside '48.* He was not half the teacher Avital had been. I didn't like him one bit.

I was not allowed to play until my homework was done. After eating lunch, I rushed to Abu Manar's house. His daughters were eighteen and nineteen years old and helped me with my studies. They thought I was a cute, innocent little kid; little did they know that when Amani sat next to me and clarified an arithmetic problem, I felt my heart dancing. I did not say a word to anyone about my crush on Abu Manar's daughters. I didn't want the girls to laugh at me. But there was no harm in looking at them as they explained grammar to me, and to let my heart dance a little bit.

---

*"Inside '48" signifies Palestinians who live inside the 1948 borders of Israel, as distinguished from Palestinians living in the Occupied Territories. Roughly 20 percent of Israel's citizens are Palestinian. The community of Palestinians inside Israel are referred to by different names, often with political implications, including "Arabs of '48," "Arab-Israelis," "Palestinians inside Israel" (or simply "Palestinians inside"), and "Palestinian citizens of Israel."

I was tempted to stretch homework time until evening, but that would have interfered with my other passion: marbles. My friends and I gathered on the steps of the neighborhood shops and played for hours. We lost and gained marbles between us at lightning speed. I stored my growing collection in a glass bottle. In the evenings, I often spread the marbles on my mat, enjoying the feel of their cool, smooth surface and the beautiful swirl of colors. My shooter was dark blue. I could always count on Lucky Blue to bring me more treasure.

One afternoon, I was so intensely involved in the game that I did not hear the evening call to prayer. My father came out on the street, grabbed me by the shoulder, and dragged me into the house.

"You're out playing marbles until this time of night? As if you don't have a home? Everyone will say we raised you to be a street kid!"

His switch slammed hard against my behind over and over, until my mother pleaded with him to stop. But much worse than the sting of the switch was the fate that befell my treasures. My entire collection of beloved marbles was dumped into the well, for the third time in as many months. I knew that I would start my collection from scratch the very next afternoon, but the knowledge brought little comfort. I wept in fury until late at night, grieving for the hundreds of brightly colored marbles now floating in the waters of the Old City.

CHAPTER THREE

⁓⁓⁓

IT WAS RAMADAN 1973. School days were short during Ramadan, so my friends and I could devote more time to marbles. Phrases such as "Arab unity," "Israeli occupation," and "liberating Palestine" floated above our heads as we set up our ring outside the neighborhood shops. UN Resolutions 242 and 338 were invoked as we played. I loved listening to the men talking about these serious matters. They seemed to know everything.

On October 6, Abu Fakhri came to the shop, but before he could take his customary seat on a stool, Abu Manar approached him holding up an Israeli lira. "You see this?" he said to Abu Fakhri. "This will soon be worthless. The war has begun! We won't be using Israeli money anymore!"

"I have to go now," I said hurriedly to my friends, scooping up my marbles. I began running home. *Iftar** was approaching and the narrow streets were packed with women shopping for last-minute ingredients, men talking with excitement about the attacks, and children scurrying on errands for this or that forgotten item. I skillfully navigated the small spaces between people's legs and, in record time, I reached the skinny alley that led to our house. I thrust open the metal door to the small courtyard and bounded up the stairs, taking the final three steps in one giant leap.

I went directly to my orange plastic bank, sitting on top of the radio. Every day I had been putting my pocket money inside the bank, saving it for *Eid il Fitr.***

"Samira!" I called to my sister, who was in the kitchen helping my mother prepare *iftar*. "Bring me a knife, please!"

---

*The evening meal that breaks the daytime Ramadan fast.

**The three-day celebration marking the end of Ramadan.

Samira handed me the knife, watching curiously as I sawed open my plastic bank and shook the coins out on the floor.

"What are you doing, Sami?" she finally asked. My mother joined her as I quickly counted my money.

"The Israelis will be gone soon," I said, gathering the coins into my hand. "I have to spend my money now."

My mother burst out in laughter. "Nothing is going to change by the end of Ramadan, *habibi*. Your money will still be okay."

"It's my money! I can do what I like with it!" I protested.

"Of course, of course you can." My mother shook her head, smiling. "Spend it in good health, my son."

With my loot held tightly in my fist, I sprinted down the stairs, through the courtyard, and back to the store. A large crowd had gathered, estimating how quickly Palestine would be liberated. I wanted to linger and listen, but I had an important task at hand. How many balloons, cookies, and candies could I purchase with my money? As talk about tanks and warplanes swirled around me, I walked happily back to my house with an entire carton of balloons and a big paper sack stuffed full with sweets. Maybe I would share some with my family. But if they continued to laugh at me, I would be forced to eat it all myself.

My mother stockpiled rice, lentils, beans, flour, tea, and sugar. The war was all anybody could talk about. The surprise attacks launched by Egypt and Syria were sure to liberate our land! Everyone in the Old City huddled around transistor radios at every shop or street corner, keeping track of how many Israeli airplanes the Arab armies had shot down and how many Israeli tanks had been destroyed.

Abu and Um Mustafa in the room downstairs had a small black and white television set. Thirty of us crowded like sardines into their twelve-square-foot room for the 8 p.m. news broadcast from Jordan. The adults, sitting on wooden chairs or the edge of the beds, drank cups of tea while the kids jostled for the best spots on the floor. Um Mustafa teased Abu Fakhri for insisting on a little extra space for his *narghile*.* When the broadcast began, the kids were immediately shushed.

The quiet in the room never lasted. We clapped and cheered loudly watching images of Israeli planes falling from the sky. A few days into the war, the

*Glass-based water pipe or hookah, also called *arghile*.

newscaster reported that Syria had liberated the Golan Heights and that Egypt liberated the Sinai Peninsula. We rose to our feet in jubilation. The Israeli occupation was almost over!

"Finally!" Abu Fakhri said over and over to anyone who would listen. "The Arabs are uniting in one front! It's about time!"

"Soon we'll be raising the Palestinian flag!" Um Mustafa shouted. I stamped my feet and whistled and cheered. Abu Manar and Abu Mustafa began formulating plans for their families to come back home from refugee camps in Lebanon, Syria, and Jordan.

Night after night, the television reported that we were winning. But after several days, the adults grew increasingly tense and nervous. The comments over our heads started to focus on how American military support for Israel was upsetting the equation. The television announced the October 25 ceasefire as if it was an enormous victory for the Arab armies. But the anger creasing Abu Fakhri's face bespoke a different reality.

"Nothing will change," Abu Fakhri announced bitterly to passersby as he perched on his stool by the shop. "We were sold out by the Arab governments. They caved to the demands of the Americans. They sold Palestine."

"Negotiations!" Abu Mustafa spit disdainfully on the sidewalk when talk began circulating that there would be an Arab-Israeli summit in Geneva. "Agreements are nothing but a waste of ink on paper. Like Gamal Abdel Nasser said: what was taken by force can only be restored by force."

The Eid came and went, and we were still using Israeli money.

In 1974, I visited the Ibrahimi Mosque in Hebron with my sixth-grade class. The mosque was the burial place of Ibrahim, the holy prophet for Muslims, Jews, and Christians. It was one of the Palestinian people's most treasured sites. I stared at the tombs of Ibrahim and his wife, Sara, covered with green silk and verses from the Qur'an. I pictured them dwelling in their small house in Hebron, perhaps not far from where my Aunt Fatmeh now lived. I stroked the lush woven fabrics decorating the walls and imagined the architects sketching the painstaking details of every magnificent arch. Ancestors of mine, dating all the way back to the Herodian era, had transported these stones from the quarry, lifting one on top of the other. Those men had been building civilization. I thought about the images of the recent war. We were not building civilization anymore. We were destroying it.

The ritual of watching the news continued. In June 1974, we sat, stunned, as reports described how the Israelis had started to dig tunnels under the gates around the Ibrahimi Mosque.

"This is one of our holiest places!" Abu Fakhri sputtered with rage. "The Jews will stop at nothing!"

Demonstrations began. I watched them on the nightly news: men and women, old and young, in Hebron, Nablus, Gaza, Jerusalem, protesting the intrusion into our sacred mosque. Sadness and anger intermingled in the crowds.

Samir stood up suddenly, pointing at the TV. "Um Mustafa! It's you!" he shouted. The cameraman had filmed our downstairs neighbor leading the march through the Old City *souq*,* chanting loudly with her arms spread wide. Every two hours the news was repeated; we remained glued to the TV set all night. We wanted to see Um Mustafa lead the demonstration again and again.

The Ibrahimi Mosque crisis worsened over the next year. In August 1975, Israelis divided the mosque in two: half for Jews, half for Muslims. Next, an Israeli flag was hoisted over the mosque. Then settlers desecrated the holy Qur'an by stomping on it. With each fresh provocation, the crowd at the demonstrations grew and the rage intensified.

If a demonstration erupted during school hours, our teachers locked us inside the classroom. But trying to concentrate on studying was pointless. We staged our own pseudo-demonstrations right inside our class.

"Go to hell, Israel!" one classmate shouted. "You stole our homeland!"

"There are more of us than there are of them. Why can't we kick them out?" another responded.

After school hours, our teachers could not control us. The moment I heard that the *shabab*** were congregating in the Al Aqsa compound or at Damascus Gate, my best friend, Abbas, and I ran there as fast as we could. The kids hurling stones and running away from the gas bombs were Samir's age and older. But even if we were young, we could still chant with the crowd, "*Falestina Arabiyya, Faltaskut assahyuniyya!*"***

"Get out of here, Sami!" Samir shouted when he saw me on the sidelines. He kicked me for good measure. "Go home!"

I positioned myself farther from where Samir and his friends were throwing stones and continued to shout until I was hoarse, "*Biruh, biddam, nifdiki Falastin!*"‡ and "*La lil-ihtilal!*" §

---

*Arabic for "market."

**Arabic for "youth," equivalent of the American "the guys."

***Arabic for "Palestine is Arab land; Zionism will fall!"

‡Arabic for "With soul and blood, we give Palestine to you!"

§Arabic for "No, no to occupation!"

I loved the rush of adrenaline when I marched with the *shabab* from Al Aqsa to Damascus Gate, shouting until my throat became sore. I chanted with even more fervor whenever I saw someone waving a large Palestinian flag. The *shabab* marching with the flags were my heroes. They were risking three or four years in prison just by waving our flag on the street.

I was skilled at avoiding the soldiers' clubs during the demonstrations. Darting away from their sticks was a game. If there was no place to run, I took cover behind an old woman, whom they were less likely to strike. If the demonstration moved through Damascus Gate to the street outside, I did not follow. I could not be sure of what might happen outside the Old City walls.

Later in the evening Samir and his friends Hisham and Ibrahim would return to the neighborhood.

"Wow, that was rough today," Hisham remarked nonchalantly in front of Abbas and me.

"Did you get hurt?"

"Nothing too bad."

"Let us see!" we begged them.

They lifted up their shirts and proudly showed off their purple bruises and red welts. Abbas and I were suitably impressed. Ibrahim limped back to his house. A soldier had crunched his baton on Ibrahim's foot to prevent him from running away.

I should have known better than to go to a demonstration when Aunt Fatmeh was visiting. She spotted me on the periphery and pushed her way toward me through the crowd, yelling so loudly that all the Old City could hear. "What do you think a small boy like you can do for the resistance? Let the powerful countries take care of politics! You're just a child!" She grasped me firmly by the ear and marched me into the house. "Look who I found in the *souq* today," she said grimly as I squirmed to get away. "Shouting slogans, facing the Israelis!"

My father grabbed me by the shoulders and shook me as hard as he could. "What were you doing there?" he shouted. "Don't you know how dangerous that is?"

If my teeth had not been rattling inside my head, I might have mentioned that before Aunt Fatmeh snagged me, she had been right up in the soldiers' faces herself, scolding them as only an old woman could: "To hell with you and your fathers! Stop beating those kids! Get out of here and leave them alone!"

The second time Aunt Fatmeh caught me, my father punished me with the switch; the third time he used his belt, beating me until I bawled. "I won't go again! I promise, *Yaba!*"*

My mother cried even harder than me. "Stop hitting him, *khalas,*** Saber! You punished him enough!"

My father's face was full of anguish more than anger. "How else will he learn? If he doesn't respect my words, maybe he will respect my belt!" He struck me again. "It's hard enough as it is to feed him. The last thing we need is for him to be in the hospital with broken bones!"

"I won't go ever again!" I blubbered.

But by the time the chanting and excitement of the next demonstration began, the beating was already a distant memory. Plus, my Aunt Fatmeh was back in Hebron. I was not so likely to be caught this time.

"*Assalamu 'alaikum,**** Abu Fakhri." My old neighbor was on his usual perch outside the shop.

"Look at this!" Abu Fakhri thrust the evening's newspaper at me. "Can you believe this?"

I looked at the article. Montaha Horani, fourteen years old, had been shot and killed by soldiers at a demonstration in Jenin. She was staring right at me from the photograph in the paper, wearing her school uniform. Montaha Horani was still just a child. I could not take my eyes off the photo. She must have been scared when they shot her. She probably cried. I knew I would have. I wondered how long she had suffered between the moment they shot her and the moment she died.

"Montaha Horani is a *shaheedah,*"‡ Abu Fakhri said gently, sensing my distress. "Allah *yerhamha.*"§

Montaha was the first *shaheed* I had ever heard about.

Abbas and I talked about Montaha in hushed voices as we walked to school the next morning. Abbas's cousin had died a few years ago while making a bomb. Abbas was proud of his cousin; we should be proud of Montaha,

---

*Arabic for "Papa" or "Dad."

**Arabic for "enough" or "stop."

***Arabic greeting, meaning: "Peace be upon you." Usually responded to with "*Wa 'alaikum assalaam,*" meaning: "And peace upon you!"

‡The feminine equivalent of "shaheed," Arabic for "martyr."

§ The feminine equivalent of "*Allah yerhamo,*" Arabic for "God have mercy on her," said when someone has died.

he told me. But all I could think about was Montaha's family and classmates. Were they proud? Or were they grief-stricken? Montaha was not walking to school as we were. There was an empty desk where she used to sit.

That afternoon, there was a huge demonstration for Montaha. Abbas ran to the *souq* to join the action. I followed him slowly, my feet dragging. Maybe this time the soldiers would kill me. I thought about the nightly news we watched in Abu and Um Mustafa's room. North Vietnamese kids no older than I were using Kalashnikovs against the American occupation. If they were brave enough to shoot the American soldiers, I should be brave enough to stand up to the Israelis. I caught up with Abbas at the *souq* and began chanting and shouting. But when the soldiers started swinging their wooden clubs, I scurried away as fast as I could. Let the older *shabab* face the soldiers. They could absorb the blows more easily. Their bodies were big and strong, not small and skinny like mine. The soldiers' sticks were heavy. They could bash my brains out. This was no longer a game.

⁂

"I'M NOT going to stand around with my hands in my pockets!" Samir's friend Hisham declared. "We have to do something!"

Samir and his friends stood on the corner planning huge actions, something that would put a real dent in the occupation. They imagined throwing Molotov cocktails at army jeeps from the Old City walls. The only time their talk about resistance paused was to eye the girls walking by. The girls blushed and giggled as they passed. I wanted to be respected like that by girls. Girls never seemed to notice me. Samir and his friends marched in the demonstrations with overflowing confidence as the girls marched behind them. Like they owned the streets. If they kept on like this, they could free Palestine for sure. They could change the world.

I soaked up as much of their bravado as I could, taking note of their clothes and how they styled their hair so I could imitate them. If I was silent as a cat, they tolerated my presence. But if I so much as sneezed, Samir chased me away, making sure to get a kick or punch in.

I liked to hang out with older kids at school as well. Ramzi, an eleventh grader, saw me borrowing a stack of books at the library.

"You like to read, Sami?" Ramzi asked.

"Yeah."

"You should come to our book group meetings at the Mozafin Club."

The only club I knew was the one in the Old City where we played sports. I had no idea what a book group meeting was, but I decided to attend.

I entered Mozafin hesitantly. Ramzi greeted me warmly, but he was busy talking to other youth. At fourteen years, I was by far the youngest there. The dozen of us made a circle with folding chairs. They were discussing a book about psychology. I understood very little of the discussion, but I sat quietly, trying to absorb as much as I could. I had never been in a group like this: boys and girls together, expressing their opinions seriously. Everyone sounded so intelligent.

"Remember to come by nine in the morning on Friday," one of the group members called out as the meeting was breaking up.

"What's on Friday?" I asked Ramzi as we stacked our folding chairs against the wall.

"We're going to Jalazone refugee camp. There's no proper street linking the camp to the main Ramallah–Nablus road. They asked us to help build one. You want to come?"

Dheisheh was the only refugee camp I had been inside. I liked the idea of helping our poor people in the camps. "Sure, I'd love to come!"

Fourteen people gathered at Mozafin on Friday morning. Once again, I was the youngest. We took a bus heading to Nablus and got off at the junction near Jalazone camp. I understood why Ramzi said there was no proper street linking the camp to the main road. We had to pick our way between stones through the valley to get to the camp.

An older man and a group of *shabab* from the camp greeted us and gave us tools and instructions. We broke into several small groups of three: one to break the large stones into pieces, one to carry the pieces to the road, and one to place them in the correct spot. Each group of three was responsible for thirty feet of the road.

Before long I found myself side by side with two older girls. We had been given a twenty-pound iron hammer to break the stones. Without hesitation, one of the girls lifted the heavy hammer and shattered a stone with the force of her blow. I watched in amazement. This girl was stronger than any boy I knew in my neighborhood! We rotated the three jobs between us. The second girl was just as capable. When it was my turn to break the stones, I lifted the hammer high above my head, bringing it down hard and fast, just as I saw the girls doing. Within fifteen minutes my back and shoulders were sore, my hands were blistered, and I was covered in sweat.

What is Abbas doing right now? I wondered. He was probably trying to hang out with the older boys, who would be boasting about how they were going to do something big. But here I was actually working, side by side with other youth, including young women! This felt good.

Older folks watched the work progress. "Making a street now, are they? As if we're going to stay here forever!" one old man said.

"Why shouldn't we have a street?" his wife retorted. "Even if we return to Al-Lyd next week, at least we can put our things in a truck and drive to the main road!"

We took a break in midafternoon. People from the camp invited us to sit in the shade and gave us falafel sandwiches and cold water.

"Can I walk around inside the camp?" I asked the group leader.

"What for?"

"I don't know. . . . I just want to see the people . . . see how they live."

"Sami . . . our objective is to build the road, not to go and stare at the people inside the camp."

Flushing a bit from his comment, I went back to gathering broken bits of stone in a plastic bucket. I had not intended anything disrespectful by wanting to see the people inside the camp. I felt sorry for them. They did not have the opportunity to work. They depended on the United Nations for food. The kids didn't have sneakers to wear when they played soccer. Refugees deserved our sympathy.

As I hauled the bucket to our section of the road, it occurred to me: I am the same as the residents of Jalazone. I didn't grow up in a camp, surrounded with stories about my native village, but that was the only difference. I was a refugee, too, exactly like them. Their families had been displaced from Al-Lyd, mine from Zakariyya and Deir Yassin.

I had seen Deir Yassin for the first time a few months earlier. My Uncle Zaki had come from Jordan to get married. One afternoon, Uncle Zaki took me past Deir Yassin. We did not enter the village, which the Israelis now called Givat Sha'ul, a neighborhood of West Jerusalem. Uncle Zaki simply pointed it out from the road. My father had been in the blind school in Ramallah on April 9, 1948, when the massacre in Deir Yassin took place. Uncle Zaki told me about our cousin, a toddler named Fou'ad Al Jundi, whose two-year-old throat was slit by a knife while his mother clutched him in her arms.

I swung the hammer forcefully, scattering pieces of stone around me. Zakariyya and Deir Yassin were reminders of who I really was, a refugee. I paused to wipe the sweat off my brow, staring at the entrance of the refugee camp. I come from here. I am part of this larger story. I passed the hammer to one of the girls and took my turn with the bucket.

Late that afternoon, we stood at the top of the valley and surveyed our work. Professional workers would still have to pave it with a layer of pebbles, but we had laid a good foundation. I thought about what the old man watching us had said. He was right. This road should be temporary. The people in Jalazone should be allowed to return to Al-Lyd! No one has the right to separate my people from our homeland.

The next day, I tried to explain to Abbas the powerful feeling that came from accomplishing such a huge task as part of a group. I wanted Abbas to join me next time.

But Abbas snorted in disapproval. "That group is a bunch of communists. They don't even believe in God."

I had never heard of communists before. Didn't believe in God? I was shocked. I had never known anyone who did not believe in God. I thought about the people in my neighborhood. Many of them were religious Muslims, but I didn't see them doing for our people half of what my new friends in Mozafin were doing. I did not have to share their opinions about God in order to break up stones to build crude roads. The following Friday, I went with the club to clean the cemetery outside Lions' Gate. As I pulled out thorny weeds, questions began to swirl in my own brain. Did I believe everything I had been taught about religion? Wouldn't God judge people according to how they treated others, rather than how often they prayed and fasted?

Abbas and my other friends made fun of me, joking about the nonbelievers and communists. Gradually I stopped going to Mozafin. My friends from the neighborhood were more important to me. And I was very busy. There were a lot of girls to look at and demonstrations to attend.

I had learned a thing or two from my experience with Mozafin. I offered to help break up big stones into smaller ones and to carry them in buckets to where the older kids were hurling them at soldiers. Sometimes Abbas's cousin Badawi joined us. Badawi was a year older than us and was Abbas's opposite. Abbas had puppy-dog eyes, was pale, tall, and thin, and spoke slowly and quietly. Dark-skinned and short, Badawi loved to be the center of attention, smiling, joking, and talking with animation. Badawi made Abbas and me laugh.

I arrived at Abbas's house one Friday with my bathing suit and towel. "*Yallah*, let's go to the pool in Katamon," I said. The pool in Katamon was nicer than the one in East Jerusalem. Abbas did not need much encouragement. It was a hot day. Abbas and I took Egged, the Israeli public bus service, from outside the Old City to the Katamon neighborhood in West Jerusalem. We paid the entrance fee and went inside.

We goofed off for an hour or so, jumping off the diving board to see who could make the biggest splash. I was getting ready to do a backflip when a group of ten Israeli teenagers entered. They looked about a year or two older than us and a year or two bigger. One of the boys pointed at us and said something to his friend, who laughed loudly.

Abbas and I decided to leave. "I'll get our towels," I said to him in Arabic, as I began walking to where our belongings were lying on the grass.

"Bring our clothes too!" Abbas called after me.

But before I could reach our things, the group of boys had surrounded me. "What are dirty Arabs like you doing here?" the ringleader asked in Hebrew.

"We came to swim. We bought a ticket just like you." I tried to keep my voice level. I didn't want to provoke them. But violence was flashing in their eyes. It didn't matter what I did or said; I was going to get beaten up and I knew it.

The circle of boys began shoving and pushing me. "Fucking dirty Arab. We don't want garbage like you here!" One boy spit on me.

"I did something to you just by being an Arab?" My Hebrew was weak, but I could say that much. I blocked one boy's arm as he tried to slap me. The whole group fell on me, punching and kicking. I fell to the grass, trying to shield my stomach and face as blows from their fists and feet landed on my head, back, shoulders, and legs.

I heard a man shout in Hebrew, "What are you kids doing? Leave him alone!" I felt him pull one boy off me, and the rest stepped back, breathing hard. "You should be ashamed of yourselves."

"Fucking Arab—he's the one who should be ashamed," the ringleader retorted weakly. The boys sauntered to the other side of the pool, laughing. Abbas helped me to my feet.

"Are you okay?" the man and Abbas asked me at the same time, one in Hebrew, the other in Arabic.

"I was just getting our stuff . . . that's all I was doing . . ."

Abbas and I threw our shirts and pants on quickly. The man walked us to the entrance of the pool.

"Fuck them!" I said as soon as we got out, trying to hide my shaking.

"Who needs their stinking pool anyway? I never want to go there again!" Abbas spit on the side of the road.

A few days later, when the humiliation was a little less acute, Abbas and I told Badawi what had happened. He immediately put down the cards that we had been playing.

"Sami! Why didn't you tell me right away? They can't do this to you and get away with it!" Badawi scratched his chin thoughtfully. "Okay then. We need to get one of them in return. Let's go to the New Gate. One of them will pass by . . ." Badawi pounded his fist into the palm of his hand, demonstrating what we would do.

We tossed our cards onto Abbas's bed and left his house, cutting through the alleys from the *souq* to the New Gate. We sat on a low wall inside the entrance of the gate and waited. At first the only Israelis who passed by were adults or girls. We didn't want to hit girls. Then—after ten minutes—we had our chance. Two Israeli boys walked in. They were a year or two older than us, but we had the advantage of surprise. We pounced on them, getting in a few slaps and kicks each. They began to cry and shout. We chased them five or six steps to scare them more and then we sprinted into the *souq*, getting lost in the stream of people. We ran until we reached the Church of the Holy Sepulcher and leaned against the church wall, panting and exchanging high fives. I felt good, strong. If we ever saw any of them in our neighborhood again, they could expect more of the same. They had no right to be on our turf.

"Did you hear about Elon Moreh?" Badawi asked Abbas and me a few weeks later when we came over to play cards. Abbas and I looked at each other blankly.

"No, what's that?"

"It's going to be the biggest settlement yet. They're building it on olive tree groves they confiscated from villages in the Nablus area."

They were taking people's olive groves? Ripping out the ancient trees and then building homes on the land and settling other people in those homes? I was horrified.

The commentators on the Arab news channels spewed harsh words against the fresh theft of our land, but that did not fool Abu Fakhri, puffing in despair on the end of his *narghile* in Abu Mustafa's room. "Mark my words," he said. "The Arab countries won't lift a finger. We've got double trouble: Israeli occupation and Arab governments that don't give a damn."

I thought about Abu Fakhri's words in bed that night. He was absolutely right. It was up to us. We had to raise our voices and let them know this was our land. This was our home.

A fresh wave of demonstrations erupted. Abbas, Badawi, and I continued to collect stones, gathering them in buckets from the streets and under the trees and leaving them at all the crossroads in the *souq* where the older *shabab* would need them.

These demonstrations were bigger than the previous round, with hundreds of people participating in each one. We congregated at Al Aqsa and began to march, shouting, "*Allahu Akbar!*"* and growing larger along the way like a snowball rolling down a hill. Our *shabab* threw stones more boldly and the soldiers answered them not only with gas bombs and clubs, but also with bullets. Fifteen-year-old Leena Nabulsi from Nablus was killed on May 15, 1976. In the next day's demonstrations, nineteen-year-old Mustafa Hawas from Qalandia refugee camp was killed.

On May 17, Abbas and I waited in the Al Aqsa compound for the demonstration to begin, protesting both the construction of Elon Moreh and the deaths of Leena Nabulsi and Mustafa Hawas. The crowd we expected to gather had not arrived.

"Maybe it's starting in the *souq*," I said. Suddenly, a young man burst into the compound. His white T-shirt was drenched with sweat and covered in blood.

"They killed him! The Israelis killed Mahmoud! Fuck them! Fuck their fathers!" Tears streamed down the young man's cheeks as he washed his bloody hands and face in the faucet.

Abbas and I stared at him, shocked. "Are you wounded?" Abbas managed to ask.

The youth turned on Abbas fiercely. "It's not my blood, it's Mahmoud's! I had to carry him to Damascus Gate . . ." The water flowed a rusty red from his hands. He couldn't get the bloodstains off his shirt or his pants. Wiping the tears off his face, the boy ran off to tell others.

People began to gather, a few at first, and then more and more.

"Who was it? Do you know which Mahmoud was killed?" I asked a kid I had seen in other demonstrations.

"Mahmoud Al Kurd! And they will pay for it!" The kid dashed off to break up stones.

Mahmoud Al Kurd was the new *shaheed*? Mahmoud Al Kurd was not just anyone; he was a local celebrity. Mahmoud was last year's bodybuilding champion of the West Bank. He lived in the Old City and my friends and I

*"God is greater!"

ran into him often. Whenever we passed him at the juice stand near the Church of the Holy Sepulcher, he returned our starstruck greetings with a smile and shook our hands. One time he even let me sip from his glass of carrot juice. We pumped the next arrival for more information. Mahmoud had been shot, he told us, right outside that very juice stand.

Rumors began to fly as more and more people arrived, each new rumor replacing the one before.

"Mahmoud punched a soldier in his face!"

"No, the soldier hit him first and Mahmoud was attacking back!"

"He was shot from fifteen feet away."

"No, it was five feet! I was there, I saw it!"

Everyone agreed on the following: Mahmoud had taken three bullets in the chest and one in the forehead.

"Mahmoud's still alive. He's in the hospital now. They're going to save him!"

"No, he's dead—it was the bullet in the head that killed him!"

People poured into the compound from all over East Jerusalem. Badawi found us in the crowd. Men, women, old people, kids, all of them waiting to bury the BodyBuilding Champion of the West Bank.

Updates circulated: "The car from the hospital is outside Lions' Gate!"

"They're bringing his body now!"

Badawi, Abbas, and I scampered up steps so we could get a good view. We wanted to know what a *shaheed* looked like. A group of Mahmoud's friends carried his body into the compound on a stretcher. Even from our elevated position, we could barely see him over the swelling crowd. Mahmoud's body looked big on the stretcher, draped in a large Palestinian flag. His head was covered with white bandages and a black and white checked *kuffiyeh*.* The funeral prayers finished and Mahmoud's friends hoisted the stretcher high above their heads. We jumped down from the steps as the funeral procession began, heading to the cemetery outside of Lions' Gate. People streamed in from every direction, joining the procession. The stretcher looked like a canoe bobbing on water as it passed from one raised hand to another in the crowd of thousands. I had never seen that many Palestinian flags before. The flag carriers knew they could be arrested, but nobody cared. They had killed Mahmoud Al Kurd, the BodyBuilding Champion of the West Bank. Grown men and older youth were crying. Tears wet my cheeks as well.

---

*Traditional Arab headdress or scarf.

The funeral procession surged toward the cemetery, the shouting and crying growing louder and fiercer. I kept my eyes focused on the stretcher bearing Mahmoud. I barely had to move my legs; the throng lifted me up and carried me in its belly. It was impossible to enter the cemetery itself; it was already overflowing with mourners. Just as I saw Mahmoud's body disappear behind the cemetery wall, a warm drop of water landed on my head. Then another. I looked up in surprise. Rain? In the middle of May? The teardrops from the sky continued. As if even God was grieving for Mahmoud Al Kurd.

"*Ya shaheed irtah irtah, ehna binkamel el-kefah!*"* the mourners chanted.

Suddenly shots rang out. People bolted toward the road. I grabbed Badawi. "What's going on?" We started to run across the street, but Israeli soldiers on horseback were there.

"*Yallah!*" Badawi shouted and the three of us ran back to Lions' Gate and inside the Old City.

The Old City ramparts were packed with *shabab* hurling stones. We couldn't see the soldiers they were trying to pelt, but we heard the gas bombs detonating, followed by the unmistakable sound of live ammunition.

"Just shooting in the air," Badawi said when he saw me jump.

"How do you know? Bullets like that hit Mahmoud Al Kurd right here"— I poked three fingers on Badawi's chest—"and here!" I poked one more on his forehead. "Let's get the hell out of here."

Abbas, Badawi, and I walked quickly to the *souq* and stood in the softly falling drizzle. Abbas kicked a small pebble. "We should go to his house. Everyone will be going there."

We knew where his house was; Mahmoud lived just inside Damascus Gate. We walked to his house in silence.

Mahmoud's younger brother, Khaled, was sitting on the stoop outside. We sat down next to him, trying to summon words of comfort. Badawi put his arm around Khaled and broke the silence. "We are your brothers, too, Khaled. Mahmoud was a brother to all of us," he said.

"You should be proud of him," Abbas added. "He's a *shaheed* now. He'll get a good place in heaven."

I had no idea what to say.

Khaled wiped his eyes roughly with the back of his hand. "My brother was nicer to me than anyone else in the world. And now he's gone," he said simply and went back inside the house.

---

*Arabic for "Rest in peace, oh martyr, and we will continue the struggle!"

Abbas, Badawi, and I sat outside Mahmoud's house for a long time watching people come and go to offer their condolences. When I finally got home, I saw Samir sitting in a chair in the salon. He was looking straight ahead of him. His eyes were blank and rimmed with red. Suddenly I realized—"Mahmoud was a friend of yours?"

Samir nodded silently.

The following day, photocopies of a picture of Mahmoud were pasted on every Old City shop door. He was holding up his trophy with a wide grin. Badawi, Abbas, and I stared at one at the juice stand where Mahmoud had been shot. Abbas ordered carrot juice.

"You hate carrot juice," I reminded Abbas.

"Mahmoud Al Kurd always drank carrot juice," he answered.

The next week, Abbas went to the club to work out and lift weights, though he had never been interested in physical fitness. In conversations, where Abbas used to mention the *shuhada** in his own family's history, he now made reference to Mahmoud.

Abbas, Badawi, and I became bolder in the demonstrations. Rather than just breaking up stones, we began to throw them ourselves. No one had been killed in Jerusalem since the war of 1967. Mahmoud Al Kurd, the Body Building Champion of the West Bank, was the first.

THE OCCUPATION entered every corner of my existence. The streets in West Jerusalem were well maintained, cleaned regularly, and there were dumpsters for garbage. Our roads were full of potholes and cleaned much less frequently. I had to go to West Jerusalem if I wanted to sit on a bench in a green park. Despite these second-rate services, our taxes were higher and enforced more stridently; Palestinians were approximately one-third of the population of Jerusalem, yet we paid 40 percent of the taxes and received only 8 percent of the budget. We did not get any of the social or monetary benefits that Israelis received for serving in the army.

The occupation infiltrated my education. The curriculum was determined by the Israeli Ministry of Education. Why was I forced to study about the Bar Kochba revolt?** This was not my history! These were not my people! My eighth-grade history book was called *The Israeli State*. But no textbook could fool us. We knew who we were.

*Plural of *shaheed*; martyrs.

**A Jewish rebellion against the Roman Empire led by Simon Bar Kochba.

Everywhere I went, I was stopped and questioned by soldiers with guns. Damascus Gate, Salah El Din Street . . . "Where are you going? What are you doing?" I seethed inside each time I had to justify my comings and goings to soldiers who had stolen my people's land and killed Mahmoud Al Kurd.

Abbas worked with his father on Jaffa Street in West Jerusalem, restoring antique furniture. One day he came home furious. Eighteen-year-old soldiers had sneered arrogantly at his fifty-year-old father. His father could do nothing but lower his eyes deferentially. Abbas wanted to smash them, but he couldn't. We set out to the Jewish Quarter to find something else to smash instead. I led Abbas to my old neighborhood from before '67. Pristine new houses had taken the place of the home my family had been kicked out of. There were tidy rows of flowers planted in ceramic pots outside the doors. Abbas and I lifted the pots up over our heads and dashed them on the stone steps, watching with satisfaction as ceramic shards, dirt, and flowers flew in all directions. We smashed the doorbells with stones, running away quickly before we got caught.

In August 1976, news of the Tel Al-Za'atar massacre spread like wildfire. Tel Al-Za'atar was the largest Palestinian refugee camp in Lebanon and was the heart of Palestinian resistance. I watched the news each evening in horror as fresh stories of atrocities poured out of the camp. What separated us from them? Nothing! We were all Palestinian! And who was slaughtering them? Lebanese, backed up by Syria and by Israel! I could not concentrate on my studies when ninth grade began a few weeks later. Why bother preparing for exams? We would all be killed anyway if we did not defend ourselves.

"How will throwing stones in the Old City help?" Abbas complained, as we stood on the street corner waiting for girls to pass by. "The real war is happening in Lebanon."

"If kids in Vietnam can resist the Americans, we can go to Lebanon and fight too!" I had no money. I didn't have a passport. I had no idea how to enlist in a militant group. But I didn't care. I was going to become a fighter and go to Lebanon to defend my people there. And it would not be scary like confronting soldiers in the Old City. We would not be little kids with stones. In Lebanon, we would have weapons.

A few weeks after my fifteenth birthday, Abbas pulled me aside outside my house.

"How much pocket money do you get?" he asked me.

"A few lira a day," I answered. "Why?"

"I get to keep a few lira a day from my salary. If we pool our money for a month"—Abbas looked around dramatically to make sure Azzam was not snooping nearby—"we'll have enough to go to Lebanon!"

"We will?"

"Well . . . we'll have to do a lot of walking," Abbas admitted.

We made a solemn pact, shaking hands. From that point on, we spoke of nothing else. Our friends at the club became irritated that the two of us always had our heads together, whispering. We kicked Azzam and Riyyad away from us even more than usual. Several times we wanted to tell Badawi, but we had sworn not to tell another living soul. I left the house every morning with money for the bus and to buy hot falafel for lunch. I pocketed the coins instead, walking over a mile each way and taking bread and cheese from the kitchen while nobody was watching.

I ripped out a map from an Israeli atlas at school. Abbas and I studied it, strategizing how to get across the border into Jordan.

"What about crossing here?" Abbas pointed to the middle of the Jordan Valley.

"Are you kidding? It's totally militarized!"

Abbas and I pored over the map every afternoon for weeks, plotting out the route. We would travel to Hebron, we decided, and from Hebron to Beer Al-Sabe', and then to the Bedouin area of Tel Arad. From there, we would walk around the southern tip of the Dead Sea to Jordan. We would use the rest of our money on taxis, first to Amman, then to the north of Jordan, and then cross into Syria and finally Lebanon. The plan was simple—and brilliant.

Abbas and I met at the jitney station at 7 a.m. We had six pounds of cucumbers each, a few tomatoes, olives, and some pita bread—enough to last us two days. I had a butcher knife I had swiped from the kitchen, stashing it in the thick green plastic bag with the vegetables. Abbas brought a flashlight and a bottle of water.

We were somber and quiet until the bus to Hebron rolled out of the station, heading south. Only then did Abbas poke me in the ribs with a wide smile.

"Take a last look at Jerusalem, Sami! *Khalas* to this city!"

We arrived in Hebron after an hour and quickly found transport on a service taxi to Beer Al-Sabe'. We found a minibus from Beer Al-Sabe' to Tel Arad easily. We were tense each time we paid a driver, expecting to be stopped or questioned, but we never were. By the time we pulled into Tel Arad at 11 a.m., we were almost giddy with our success.

"Can you imagine our parents' reaction? My dad will go absolutely insane tomorrow morning when he realizes I'm really gone!" I grinned at the image as Abbas and I disembarked from the minibus.

"They'll be going nuts now, but think how proud they will be someday soon. They'll be calling us heroes . . . just like Mahmoud Al Kurd," Abbas answered.

From Tel Arad, we walked straight into the desert, using the sun as our compass. We avoided the roads, making our way through the mountains instead. We wanted to be far from anyone who might wonder what we were doing.

"When do you think we'll make it to Lebanon?" I asked as we navigated between the desert rocks.

Abbas thought for a moment. "Day after tomorrow, I'd say."

"You think? I'm guessing one day more than that."

"Do you think they'll begin training us immediately?"

"I don't know. Maybe they will want to wait a few days. How long do you think our training will last?"

Abbas shrugged. "I have no idea. But I can't wait until I'm carrying my own Kalashnikov like the kids in Vietnam!"

We talked for hours until we noticed the sun beginning to sink behind us. The yellow desert mountains shimmered to orange and red. Dark would be upon us in a few hours. We were not entirely confident that we were going in the right direction. With the sinking sun, it would be even harder to keep our bearings. Bedouin tents were sprinkled all across the mountains. One was not far away.

I nudged Abbas. "Let's ask the Bedouins in that tent where Ein Jedi* is. And then we'll go in the opposite direction!"

We felt very clever as we approached the tent. An old man sat in the entrance.

"*Assalamu 'alaikum,* Uncle."

A white moustache and salt-and-pepper beard covered the Bedouin's wrinkled, leathery, dark face. The white *kuffiyeh* wrapped around his head looked as old and worn as he. His eyes were small, bright, and dark as a bird's.

"*Wa 'alaikum assalaam.* Come, boys, sit and have some tea."

---

*In Hebrew and English, called Ein Gedi, a desert oasis next to the Dead Sea.

"*Shukran,** Uncle." We had nearly finished our water and eaten nothing but cucumbers and half a tomato all day. The thought of warm tea was very appealing.

The old man did not take his eyes from us as he poured sweet, thick tea into small glasses. "Where are you boys heading? Night will be here soon."

"We're going to Ein Jedi. Can you show us the way?" The old man confirmed the direction with a gnarled hand. "But Ein Jedi is still a day's walk from here. Where will you sleep?"

We gave him a vague answer, gulped down the rest of our tea, said goodbye, and continued walking, heading in the opposite direction he had indicated as soon as we were out of sight. Hour after hour slipped by as the sky turned dark blue, darker still, and finally a silky black. The mountains surrounding us, beautiful in the daylight, had transformed into black and menacing silhouettes.

Abbas dug his flashlight out from between the cucumbers. The light was barely enough to keep us from stumbling. After we walked for another hour, the flashlight revealed a large mound of small gray rocks just ahead of us. Gray? That was strange. All the rocks in this area were yellowish orange and white. I picked one up to examine it. Its sides were smooth and uniform, as if it had been cut by a machine. It didn't feel right. We went around the mound as quickly as we could.

By the time we stopped to eat our piece of pita and finish our tomato, it was late at night. The tea felt like a long time ago. I had never walked this much in my life.

"Should we keep going?" I asked, hoping Abbas would reject the suggestion.

"Let's just sleep here," Abbas said. "We need to save our flashlight batteries. We can continue at sunrise."

We found a soft piece of ground under a protective overhang against the side of the mountain. It would do for the night. We tried to make ourselves comfortable on the sand. I leaned against the rock wall and stretched out my legs, feeling my tired muscles begin to relax when the sound of barking made us both jump.

"Just a dog," I said, to reassure myself as much as Abbas. It barked again. "Sounds pretty far away."

"I'm not worried about dogs," Abbas said. "It's the hyenas we have to be careful of."

---

*Arabic for "thank you."

We gathered a pile of stones near us so we could chuck them at approaching hyenas. But I had heard that a hyena could smash a big rock between his jaws. I took the knife out of the bag. If hyenas were in the vicinity, could they smell us? Did they know there was fresh meat in these hills? I clutched the handle of the knife tightly. The dogs continued to bark, but no signs of hyenas. Gradually my grip on the knife loosened and I started to breathe a little deeper.

Then we heard a muffled explosion. Followed by another one. It must have been the Israeli army. The mound of strange rocks we had passed was part of some kind of training base. There was no other explanation.

"Shit," I heard Abbas mutter under his breath. "What are we doing here?"

We listened to the explosions in silence, trying to gauge their distance. The dogs began to bark again, and a wolf emitted a mournful cry, answered by another. The wind started to howl, adding to the frightening chorus. It seemed that morning would never come.

Finally, the black dissolved into gray and before long we could see the outlines of the surrounding hills. Abbas and I put the knife and flashlight back in the plastic bag, stood up, and stretched the painful cramps out of our stiff legs and backs. We looked at each other. We each knew what the other one was thinking. But neither of us wanted to say it first.

"Do we even know if this is the right way?" Abbas finally asked.

I chimed in quickly, "No, I'm not sure at all."

"And those bombs . . ." Abbas added. "We're in a damn military zone!"

"Let's get the hell out of here."

We crammed a few bites of cucumber into our mouths and started to walk as quickly as we could, trying to trace our steps back through the mountain. Every time I thought we were hopelessly lost, I saw a rock formation that looked familiar or a clump of prickly vegetation that I felt sure we had passed on the way. At last we reached the area where the Bedouin man had given us tea, and finally, Tel Arad.

I silently cursed our stupidity on the ride from Tel Arad to Beer Al-Sabe'. The route, the neatly drawn borders—it had all looked clear and simple on the map!

By the time we reached Beer Al-Sabe', we were truly scared. The army and hyenas were one thing—facing our families was another. They had probably turned Jerusalem inside out by now searching for us. What would we tell them? We tried out a dozen excuses on each other, each one sounding lamer than the one before.

"*Khalas,*" I said. "We'll just tell them we went to Ein Jedi to swim in the Dead Sea."

We tossed the knife and remaining cucumbers into a rubbish bin in Hebron. Why would we have brought a butcher knife with us to the Dead Sea? We made sure our stories matched exactly as we sat on the bus to Jerusalem. We lingered for a few moments at Herod's Gate.

"Well, I'd better get home," I finally said.

"See you later. Good luck."

"You too."

I walked home as slowly as I could. My heart was pounding when I stood outside the house. Maybe they would be relieved rather than furious. I tried to slip into the courtyard as invisibly as a cat, but Riyyad was coming out of the bathroom and saw me right away.

I smiled weakly. "Hi. I'm home."

"Mom! Dad!" Riyyad called out loudly. "Sami's back!"

My parents could move very quickly for blind people. Within seconds my father had a deathlike grip on my shoulder and my mother was feeling my face with her hands, crying. "Where were you? We were so scared! We thought you had died!"

Then I saw Abbas's parents in the salon. The families had been waiting together.

I tried to shrug my father's hand off my shoulder, but it tightened like a vise.

"Abbas and I went to the Dead Sea. But it got dark and we didn't have a way to get back, so we slept at Ein Jedi . . ." It sounded idiotic and I knew it.

"You expect us to swallow that? No one with half a brain would believe that!" My father slapped me across the face. "Tell me the truth!" He hit me again, across the neck.

"I swear! We went to Ein Jedi! Where else would we go? We didn't mean to worry anybody!"

Abbas's older brother stormed into our house dragging him by his arm.

"I can't believe how selfish you are," he snorted at us. "Kids the same age as you are dying in Lebanon, in Vietnam. And you go to Ein Jedi to swim and have fun!"

Abbas and I avoided eye contact with each other. We said nothing to correct his brother, either then or later. We could handle his brother's contempt, thinking we were selfish. But we did not want him to mock us or call us stupid little kids for trying to walk around the Dead Sea to Jordan and join the resistance in Lebanon.

CHAPTER FOUR

I FOUND MY MOTHER leaning back on the couch. Her book was open in front of her, but her fingers were not devouring the words as usual. Her head was hanging down.

"*Yamma?* Are you okay?"

She didn't answer. When I came closer, I saw greenish drool coming out of the side of her mouth. She was groaning softly.

I ran out to the courtyard where Mazin was playing. "Mazin! Something's wrong with Mom—go get Dad!"

Mazin jumped up and took off at a run for the Arab Blind Organization. Minutes later, he returned leading my father. By then, my mother was sitting up again, gripping her head.

"Are you okay, Myassar?" My father sat next to her, taking her hand.

"Yes, yes, fine. Just a headache, that's all."

Two days later, my mother's fingers stopped moving in the middle of cleaning lentils with Samira. Her hands clutched her head and she started moaning. Light green drool again emerged from her mouth. Samira helped her to the sofa, where she collapsed in a state of semiconsciousness. Mazin ran to get my father again. This time we went directly to Al Makassed hospital. The doctors examined her, but they had no equipment to run any kind of tests.

"Just make sure she gets plenty of rest," was the only advice the doctor could offer.

After a few weeks, the headaches plagued my mother nonstop. When they grew especially fierce, she became like a crazy person, her neck rolling on her head and her limbs flailing. We took her to Hadassah hospital, which had more modern equipment. Doctors there were able to help as little as Al Makassed's.

My mother grew worse. She was in her altered state more often than not, with only brief windows of lucidity. My father took her to Hebron to visit one of the *fattaheen** who was famous for dispelling the evil eye. For payment of one gold bracelet, he gave my mother a leather pouch to wear around her neck. Inside the pouch was a slip of paper on which the healer had written words from the Qur'an. My father put the amulet under her pillow at night as he had been instructed. But she continued to grow worse. The next week he took her to a different healer in Jenin. Week after week, *fattah* after *fattah* took her gold bracelets and gave her amulets. But her fits grew more severe.

She stayed in bed most of the time now, groaning and writhing, screaming words that made no sense. My brothers, sisters, and I stood around her bed helplessly watching her. Weeks turned into months. My mother continued to deteriorate. Neighbors and relatives came to visit and left her bedroom shaking their heads with sorrow.

"It would be better if she died," I overheard Abu Fakhri say to Aunt Fatmeh. "At least her suffering would end."

Azzam, Riyyad, Samira, and I sat on her bed during a lucid moment. "*Ya masakeen,***" she said, gathering us in a hug. "Who will take care of you when I go?" I squirmed out of her embrace and ran out of the room to hide my tears.

Late at night, I passed by her room. My father was sitting on the side of her bed, stroking her hand with tears running down his face. I had never seen my father cry before.

My father treated us with extra tenderness in his own way. It gave me the confidence to broach an important subject.

"*Yaba,* there are these boots that everyone in school is wearing. Maybe I can get a pair?"

My father took a sip of his tea. "I just bought you shoes a few months ago, Sami."

"I know, but these are special. I really need them . . . " They were made from a sturdy, sand-colored canvas.

---

*Plural form of *fattah*, a traditional healer, fortune-teller, or someone who deals in black magic.

**Plural for *ya maskeen*, Arabic for "poor thing."

He put the cup down. "Luxuries like this are not in our budget! You have perfectly good shoes on your feet—*khalas!*"

He did not even try to understand how crucial the boots were to me. I refused to talk to him the rest of the night. The next day, I wordlessly delivered his lunch at the Arab Blind Organization. He mixed the rice and *mlukhiyyeh** together in silence, squeezing lemon on top.

"You are still angry with me about the boots?" he finally asked.

"You still didn't change your mind about them?" I asked back.

"No," he said, taking a bite of his lunch. "Maybe in a little while, but right now I can't."

I dug deep inside myself to find more anger, but I just couldn't. I knew our situation.

"Never mind, *Yaba.* I understand. *Oyooni elak.*"** I walked toward the door.

"Come here, Sami." I turned, my heart leaping. The love coming from his face took me off guard. Perhaps it was because I had never said anything like that to him. Perhaps it was because I had, quite literally, served as his eyes so many times. He had put the *mlukhiyyeh* aside and was holding bills in his hand. "Here's the money for your shoes."

"No, don't worry, *Yaba.* I know we can't afford it."

"Take the money and get the shoes, Sami! No one will starve at home because of your shoes."

I ran right to the shoe store on Salah el Din Street. But my stylish new footwear brought me little satisfaction. My mother was sick, my father had eight children to feed, Samir would be starting college soon, and I had just bought myself a pair of fancy boots to be like my friends. The image of my father's face as he handed me the money floated in front of my eyes. I forced myself to wear the boots every day, swearing never again to ask my father for anything expensive.

My mother had been sick for more than a year. The house was in chaos. My mom had done everything for everybody: cleaning, cooking, washing our clothes. Samira took on some of the tasks, but she was still only twelve years old. Aunt Fatmeh stayed with us as often as she could, but she had her own husband to care for.

---

*Mallow leaves, cooked often as a soup with a taste and consistency somewhere between okra and spinach.

**"My eyes belong to you"; an Arabic idiom used to mean "Anything for you."

My father sat us down one evening. "We are praying to God your mother will get better, but we don't know what God's plans are," he said. "A man my age still needs a wife."

It was several minutes before I understood. My father intended to take a second wife. "She's from Nablus. Her name is Mariam. I know her from the Arab Blind Organization."

"No!" Samir stood up, his eyes flashing. "You can't do that to our mother!"

"Mom is going to get better!" I shouted at him. "We don't need another mother and you don't need another wife!"

Azzam and Samira sat stone-faced. Riyyad and Mazin began to cry. Hanadi and Sa'ed, aged five and three, knew something was terribly wrong. They ran to Samira for comfort.

Aunt Fatmeh came the next day. "This will be better for everyone, Sami," she said to me. "Mariam can help take care of the home and the little ones. You may not need another mother, but think about Hanadi and Sa'ed." Aunt Fatmeh could see that I was not convinced. She tried a different tack. "According to Islam, your father has every right to take another wife."

Aunt Fatmeh was my father's sister; naturally she would advocate for what he wanted. But the next day my mother's brother, Uncle Mustafa, also gave his agreement to the marriage.

Aunt Fatmeh went with my father to Nablus to make the arrangements with Mariam's family. Within a few months they were married.

"I won't talk to that woman!" Samir hissed at me through clenched teeth as Mariam's brothers carried her boxes into the room Abu and Um Mustafa had vacated.

Riyyad and I were with my mother during a rare window of consciousness. Somehow she knew about Mariam. "Don't be angry, boys." Her voice was so weak I had to lean over her and strain to hear. "It is your father's right to have a healthy wife."

How could I continue to object if my mother herself consented? But when she told us not to be angry, I saw an unmistakable look of hurt in her eyes.

⁂

IN 1978, with my family consumed with my mother's illness, I had more freedom to participate in protests, which began spontaneously whenever a group of *shabab* gathered outside Al Aqsa Mosque or Damascus Gate and started to shout slogans. If there was no demonstration in Jerusalem, Abbas, Badawi, and I went to Ramallah to throw stones. If Ramallah was quiet, we continued north to Nablus or went south to Hebron. Maybe Abbas's and my plan to walk around the Dead Sea had been ill-conceived; perhaps we were still too young. But eventually we would make it to Lebanon or Syria and join the resistance.

People identified with the PLO* as a whole more than any particular movement under its umbrella. Even so, Abbas, Badawi, and I paid close attention to conversations about movement ideologies in coffee shops where we sat playing cards. The Communist Party was not for us. They were engaged solely in community service and building civil society. The Marxist PFLP** sounded more promising; they supported revolution. Mao Tse-tung and Che Guevara were among their heroes. We liked Che Guevara. Fatah was the largest movement in the PLO. The word *fatah* means victory and is also a reverse acronym for *Harakat al-Tahrir al-Watani al-Falestini.**** Like PFLP, Fatah also called for armed resistance, but it seemed Fatah had a policy of not getting involved in politics internal to the Arab states. PFLP, from what we heard, was not afraid to criticize corrupt Arab leadership. Plus, Badawi and Abbas's cousin was a member of PFLP. "PFLP," Badawi said thoughtfully as we walked home from the coffee shop. "This is the way to liberate Palestine."

It was March 11, 1978. Abbas and I were playing cards in his room and talking about girls. Badawi burst in.

"Did you hear what happened?" he panted, leaning against the wall to catch his breath.

"No, what?"

Badawi relayed the day's dramatic events to us. Fourteen heavily armed Fatah militants had left south Lebanon in a rigid inflatable boat in the early morning hours, heading toward Israel's shores. The group's leader was an eighteen-year-old girl named Dalal Mughrabi. The water rose sharply that morning. The group lost three of its fighters on the sea. Their goal was to launch an attack on the Israeli Ministry of Defense in Tel Aviv and to kidnap soldiers for a prisoner exchange. They landed in the north of Israel and hijacked a taxi and then a bus along the coastal road to Tel Aviv, commandeer-

*Palestine Liberation Organization, founded in 1964 and recognized in 1974 in Rabat as the sole legitimate representative of the Palestinian people. The PLO is made up of multiple factions.

**The Popular Front for the Liberation of Palestine.

***Arabic for "Palestinian National Liberation Movement."

ing a second bus on the way. A lengthy chase ensued, ending with a shoot-out with Israeli police at a roadblock. Nine of the eleven Fatah fighters were killed, including Dalal. Thirty-seven Israelis were killed and more than seventy wounded.

Abbas and I jumped up, whooping with joy. "You see?" Badawi shouted as we danced around the room. "We can beat the Israelis! They made it to the heart of Israel! Pow! Pow! Pow!" Badawi imitated Dalal and her fighters in the shoot-out.

"This is what resistance should be!" Dalal Mughrabi was only eighteen years old! If she led this group of fighters, then maybe Badawi, Abbas, and I would lead the next attack!

"PLO! Israel no!" Abbas, Badawi, and I shouted every slogan we had ever heard.

Delirious in our excitement, we spilled out onto the street, joining other *shabab* who were similarly celebrating. Israel was finally being taught its lesson. If they continued to inflict pain on us, we could inflict pain right back. How else could we teach the Israelis they could not steal our homeland and trample our rights? This was the only language the Israelis understood. Badawi, Abbas, and I sat glued to the radio for days, listening to every new song composed about Dalal Mughrabi.

Three days later, on March 14, Israel invaded Lebanon. By the end of the weeklong offensive, the Israeli army had reached the Litani River. Each hour, the number of Palestinian and Lebanese casualties mounted. In response, youth all over Palestine were taking on small acts of resistance. Abbas, Badawi, and I climbed up the Old City ramparts after dark, each carrying a few stones. An Egged bus stop was right underneath Herod's Gate. We waited patiently. When the bus pulled up, we dropped the orange-size stones onto the roof of the bus—one, two, three!—jumped down, and ran away as quickly as we could. We wanted the Israelis sitting inside that bus to know: whether they like it or not, we are here. We wanted them to feel afraid.

Strikes were called on a regular basis, protesting the killings. The shops in East Jerusalem were closed and shuttered. Abbas, Badawi, and I wandered aimlessly through the quiet and still Old City. We passed old Abu Hazem's shop, where we'd bought candy and Coke for years. His door was cracked open, an invitation to slip inside and buy something.

"That asshole," Abbas grumbled in disgust. "Not willing to do even his small part for our freedom."

The next day was business as usual; the shop doors in the Old City were wide open. Abu Hazem greeted Abbas, Badawi, and me as we walked by. He was met with a stony silence.

"Boys!" he called after us. "Why do you act this way, ignoring me?"

"You can crawl up my ass! Leave us alone!" Badawi yelled over his shoulder. We stifled our laughter until we were out of earshot. We didn't care if we hurt Abu Hazem's feelings or that he had been kind to us on many occasions. He had been more interested in making money than in participating in yesterday's strike; that was all we needed to know.

The next strike day, we made note of which shop doors were ajar. The following morning, those shopkeepers found they couldn't unlock their stores; the keyholes had been jammed with matchsticks.

Abu Zaki owned a shop in our neighborhood. He called himself the Rooster and it was an apt moniker; he was rude and arrogant. The Rooster's door was ajar one strike day. The next morning he shouted curses as he confronted his lock jammed with a matchstick. He picked at the keyhole with a needle until the matchstick was removed. His door was open even wider the next strike day. Badawi, Abbas, and I would have to punish him more severely. We dabbed the end of the matchstick in superglue before pushing it into the lock; no amount of needle-picking could extricate it.

But the following morning, the Rooster ripped the entire lock right out of the door, holding it up triumphantly. "That will show those hooligans!" he shouted and spat. The Rooster had not learned his lesson.

I waited for Abbas and Badawi outside the Rooster's shop just after midnight. Our faces were wrapped in *kuffiyehs* so that we could not be recognized.

"You got yours?" I held up my black plastic bag, loaded with self-made ammunition.

"You bet!" Abbas and Badawi each held up theirs. "A bag of shit for that piece of shit!"

We jammed his shiny new lock with two matchsticks, supergluing the entire keyhole for good measure. Then we dipped pieces of cardboard into the plastic bags and smeared our feces all over the Rooster's shop door.

The three of us sat at a shop across the street the next morning, innocently drinking Cokes. Soon enough, the Rooster came strutting down the street, calling out, "*Sabah el khair!*"* He did not seem to notice people snickering behind their hands.

---

*Arabic for "Good morning."

His nose twitched in disgust as he neared his shop. "What the? . . ." Then he saw the door, covered with thick globs of our dried excrement. The Rooster exploded in rage. "Who did this? I will kill those fucking bastards! Maniacs! Their sisters are whores!" He stormed down the street, returning with a can of kerosene and a bucket of rags. He began wiping the entire door from top to bottom with kerosene, all the while spewing curses at God, the resistance, and the unknown assailants.

Badawi winked at Abbas and me and approached the Rooster. "Uncle, what's that awful smell?"

The Rooster scrubbed the door with a vengeance. "Some fuckers did this!"

Badawi shook his head in mock sympathy. "Don't worry, Uncle. If we find the culprits, we'll take care of them for you!"

We left the Rooster to his scrubbing and cursing. Many of the other shop-keepers discreetly winked and smiled at us as we walked by. Maybe the Rooster did not know who was responsible, but apparently others had fig-ured it out.

"It's time to stop talking and start planning," Badawi said as we walked home from the club. "We won't make it to Syria and become part of the PFLP if we don't do something about it."

I did not want to admit it, but I knew in my heart that I could not go. Badawi and Abbas had more independence and pocket money than I did. Sixteen-year-old Abbas was working full-time on Jaffa Street and seventeen-year-old Badawi was employed in an iron workshop in Wadi Joz.* I was still a student. Not only was I in school, but also I was first in my tenth-grade class. I sometimes fantasized about going to university to study medicine or engineering. My Uncle Omar in Kuwait was an engineer. We had a black-and-white photo of him on the wall. He was dressed in dapper clothes, smil-ing from the frame like a movie star. My mother used to finger the photograph lovingly, as if she could see it.

"You'll be an engineer like your uncle, Sami," she would say.

"Engineer?" my father would retort. "Why not a doctor?"

The only doctor I knew was Dr. Amin, with a clinic on the Via Dolorosa. My mother used to take us to Dr. Amin at the first sign of a cough or fever. He always greeted us with a smile and accepted only small coins for his ser-vices. I would love to be useful to my people like Dr. Amin.

---

*A neighborhood of East Jerusalem, close to the Old City.

I never permitted myself to get too carried away with my fantasies. I saw how hard my father had to struggle to help Samir pay for college in Amman, where he was studying arts and sports education. I did not want to be a burden. Better just to drop out of school, find work, and help my family. With my mother's strange disease progressing, any other choice would be selfish. Besides, Abbas, Badawi, and I were going to join the PFLP. Of what use was education?

My father sensed my thoughts. "Take care, son," he cautioned me one night, as I was reading aloud to him. "Politics is a dangerous game. The Israelis show mercy to no one. And if you get in trouble, you think the PLO will lift a finger for you?" I pretended to agree with him. But the next night he interrupted my reading again. "The best way to serve your people, Sami, is to study hard and get good marks."

Aunt Fatmeh always nodded approvingly when she saw my head bent over the books, preparing for my exams. "This boy was born to study," she said, patting me on my head. I hated to dash their high hopes for my future. But every day the news reported more and more people arrested in Tulkarem, Jericho, Jerusalem. My future would most likely find me in prison, wounded, or killed.

I worked with my father at the Arab Blind Organization that summer. It was the last day of August. "Do you have everything you need for the start of eleventh grade?" my father asked me as we walked home from work. "You have enough pencils and notebooks?"

I took a deep breath. I had to tell him sooner or later. "I'm not going back to school, *Yaba*."

"What is this nonsense? With your marks, you can become a famous doctor!"

"It's better if I work."

My father stopped walking and placed his hands on my shoulders. "Is this because of money? Sami, put this far from your mind. We will manage to find a way to send you to university. I will do the impossible."

"*Yaba*, you've always done the impossible, feeding us all and providing us with a good home. It's time for you to depend on me."

My father's voice grew a hard edge. "Is this because of your friends? Abbas and Badawi have been working for a long time and now you want to be like them?"

"This has nothing to do with them. It's my decision alone."

There was an additional reason I wanted to work. I wanted to get engaged to my cousin Sanaa, in Jordan. We'd met a few times in Jordan and a few

times when her family came to Jerusalem. She was smart and animated—
and beautiful. In order to get engaged, I needed money.

My father and I walked the rest of the way home in silence. Before entering the house, he turned to me mournfully. "You know, Sami, a chicken who
digs a hole will be covered by its own dirt."*

We received a call from Hadassah hospital on an icy winter day. A team of
brain specialists had been invited from the States to perform surgeries re-
quiring expertise that no doctor in Israel had. They had looked at my
mother's files. They wanted to examine her.

With the number of doctors and *fattaheen* who had already poked, prod-
ded, or taken her gold bracelets, I was not very hopeful. Nevertheless, we
took my mother to Hadassah the following morning.

After a battery of scans and tests, an American doctor sat down with my
family. "It's a brain tumor," he told us with a nurse translating. "And it's large.
She needs surgery. Her prognosis is not very good. With the surgery, she has
about a 35 percent chance of survival. But without the surgery, she has no
chance at all."

There was nothing to lose. The surgery would be successful, or she would
finally rest in peace. They needed a week to prepare her. We checked her in
right away. I stayed with my mother in the hospital that night. She took labored breaths and her face twitched with pain as I sat next to her bed, watching snowflakes drift toward the earth.

A nurse came in. "How is she doing?" she asked me in Hebrew.

"Sleeping," I answered.

Deep in her unconscious state, my mother heard the Hebrew. "Where am
I?" she started shouting. "The Jews will kill me! Take me home!" She tried to
sit up and get out of bed.

I did my best to soothe her. "Shh, *Yamma,* no one is trying to kill you . . ."

"They will kill me! Why did you put me here?"

I had to restrain her. "You're going to have an operation, *Yamma,* and after
that everything will be okay."

She stopped struggling and returned to a fitful sleep. I sat back on my
chair, breathing hard. The snow continued to fall outside the window, covering the hospital grounds with a thin white blanket.

The next night, the same thing happened. "The Jews will kill me! Take me
home!"

*An Arabic idiom, meaning "Be careful when you create your own problems."

Other patients began tossing and turning in their beds, agitated at the shrieking. In broken Hebrew, I tried to explain her fears to the doctors and nurses. I knew the hospital personnel were doing everything in their power to save my mother's life. I was embarrassed that in her delirium she was accusing them of trying to murder her.

"Don't worry. This kind of thing has happened before," the doctor told me kindly. They moved my mother to a private room so that other patients would not be disturbed by her outbursts.

We faced another problem: at home, my mother had compliantly opened her mouth when any of us fed her. But in Hadassah, she refused to open her mouth for anyone but her brother Mustafa. Uncle Mustafa had to come from Bethlehem every day just to make sure my mother ate.

The morning of her surgery, my father, the eight of us kids, Aunt Fatmeh, and Uncle Mustafa all gathered at Hadassah by 7 a.m. Mariam waited at home. We paced the lobby while the doctors cut open my mother's head and removed the cancerous growth inside her brain. At 8 p.m. the doctor emerged from the operating room with a tired smile.

"She survived. You can go see her now." Before the words sank in, he continued, "But she's still in critical condition."

We crowded into the recovery room. Her head was swathed in white bandages, with her eyes, nose, cheeks, and mouth just barely protruding. She was in a deep, deep sleep, from which she might never emerge. But even though I did not pray, I felt certain that God and his angels would wake her so that she could continue her life and care for her children.

After a few hours, her eyelids began to flutter. Then her fingers moved, ever so slightly. "The chloroform is wearing off!" Samira announced in an excited whisper. Her fingers began to explore the bedsheets and the thin white blanket, trying to ascertain where she was. Nothing felt familiar. Her fingers were confused. Moments later, she dropped again into a deep sleep.

The nurse entered. "She needs to rest," she said gently. "And so should you. One of you can stay with her for the night, but the rest of the family should go home."

I volunteered to stay. I dropped exhausted into the chair next to my mother's bed, trying to count the winter stars from the hospital window. Maybe one of those stars was the angel who had protected my mother during the surgery.

An American and an Israeli doctor entered the room. The American doctor asked me something in English. I looked at the Israeli. "He wants to know if she's shown any signs of consciousness," he told me in Hebrew.

"She moved a little before, but she has been sleeping again for hours," I managed to say in primitive Hebrew, which the Israeli doctor translated into English.

My mother stirred in her bed. "Sami," she said. We all froze. She continued in Arabic. "Sami, *habibi*. Don't be silly. Why are you translating back and forth from Hebrew to English? I can talk English with the doctor directly." She switched to English. "Thank you for all you did. I am aware that I screamed terrible things and my son was trying to help me. I am very sorry for this. This tumor was controlling my brain. I understood everything, but I could not control my behaviors. Now, what would you like to ask?"

"Umm . . . umm . . . ," the American doctor stammered in shock. He motioned for me to follow him to the hallway and, with the translation help of the Israeli doctor, asked me a new question. "Did your mother speak English before the surgery?"

I burst out laughing. "Yes, she learned it in the school for the blind! The brain surgery may have saved her life, but it didn't give her a new language!"

My mother was asleep again when I returned to her bedside, but I was filled with joy and relief. She would come home with us; she would look after Hanadi and Sa'ed; everything would be back to normal!

A week later, my mother was recuperating in her own bed. Within three weeks, she was up and around, though she moved slowly and rested often. Within two months, my mother was fully back to herself. She handled the adjustment to Mariam with more grace than I would have imagined possible, tucking her hurt inside her heart and treating my father's second wife as a younger sister. My father rotated between my mother's bedroom and Mariam's. Within months, my mother had an announcement for the family.

"I'm pregnant again!"

Mariam added to the surprise. "I am, too!"

I was pleased with the news and gave credit to my father. If both women were pregnant, it meant he was giving my mother equal attention to Mariam. But as my mother's belly grew larger, she ended her physical relationship with my father. "Go, be with Mariam," I heard her tell him on several nights. "I don't want you in my bedroom." I looked for other signs of tension but found none. My father and mother continued to treat each other as intimate friends, and my mother and Mariam seemed to grow closer as well.

I could move ahead with my life. I told my father that I wanted to get engaged to Sanaa. My family made the engagement contract with hers. Now we could take walks together when she visited Jerusalem. She even let me give her a small kiss on the cheek, but I was still not permitted to hug her or touch her body.

"Come on, Sanaa, we're engaged! This is legal now!" I pleaded with her, but she pushed me away coyly.

"'Legal' does not mean 'appropriate,'" was all she would say.

Within months of my engagement to Sanaa, I had two new baby sisters: Sa'eedah from my mother and Samiah from Mariam.

IT WAS 2 A.M. on a hot summer night, 1979. I was awakened by footsteps on the roof. Who could be up there in the middle of the night? Then I heard voices, speaking Hebrew. There were more footsteps, more voices. There must be twenty of them! Had someone ratted out my stone-throwing?

Three border policemen barged into my room. Before I could sit up, there was a pistol poking me in the chest and a bright flashlight shining directly in my eyes.

"What's your name?" the one with the gun barked at me in Arabic. He wanted me to feel afraid. I would not give him the satisfaction.

"Sami."

"How old are you?"

"Seventeen."

They left my room and joined the others in the courtyard. "This isn't the one."

I heard my father on the steps. "What's going on?"

"Where is Samir Al Jundi?" they asked him.

"What do you want with my son?"

"We just need to ask him some questions. He'll be back in half an hour."

My father had no choice. They would find Samir, who was home for summer vacation, whether he showed them the room or not.

"Why are you taking him? He didn't do anything wrong. He's just a student!" my mother shouted to them. "Leave him alone!"

"*Khalas,* Myassar, *uskuti,*"* urged my father. "He'll be back in a few minutes."

I stayed in my room. I did not want to see Samir being put in handcuffs and taken away.

My parents sat in their room upstairs, counting the minutes. Samir did not return in half an hour, an hour, or two hours.

---

*The feminine conjugation of *uskut,* Arabic for "Be quiet!" or "Shut your mouth!"

In the morning we learned that Samir's friends had also been taken. Arrested for throwing stones. Days passed. No Samir. Weeks passed. My parents went daily to the police station. "He's under questioning," was all they were told.

Now that I had dropped out of school, I needed work. Our neighbor Abu Ahmad had a job in a large Israeli factory making kitchen cabinets. They needed more workers. Abu Ahmad and I took an Egged bus to the factory to talk to the supervisor, Giora, about a job. The factory was in Givat Sha'ul. Givat Sha'ul had been built on the ruins of my father's village, Deir Yassin.

Giora, a big blond man with thick glasses and the knitted skullcap typical to settlers, looked at me disdainfully but hired me right away. My job was to deliver sections of cabinets to their next destination on the assembly line, shuttling back and forth with a small forklift. I also wrapped the finished cabinets in thick plastic, preparing them to be shipped to Europe.

Giora barked orders and shouted at us, even at workers older than his father. The word *Arab* was added to whatever other adjective he slung at us, whether *dirty* or *lazy*. There was only one non-Arab working with us—an old, balding Iranian Jew named Rahamim. Rahamim was quiet, gentle, and a bit peculiar; he combed his thinning hair over his bald spot with a toothbrush. Giora did not spare Rahamim his abuse; Rahamim was *Mizrachi** after all, only one step away from being Arab.

More than hating Giora, I hated working in an Israeli factory located in Deir Yassin.

"Where's your job, Sami?" people in the Old City asked me.

"Deir Yassin," I had to tell them.

"Deir Yassin? Aren't you from Deir Yassin?"

I lowered my eyes and shrugged.

My grandmother visited from Jordan. Tears sprung to her eyes when I told her where I worked. "Is your Uncle Abu Ismail's house still there?" I did not know how to tell her that only a few buildings from the original Deir Yassin remained, and the Israelis had turned them into an insane asylum.

My grandmother gripped my arm tightly before I left for work the next morning.

"Sami, please. Bring me a fig."

---

*Hebrew term for "Eastern," referring to Jews of Middle Eastern or Arab descent.

During my lunch break, I walked to the heart of Deir Yassin. I watched the crazy people wandering in the yard between the homes of my people. When no one was watching, I plucked a fig and a lemon from nearby trees. I gave them to my grandmother that evening. She held the lemon to her nose, breathing deeply the fragrance of her village. Then she cradled the fig to her cheek. "The figs in Deir Yassin," she said. "There are no figs in the world like those from Deir Yassin."

The next day I wrapped the cabinets, staring out the large window overlooking the valley covered in fruit trees. All the workers here were nothing but traitors, and I was the worst of all. We were disrespecting the blood that had been spilled here. Maybe the souls of the massacred were still hovering in their demolished village. How could I possibly justify myself to them?

Before wrapping the next cabinet in the thick plastic, I carved words across its face with a screwdriver. I did it again the next day, and the next. The following week, I plugged the forklift backward into the charger, mixing the electric signals and blowing out its circuits. Each time shame overwhelmed me, I found some new way to sabotage the work.

Abu Ahmad figured out what I was up to. "Sami, you have to stop this. You're going to cause problems for all of us."

I looked straight into Abu Ahmad's eyes. "I have no idea what you're talking about."

The manager began to receive phone calls from Europe about defective cabinets. It was obvious that I was the culprit; I was the only one with access to all stages of the assembling.

"You piece of rubbish, you disgusting Arab, I'm going to fire your ass! I'm calling the police!" Giora shouted at me.

I shouted right back, "You want to call the police, you fucking settler, fine! Call them! But you can't fire me, because I quit!"

I stormed out of the factory and never returned. But I smiled each time I imagined customers in Belgium and Italy unwrapping their new kitchen cabinets, only to find the Arabic words I had carved deeply across their doors:

Made in Deir Yassin!

⁂

ABBAS AND BADAWI WHOOPED with laughter at the havoc I had wreaked at the factory. "Way to go!" Badawi slapped me on the back. "Damaging the Israeli economy!" But the discussion took a more serious turn. "We're leaving next month, Sami. In May. Are you coming with us?"

"I just don't see how it's possible. My father still controls my movements. I don't even have a passport."

Badawi scratched his chin, thinking over the dilemma. "Okay, we'll go without you. Don't worry about it. You'll still be a part of whatever we do."

My neighbor Abu Manar knew that I was looking for a new job. He worked as the janitor in an office building in West Jerusalem. There was a small café on the ground floor. They were currently hiring. How many plates and ashtrays could I "accidentally" drop before getting fired from this place, I wondered?

The next day, Abu Manar introduced me to Morris and Reuven, the café owners. They were cousins from Argentina and had immigrated to Israel a few years earlier.

Morris, a middle-age man, shook my hand warmly. "This is a family-run business, Sami," he told me. "If you work here, you'll be part of the family." He began explaining the routine of the restaurant. Reuven demonstrated how to make the different sandwiches on the menu.

"How did it go?" Abu Manar asked me when we met late that afternoon to walk back to the Old City.

"They're nice, this Reuven and Morris, right?" I said. "They treated me like I was one of them."

"Ahh, this is because they are from Argentina," Abu Manar said. "They didn't learn hatred, like everyone else here."

Reuven, Morris, and I would chat casually as we cut the tomatoes, cucumbers, and red peppers that I would use throughout the day. I took pride in making the toasted sandwiches. I liked it when the regulars said, "I'll have the usual, Sami, thanks!" and I knew it meant no tomato for this one, extra cheese for that one.

Morris and Reuven hired a young woman named Galit. Galit was also from Argentina. She had come to Israel for the year to decide whether she wanted to immigrate. We talked throughout the day as we sliced vegetables and toasted sandwiches. She asked me about my family, what I liked to do, why I had left school. She told me about her parents, brothers and sisters, and the life she had left behind.

Days passed quickly slicing vegetables and cleaning plates. I looked forward to going to work each day, I realized. I looked forward to seeing Galit. I liked how her light brown hair fell on her shoulders as she cut the tomatoes and how her green-blue eyes sparkled when she laughed. I liked how her voice turned low and soft when she was talking about something serious.

She was lonely here without her mom and dad, she told me. She was not sure if she wanted to stay in the country or not.

"Actually, here in the restaurant is where I'm happiest," she confided. "I feel like I'm with family when I'm here." She glanced at me over the cucumbers. "Especially with you, Sami."

My heart skipped a beat. I had to restrain myself from reaching out and touching her shoulder. Galit had just told me that I was like family. I had to protect her like a sister and show her nothing but kindness and respect.

I left the café every day and walked back to the Old City. The nightly news was full of stories about clashes in Lebanon and humiliations suffered at the hands of the Israelis in the Occupied Territories. Everyone agreed: peace was impossible.

But it didn't feel impossible when I greeted Galit, Morris, and Reuven the following morning, making the regular customers their favorite sandwiches. Was I a traitor, developing warm relations with the enemy? But who exactly was my enemy? I had always considered people like Giora at the factory to be my enemy, or the kids who had pummeled me at the swimming pool, and the soldiers who harassed me daily. I could not conceive of Galit, Morris, and Reuven as my enemies.

In May, Abbas and Badawi went to Amman. For a cousin's wedding, they told me. They returned a week later.

"Welcome back!" I greeted them when they showed up at my house. "How was the wedding?"

"Let's get something to drink," Abbas suggested, avoiding my question. We walked to the coffee shop at Herod's Gate. Only after Badawi had dealt the first hand of cards did he lean toward me with a wide grin and say in a lowered voice, "We did it!"

"What?"

"We went to Syria! We signed up! We're *fedayeen** now!" Badawi patted me on the shoulder. "Don't worry, Sami, you are with us. We made sure they knew that you're a part of our group."

I was not sure how I was supposed to feel. "So—we're all members of the PFLP now?"

Abbas and Badawi exchanged looks. "Well, we didn't exactly sign up with PFLP," Abbas started to explain. "We got to Damascus and were looking for

*Literally translated as "those who self-sacrifice," *fedayeen* is used to mean "freedom fighters."

someone connected with the PFLP. We couldn't find anyone. So we were sitting at an ice cream parlor near the river—"

"The ice cream in Syria was fantastic, Sami!" Badawi cut in. "You really missed out!"

"And we started talking to this guy and he was with Fatah. So, we joined Fatah."

I digested the new information. "Okay, Fatah. No problem. It's all fighting for the same cause."

They filled me in on more details. Badawi, who was nineteen, would be the leader of the group. Abbas and I, at eighteen, would be the only other members.

"When do you go back for more training?" I asked.

"We don't. We learned everything we need to know," Abbas answered.

"How is that possible?"

"Oh, it's possible," Badawi said confidently. "We learned how to use Kalashnikovs, M16s, Uzis. They showed us how to throw hand grenades, rocket-propelled grenades . . ."

"We learned how to make bombs," Abbas added.

I was skeptical. "You learned all this in a week?"

"Less than a week! The training took three days—we spent the rest of the time in Amman!"

"Are you sure you know how to do everything safely?"

"Yeah, Sami, don't worry! We learned it really well!" Abbas elbowed Badawi. "Badawi, tell him about the dog!"

"The dog!" Badawi almost choked on his laughter. "Sami, get this," he said. "When they were teaching us how to use the RPG launchers, they put a big rock in the field. 'This rock is your target,' they told us. This guard dog was only fifteen feet away from the rock. Abbas hit the rock with the grenade. And the grass around the rock caught on fire and then . . . " Badawi had to stop talking; he was laughing too hard.

"The dog caught on fire!" Abbas finished Badawi's sentence. "He started barking and rolling around on the ground! 'Look, the dog, help the dog!' we shouted. But the instructor said, 'Don't worry about the dog, he's immune to fire. This is a game for him.'"

"And the dog was fine!" Badawi jumped back in again. "He didn't even get scared when we shot the next grenade. That dog was the bravest thing I ever saw in my life! If only all Palestinian fighters could be as brave as that dog!"

All their stories led to jokes about the dog. I felt sorry for this dog. What kind of dog just sits quietly while grenades explode all around him? What kind of explosions, I asked myself further, can't even hurt a dog?

"So—what happens now?" I asked.

"We wait," Badawi answered. "And we listen to the news. We'll get our instructions from *Sawt Ath-Thawra Al-Falestiniya*."* We had been listening to the radio program, broadcast out of Baghdad, for years. At the end of each broadcast, we often heard strange messages. It had never occurred to me that these were code to resistance fighters.

A knot formed in the pit of my stomach. How could Abbas and Badawi have possibly learned everything with only three days of training? And even more absurd was the notion that we would receive our orders through the radio. I tried to push for more details about the message. What would it say? How would we know it was for us? How would we decipher what we were supposed to do?

"Relax, Sami!" Badawi smiled widely, as always. "The message will tell us everything we need to know."

I left Abbas and Badawi in the coffee shop still laughing about the dog as I walked home. What the hell were we doing? This was not a little kid's game. Where could this possibly lead us? Prison, death, or exile. Did I want out? For years I had been dreaming of fighting to liberate Palestine, and now we were on our way! I could not tell Abbas and Badawi that I was having second thoughts. They would think I was weak. Anyway, they had already signed my name with theirs. I was past the point of no return.

The next morning, Abbas went back to restoring antique furniture, Badawi welded doors and windows in the iron workshop, and I went to Morris and Reuven's café. The three of us met up after work to play cards at the coffee shop as though nothing had changed. The next day was the same, and then the next. The knot in my stomach began to loosen. Days turned into weeks and then into months. After a while, I nearly forgot that we were listening for a cryptic message at the end of the *Sawt Ath-Thawra Al-Falestiniya* news broadcast.

I loved how Galit flipped her hair after giving a customer his sandwich. Sometimes I could smell her shampoo as we stood side by side chopping vegetables. I loved laughing and telling stories with her throughout the day.

---

*Voice of the Palestinian Revolution.

Galit and I were wiping crumbs off the tables. She turned to me casually. "We should do something after work someday," she said. "Go to the cinema or get something to drink. What do you think?"

I immediately envisioned myself walking into the cinema with Galit by my side. Maybe it would be a horror film and Galit would scream during the bloody parts, grabbing onto my arm for protection. Maybe it would be a romantic film and afterward she would permit me to hold her face tenderly in my hands and kiss her. I was dizzy with excitement. Aside from the pecks that Sanaa had allowed me, I had never touched a girl.

Sanaa. How could I go with Galit when I was supposed to marry Sanaa? Our wedding was set for the following summer. But Sanaa never opened up her heart to me the way Galit had. I knew nothing of Sanaa's hopes, her fears, her dreams. I didn't know what Sanaa's shampoo smelled like. If I had to choose between Sanaa and Galit, I would choose Galit.

But how could I? Badawi, Abbas, and I were now members of the Fatah movement. How could I go for coffee with the enemy? There were Palestinians I knew of who had relations with Israeli girls. But those relationships were only about sex. I did not know anyone who felt about an Israeli the way I felt about Galit.

Galit was waiting for my answer. The blood pumping from my heart felt warm as it flowed through my veins, carrying strange, prickly sensations throughout my body.

"Sure, let's do that," I responded with as much nonchalance as I could muster.

It was a Tuesday in the middle of August. We were lying on the floor of Abbas's room, listening to the radio and playing cards. After the broadcast wrapped up, the announcer had a message from Abu Majd. Badawi and Abbas bolted upright.

"What? Who is Abu Majd?" I asked.

Abbas shushed me while Badawi quickly explained. Abu Majd was the code name we had been waiting for. This message was for us. "To the group of Leena Nabulsi," the message from Abu Majd said. "You must go to receive your gift."

"That's it?" I asked impatiently. "What does it mean?"

"Leena Nabulsi was from Nablus. Weapons are waiting for us in the Nablus cemetery!"

Badawi turned off the radio, smiling triumphantly. "We'll go on Saturday."

Saturday. Three days away. The pit in my stomach immediately returned, tighter than ever. As I lay in bed that night, swirling doubts overwhelmed me. Why now, God, why did the message come now, just when Galit and I were making plans to go out? And if we found a bomb or a gun in the cemetery, did Badawi and Abbas really know what to do with it? Is it possible that the message was a trap? I made myself sick with worry. *Khalas*, I finally told myself sternly. *You're taking your place on the front line for Palestine, against occupation. It's what you've been waiting for!* I had to turn myself into a horse wearing blinders and move straight ahead. I was going to Nablus to find weapons because a cryptic message over a Baghdad radio station from an unknown Abu Majd told me so.

Badawi and Abbas's anticipation mounted.

"What kind of weapons will be waiting for us?" Abbas asked over and over.

Badawi's guess changed each time. "Pistols, probably. Maybe TNT. Bullets."

Early Saturday morning, we boarded a bus to Nablus. Once in Nablus, we walked to the small cemetery across the street from the hospital. The rows of marble stones were surrounded by a stone wall.

"Sami, you wait outside," Badawi instructed me. "If you see anyone coming, give us a signal."

I waited with dread, keeping my eyes peeled for Israeli soldiers or people who looked like collaborators.* The street was empty. I stared at the hospital, suddenly thinking about the Israeli doctors at Hadassah who had helped save my mother's life. The conflict had not affected the treatment they gave her; was this any way to thank them? I shook those thoughts away quickly. It was unrelated. Politics were not a factor in hospitals and the care my mother had received could not be a factor in my decision to fight occupation. Those same Israeli doctors probably served proudly in the army! Why shouldn't I be a proud fighter against the occupation?

Abbas came to get me. "*Yallah*, Sami, I think we found it."

He led me across the cemetery, where Badawi was using a switchblade to pry out a mostly deflated plastic soccer ball from a hole in the wall.

"There's probably something behind it," Badawi grunted as he worked to loosen the ball.

---

*Term used to mean Palestinians who secretly worked with the Israeli military, often informing on other Palestinians.

With a final tug, the stone wall released its grip on the soccer ball. We peered inside the hole. Nothing. Abbas reached inside and felt around with his hand. Still nothing.

Badawi shook the soccer ball. "There's something inside!" He carefully sliced the plastic ball with the switchblade and stuck his eye into the crack.

"Dirt," he said. Crouching, we dumped the dirt out on the ground to see what it concealed. There was nothing.

"They pulled a fast one on us," I said, hoping that my faked frustration masked my relief. "We came all the way from Jerusalem for nothing! They must think we're really stupid!"

Badawi fingered the dry dirt thoughtfully. "No, Sami. This means we have to do something on our own."

"Something on our own? Like what?"

"We can make a bomb."

"But they didn't give us any materials!"

"No big deal. The main material we need is match tips."

We returned to Jerusalem. "Maybe we should wait for another message?"

But Badawi and Abbas were adamant. We were on our own and we had to act now.

⁂

BADAWI, ABBAS, AND I bought boxes of matches. We sat in Abbas's room, twisting the match tips off the wooden sticks as we brainstormed ideas. We all agreed that our target would not be civilians. The Israelis killed women and children. We would not be like them.

"We have to do something to damage the Israeli economy," Badawi said.

"We can bomb a supermarket!" Abbas suggested.

"But there are people at a supermarket!" I protested. "Maybe even Palestinians!"

"We'll do it on Saturday when Israeli shops are closed." Badawi draped his arm around my shoulder. "*Yallah*, Sami, you're the inspiration for damaging the economy. Remember those cabinets in Deir Yassin?"

We continued twisting match tips off the wooden sticks. They didn't come off easily. Our fingertips were raw and blistered by the end of the night. The next day, we resumed the work in my room with the door locked. Abbas brought a can of gasoline and dumped the matches inside.

"Easier to twist off," he said. "That's what they told us in Syria."

The window leading to the courtyard was cracked to give us some air. My father put his face to the window. "Sami, what are you and your friends doing in there?"

"Playing cards!"

He clucked his tongue suspiciously. "*Wallah,* I'm worried you're doing something dangerous . . ."

"What could we possibly be doing that's dangerous? We're playing cards, that's all."

My father walked slowly downstairs. We laughed nervously and Abbas shook his head incredulously. "How could he possibly have known anything?" he asked.

"Never underestimate a blind man," I said, twisting a match tip off of the gasoline-soaked stick. "Maybe he can't see, but his other senses are razor sharp."

"He'll know he was right soon enough!" Badawi laughed.

The next day, Abbas scouted out the small fruit and vegetable market we would target. He passed it every day on Jaffa Street. In the dirt parking lot behind the market, there were gas canisters surrounded by a low wall. We would place the bomb there. The wall of the market would definitely be damaged in the explosion. If we were lucky, the gas canisters might ignite as well, setting the whole market on fire.

After four days, we had twisted off a pound of the red, flammable material. Badawi held the plastic bag in his hand, as if weighing it. "Enough," he finally proclaimed.

We met at Badawi's house on Saturday afternoon. Badawi had a half-inch water pipe, camera flash, a windable wristwatch, and batteries, carefully concealed in a black plastic bag. Abbas brought the bag with the match tips. I watched Badawi and Abbas carefully as they assembled the materials. It took them only an hour. I stared at the contraption in fascination and repulsion. This half-inch pipe would be able to help end the Israeli occupation?

It was 5 p.m. Badawi picked up the bomb gingerly and set the watch.

"Thirty minutes," he said, sounding more serious than I had ever heard him. He put the bomb in a black plastic bag.

"Here, you hold this, Sami." Before I knew it, the bag was in my hands.

On our way out the door, Badawi swiped a few pieces of pita bread from the kitchen. He gently placed the bread on top of the bomb, so that pita could be seen emerging from the top of the bag.

"Nothing wrong with bringing some bread home for our families, right, Sami?" he said with a wink.

We left the Old City, walking slowly and nonchalantly, just three friends out for an evening stroll. The West Jerusalem streets were empty. It was still Shabbat for Israelis. I carried the bag as casually as possible. We arrived to the market in ten minutes. I gave Abbas the bag. He laid it on the small wall surrounding the cylinders.

"5:15," Badawi announced. Time was running. My hands were shaking and my heart was pounding inside my T-shirt. I was sure that Abbas and Badawi could hear it.

"Let's go!" I tugged on Badawi's sleeve, urging him to run.

"Relax!" Badawi commanded. "We don't want to attract attention!"

We walked out of the parking lot as normally as possible, continuing to place one foot in front of the other, until we reached Damascus Gate.

"Well . . . guess I'll go home now." More than anything, I wanted to be safe inside the house with my family.

Abbas looked a little paler than usual. "Yeah, me too!"

"We can't go home yet," Badawi said. "We have to be in public when the explosion happens."

We went to our usual coffee place inside Herod's Gate and shuffled the deck of cards, all the while straining our ears to hear the thud of the explosion. We heard nothing.

"We're probably too far away to hear it," Abbas said. "They'll announce it on the news."

The news came and went with no mention of a pipe bomb at a fruit and vegetable market on Jaffa Street in West Jerusalem. We talked in hushed voices about what might have gone wrong. Had there been a problem with the timer? Had the bomb been discovered and defused before exploding?

"Should we go and check it out?" Abbas asked.

"No," Badawi answered firmly. "The last thing we need is to be seen sniffing around that place right now."

After three days, we decided we could safely go and investigate. We arrived at the market just after dark. The gas tanks were in the same place, and the wall surrounding it was intact.

"Look at this!" I crouched down and collected some pieces of stale pita strewn around.

"Yeah, and how about this?" Abbas pointed to a Frisbee-size black mark on the wall.

The bomb had exploded after all! And the only damage it caused was leaving soot on the wall and scattering our bread as if we had intended to feed the birds. The Israeli economy was not damaged; it had not even heard the sound of the explosion.

A week later, I was washing cups while Galit toasted cheese sandwiches.

"So are we ever going to do something outside of work or not?" she asked.

"Yes! Of course!"

"Well . . . when do you want to meet?"

We set a date for the next Saturday. We would go to the cinema and have coffee afterward. I floated back to the Old City. My date with Galit was all I could think of as I played cards in Abbas's house that night.

Badawi interrupted my reverie. "We have to make a bigger bomb this time, one that will really cause damage."

"Should we try the *Masyadet El-Moghaffaleen?*"* Abbas asked.

"Yeah. Good idea!"

"What's that?" I asked.

Abbas explained, "We'll take a can and put a battery and a timer with tape and electrical wiring outside of it. We'll put it in a crowded, visible place. Someone will see it and will call the police. The police will come and will cut the electric wiring. He'll think he disabled the explosive, so then he will pick up the can."

"But aha!" Badawi interrupted with excitement. "The can is a decoy! The real bomb is inside the can! And when the policeman picks it up, it will activate a button on the bottom of the can and then . . . " Badawi made a noise and gesture of an explosion.

We started twisting tips off matches again. We needed more this time, but we were faster. Abbas said we had enough after four days.

"Are you sure?" I asked lamely. I would not mind twisting match tips for another week or two; if it delayed the next step, I'd twist match tips for the rest of my life!

"Yeah, we have enough," Badawi said definitively.

Galit and I continued to make our plans for Saturday. Should we go in the afternoon or evening? What café should we go to afterward? I tried to hide how jittery I was. What would happen, I asked myself, if I told Badawi and

---

*Literally translated: "trap for the sleeping"—i.e., booby trap.

Abbas that I wanted out? There was no way to do that without making enemies of my best friends. Besides, I already knew too much. I was involved no
matter what.

On Friday, my family went to the beach in Asqalan. Everyone except Azzam, who had broken his leg when a large piece of timber fell on him while
he was working with my father. He was watching TV downstairs with his leg
in a cast propped up on a pillow. He would not be able to bother us as he
usually did.

We started in midmorning. Badawi placed the pipe on my bedroom win-
dowsill. It was an inch and a half in diameter, three times bigger than the
first bomb.

"If anything goes wrong," Badawi instructed us as he laid out the other
materials, "go to Nablus right away and listen to the radio for a message.
Sami, can you make us some coffee?"

"Sure!" I jumped up, eager to get out of the suffocating room, even if for
just a few minutes.

"What are you up to?" Azzam asked me when I went downstairs.

"What are you talking about? We're just hanging out and playing cards."

"Don't bullshit me. Everything is totally silent up there."

"You want to come up and see for yourself?" Azzam could barely make it
to the toilet, much less up a flight of stairs.

"Fuck you very much indeed!" Azzam said, giving me the middle finger
with a flourish.

I returned to the room with the coffee.

"I forgot tape—we need tape to cover the electric wires," Badawi said.

I jumped up again. "No problem! I'll buy some!" I offered.

"That's okay," Badawi said. "Just give me some paper. We can use that." It
did not seem wise to me, but what did I know? I hadn't been to Syria to get
training. I ripped a few sheets out of Mazin's school notebook and handed
them to Badawi.

Badawi and Abbas worked for another hour in near silence. I alternated
between hovering over their shoulders and leaving the room as often as possible to fetch more coffee or tea. Each time I left I thought about running out
of the house and not returning. Each time something drew me back inside
my room.

"Almost done," Badawi said. "Just need to put the nails in." Badawi picked
up a plastic cup of tiny nails. "This is the dangerous part," he said. "Only one
of us should be in here. Sami, Abbas, you wait outside."

"No, I'm staying with you," Abbas said. "We did this together during train-ing and we'll do it together now."

I moved back a few feet and sat on a chair next to my bed. I craned my neck to see, but Badawi's and Abbas's bodies were right in front of the bomb.

I heard the clink of the nails as Badawi slowly began pouring them in. Gradually, he tipped the cup more, so the nails could slide in faster.

"Just a few more nails to go," muttered Badawi.

A deafening noise ripped through my eardrums. I was knocked off my chair. The world turned pitch black.

CHAPTER FIVE

✧

IT WAS DARKER THAN NIGHT. My ears were ringing. The smell of sulfur and singed flesh overpowered me. I groped for the door in the blackness and stumbled out of the room. Blood was streaming from my arms and hands. It was all over my green T-shirt. My hands flew to my face. It was wet and sticky with blood as well. I must be badly injured! The next thing I knew I was running as fast as I could to Herod's Gate. *Get to Nablus, get to Nablus, get to Nablus*—Badawi's instructions replayed in my mind.

I ran outside of Herod's Gate and frantically jumped into a waiting cab.

The driver recoiled in his seat. "What happened? Where are you going?"

"Nablus!" I said. "Nablus hospital!"

The driver turned on his engine. "I'll take you to Al Makassed. I'm not driving you to Nablus in your condition." I looked at my hands and arms. I had never seen gashes so deep. I tried to wrap the end of my T-shirt around them to stop the bleeding. *Why doesn't it hurt?* I wondered.

The driver sped to Al Makassed hospital and dropped me off at the entrance. He peeled away before I could figure out how to reach into my pocket to give him some coins.

I stumbled inside the hospital. A girl screamed in horror. "Nurse! Come quickly! We have an emergency here!" a woman called. Their voices sounded like they were coming through a tunnel ten miles long. I looked around frantically. I was desperate to find someone I knew.

I spotted my former classmate Abed sitting in the reception area with his grandfather. Abed jumped to his feet.

"Sami! What happened to you?"

"Abed, can you go to my house? Get the stuff we were using—quickly! And throw it all down a well!" I realized that I was shouting.

The nurses pulled me onto a gurney and a doctor immediately began pulling pieces of nail and pipe from the open wounds in my hands and arms. "Is my face okay? It's bleeding!" I said to the doctor.

"Your face isn't injured," he answered. "You're going to be fine."

Maybe some of the blood covering me wasn't my own. "My friends . . . what happened to my friends?"

"Just lie down and keep your arms spread wide." The doctor continued to stem the flow of blood. "Nurse, prepare a room for surgery."

Moments later, medics carried in a body drenched in blood on a stretcher and laid him on a gurney next to mine. People from the neighborhood flowed through the hospital doors after him. It was Abbas.

"Abbas! Are you okay?" I waited for a third stretcher to come through the hospital door but it didn't. "Where's Badawi? What happened to Badawi?"

"He's dead!" Abbas shouted in a high-pitched, strangled voice. "Badawi's dead!"

Four soldiers entered accompanied by two men in civilian clothes; *shabak*,* I knew instantly. They were by our gurneys in a flash. The doctor placed himself between us and the soldiers. "These men need immediate medical treatment," the doctor told them.

"We're taking them to Hadassah. They'll get treated there."

The soldiers loaded us inside two waiting ambulances. A medic continued to clean and bandage my wounds under the guard of an armed soldier as the ambulance drove to Hadassah hospital, followed by an army jeep. Stabbing pain seared through my arms and hands. The shock must be wearing off. I gritted my teeth against the pain. We reached Hadassah. Nurses put me on another gurney and began to wheel me down the hall. The soldiers and *shabak* followed the gurney until a doctor stopped them.

"You can't go inside. When we're finished with the surgery, he's all yours, but until then, wait here."

I remembered the treatment my mother had gotten at Hadassah from Israeli doctors. Abbas and I would be well cared for here. We would be okay.

A male nurse began to undress me in the operating room. "Brother, roll over just a little bit so I can put this under you," he said in Arabic, holding up a container of blue gel. I was relieved to hear Arabic.

"What will you do to me?" I asked him.

*Hebrew acronym for *Sherut ha-Bitachon ha-Klali*, translated as "General Security Service," also known as "Shin Bet."

"There's shrapnel that needs to be extricated," he said as he applied the gel. "In your left forearm, both your wrists, and a few nails in your ribs, chest, and neck. Here—this will make it easier." He put a mask over my face, holding a bottle of chloroform over it. "Just breathe deeply and count to ten." I followed his instructions. One . . . two . . . the pain floated away on a cloud. Three . . . four . . . I was peaceful, relaxed. Somewhere between five and six, I lost consciousness.

The gentle slap across my face felt as if it came from another world. I tried to open my eyes but my eyelids were made of lead. I sank back to that peaceful place . . .

Another slap.

With great effort, I forced my eyes to open. The room swam in front of me, dark and blurry. Another slap and the world began to sharpen into focus. Inches from my face were large eyes behind thick glasses. A bald head. And the barrel of a pistol.

"Who was in your group?" Spoken in Arabic with a Hebrew accent.

Before my mouth could form words, I was drifting back to a deep sleep.

The slap was a bit rougher this time. "Wake up. Look at me! Who was with you?"

Mr. Eyeglasses waved the gun slightly in front of my face. I smiled inside. This was not the first time I had woken up to a gun pointed at me. This pistol was smaller and more modern than the one poking me in the chest the night Samir had been arrested.

"No one—just the three of us." Gravity was pulling my eyelids shut again, but Eyeglasses leaned in so close that his mouth nearly touched my ear. This kept gravity at bay for a moment. He spoke softly, almost gently. "I can kill you right now and tell the press that you died in your 'work accident.' Tell me about the others in the group!" He pressed the gun into the side of my skull and cocked it. "We already know that there were five of you—who were the other two?"

I fought through the cotton in my brain and grasped the memory of entering Al Makassed: witnesses both there and here at Hadassah had already seen me alive. His attempts at intimidation were silly and weak. He was not going to shoot me here in the hospital bed. "No one."

"Give me names!"

"There was no one else . . ."

If I closed my eyes one more time, maybe Eyeglasses would go away. Maybe that doctor would come in and tell him to leave me alone, to let me sleep . . . sleep . . . maybe it would all turn into a bad dream . . .

Slap. "Who helped you?"

As I drifted back down to the peaceful place, I mumbled something about Abed.

"What exactly did you tell him to throw down the well?"

"Just some pipes . . . matches . . . wires . . . " I closed my eyes until the next slap.

Slowly, the chloroform wore off and my consciousness returned. When it did, the full force of the pain swept over me. Eyeglasses left the room and returned moments later with two policemen.

"Sit up!" one of them ordered me. I sat on the edge of the bed as he put metal cuffs around my ankles. I groggily held out my arms, expecting them to be cuffed as well. Both my hands and arms were entirely covered in thick white bandages. No wrist cuffs for me. Eyeglasses led me down the hospital corridor, one policeman holding me on either side. My ankle cuffs permitted me only to take small, shuffling steps. People were gawking at me. I looked straight ahead, avoiding eye contact. I hoped they did not think I was a lowly criminal, injured during a violent robbery or a drug-related murder. I wanted them to somehow know that I was being arrested for a politically motivated action.

It was dark as the policemen led me to their car. It must be Friday night, or could it be Saturday night already? I was sure we were heading to the police headquarters, housed in Jerusalem's Russian Compound district. I could not see anything from inside the car but soon enough, I knew I had guessed right.

We walked inside the police station. An exposed bulb cast a weak yellow light over the bare and empty room. The policemen led me down a dark corridor, ending at a thick steel door.

The policeman rapped on the door with his heavy metal key ring. "Arkadi! Open up!" he called.

The iron panel on the top of the door slid open and a pink face appeared in the window, middle-aged and heavyset. "Who is this ugly one?" Arkadi asked gruffly.

"He belongs to the *shabak*," the policeman answered. Arkadi opened the door, grabbed me by the back of my shirt, and pulled me inside the *shabak* side of the door.

"He's injured," the second policeman added. Arkadi nodded his comprehension, then closed and locked the steel door. He began pushing me down the corridor. Still in shackles, I shuffled ahead of Arkadi.

A soft moan. I turned my head quickly toward the sound. We were passing a small, unlit courtyard. A second moan. My eyes adjusted to the darkness. Silhouettes of bodies emerged from the silky blackness. Hands bound behind their backs. Ankles shackled together. Foreheads pressed against the walls. I could make out their torsos, arms, and legs, but from the shoulders up they were shapeless. There were sacks over their heads, I realized with a shudder. Arkadi let go of my shirt and stepped quickly into the courtyard. He kicked a silhouette whose entire body had slumped against the wall. "Wake up, you shit!"

Within seconds Arkadi was behind me again. Then everything went entirely black. Thick, scratchy material pressed against my face. The stench of filth and urine forced its way into my nose and mouth. I tried not to gag. Arkadi grabbed the back of my shirt again and pushed me a few more stumbling steps. I heard his keys unlock a door. He shoved me inside a room, removing my ankle cuffs and the sack. He slammed the door behind him. I heard the key turn quickly and firmly in the lock.

I stood alone in the middle of a tiny cell, about seven feet long and less than five feet wide. It was dirty and smelled of urine, though not as strongly as the sack. In the corner, there was a Turkish-style toilet, a shower head, and a metal sink. The door was solid steel sealed firmly around its edges. The only opening was more than six feet up: an iron sheet with tiny holes through which the soft moaning from the courtyard wafted. Neither daylight nor fresh air could penetrate. There was one caged lightbulb fastened to the ceiling. It emitted a weak, flickering yellow glow. I looked for a light switch. There was none. The walls were crude; chunks of protruding cement would bite into my back if I tried to lean against them. The only option was to lie down on the thin foam mat that covered most of the floor. I did, trying to ignore the stench of feces embedded in the mat and the flickering half-light that I could not extinguish. My head was still fuzzy from the chloroform, but anytime a wave of sleep started to overtake me, sounds yanked me back more abruptly than Eyeglasses's slaps: Arkadi's keys jingling as he strode up and down the corridor; locks being opened and closed; a steady stream of soft groans. Sometimes the sound of a boot or fist striking flesh, followed by a cry or a scream.

"I have to go to the bathroom!" one silhouette called out.

"Shit in your pants!" from Arkadi.

Dried blood was caked on my hair, neck, and chest. Knives of pain stabbed my arms and wrists. My neck pulsed where the nail had punctured it. Here I was, lying in a cell that was like a tomb. No, I corrected myself, it was a cave, not a tomb. Unlike Badawi, I was still alive.

Badawi.

I imagined Badawi at parties or playing cards; laughing, dancing, loving life—and now, because of making this stupid bomb, he was dead. I curled up into the fetal position and wept. I tried to muffle my heaving sobs in the shit-smelling mat; I didn't want Arkadi to hear me. Finally exhaustion and the remnants of chloroform conquered my pain and grief. I drifted off, the sound of Arkadi's heavy footsteps and jingling keys punctuating my restless dreams.

THE FLICKERING, dim, yellow bulb ensured that I was never fully in the light or totally in the dark. I knew it was morning only when I heard the door open at the end of the corridor and a voice call out, "Breakfast! How many people you have in there, Arkadi?"

"Twelve," Arkadi answered. A cart was rolled through the door to Arkadi. My stomach rumbled, reminding me that I did not know when I had eaten last. I sat up on the mat, waiting for the meal to arrive. Half an hour passed, maybe an hour. There was no way to monitor time. Finally I heard Arkadi's keys in the door and he slid a tray with two plates inside, pushing another prisoner into the room with me and locking the door.

"I thought they put me here to rest from the *sahat al-tahqeeq*."* The prisoner looked at my bandaged hands. "But I guess I'm supposed to help you eat as well. I'm Ahmad. I'm an actor from Jerusalem."

"*Sahat al-tahqeeq?*"

"That's where they keep us standing with the damned sack. Now let's see what Arkadi brought us this morning . . ."

Ahmad fed me half a hard-boiled egg, a piece of bread with jelly and margarine, and tomato and cucumber salad. The egg was not fresh and the bread was stale but I was hungry enough to choke down a few bites. Ahmad held a cup of tea to my lips. I took a sip and spit it out immediately.

"What kind of tea is this?" I said. It was dark, bitter, and stone cold. It tasted like it had been brewed from a strange substance.

*Arabic for "interrogation courtyard."

Ahmad was instructing me on what I should do to protect my rights when Arkadi entered. "Let's go." He fastened the ankle cuffs, led me through the corridor, and transferred me into the waiting hands of two policemen and a *muhaqeq*.* As soon as we stepped outside the door, the sack was thrust over my head again. In darkness that smelled like urine, they led me across the compound.

The sack was removed inside a judge's chambers.

The *muhaqeq* put a paper on the judge's desk. "This is one of the suspects involved with the explosion in Jerusalem Friday. We need permission to detain him for questioning."

The judge turned to me. "The state will provide you with a lawyer," he said.

"I don't want your government-appointed lawyer," I answered, following Ahmad's advice. "I want Lea Tsemel to represent me."

Lea Tsemel was an Israeli lawyer renowned for defending Palestinian political prisoners with passion and conviction. She had been Samir's lawyer as well, when he had been arrested and detained six months for throwing stones.

"So you refuse the appointed legal representation?"

"Yes."

The judge signed the *muhaqeq*'s paper without asking further questions. Within minutes, Arkadi was pushing me inside a new room. This room was clean and slightly bigger than the cave, with a small desk and chairs. A fluorescent light was installed in the ceiling. Eyeglasses was waiting for me, with two other *muhaqeqeen*. The one sitting behind the desk smiled at me warmly, introducing himself as Yossi. The one sitting next to the desk snarled.

"Have a seat," the *muhaqeq* named Yossi said, indicating the empty chair. I sat.

"Would you like some coffee? Good coffee, not like the crap you got this morning."

"Sure." Yossi sent Eyeglasses to bring me some. In the meantime, he took out a packet of cigarettes, pulled one halfway out of the pack, and slid it across the desk to offer it to me. Though I rarely smoked, I took it with the free fingers in my left hand. "Thanks."

---

*Arabic for "interrogator." Refers to *shabak* officers involved in interrogation. Plural is *muhaqeqeen*.

I had already decided: I would tell them everything. What did I have to hide? Abbas was already in their custody and Badawi was dead. There was no one else to implicate. Coming clean might make my time here easier.

Eyeglasses returned with the coffee and held it up to my mouth so I could take a sip. It was hot and tasty, like Yossi had promised.

"Now . . ." Yossi moved from behind his desk and sat on top of it, directly in front of me. "We'd like to hear the entire story from A to Z. How exactly did the explosion happen?"

I told them the story.

"Now, tell me again, please, who was involved?"

"Just the three of us: Badawi, Abbas, and me."

The third *muhaqeq* jumped in with a grimace. "We told you not to bother being nice to this one. Let me make him tell the truth!"

Yossi leaned toward me. "My colleague, Rani, is angry. He thinks you are lying."

"Every word that I've said is true, I swear!"

Yossi held up his hand. "I believe you, my friend, but the problem is my colleagues. They don't believe you."

At that moment there was a knock on the door. "The judge needs to talk to you, Yossi," Arkadi said.

Yossi got down from the desk. "Continue to talk to him," he said to Rani and Eyeglasses, leaving and closing the door behind him.

Rani thrust his face right into mine. I could smell onion on his breath. "You don't want to tell us who else you were working with?" He slapped me across my cheek, hard.

"I already told you everything there is to say."

He turned to Eyeglasses. "Get the water," he told him.

Eyeglasses went out, returning moments later with several one-liter glass bottles of water. Frost covered the glass and pieces of ice were floating inside.

Rani held one of the bottles over me and tipped it slightly. Freezing-cold water trickled down my back. I began to shiver involuntarily. My spine turned numb.

"Who the fuck else was involved with you?"

"It was just the three of us!"

The cold water came faster, soaking me. I gasped in shock. The first bottle of freezing water was followed by a second, then a third. The numbness spread from my spine to the rest of my body. Rani kicked me in the legs and Eyeglasses hammered me with his fists on my shoulders.

"Tell us the truth, you bastard!"

Hours later, back in the five- by seven-foot cave, I assessed the damage. I had some bruises from the kicking and beating, but not worse. My main concern was the drenched bandages. I had to somehow protect my open wounds.

Dinner that night was vile. It must have been sitting out for hours. The chicken, still sprinkled with feathers, smelled rotten. The mashed potatoes were dry and crusty and had been mixed together with cabbage salad. With Ahmad's help, I nibbled only at the stale bread.

Lying on the mat, I imagined what my family was doing at that moment. My mother would surely be crying, heartbroken. My father would be worried out of his mind. How could I have done this to them? Then, without warning, thoughts about Badawi invaded my mind and sobs overwhelmed me again.

A few hours later, it was just Yossi and Rani in the fluorescent-lit room. Yossi coaxed and cajoled again, finally getting called out of the room by Arkadi, leaving me with Rani. The kicks and blows were less restrained this time. I fell off the chair as Rani continued to strike me. I looked at the bandage on my right hand with alarm. Blood was seeping through.

"You're bleeding, are you? Maybe we can make you bleed more!" He grabbed the edge of the bandage and ripped it off my arm. I screamed in pain. Blood from my wound began to flow freely again. I tried to get back on my feet, but Rani kicked me, knocking me down. I clenched my jaw so that another scream would not escape.

Rani sent for Arkadi. "Take him to the clinic," he told him. The army doctor put a new bandage on my wound and gave me antibiotic pills to prevent infection.

When Arkadi led me back to the cave, Ahmad was there, lying on the mat. "*Ahlan,** Sami."

I didn't say anything. All I wanted was to be alone. I put my head between my knees. Ahmad sat up and began massaging his legs.

"Sixteen straight hours in *sahat al-tahqeeq*," he explained. I buried my head deeper in my knees. I forced myself not to think about Badawi. I did not want to cry in front of Ahmad.

Arkadi delivered a cold and nasty dinner on a tray. Ahmad tried to feed me a bite of the meat, but I turned my head away from the peculiar smell in disgust. "Just the bread," I told him.

---

*Shorter, less formal version of *ahlah wa sahlan,* meaning "welcome."

He offered me a bite of bread before speaking. "Sami, look. I'll be out of here in a few days. But you're going to be in prison for a long time. Don't become thin and weak! You must eat everything they put in front of you! This is your life now."

Ahmad stretched out on the mat again to try to get a few hours of sleep before returning to be shackled in the *sahat al-tahqeeq*. I thought over his words. He was right. I knew I would be in prison for many years. This was my life now. The nearly inedible food was an attempt to weaken us physically and psychologically. It would not work on me, I decided. The next morning, I convinced myself that everything on the breakfast tray tasted like it came from my mother's kitchen. I cleaned my plate.

Arkadi took me out of the cave after breakfast, shackling my ankles as usual. A few feet down the corridor, he forced the urine-covered sack over my head. I was headed for the *sahat al-tahqeeq*. I stumbled blindly as Arkadi pushed me into the courtyard. He shoved my forehead against the wall, instructing me not to move. I could hear breathing around me. I knew that the others' hands were shackled behind their backs while mine were free of cuffs. The injuries brought some benefits.

"Who's there?" I heard a whisper muffled as a cough after Arkadi's heavy footsteps moved down the corridor.

"It's Sami," I coughed low in return.

"*Ahlan,* Sami."

Conversation ceased. Arkadi would strike us if he detected any attempt to communicate.

I stood for one hour . . . two . . . three . . . four . . . The sack smothered all my senses. I could barely breathe. Five hours . . . six . . . My legs fell asleep and my body grew heavier than lead. I leaned against the wall for physical support. A strong blow from Arkadi's boot was delivered to the side of my leg. "Stand up!" was the growled command. I straightened up, shifting my weight from one leg to the other to reduce the pain. Seven hours . . . eight . . .

"I have to use the bathroom."

"Piss on yourself, what do I care?"

I tried to hold it in but I couldn't. I relieved myself in the courtyard with my forehead pressed against the wall. My body and clothes now smelled like the sack.

I had no idea what time it was when Arkadi roughly grabbed the back of my shirt and pushed me toward my cell. I collapsed flat onto my aching back. I moved my ankles in circles. Pain pierced them like needles as the blood started circulating again.

Arkadi opened the door and pushed in a tray with half an egg and bread and butter. Breakfast again? That was the last meal I had eaten. Surely I had not been standing for twenty-four hours. Were they trying to confuse me? I swallowed the egg and bread as fast as I could so I could return to lying prone on the mat. But ten minutes later, Arkadi was at the door. "Get up," he said, shackling my ankles.

Arkadi pushed me into a metal chair facing Yossi and Rani. This time he locked my ankle cuffs around the legs of the chair.

Yossi took the lead, talking calmly as always.

"What do you know about the bus bombing a few months ago?"

"Bus bombing? Nothing!"

"Lying sack of shit!" spit out Rani. "Your friend already told us that your group planted that bomb!"

I understood the game immediately; they did not have any solid leads about this incident. They were trying to squeeze any relevant information out of Abbas and me. Arkadi summoned Yossi quicker than usual, leaving me alone with Rani.

The kicking and the hitting began intensely, Rani punching me on every place of my body where marks wouldn't show.

"You see this bottle?" Rani held up a glass Coke bottle. "Tell me about the bus bombing or I will shove this up your ass!"

I fixed my eyes on the wall directly in front of me. I forced my voice to stay steady. "Shove whatever you like up my ass. I know nothing about the bombing." *They will not break me. They will not break me. They will not break me. I am a donkey, able to endure anything.*

Rani put the bottle down. "How's that arm doing today? Let me see it."

I held out my arm. He ripped the bandage off again, taking hair and fresh pink skin with it. "Fucker!" I spat through gritted teeth. Blood began to ooze out again.

"We can cut your arm off, you know. We'll say that you lost it in the explosion." He took a salt shaker out of the desk and a two-liter bottle of ice water. "Better yet, maybe we'll just get it so infected that it needs to be amputated." He poured salt into my open, bleeding wound, dumping the bottle of water directly into it as well. I bit the inside of my cheek until I tasted blood, hoping this new torment would distract me from the agony.

Arkadi brought another two-liter bottle of frozen water. I braced myself for the shock as it was dumped down my back, followed by pummeling on

my shoulders from Rani's thick fists. "You piece of shit!" the *muhaqeq*
shouted, slapping me across the face and storming out of the room. I was
shackled to the chair with teeth chattering, but alone for a small, treasured
moment. I had never been so tired. Just as my eyes closed, I heard the door
open behind me.

"Ah, if it isn't my friend Sami!" Yossi said. "I see that you're wet and cold. I
want to help you. Just tell me about the bus bomb. Then I'll let you rest."

"I had nothing to do with that bombing."

"I'm sorry about my colleague—he's angry and I can't control him. But if
you tell me the details of the bombing, I can help you."

How could he help me when I didn't know anything? Arkadi called Yossi
out. Rani returned with a fresh two-liter jug of ice water. He dumped it down
my back and kicked the chair. The chair and I fell over together.

"Your friend told us it was you. You might as well stop lying!" Kick to the
back. Another to the shoulder.

"If he said it, he was the one lying," through gritted teeth.

"Maybe a refreshing drink will help you remember?" Another can of ice
water.

"There's nothing for me to remember!"

Rani summoned Arkadi, who took off my ankle cuffs and left.

"Stand up," the *muhaqeq* said softly. I did, painfully. "Take off your
clothes." I struggled to take them off quickly and calmly. I would not show
any sign of shame. I stood naked for one long minute, staring directly at my
tormentor without flinching.

"Put your clothes back on," he said finally.

Arkadi took me to the clinic to re-bandage my wound. I was desperate to
sleep. But the piss sack was slammed over my head again. Back to *sahat al-
tahqeeq*, pressing my forehead against the wall, trying not to let my legs
buckle underneath me. One hour . . . two hours . . . five hours . . .

Arkadi grabbed me and I stumbled ahead of him, barely able to walk, until he shoved me back into the room with Rani and Eyeglasses and slammed
me down on the chair.

"You still know nothing about the bus bombing?" The bandage was
ripped off again. A howl of pain escaped my lips before I could stop myself.
Another can of ice water followed by an immediate shower of blows raining
down on my back, my shoulders, my head. I fell to the floor. Rani brought
out the salt shaker and poured it over my wound.

"Yes, I did it!"

The beating stopped immediately. Yossi, Rani, and Eyeglasses stood with their hands on their hips, looking back and forth at each other and then at me, lying on the floor, breathing heavily. I had not even noticed that Yossi had entered the room.

"Thank you, my friend, for being willing to cooperate with us. You will be glad you did." Yossi helped me up and led me to another room with a desk, a comfortable chair, and an electric kettle. "Do you want a cigarette? Some coffee?"

Cigarette. Coffee. "Sure, why not?" My mouth watered as Yossi boiled the water to make coffee. I knew I would pay a heavy price for this reprieve, but at the moment it was worth it. As the *muhaqeq* added the sugar, I began to invent the story that I would tell him. It had to be a good one, long enough to have time for a second cup. Who worked with me, how we made the bomb, where we placed it . . . my imagination filled in the details.

Yossi's first question took me off guard. "What color was the clock inside the bomb?"

I had not yet taken a single sip of the coffee. "The clock? It was . . . white."

He leaned forward eagerly. "And which Egged line were you trying to bomb?"

"Line number . . . four, I think."

Yossi's face changed in front of me, becoming as harsh and ugly as those of his friends. He backhanded me across the face, spilling the hot coffee all over me. "You liar!" he snarled. "You're making this up!"

"You wanted a story!" I managed to gasp out. "I'm giving you a story!"

When Yossi tired of beating me, Arkadi dragged me to the clinic to get re-bandaged yet again, and then back to *sahat al-tahqeeq*, shoving the sack over my head.

Hours later, Arkadi pushed me back in the cave. I collapsed on the mat. My back was screaming, my arm was throbbing, and I was shaking uncontrollably. But I permitted myself a brief smile. They had given me their worst and I had survived. Human beings are capable of enduring more than we ever imagine we can.

The pain in my arm woke me up. I dragged myself to a sitting position and looked at the bandage. Pus was oozing out of it. I held it up to my nose. It smelled rotten. I was panicked. Thankfully, Arkadi entered moments later with ankle cuffs.

"It's time for your checkup at Hadassah. Let's go."

The doctor in Hadassah unwrapped my bandages gently. "Hmm . . . looks like you've got the start of a nasty infection here," he said with concern. "Are you taking the antibiotics daily?"

"Yes . . . but I don't think it helped when the *shabak* ripped the bandages off and poured water and salt on them."

"They did this to you?"

"Yes."

The doctor turned angrily to the accompanying police officers. "This man is still undergoing medical care! After his treatment is over, you can do what you like with him, but while he is under my supervision, I won't tolerate this."

That evening was Friday. Shabbat brought a bit of relief. But on Sunday it began again.

This time Eyeglasses confronted me in the chair. "Who is Galit?" he asked.

I startled but quickly tried to cover. "We worked together at a café in West Jerusalem."

Eyeglasses smiled. "Just work?"

"Yes, just work!"

The smile turned into a sneer as Eyeglasses poked his nose into mine. "You're trying to kill as many Jews as you can, and at the same time you're planning to fuck a Jewish girl?" He lit a cigarette, blew the smoke in my face, and looked at me with disgust. "This Galit of yours is very upset, you know."

I was unglued. "We weren't going to kill civilians!"

Lying on the mat later that day, I tried unsuccessfully not to think about Galit. I was sure that Eyeglasses was speaking the truth; Galit would be sad. Sad and disappointed. I prayed inside myself that Galit would understand that what I did was against occupation and not against her, that she would not regret having befriended me, that she and Morris and Reuven would not nurture a hard spot against me in their hearts. I hoped Galit somehow knew that I was lying in a cell in the Russian Compound police headquarters, fervently wishing her a safe and happy life.

Arkadi took me from the cave and led me to a new room. I expected to find Yossi, Rani, or Eyeglasses inside, but to my surprise a thin woman in her thirties with shoulder-length brown hair awaited me.

"My name is Lea Tsemel," she said. "Your parents asked me to be your lawyer. Do you agree?"

Her bright eyes, open countenance, and warm voice reminded me of my fifth-grade Hebrew teacher, Avital. I trusted her immediately.

"How are my mom and dad?"

"They're concerned about you. They've come here several times to try to see you."

It was too painful to talk more about my family. I quickly asked Lea about my case.

We'd be judged in a military court in Al-Lyd, Lea explained. The military court still operated under the British Mandate Emergency Law enacted in 1945 against Jewish terrorist groups. Anyone who committed acts against the state was judged under this system. Israelis who committed acts of violence against Palestinians, however, were judged in civilian court.

Lea offered me a cigarette. "There are fourteen witnesses in your case," she told me as I inhaled. "Doctors and nurses in Al Makassed, neighbors who heard the explosion. It's certain you'll go to prison. The question is, for how long?"

"What do you think?"

"Well . . . " She paused, considering. "Most likely ten to twelve years."

I nodded. It was what I expected. Merely being a member in an illegal organization would mean three years.

I told Lea what I had undergone during the interrogations. Lea had defended dozens of Palestinian political prisoners; she knew the details of my abuse as well as I did. She said she would address it with the judge but that the treatment was not likely to improve.

Lea reached inside her leather briefcase and began shuffling around. She pulled out a stack of papers and handed them to me. I expected legal documents, but instead I was looking at childish drawings made with colored pencils and markers. The first was a tank. The second depicted soldiers on a bloody battlefield. I looked at her quizzically.

"My nine-year-old son, Nissan, drew these. He was born into this bloody conflict, just like you."

Nissan was just a year younger than my little brother Mazin. I examined the images more carefully. One portrayed the little boy's family outside his house next to a large, leafy tree. Upon closer inspection, even this scene of domestic tranquility showed evidence of war; Nissan had sketched a bomber plane overhead. Looking at drawing after drawing, I felt a strange combination of tenderness and jealousy for this nine-year-old boy. I was locked up; he was going to and from school, playing with his friends, being cared for by his family. I had also sketched pictures of war at his age. I had also painted trees and my family and the river and the sun. In all of my drawings, I had included a Palestinian flag. I searched through the stack of papers. There were no flags in any of Nissan's pictures. I was not sure what meaning to draw from that.

This little boy drawing tanks and battles . . . he still had a chance to grow up and have a normal life.

Nine days, twelve days, sixteen days. Back and forth from the cave, to the *sahat al-tahqeeq*, to the interrogation room, to the clinic. With each passing hour, I was closer to getting out of this hellhole. On day nineteen, Arkadi shackled my ankles and led me to a new corridor. I caught the cell number as he opened the door: number ten.

"Don't open the window, Sami," he said before he closed and locked the thick steel door. Arkadi himself, however, left the small window of the door ajar. I knew he would; I had already been warned by Ahmad about cell number ten. Cells nine and ten were where the Israelis put us when they wanted to hear what we said to each other. I heard the door of the neighboring cell as it was unlocked and Arkadi's voice said, "Don't open the window, Abbas."

Knowing Abbas was in the cell next to me almost brought tears to my eyes. I had not seen or spoken to Abbas since the day we made the bomb. I knew that every word we said was being monitored. But I didn't care. "Hey, Abbas," I said quietly.

"Sami. How are you?"

"Surviving. How about you?"

"I'm okay. I lost three fingers, and a nail pierced my heart. I almost died."

"I didn't know that." What could I possibly say? "Are you in a lot of pain?"

"Yeah. You?"

"Nothing I can't live with."

Fifteen minutes later, Arkadi took me to the interrogation room. Yossi was waiting for me with a smile.

"So, did you see your friend?"

"Yes."

"I hope you enjoyed Arkadi's stupid mistake. And what did you talk about?"

"Nothing, just asked how the other one was."

"Fine, fine. Now tell me your story one more time, from beginning to end."

For the thousandth time I regurgitated the details. But this time I sensed that I would not have to repeat the story much more. I saw it in Yossi's eyes; the *muhaqeqeen* were convinced that they had squeezed and twisted every drop of possible information from me.

A few days later, Arkadi took me to an office. A different *muhaqeq* was sitting behind the desk. He had a notepad and a pen.

"I'm going to write your confession," he told me. "Tell me everything and I will write down exactly what you say."

Relief flooded over me. The *muhaqeq* took copious notes as I recounted the incident. When I was done, he slid a paper over the desk to me.

"Sign this, please."

I almost laughed aloud when I read the paper. They were smart all right. I signed the paper testifying that my confession-taker had not used any coercion. It was true in a literal sense; I had never seen this particular *muhaqeq* previously. I signed the paper.

"Thank you," he said politely. "That will be all."

⁂

YOSSI INFORMED ABBAS and me that we would be sent to Jalameh prison in Haifa within a week to await our trial.

"Listen, Sami, Abbas, a piece of advice . . ." He leaned toward us confidentially. "It will be better for you if you don't mention anything that happened while we were questioning you. We'd like to help you in court." He smiled. "We're friends, right?"

We assured him that we were friends.

The prison system truck rolled into the Russian Compound to transport us to Jalameh. A soldier cuffed Abbas's ankles to mine after we climbed into the back of the truck. Our hands were cuffed to each other behind our backs.

Two armed soldiers rode in the back of the truck, separated from us by a metal door with a panel of small airholes. There were four rows of long, metal benches. Abbas and I sat on one. As the vehicle pulled out onto the street, I twisted my body around and stood, forcing Abbas to stand with me. I wanted to peer out of the small airholes on the side panel to get my last view of Jerusalem.

"Get down!" the prisoner next to me hissed. I did, quickly. "First time in the truck, I take it?" I nodded. "If the soldiers see you do that, they'll close all the air panels."

It was a warm day for the end of October. Sitting on the metal bench already felt like being inside an oven. If they closed the panels, we would suffocate.

"What are your names?" the prisoner next to us asked.

"Sami."

"Abbas."

"I'm Fat'hi. I'd shake your hand, but . . ." He smiled ruefully.

There were thirty-five other prisoners in the truck. Some of them had their ankles bound with hands cuffed behind their backs like ours. Others had their hands cuffed in front of them and their ankles were free.

"Why are the cuffs different?" I asked Fat'hi.

"Criminals get a bit more freedom than political prisoners."

The political prisoners were all Palestinian. The criminals were a mixture of Jews and Arabs. As Abbas and I were still awaiting our trial, we were the only ones in civilian clothing. Everyone else had blue or brown pants and orange shirts.

The criminal sitting across from me picked open his lock, using a paper clip he held in his teeth. I watched in amazement as he took a small plastic bag out of his pocket and began to roll a greenish brown herb in paper.

"Is that what I think it is?" I asked Fat'hi in a low voice.

The man rolling the hash overheard me. He grinned. "You want me to get your cuffs off?" Fat'hi turned around so that he could be sprung loose. Throughout the truck, criminals were helping the political prisoners get their wrist cuffs off.

The tight plastic cuffs were biting into my injuries painfully, but I thought it would be wiser not to break any rules before we got our sentencing. "No thanks," I said.

"Suit yourself." The man lit the joint, inhaled, and passed it. Fat'hi declined politely. The criminal across the bench took it next.

My eyes grew wider. "Don't the soldiers smell that?"

Fat'hi laughed. "Of course, but as long as we're quiet, they don't care. They're probably enjoying the contact high!"

"And if we don't stay quiet?"

"Then they pump pepper spray into the truck and close all the panels."

An hour later, the truck pulled into another station. "Must be Ramle," Fat'hi said.

A few prisoners were unloaded, and others took their place. The truck rolled on. We passed the hours peppering Fat'hi with questions on what to expect inside the prison system, which he referred to as "university." He described the education and democracy system that the political prisoners had built across factional lines. Abbas and I would not be a part of that, however, until we received our sentencing.

It was late at night by the time we arrived in Jalameh. The guard led Abbas and me inside the prison and directly to our cell. "Look how big it is!" I whispered to Abbas. There were three steel bunk beds. The windows, though still only panels with tiny holes, gave more fresh air than the windows had in the Russian Compound. The fresh air, however, had a disadvantage; it was colder in Jalameh than it had been in Jerusalem.

A guard brought us dinner. The food was more plentiful than it had been, but it was prepared in a very dirty kitchen. Abbas and I scooped bugs out of our soup before eating it.

Our four cell mates, all criminals, told us more about Jalameh. Everyone here was Palestinian and under twenty years old. All were still waiting for trials. Abbas and I were two of only a handful of political prisoners; the rest were criminals, arrested for shoplifting, burglary, and other non–politically motivated criminal acts.

I was surprised when our cell mates told us there was a common room to smoke, drink coffee, watch TV. Abbas and I enjoyed the relative leniency the next night, meeting the other young men. Though two policemen guarded the common room, they left us alone. The prisoners purchased coffee and cigarettes from a small canteen with a monthly allowance received from their families. Political prisoners were permitted less allowance than the criminals, but our new friends were generous.

"You two are heroes," one young man said to us as he bought us cups of instant coffee. "I'm here for stealing cars. But you did something for our people." I was far from being a hero. But it felt good to command so much instant respect.

It didn't take Abbas and me long to notice tension between the prisoners. It seemed to be along geographic lines. The guards intentionally stoked this tension. Keeping the prisoners divided against each other made them easier to control. With their encouragement, the Jerusalem criminals often teamed up against the criminals from the north. The Jerusalemites lobbied hard for Abbas's and my support.

"We need you with us. You'll make us stronger," one took me aside to say.

"Those people from Nazareth are bad; they hate us!" another tried to convince Abbas.

Fat'hi had warned us never to take sides in disputes between different groups of criminals. Our protected status would remain intact only if we stayed above their internal conflicts.

Though my injuries were not yet healed, Abbas was much worse off. He had only two fingers on his left hand and his wounds were still deep, including the punctures in his heart and lungs. But Abbas was not only damaged physically. His personality was completely altered, whether due to depression or trauma, I did not know. He was quieter than ever. Some nights, as we sat in the common room, he stared off into space for hours. I assisted my friend physically, helping him wash and dress. But I was at a loss about how to bring the old Abbas back from the shell he had become.

Abbas was not the only one experiencing psychological difficulties. I dreaded night. Sleep was hard to come by, and when it finally did, explosions tore out my eardrums, waking me in a cold sweat with a pounding heart. After falling back to sleep, I was shackled in my dreams, beaten, doused with ice water. Night after night, I struggled to open my eyes in order to wake myself from the horror, and when I did, I found a bald head, thick eyeglasses, and the barrel of a pistol in my face. Nightmares within nightmares. I would lie awake for the rest of the night, berating myself over and over for having decided to join with Abbas and Badawi in making the bomb.

There were only a few books in Jalameh. I picked one up in the common room and began idly flipping through it. The title of the first chapter jumped out at me: how to resist suffering. The second chapter: the mind is stronger than the body. I read the book from cover to cover the next day, sleeping with it under my mattress. I read it again the following week, and a third time as well. The nightmares continued, but I stopped punishing myself. *Khalas, it's done,* I instructed my brain to convince the rest of me. It's time to turn the page.

In Jalameh, I was able to see my mother at last. She took the long ride up from Jerusalem with the Red Crescent.* I stared at her through the glass window, communicating via phone. My mom was here. I was still cared for. I was not alone.

The guards came to our cell every morning for inspection. We stood by the sides of the steel bunk beds with our hands in front of us when they entered.

---

*Part of the International Red Cross and Red Crescent Movement.

"Is everything okay?" the head guard, Kamal, a Druze man with bright green eyes, often asked Abbas and me. "Do you need anything?" There was an unmistakable tone of respect in his voice. I was amazed. He rarely addressed the other prisoners in the cell.

"They trust political prisoners more than they trust us," one of my cell mates explained. "Maybe you were building a bomb, but at least they know you're honest."

We did not always get special treatment. If there were disturbances in the prison, Kamal went from cell to cell.

"What happened?" Kamal roared at each of us. Abbas and I learned fast from our cell mates. We heard nothing, saw nothing, knew nothing. We were, therefore, not spared the collective punishment.

Sometimes the guards lashed out at us with a slap or a kick when we were on our way to the courtyard. But other times the guards seemed hungry for conversation, especially with Abbas and me. Bisan, just a year or two older than us, often brought coffee from the outside that he would share. Bisan was also Druze, from the nearby village of Isifia. I had never met Druze before. Unlike other Arab citizens of Israel, Druze men served in the Israeli army and police forces.

"You know why I'm working here, Sami?" Bisan said as he handed me a cup of coffee. "I couldn't get any other job. Without a university degree, there's no work available to Druze except to be a guard or policeman . . ."

There were many types of prisoners in Jalameh. Kamal and Bisan were prisoners in a different way. I thought about Arkadi, his heavy steps patrolling the *shabak* corridor. He had been a kind of prisoner too.

Abbas and I were loaded onto the prison trucks to go to Al-Lyd. There, we met with Lea and had our initial session in court. We spent a few nights in Ramle, the transfer prison. Other political prisoners heaped advice on us about how to handle our trial.

"When they ask you if you are guilty, never say yes!" we were instructed. "There is no guilt in fighting occupation!"

The court building had been constructed during the British Mandate. The courtroom itself was small and painted white. The only windows were covered by black draping. Abbas and I were led to a box in the corner of the room and instructed to sit on the wooden benches. Police officers sat next to us. My mother was there. But to my disappointment, my father was not.

There were three military judges, sitting on a raised platform behind a dark wooden desk. The head judge was an old, thin man with deep wrinkles creasing his forehead. He had thick, large glasses and a wooden gavel. An Israeli flag was behind him. The other judges were both middle-aged men, with gray hair and glasses. They all wore army uniforms.

Lea and the army lawyer sat at tables in another area of the room. I looked at Lea. She nodded slightly as if to say, "I'll do my best for you."

The lead judge initiated the proceedings. His voice was so soft I was not aware he had begun, until he banged his gavel on the desk to get everyone's attention.

The army lawyer went first, asking that Abbas and I each get twenty-five years in prison. Lea had forewarned us that they would be asking for the maximum sentence.

Lea, who had always been gentle in our meetings, surprised us in court. She spoke forcefully—almost shouting, "The reason these young men are here today is because of the occupation. That's the central issue here!"

Then her voice suddenly grew calm and measured. She put her notes on the table directly in front of the judges and pointed out the text of a law she had copied.

"These young men are from Jerusalem," she said. "How is it you're judging them with British Mandate Emergency Law rather than Israeli civil law?"

Lea moved around the room constantly as she spoke, a master of the art of when to be gentle and when to be commanding.

"The only people injured by their actions were themselves!" she concluded forcefully. "They should receive the minimum sentencing!"

The judge asked us only one question in a voice so quiet it seemed he did not want to expend energy on speaking. "Do you plead guilty or innocent?"

Abbas and I followed the advice we had been given. "We were making a bomb because we wanted to end the occupation."

Abbas and I had been taken to the military court in Al-Lyd every few months, returning to Jalameh after a few days. Now, our final court day was in less than a week. After fourteen months, it was time to leave Jalameh for good. We would be taken to Ramle in the morning. After our sentences were given, we would be assigned our permanent prisons.

Bisan looked as if he might cry when he said goodbye to us. "You're different from the other prisoners here," he said. "You are like brothers to me." The incidents where Bisan had struck me for no reason flashed through my mind. But so did the times he had shared his coffee, eager to talk with Abbas and me for hours. I was not sure how to respond. The guard/prisoner relationship was complex.

"Take care of yourself," I finally said.

In Ramle, the other political prisoners pumped us up with advice about the upcoming sentencing.

"Make sure you stay quiet and respectful, no matter what," one told us. "I jumped up and shouted 'Free Palestine!' All of a sudden, my five years turned into eight . . ."

They described the highly organized prison system that we would be entering. "Get ready for university!" we heard more than once.

On December 13, 1981, Abbas and I were led into the courtroom. I looked out at the rows of benches filled with people. Abbas's family. Azzam, Riyyad, Samira. I tried to send each one a silent message of gratitude. My mother smiled at me the moment my eyes landed on her face. As if she knew. And next to her, my father! My gaze lingered on my father so long I almost did not notice the young woman sitting next to him—my fiancée, Sanaa. I tried not to wonder if Galit had any way of knowing about the court date and if she would have come if she did. Instead, I stared at Sanaa in amazement that she had made the effort to come all the way from Amman. I wanted to hug her in appreciation, but all I could do was mouth "*Shukran*" when I caught her eye.

The room sat in silence as the head judge shuffled through his papers. I tried to prepare myself for the worst.

The judge stood up, with the air of someone who just wanted to get his job done and go home. He read with his customary weak voice. The first defendant, Abbas Hosni Hassan Kashour, the judge read, is found guilty for membership in an illegal organization, for undergoing training in Syria, for making and planting one bomb, and for attempting to build a second bomb.

The second defendant, Sami Saber Al Jundi, he continued, is found guilty for membership in an illegal organization, for making and planting one bomb, and for attempting to make another bomb.

The first defendant is more dangerous than the second, the judge concluded. Defendant 1 went to Syria for training and was more directly involved in all the activities of the group. Defendant 2 was recruited by Defendant 1 and his cousin, Badawi Kashour. However, he still participated of his own free will.

The judge's voice grew even more quiet. I had to strain to hear him. "Defendant #1, Abbas Kashour, is sentenced to fifteen years of prison, starting from September 13, 1980. Defendant #2, Sami Al Jundi, is sentenced to ten years of prison, starting from September 13, 1980."

I sat quietly, remembering the warnings I had been given. The judge closed his book quickly.

"All rise!" the policeman called out and everyone stood as the judge left through the black curtain behind his platform. The entire sentencing had taken exactly fifteen minutes.

"Be strong, Sami!" my father shouted out while the policemen led Abbas and me away.

"*Al sabr jamil,** my son! Don't lose hope!" my mother called after us. I turned my head as we left the courtroom to get one last look at them, and one last look at Sanaa.

I read the walls in Ramle that night. Every prisoner passed through Ramle at one time or another. They scratched their names and the dates they were there on the cells. I ran my fingers, free of bandages for a year now, over the etched evidence of their presence. These men were my brothers. How many years of locked-away life did the walls of this one cell in Ramle represent? I contemplated the next decade calmly. I would be twenty-eight when I was freed. I had no other choice but to accept my fate. Inside or outside the prison, there are still twenty-four hours in a day. How to best spend that time would be my new challenge.

*Arabic for "Patience is beautiful."

CHAPTER SIX

⁓⁓⁓

EARLY THE FOLLOWING MORNING, a truck pulled into Ramle. I raised my eyebrows at Abbas and he flashed back a quick grin. We were going to start our life as political prisoners. Abbas and I sat next to each other in silence on the freezing metal bench as the truck stopped at one police station after another. I wanted to sit on my hands to warm them, but the tight plastic cuffs made that impossible. The chill increased as the truck rolled on and on. The late afternoon sunlight was filtering through the tiny airholes when we finally approached Beer Al-Sabe' prison. I knelt on the bench to peek through the holes, though I knew I was risking the pepper spray. The cement walls and sniper tower loomed large and high. I let out a long, low whistle. The truck came to a halt at an enormous electric gate. The soldiers driving checked their guns with the prison guards; aside from those of the soldiers on the sniper towers, no weapons were permitted inside the grounds. The gate slowly swung open and the truck rolled inside. This gate would be the point of separation between me and everyone on the outside. I held my breath as the gate closed silently behind the truck.

The soldier opened the back of the truck and glanced at his list. "Sami Al Jundi!"

"Take care of yourself," I said quietly to Abbas before standing up. Abbas would be continuing on to Nafha prison, eighty kilometers deeper into the Negev Desert.

"You'll be fine," Abbas reassured me. "You'll be with the brothers."

I shuffled toward the door of the truck as names of a few other prisoners unloading in Beer Al-Sabe' were called. A guard signed a form certifying that he had taken custody of me. He removed my cuffs. My heart racing, I climbed off the truck and into the grounds of Beer Al-Sabe' prison, an enormous grave for the living. I followed the guard through the courtyard, straining to try to decipher signs of life outside. I heard a donkey bray and imagined an old Bedouin man walking with him. I could make out the sounds of cars and semi-trailers driving past. Did the drivers ever wonder about the people inside the imposing walls? Perhaps to them, Beer Al-Sabe' prison was simply part of the desert landscape.

The guard led me to the supply room and handed me a plastic cup, toothbrush, soap, seven thin blankets, and a rubber pad. I was given two long-sleeved orange T-shirts with "Service of Prisons" printed on them. Two pairs of brown cotton pants. A dark blue wool sweater. Plastic slippers. Boots. A jacket identical to police jackets but with "Prisoner" inscribed on the back instead of "Police." I wrapped it all inside a beige foam mat, tying the load together with a rope. I signed for my new possessions, hoisted the bundle onto my back, and followed the guard to Section Nine.

A middle-aged man with the same orange shirt was pushing a cleaning cart and a broom down the corridor. He saw me approaching and leaned the broom against the wall.

"*Ahlan wa sahlan,* Sami Al Jundi!" I started in surprise as the prisoner hugged me and lifted the bundle off my back. How did he know who I was? My companions on the truck must have spread the word about my arrival as I was getting my supplies.

I followed the guard down the long hall, lit by exposed yellow bulbs protected by iron grates. The floor and walls were gray concrete. Both sides of the corridor were lined with cells, the doors of which were iron bars. Faces crowded around the doors of each cell with hands extended through the bars to shake mine.

"Welcome, Sami!"

"*Ahlan!*"

Warmth poured over me. This would be my home for the better part of the next decade. Though my heart was still pounding, I could not contain my smile.

Among the faces pressing through the bars of cell number two, I spotted a familiar one: Zakaria Kashour, Badawi's older brother. He was serving four years for his involvement in a relatively small movement called the Popular Struggle Front, a splinter group of the PFLP. I looked at Zakaria anxiously. Did he blame me for Badawi's death? He smiled as he silently enveloped my hand in both of his, but his smile was sad. He looked more like Badawi than I had remembered.

The guard mechanically pulled out a ring of large, heavy iron keys and unlocked cell number eleven. The seven men inside the fourteen- by ten-foot room stood up as I entered. They were clearly expecting me.

"*Ahlan,* Sami! I'm Abu Sadeq, the leader of the cell." A short, stocky man with sharp, black eyes and a salt-and-pepper moustache greeted me as he took my rubber sheet and mat, laying it between the other seven mats, covering the only blank space on the cement floor. He patted it. "This is your place."

Someone else spread the blankets on the mat and a third put my cup and toothbrush in a small plastic cupboard propped under the window.

My cell mates began to make a circle on top of the mats. "Come, Sami, introduce yourself!" Abu Sadeq said. I joined them.

"I'm Sami Al Jundi. I've served sixteen months so far of a ten-year sentence," I told them proudly, remembering how much reverence our status had afforded Abbas and me in Jalameh.

Some of my cell mates smiled at me indulgently; others laughed outright. "We should put your mat next to the door," one joked. "Compared to the rest of us, you're practically a free man."

My pride deflated instantly. I surveyed the circle, realizing quickly that at nineteen years, I was by far the youngest.

Abu Sadeq sat quietly chewing the end of his moustache as the others introduced themselves. Abu Abdallah, nearly bald and with a plastic brace on his neck, was the oldest man in the cell. "I've been here for thirteen years," he told me. "My only hope for freedom is a prisoner exchange."

"I'm Mousa Sheikh." Mousa was also bald, with jowls like a bulldog. "I've also been here thirteen years. And I will stay for the rest of my life, or until God opens the door—whichever comes first."

"We call Mousa Sheikh the 'Military Reporter,'" Abu Sadeq explained. "He's constantly analyzing and writing about war strategy and battles."

"Unless," added Abu Abdallah, winking, "we call him 'Private'!"

"*Uskut!*" the Military Reporter growled good-humoredly. He had been low-ranking in Fatah's militia before he was captured, he explained, an embarrassment that the other prisoners enjoyed teasing him about.

Nearly everyone in the circle had been in prison for thirteen years. Shortly after I had fled from our home in the Old City as a tiny boy, Mousa Sheikh, Abu Abdallah, and Abu Sadeq had been part of guerrilla operations based in Jordan. On March 21, 1968, the IDF* attacked a PLO stronghold in

*Israel Defense Forces; the Israeli military.

al-Karameh refugee camp in Jordan in retaliation for raids against Israel, chiefly perpetrated by Fatah fighters. Hundreds had been killed or captured during the Battle of Karameh, many of my cell mates among them.

"Sami, tell us how you were arrested."

I began the story with gusto, but Abu Abdallah interrupted me, adjusting his neck brace. "Please, Sami, leave out the small details. My soul can't bear more stories."

I gave the condensed version, to a circle of nodding heads. They had heard many similar tales before.

Abu Sadeq took the moist end of his moustache out of his mouth. "Tomorrow, we will put you in a cell with other new prisoners from Fatah."

"We can switch cells?"

"Within the same section, yes. We are holding an elective course on economics in this cell. You have to take the mandatory course for new prisoners."

The old prisoners told me about the years from 1967, when they painstakingly built the prison society. Many Palestinian political prisoners had been forced to work in Israeli military factories. They did hard physical labor, building crates for missiles and netting for tanks, eroding not only their physical strength but also their self-respect, as they created the infrastructure of the weaponry used to enforce the occupation.

According to my cell mates, Moshe Dayan, a leading Israeli general and politician, had proclaimed with pride in 1979 that the hand that had killed Israelis was now developing the Israeli economy. The prisoners did not share his enthusiasm. They set fire to a prison factory. From that point on, they declared, all their efforts would benefit their people.

Prisoners had always discussed books and political issues in their cells. Now, the meetings and education system became more formalized, especially in Beer Al-Sabe', Nafha, and Asqalan prisons. Initially, prisoners wrote with smuggled pens on thin pieces of cardboard that they peeled off of margarine or cigarette wrappers. Numerous hunger strikes undertaken in the '70s earned them more rights; now we had paper and pens, and due to years of struggle and the support of the Red Cross and UNESCO,* the Israelis placed no restrictions on our books. Though rights to study were tolerated, it was clear that the Israelis did not like our program. Anytime the guards punished us, the old prisoners told me, books and paper were the first hard-won privileges to be revoked.

*United Nations Educational, Scientific, and Cultural Organization.

I spent much of the first night too excited to fall asleep. The political prisoners Abbas and I had met always referred to prison as "university." And now, my real education was beginning! In the stillness of the early morning hours, I slowly drifted off to a few hours of sleep.

Abu Sadeq helped me repack my bundle before I was led to the new prisoners' cell and introduced to my cell mates there: two old prisoners, who were teaching our courses, and six new prisoners, including me. Talal and Asim, both from Khan Younis, Gaza, had a story similar to mine. The bombs they were making exploded prematurely. Talal was missing his left arm below the elbow. Asim continued to write with his right hand, though only his pinky and ring finger remained. Abu Ali had been in prison in Hebron before being transferred to Beer Al-Sabe'. He was serving a life sentence. They called him Abu Ali Salumi in Hebron prison, he boasted, because he had murdered a settler named Salumi. He also bragged about killing a collaborator in Hebron prison. I understood Abu Ali's violence against a settler; there was a distinction between civilians inside Israel's 1948 borders and settlers in the West Bank and Gaza. Abu Ali's killing of an alleged collaborator was far more disturbing to me. Vigilante justice was not justice.

I woke up at 5:30 the next morning, eager to start my new routine. Only Abu Ali and our teacher Diab were awake, praying. I lay on my mat alongside the others until just before 6, when the guards began moving from cell to cell.

"Count!" they called as they entered our cell. Following my cell mates' lead, I stood up until they finished.

The toilet, sink, and shower were separated from the rest of the cell by a nylon curtain. Everyone read as he waited for his turn to use the bathroom. Everyone except for Abu Ali.

"There's no rush. I'm here for life," he told me with a shrug when I asked him why. "I've got all the time in the world to study."

By 7 a.m., the top halves of our mats were pushed up against the walls, creating space in the middle of the concrete floor for breakfast. Bread with margarine and jelly, an egg, tomato, cucumber, olives, and coffee. I ate enthusiastically. Sitting in a circle around breakfast, I felt like I was eating with my family. I could almost hear my brother Azzam's voice asking me to pass the jelly.

After breakfast, I had my first lesson in prison democracy. As the newcomer, I assumed that I would do the grunt work. But instead, I found a rotating schedule; one person each day was responsible for washing the dishes, cleaning the cell, and making the tea—two tea bags in a pot with warm tap water for the eight of us. Everyone's name was on the schedule, including the teachers; we were all the same.

"But Abu Ali usually offers to make the tea," Asim told me as he explained the system. "He likes to get out of the discussions!"

Over breakfast I learned that we met for three hours a day with each of the two teachers for the new prisoner course. Our session with Diab, a tall, thin, quiet, religious man, was first. Diab instructed us on the history and ideology of Fatah from its inception as a Palestinian national movement. He taught slowly, gently, and patiently. He did not smile often but when he did, we could not help but smile with him. I was immediately fond of him.

Abdel Fatah, our teacher for politics and global revolutions, had been one of the *fedayeen* in the mountains around Nablus. He had been arrested in 1970, eleven years ago. As he settled himself in our circle, Talal nudged me and whispered, "Everyone respects this guy! If anyone in the prison has an argument, it's brought to Abdel Fatah to resolve."

Abdel Fatah greeted us with a broad smile and handed Talal a book about the Bolshevik Revolution, quietly asking him to read aloud from a certain page. Talal scarcely got through a paragraph when Abdel Fatah stopped him, providing in-depth background about each sentence. Asim read next, and Abdel Fatah also stopped him a few sentences later, connecting the information in the passage to Cuba and Vietnam. Questions from my cell mates arose about Argentina, the French Revolution, Ireland, and South Africa. Abdel Fatah answered them all in great detail. I listened in amazement. Our teacher seemed to know every single thing in the world. He interjected stories about his days as an underground fighter in Nablus and slipped in a joke or two. His grin was quick and wide, yet his eyes betrayed a deep sadness.

After the six hours of meetings, everyone retreated to his mat with a book.

"Here, Sami." Diab handed me the first book I was required to read, as part of the curriculum that the education committee had developed. My early reading would focus on the history of the Palestinian people and our struggle, Diab explained. Later, the curriculum would expand to the history of all the Arab countries, Jewish and Zionist history, and world revolutions. I looked at the title of the book: *The Palestinian Issue and the Political Projects for Resolution* by Mahdi Abd Al-Hadi. "Learn it well," Diab advised me. "You'll have a lot of questions to answer."

It was the thickest book I had ever held. I sat on my mat, my back against the cold concrete wall, and began to flip through it, scanning the small print.

Names, dates, facts, figures: Palestine under the British Mandate; Revolt of 1936; United Nations Security Council Resolutions 242 and 338; the formation of the PLO and Fatah; and the origins of the Communist and Democratic movements. Seven hundred dense, dry, and detailed pages—it might take me my entire prison sentence to get through this one book alone!

After dinner each evening, the guards played an hour of an Arabic language radio station over the loudspeaker, while we drank tea or coffee. Five minutes of news headlines and then a song by Umm Kulthum, the famous Egyptian singer. She had died five years earlier, but her warm and powerful voice transported me outside the prison walls.

It was Thursday, after Umm Kulthum. I opened my book again, as usual, but my cell mates began to gather in a circle.

"What's going on?" I asked.

"Weekly criticism session," Asim explained quickly as I took a seat next to him in the circle. "We tell each other what we did wrong during the week." I sat silently, bracing myself for a list of reprimands.

Abdel Fatah started the meeting. "I am proud to be here with the new prisoners. I hope I can successfully offer you something from my experience. Diab and I prepare the course together every day for many hours. Because of that, I didn't clean the cell thoroughly when it was my turn yesterday. I'm sorry—it won't happen again."

He moved on to the rest of the circle. "Talal, you usually take an active part in the discussion," Abdel Fatah said. "But lately your mind has been wandering." My trepidation melted immediately. The critiques focused on what we were doing well, and how to add to and improve on it. Before pointing a finger at anyone else, we had to start with ourselves. If it was my day to make coffee and tea, I had to make sure each man woke from his afternoon nap with his drink by his mat. If I neglected to make the coffee, or forgot how much sugar each brother took, everyone would be waiting for me to apologize at the criticism circle. If I did not, then I would hear from each one: "Sami participated actively in all the discussions—but he forgot to make the coffee." If I addressed this mistake myself, however, everyone would thank me for apologizing and it would never come up again. Diab and Abdel Fatah were trying to build us as human beings. I looked forward to next Thursday night.

During the hunger strikes in the '70s, the old prisoners had earned the right for certain cells within a section to be opened for one hour each day.

The guards unlocked our doors and gave us five minutes to choose another cell to enter. Then we would spend the next hour locked inside that cell, before returning to our own. Our weekly political meeting took place during that hour. It was our opportunity to hear different voices and perspectives. When the war in Lebanon was the assigned topic to discuss, we all wanted to be in a cell with Mousa Sheikh. The Military Reporter gave the impression that he was delivering dispatches from the midst of battle. His years of reading and studying war made his description of warfare vibrant and alive.

I was quiet in the political meetings. When I was in my own cell, I did not hold back—but now I was with the older prisoners. I preferred to absorb their wisdom. If we were debating the benefits of negotiations with Israel, they would bring examples from Cuba, Germany, or Vietnam, reflecting a profound knowledge of history.

We argued as if the outcome of these discussions affected us personally—which they very well could. If we were analyzing how effective the PLO forces in south Lebanon were, we were also predicting how many Israeli soldiers they could capture. That could lead to a prisoner exchange. How many of us would be hypothetically freed as a result of this projected capture—the specifics were debated fiercely for hours and emotions ran high. If we reached a deadlock, Abdel Fatah was asked to determine who was right.

When I finally finished *The Palestinian Issue*, Diab handed me a Russian novel, *How the Steel Was Tempered* by Nikolai Ostrovsky. From the first page, I fell in love. I fell asleep at night holding the still-open book against my chest, dreaming about the protagonist, Pavel. Despite having suffered personal hardships, he continued to serve others. I was determined to take him as an example.

When Diab handed me my next political book, *Arab Nationalism Between the Reality of Separation and the Aspiration for Unity* by Munir Shafiq, I was much less apprehensive. I knew that another reward of poetry or literature would follow.

An Israeli officer traveled between the sections and each section had its own guard. The guard spent the majority of his twenty-four-hour shift sitting on his chair at the entrance to the corridor, smoking and drinking coffee or tea. He was not interested in creating problems for us; that would only make his job more difficult the next day. He knew his boundaries and we knew ours. Four times a day, he entered our cells to count us. Occasionally, in between counts, he patrolled the corridor. When he looked inside our cells, he saw us talking intensely in a circle or sitting on our own mats, noses deep inside a book.

Abu Ali, however, rarely read or participated in discussions. He found other ways to amuse himself. I watched him in fascination as he cut his prison-issued sweatshirt into long, thin strips and wove them together to make a ten-foot net, hanging it out the window of the cell. Abu Ali patiently leaned against the window, watching his net.

"How long do you plan to stand there?" I asked him one day, after he had been monitoring his net faithfully for three consecutive hours.

"I've got nothing but time," Abu Ali said, winking at me as he added a few more crumbs of dry bread.

"Gotcha!" he called out one day, startling the rest of us out of our books. Grinning from ear to ear, he lifted the net up through the bars of the window, grasping the top tightly in his hand. "Look, everybody, look!" he shouted. Triumphantly he held up the net with frantic pigeon squawking and more flapping wings than I could count. "Six at one time!"

Abu Ali stuck two nails inside the electrical outlet, rigging it into a makeshift stove. As the water heated in the large tin coffee can, he wrung the birds' necks one by one and plucked off their feathers. When the water was hot, he put the pigeons inside, stirring the can frequently as they stewed.

"Soup for everybody!" Abu Ali announced proudly. And by everybody, he meant all 120 of us in Section Nine. The corridor cleaner distributed a bowl to each cell, leaving one bowl for us. I ate exactly one mouthwatering spoonful.

Each section had two hours a day in the small courtyard, monitored by two or three guards. The courtyard ground was smooth stone, and above it was a cover made of mesh and wire. The mesh did not block out the mosquitoes and scorpions, which also visited us in our cells; nor, thankfully, did it block out the sunshine or birds. Rain fell rarely in the Negev Desert, but when it did, we loved it. The air smelled fresher and tasted cleaner as the rain washed over us, dampening our hair, cheeks, and clothes. We turned our faces upward and danced in the courtyard. It was also raining outside the prison walls. Maybe these same raindrops were falling on our families.

Our first hour in the courtyard was dedicated to exercise and sports. The Red Cross had provided us with a basketball and volleyball. On my first day, I watched from the sidelines, as my section mates dribbled the basketball down the courtyard. The next day, I jumped into the game with zeal, hoping my skills in soccer would somehow transfer to basketball. When the ball found its way into my hands, I tossed it into the net easily, as if I had been playing for years.

"Sami!" Abdel Fatah, who doubled as our section's coach, patted me on the back. "You're very good! You should keep playing!" I decided that I loved basketball even more than soccer. The next day I tried volleyball, discovering to my great delight that I was an excellent volleyball player as well.

After my first week, Abdel Fatah put his arm around my shoulder. "We have tournaments between the sections every month. The sports committee would like you to play on both the basketball and the volleyball teams for Section Nine."

"You want me to play on both teams?"

Abdel Fatah nodded. "What do you say, Sami?"

"I'd be honored!"

The week before my first tournament I could think of nothing else. When the day finally arrived, I was the first one in the courtyard, warming up with jumping jacks while the rest of the two sections filed in to cheer for their players.

When I sank my first basket, all of Section Nine jumped on their feet. I felt like a true hero as they cheered, "Sami! Sami! Sami!" I almost forgot I was in prison.

Section Seven consisted entirely of Fatah activists, unlike my section, which was a mixture of prisoners: seventy from Fatah, and fifty from other movements combined. There was a lot of good-natured joking between their team and ours, where I was one of the only players from Fatah. If I missed a basket, my teammate from the Democratic Front* jokingly elbowed me in the ribs. "You trying to help your brothers win?" he teased.

Similarly, when I aggressively spiked the volleyball, scoring a point for Section Nine, a player on the other side of the net called out, "If you didn't have our Fatah brother Sami on your team, we'd crush you!" I basked in the playful banter between the sections and between the movements.

We had an additional motivation to win games. We played elimination rounds. Each match we won meant our section could stay outside in the sun longer as we entered the new round.

"What cell are you in?" players from the other sections would ask. When I told them, my opponent would grin. "Ah, you're a new prisoner!" Being new had its advantages; everyone wanted to befriend me in order to have another person to tell their stories to.

---

*Democratic Front for the Liberation of Palestine, a Marxist-Leninist movement in the PLO.

The second hour in the courtyard we mingled with other people from our section. Prisoners from villages described grazing their sheep on the mountains and harvesting their crops. I recounted the mischief my brothers Samir, Azzam, and I had caused as little boys, pushing cats onto our dear old neighbor Abu Fakhri. I spoke about my fiancée, Sanaa, to anyone who would listen. How beautiful and feisty she was. I described her contagious laughter. In the privacy of my mind, I thought about Galit as well.

Abu Wahid in cell number six was also from the Old City of Jerusalem. He approached me often in the courtyard, holding my arm tightly just below the elbow and thrusting his face inches from mine. "Sami, how does the *souq* smell? Is it the same as thirteen years ago?"

Talal and Asim talked mostly with each other in the courtyard, but I tried to talk to everyone. If I interacted only with my cell mates, then my entire world would consist of seven people. If I befriended everyone in my section, my world would be large and full. I imagined living in the midst of New York City, but only socializing with one neighbor. Better to be here, in Beer Al-Sabe' prison with 120 brothers. I had the power to determine the size of my universe.

⁂

"WHAT BOOK ARE YOU READING NOW? How do you find it?" I asked Abu Wahid as we strolled around the perimeter of the courtyard. We spoke about writers as if we were talking about one of our cell mates in the weekly criticism meetings—sometimes harshly, but always warmly and intimately.

Twenty of us sat in a tight circle in the courtyard. The Red Cross had given us one copy of Soviet writer Anton Makarenko's *Pedagogical Poem*, and Abu Sadeq was recounting the work for the rest of us. I listened in fascination as Abu Sadeq described Makarenko's account of his work with orphans, abandoned children, and children of criminals in the postrevolution Soviet Union. Makarenko was firm in his conviction that these youths could become doctors, engineers, farmers—citizens contributing fully to their society. He was not willing to give up on any human being. Makarenko's belief that no human potential should be neglected excited me. Even when I discovered that his "poem" was several volumes—each one around six hundred pages in length—I was still eager to read it myself.

After three years, Diab and Abdel Fatah reported to the education committee that all of the new prisoners—except for Abu Ali—had completed our course. We continued our daily meetings in the cell, but we were now able to determine the content. The old prisoners advised us to read about Vietnam.

We analyzed it first from a military angle, next from a political perspective, and then through the writings of Ho Chi Minh. For the Vietnamese revolution to triumph, I observed, it needed support from powerful countries, such as the Soviet Union and China. We examined the relationship between the fighters in North Vietnam and the Vietnamese people. It was exactly what we needed to implement here. *Fedayeen* in Palestine should be with the people, for the people, inside the people, as in Vietnam. We needed a powerful patron state to carve out space for us and give us support to defend ourselves. We studied the 1954 Battle of Dien Bien Phu. The Viet Minh had launched the battle even after agreeing to negotiate with the French. Dien Bien Phu was decisive in the French decision to leave Indochina and grant Vietnam, Laos, and Cambodia their independence. We drew an important lesson from Dien Bien Phu: resistance must continue during negotiations, right up until a final agreement is reached.

During the course, I was permitted to read only what was assigned to me. Now I could finally begin reading the books that all the old prisoners had been talking about. The prison library, though housed in a small cell, was as vast as an ocean. Books were piled high on shelves in a highly organized system. Whenever the Red Cross brought new books, the list of titles was passed from cell to cell and we copied them into a notebook that contained our list of books. Every few weeks, I gave five or six new titles to the corridor cleaner. He delivered the titles to the librarian and, if they were available, brought the books back to me. For six months, I served as my section's librarian, organizing the books for everyone's lists and coordinating the copying of books that were in high demand. First, I located someone who knew how to cut the pages smoothly. Then the corridor cleaner distributed one page of the book and one blank sheet of paper to each prisoner in the section. Each page was meticulously copied word for word, including the page number. I gave the cut book and the handwritten manuscript to a prisoner who knew how to bind books and within two hours, we had two copies of the book, bound neatly and firmly.

Books expanded my world far beyond the prison walls. I read an average of three hundred pages each day. History, psychology, and philosophy were the serious studies. Poetry, romance stories, and French and Arabic literature were my escape. Writers were like prophets to me. Their characters dwelled inside me as if their experiences were my personal memories. I often crouched against the door of the cell until the small hours of the morning, book in hand, to make use of the small, striped square of light spilling in from the corridor.

The complete works of Dostoevsky led my seventy-title reading list. The old prisoners talked constantly about him. They admired his intense scrutiny of the human psyche. Raskolnikov from *Crime and Punishment* was invoked frequently in their discussions, his anguish mirroring their own. I had been attracted to Russian literature from the moment Diab had placed *How the Steel Was Tempered* in my hands. Ivan Turgenev and Leo Tolstoy led me to the 1917 Revolution, so I delved into postrevolution Soviet writers: Aleksei Tolstoy, Mikhail Sholokhov, Maksim Gorky, and Makarenko, as well as books about Lenin and Trotsky. Marxism led me to China, and I added books about Mao Tse-tung to my list.

I studied war. For two solid years, I avidly read every account of warfare I could find in the prison library. I analyzed the strategies of Hannibal and the Roman army. The conquests of ancient Egyptian pharaohs. Greek, Persian, Chinese, and Mongolian battles. Napoleon's victories. General Carl von Clausewitz's military classic, *On War*. British military historian Basil Liddell Hart. Battles that led to the spread of Islam. Biographies of First and Second World War generals, from all nationalities. The American Civil War.

Then I read about development after World War Two. In less than twenty years, Germany and Japan had achieved a flourishing economy and an excellent standard of living. Tens of millions of people had died in those conflicts, and countless more suffered from injuries or loss of homes and loved ones. Yet a decent life was achieved only in peacetime. I came to realize that war is a holocaust for all human beings. But was it naive to imagine there could really be life far from bloodshed?

I added the French philosopher Jean-Jacques Rousseau to my second list of seventy books, and the American Angela Davis, known for her connection to the Black Panthers,* SNCC,** and the Communist Party. I was inspired by a collection of speeches by Martin Luther King Jr. and the achievements of the civil rights movement. I read about Joe McCarthy and the anticommunist witch hunt he spearheaded. Jack London's dog Buck panted by my side. I spent several sweltering summer days with Scarlett O'Hara. I was profoundly touched by the deep connection between the black slave and the white boy in *Huckleberry Finn*. They broke all the boundaries of a society plagued with racism and oppression.

---

*An African-American organization, founded to promote justice and equality for African Americans, promoting Black Power.

**Acronym for Student Nonviolent Coordinating Committee, a lead organizer in the U.S. civil rights movement.

My third list broached the classics. I passed an entire spring with Virgil and Homer. I admired the perfect balance Homer achieved between myth and history. I read *The Odyssey* and *The Iliad* three times each. Odysseus pretended to go insane to avoid being sent to battle, because he did not want to abandon his wife and son. Eventually his ruse was discovered and he was forced to go and fight. I empathized with Odysseus. It would be far better to live one's life and be with one's family than to enlist in ten years of dark war.

Odysseus's wife, Penelope, taught me the true meaning of loyalty. Odysseus, lost on the ocean, wandered for twenty years before finding his way back home, while Penelope waited faithfully for him to return. I tucked Penelope's faith in the absent Odysseus next to my heart. For many, we were like the dead. Penelope served as a reminder that my family was still waiting for me, loving and respecting me as a living, breathing human being.

A Tale of Two Cities was delivered on a rainy, winter day. Charles Dickens painted a portrait of a ruthless war that incited poisonous hatred. I was horrified and frightened by the extent of the misery Dickens described. Men and women, driven by desperation, sold themselves into slavery or prostitution for a crust of bread. This was not the world I wanted to live in. But I also felt a measure of relief as the story unfolded. Palestinians could learn from Dickens's bleak depiction of the French masses, the kangaroo trials, the executions. Our struggle, led by our pure and just leaders, would not lead us to the same place.

I read the Qur'an, the Torah, and the New Testament. I lost myself in tales of persecuted Christian believers hiding in caves from Roman soldiers who were seeking to stone or crucify them. As with Dickens, I drew some hope from those stories. We were suffering in prison, true. But I did not have nails piercing my hands to a cross, left to die.

I read about Spartacus's slave uprising and was inspired by his commitment to freedom. Resistance from the downtrodden was inevitable. The oppressed will always rise up.

I delved into India's struggle for independence. Jawaharlal Nehru educated his daughter Indira Gandhi by writing her long letters from prison, teaching her about history and struggles for freedom and independence, in India and worldwide. I contemplated those dispatches as I listened to Umm Kulthum in the evenings. Nehru was imprisoned far from his daughter, but through his correspondence, she always felt his presence and encouragement. His efforts bore fruit years later when Indira followed in her father's footsteps and became prime minister of India. I clung tightly to Nehru's example. Even if we were locked away, we could still affect the wider world.

Every two weeks we were permitted to send one postcard. I wrote to my mother about the books I was reading and the ideas I was thinking about and discussing. My mother would need to ask Mazin or Abu Fakhri to read her the postcard; it was an opportunity to influence at least two people. I knew I could not accomplish what Nehru had. I had to be very cautious with my words, so as not to alarm the army censors. Plus, Nehru had an unlimited number of pages on which to write Indira. I had to compress my impact into one bimonthly postcard.

POLITICAL PRISONERS were kept strictly separate from criminals whose actions were not politically motivated. The Israelis were afraid that we would organize them. There had been car thieves who were released only to return later as political prisoners. It did not serve Israel's interest for pickpockets to become involved with the resistance.

There were, however, points of contact. We shared the same laundry and kitchen, and we were together in Ramle, the transfer prison. The criminals respected our unity and solidarity. And, though on most occasions we treated them respectfully, they knew if they ever caused us problems, they would pay a price. Once a seventeen-year-old Palestinian criminal attacked a political prisoner from Lebanon. We were all informed. One month later, he was spotted by other political prisoners in Ramle. They sliced his face from eye to chin with a razor blade. There were very few problems between us after that.

Criminals had previously prepared the meals, but the Israelis had decided years ago to hand the kitchen over to us. The criminals themselves preferred this. They trusted us not to steal food supplies and trade them for narcotics.

I worked as the prep chef in the kitchen for six months, cutting onions, tomatoes, and cucumbers. Once a week, the delivery truck pulled up to the loading dock behind the kitchen. We hauled cartons of produce to the industrial refrigerators. We often received boxes of surplus fruit, which helped to stabilize fruit prices inside Israel. The meat was less appetizing. Israel had stocked up on a large supply of emergency beef that dated back to World War Two. I pulled large, heavy crates of frozen blocks of ancient meat from Siberia or Alaska from the delivery truck. The meat was black-brown in color, with a hard crust on the outside. I struggled to chop it up into the 1.4-ounce-per-person lunchtime rations. Some of my cell mates refused to touch their share, but I had internalized my lesson from Ahmad back in the Russian Compound. I ate everything placed in front of me. Radishes were the only food I never touched. I had always detested them. On Fridays, we prepared chicken for lunch—one chicken for each eight-person cell. There was bread, rice or potatoes, and a cucumber and tomato salad. The dinner we prepared was similar to breakfast, supplemented with fried eggplant, potatoes, or falafel. I admired the prisoners whom I was assisting in the kitchen. They made a true art out of creating meals from the foodstuffs delivered.

I received extra allowance for working in the kitchen or library. I never used it for my personal needs. I went to the canteen with instructions from the section's treasurer to buy cartons of cigarettes for the section, while the corridor cleaner bought the pens.

I reported to the kitchen after the 6 a.m. count and would not be locked back up until 8 p.m., the final count of the day. Between meal preparations, I could ask the guard to open any cell if I wanted to join their meeting. I enjoyed the extra freedom, but I chose to stop working after my six-month shift. I missed my books.

Fridays were our free day. No room meetings or courses. We could read for pleasure, wash our underwear out in the sink, and, when the cells were open, visit each other. We were allowed to play chess or backgammon only on Fridays.

"Sami, we feel like you're always anxious to get to Friday," Diab told me at a criticism meeting. It was true. I spent hours every Friday playing chess. I loved the intense strategizing and trying to anticipate my opponent's plans. I had learned the game from my cousin Sameh when I was fifteen years old.

"You don't know how to play chess!" my brother Azzam would tease me when I was first cutting my teeth on the game. "You only know how to move the pieces!"

The old prisoners beat me easily, Friday after Friday. But I played often with Abu Sadeq, taking mental note of his moves, as he chewed the end of his moustache intently. I played with people from the Communist Party and Democratic Front, watching their strategies closely, and I learned from my own mistakes.

We made special meals on Fridays, dipping our bread into soup to soften it and spreading it out on the garbage can lid that we had scrubbed for the occasion. We put the chicken on top, making our own version of *mansaf*.*
On Saturday mornings, the kitchen prepared cake, which we softened in our

*A popular rice, lamb, and yogurt dish among Palestinians and Jordanians, *mansaf* is commonly known as the Jordanian national dish.

tea and spread out the same way, cutting fruit to place on top and covering it with the spoonful of chocolate we received weekly. We shared the sweet *mansaf* between the cells.

Fridays were also a time for communal song. We sang about land, about freedom, about the prison itself. We created our own joy during those song sessions. We felt human when we sang together.

There were reminders all day, every day, that we were not free. We were locked up in tiny cells. Four times every day we were forced to stand on a guard's command to be counted. I could not walk in the streets, grill kabob with my brothers, or swim in the sea. I did not know what it was like to be with a woman.

The medical care was gravely inadequate. Necessary medications were dispensed to ill prisoners days late, needlessly increasing their suffering. An Israeli army medic traveled from section to section every day with a small medicine bag, dispensing only aspirin no matter the ailment: broken finger, strange murmur in the heart, stomach flu.

There was a clinic, but unless it was an emergency, there was a two-week wait. If you were extremely ill, you might be transported to the hospital in Ramle. The hours on the suffocating truck with your wrists and ankles bound were sure to make you even sicker.

In 1983, word of what happened to Abu Jamal Maragha, a PFLP member in his late fifties, circulated in the courtyard. Abu Jamal had complained of sharp chest pain and was taken to the clinic. He waited in agony for an ambulance. By the time the ambulance arrived more than two hours later, there was no need to take Abu Jamal to the hospital. They took him to the morgue instead.

We mounted a one-day hunger strike, to show solidarity with Abu Jamal's family and to protest this lethal neglect on the part of the prison system. We had no power to do anything further.

I woke up before dawn one day with a throbbing pain in my tooth.

The aspirin that the medic gave me did nothing for my excruciating pain.

"A dentist is coming to the clinic soon," the medic told me after a week.

I did not want to go to the clinic. The army used the clinic to recruit spies and informers. But as the throbbing turned to searing flashes of pain shooting from my tooth to behind my eyeball, I could no longer stand it.

I sat with ten others in the clinic waiting room. It was finally my turn to enter. The army dentist, a major, tapped a large pair of pliers against the palm of his hand.

"The tooth doesn't need to be yanked. I just need medicine for the pain," I told him, eyeing the pliers anxiously.

"All I can do is remove the tooth. If you want, I can remove it. If not, you can continue to suffer." Major Dentist tapped his pliers again impatiently. "What's it going to be?"

I had not slept in a week from the pain. "Okay, yank it out."

He did, breaking another tooth in the process. Two weeks later the second one had to be pulled as well.

Bedbugs were a recurring problem. When a prisoner in one section got bedbugs, the entire prison was soon afflicted. Every inch of my skin was covered with tiny, red, itchy welts. I scratched until I bled, tossing and turning on my infested mat, receiving new bites with each passing second. The medic brought us a cream. It was hot and salty, stinging our skin when we smeared it over our bodies, but the relief it brought was wonderful. Our clothes were boiled and the foam mats changed. The Israelis took bedbugs seriously. The guards might also catch them. Prisoners and guards often shared connected fates in strange ways.

I was homesick whenever I was sick or in pain. Our hour each evening with Umm Kulthum had a similar effect. We sat in the cell listening to her voice emanate from the loudspeaker, each of us in our separate world. It was the one time of day we allowed ourselves to indulge in memories. I sat on my mat the entire hour, knees bent and arms wrapped around my legs, my head bowed down, closing myself off from my cell mates. I thought about my mother. She loved me more than anyone else in the world did—and by getting myself locked away in prison, I had broken her heart. As Umm Kulthum's rich voice filled the prison and penetrated each prisoner's heart, I wondered whether my mom was thinking about me at that very moment and whether she was crying. I cursed myself for the times I had shouted at her because I did not like the food she had prepared. I imagined her warm voice as she would caution me, "Sami, you need to take care and be gentle and kind with other people." Words coming from her mouth always sounded like prayers. Before I left the house each morning, she would ask God to protect me and remove any bad person from my path. And then, pressing her hands against my cheeks, forehead, lips, and nose, she would make a copy of my face to store in her mind. She knew instantly by touching my face whether I was happy or angry or sad. She read my face like Braille. I felt the same soothing breeze listening to Umm Kulthum as I felt when my mother read my face.

To stop the approaching tears, I forced my thoughts to my classmates and friends. What did they look like now? What were they doing? Some of them might be in university, others married and starting families. What did they think of me? Did they see me as a hero? Or had I disappeared from their consciousness entirely? Umm Kulthum made me yearn for the Old City streets, my school, the *souq*, my home, playing cards with Abbas and Badawi. Umm Kulthum finished her song and the guards shut off the loudspeaker. We sat for a moment in silence, then shook off our feelings and returned to our books.

The Red Crescent arranged transportation to bring our families every other Friday for half an hour. I was excited days in advance. When visiting day arrived, we were called by loudspeaker in groups of twenty. The security check lasted for fifteen minutes, my anticipation growing each moment. We were allowed three visitors each. Who would be coming this time? Sanaa could visit from Jordan only two or three times a year.

My mother would come for sure, unless she was visiting one of my brothers in another prison. Maybe Samira, Hanadi, Riyyad, Mazin, or Sa'ed. I loved it when my little cousins came. Tiny children were a feast for my eyes. I tried not to let myself hope that my father would be waiting for me, though I longed more than anything to see him.

Prisoners and families faced each other in two long lines with a mesh net between us. The holes in the net were big enough for just one finger to fit through. My mother squeezed my index finger, pressing the flesh around the bone to ascertain whether I was healthy.

"You are thin, Sami. Are you eating enough?" or "You're much better than last time. You feel good now . . ." She repeated over and over that her heart was with me.

"Don't worry about me. I'm fine." I hated that my mom was so anxious about me. It wore me out.

I told Hanadi and Mazin what I was reading, encouraging them to study as well.

I always sent my love to my father.

"Sami, he talks about you all the time," Mazin reassured me. "But he can't stand seeing any of us inside the prison. It breaks his heart too much."

The two times my father did visit, he was on the verge of crying the entire half-hour. It was better he not come, I decided.

It was wonderful getting good news from the family. After my mom reported that Samira had gotten married, I wanted to jump up and down.

Married! But back in the cell, even good news needed to be chewed on a little more thoroughly. My little sister Samira was now starting a family. And here I was, still counting days and counting books.

Receiving bad news was heart-wrenching. When my mother told me that Abu Fakhri had passed away, I went into a state of shock followed by deep mourning.

"Come on, he was an old man," Talal said, trying to comfort me. But he wasn't just "an old man" to me—he had shown me love and kindness since I was a small boy. I had run errands for him, helped him walk from place to place. I had pushed cats onto his dinner plate! I never imagined that death would visit Abu Fakhri before I could visit him again. And I could not even drink bitter coffee with his family.

Five minutes into the visits, I began to feel restless. Talking with a net between us, monitored by the guards, did not fulfill our need to be with our loved ones. My mom and sisters scrutinized me each moment to see how I looked and acted. There was nothing relaxed or natural about it.

We shared our family updates with our cell mates. Then we deleted the visit from our minds. We did not want to dwell on our families outside the prison walls; we wanted to be present with our family inside. We taped no photographs on the thick concrete cell walls. Photos only made us lonely for home.

Visits from Sanaa were different. It was like oxygen to see her.

"You know, Sanaa, I'm going to be here for a long time. You don't have to wait for me. My punishment doesn't have to be yours," I told her repeatedly.

Each time she would offer her beautiful smile and poke her slender finger through the net for me to take hold of. "I will wait for you, Sami," she always replied.

"As soon as I get my freedom, I will marry you. We'll be for each other."

"Ten years is not so long—I want to wait."

But now I had not seen her in almost a year. My mother came as usual one Friday.

"*Yamma*—what's going on with Sanaa?" I asked. "Why hasn't she come?"

My mother smiled and stroked my finger. "You know, Sami, it's hard for a young lady like Sanaa to come by herself from Jordan. She couldn't continue to do that . . ."

I knew the nuances in my mother's voice like she knew how to read my face. "Tell me the truth, *Yamma*. Did Sanaa end the engagement?"

There was a long silence. "She was tired of waiting, Sami. She married someone else."

I said nothing for a moment, digesting the information. "Who is he?"

"He's from Syria. He's a lot older than you . . ." My mother shook my finger forcefully. "Forget her, Sami! Who forgets you, you must also forget!"

I tried to tell myself that this was for the best. Sanaa was young; she had the right to start her life with somebody else. But it hurt all the same. I imagined what this older Syrian husband of hers looked like. I hoped that someday I would see her again—and that I would be with someone more beautiful than she.

"Wipe her out of your mind. There are lots of other girls out there," Asim counseled me.

I knew prisoners whose fiancées waited even fifteen years for their husbands-to-be. But not every woman could do that. Not every woman could be Penelope.

⁂

Each prisoner mastered the art of rolling notes into tiny plastic-covered capsules. I swallowed six capsules before a trip to Ramle for a court appointment. The following day I excreted the capsules in Ramle. I plucked them from my shit, washed them, and unwrapped the plastic. I gave the bone-dry notes to Fatah activists going back to other prisons. Extremely sensitive information was sent out with released prisoners, each of whom carried at least a dozen messages in his digestive tract.

Eventually the Israelis caught on to these methods. Returning from Ramle, we were locked in a tiny cell with newspaper on the ground until we shit. Prisoners, however, are geniuses. Perhaps dirty, but geniuses. We re-swallowed the capsules after excreting them.

Our families slipped capsules with money to us through the net on visiting day and we stealthily swallowed them. This was how we procured our first transistor radio, purchasing it from Israeli criminals. My cell was the news committee. We listened to the radio secretly at night and recorded all the events. Our "newspaper" was distributed to each cell so everyone could follow events in the outside world. We broke a hole in the concrete wall with an iron bar that we smuggled from the criminals and stashed the radio inside, re-covering the hole.

The guards put all of us in the courtyard one day while they ransacked the cells from top to bottom, searching for contraband. A tight-lipped officer led us back to our cell. Our mats had been turned upside down, notebooks ripped up, and sugar, tea, and coffee all dumped out and mixed together with our clothes on the concrete floor.

The officer held up the iron bar. He had found it under Gandhi's mat. Gandhi's real name was Batta, but he earned his nickname because he was always eager to go on a hunger strike. His health was weak. He was so thin you could see his ribs. Gandhi was only in his fifties but looked much older. Prison made people age.

"Who does this mat belong to?" the officer barked.

Eight voices chimed in simultaneously, as we raised our hands. "Me!"

"Don't try to tell me that all eight of you are sleeping on the same mat!"

Gandhi stepped forward. "Take your hands down. No one can take my resistance," he told us. Then he turned to the officer. "This is my mat. Do with me what you will."

They locked him in solitary confinement for seven days, in a cell scarcely the size of his mat. He was allowed only a cup for water, a small plastic bucket for excretion, and the Qur'an. There was not even a lightbulb. He read the Qur'an huddled near the small window on the cell door where a little light spilled in from the corridor. Gandhi spent the week on hunger strike. When he returned, we had a small "return from solitary confinement" party for him in the cell. We sang songs from the villages, national songs, songs about suffering. We had saved the weekly spoonful of chocolate to spread on our bread and margarine—our version of cake.

The loudspeaker interrupted our celebration with an unexpected announcement. All political prisoners were being transferred from Beer Al-Sabe'. West Bankers would go to Juneid prison in Nablus and those of us from Jerusalem and Gaza would be moved either to Asqalan or to Nafha.

The trucks arrived shortly thereafter. We had little time to say our good-byes. I felt like I was being torn from my family without any warning.

But Asim, next to me on the truck to Asqalan, elbowed me with a smile. "You know what this means, Sami? They must be preparing for a large prisoner exchange! First Asqalan . . . then, if we're lucky . . . freedom!"

The idea gave me some hope, but I still missed the brothers from Section Nine.

The last big hunger strike had been undertaken in Nafha in 1981 in order to get bunk beds instead of thin foam mats on the hard, cold concrete floor. During the course of the strike, Ali Ja'fari and Rasem Halawi had been beaten until they vomited blood. They were then force-fed a milk and egg mixture through tubes thrust up their noses. The mixture found its way into their lungs. Both Ali and Rasem had died.

In Asqalan, there had already been years of negotiations with the Israeli officers demanding adequate medical care for our ill and elderly. We wanted transistor radios and televisions in the cells. We called for our families to be allowed to increase our monthly pittance and to bring us clothes to sleep in and food items they did not use in the Israeli kitchen: *za'atar, mlukhiyyeh, baklaweh.** We wanted to be able to spend more hours each day in other cells within our same section. We wanted siblings to be in the same prison. My younger brother Azzam had been in Nafha prison since 1983. He and a group of friends had been throwing Molotov cocktails at a home in our neighborhood of the Old City that had been taken over by Israeli settlers. He was serving a five-year sentence. On Fridays, my mother had to choose which son she was going to visit, rather than being able to visit us together. There were dozens of prisoners in the same situation. If we could convince the Israelis to jail brothers together, it would reduce a burden for our families. Most important, we were demanding that the Israelis consider us prisoners of war, with the protections that the third Geneva Convention** afforded.

But negotiations without action were fruitless. It was time once again to embark on an "empty stomach war." All the movements created a joint operations committee in early 1985, polling every prisoner to assess whether we felt this was truly the right decision and that every other path had been exhausted. We sent surreptitious messages to our families, lawyers, human rights organizations, and the press. "We don't have the medicine or clothes we need. We're hungry. Maybe soon we will be hungrier," I wrote in my biweekly postcard to my mother.

Experienced prisoners detailed on paper how our bodies would respond day by day. The emergency committee transferred all the sick people and diabetics to one cell. They were officially excluded from the strike, though many of them planned to fast anyway. We were as prepared as possible.

I woke up the first morning dreading the knowledge that I would not be eating. I grew mildly hungry as the morning progressed, which turned into a pounding headache by late afternoon. On the second day, hunger gnawed at my insides. By day three, my energy was sapped and my head started to spin.

---

*A dessert known in some parts of the world as baklava.

**The Geneva Conventions are international treaties regarding international humanitarian law during warfare. The third treaty, updated in 1949, concerns prisoners of war.

If I moved the slightest bit, I would black out momentarily. During our regular mealtimes, the hunger intensified. In the evening, I put a little salt on my tongue, took a sip of water, and lit up a cigarette. It felt wonderful to have something solid in my mouth. But after just a puff or two, I was too dizzy to even sit up. I ground out my cigarette gently, replacing it in the carton to light again the next day.

After the fourth day, the gnawing subsided. It was persistent, but bearable. On day ten, my mother, along with mothers of other prisoners, launched solidarity hunger strikes outside all the Red Cross offices in Jerusalem, the West Bank, and Gaza. Arab newspapers reported on our condition daily. We had hoped the hunger strike would inspire the Arab world to fight with us. Though the support of the people and the press bolstered us, no leader acted on our behalf. We felt betrayed.

From the eleventh day of the strike, the clinic gave us one cup of milk in the morning and a cup of tea with a small piece of strong, brown bread in the evening. I gulped down the milk. After consuming nothing but water and salt for a week and a half, I could feel the warmth of the blood pumping from my heart through my veins.

By day twenty, the hair on my arms became brittle and began to fall out painfully. I could feel my eyelashes falling out, one by one. Reading was impossible—words in my book scampered like ants on the page, causing my head to spin. We were given fifteen minutes each day to go outside. We mustered all our strength to rise and take small, measured steps, moving like zombies. It took almost the entire fifteen minutes just to reach the courtyard. Exhausted, we placed our backs against the wall, sliding slowly, gently onto the ground. The journey to the courtyard was worth it just to exchange weak smiles with one another.

I dreamt about food. In the mornings, we stayed curled up on our beds shivering under the blankets and described our dreams to each other. The foods in our dreams were works of art. In one vivid, beautiful dream I was eating very dry bread with strong yellow cheese. I dreamt the following night about a radish. I had always hated radishes, but this one was gorgeous. I woke up with my mouth watering for just one juicy, succulent radish.

We made big plans. "You know what I'm going to do when the strike ends?" Abu Sadeq removed the end of his moustache from his mouth, where he was sucking it more than usual. "I'll make a *maqlubeh.* I'll use all the vegetables in the kitchen!"

I reluctantly pushed off my blankets and very carefully began to rise.

"Sami, where are you going?" Abu Wahid asked me.

"To the bathroom."

"The bathroom? *Ya* Allah! Have a safe trip. It would be quicker to travel from Ramallah to Nablus . . ."

The soldiers and guards used vicious techniques to try to break the hunger strike. But the security committee had already prepared us for this. The "warm heads"—those the Israelis thought were the strike leaders—were gathered up and informed that they were being transferred to a different prison. They were placed in the closed truck. The soldier driving accelerated as fast as he could and then slammed on the brakes, hurling the prisoners with their bound wrists and ankles across the truck and injuring some. But the strike continued.

Guards and soldiers came cell to cell.

"Are you going to eat today?"

"No."

The soldiers took out gas guns. "You don't want to eat?"

They pumped gas into our cells and beat us ferociously. But we did not eat.

On day forty, we refused the morning cup of milk and evening bread. We informed the Israelis that after another week, we would no longer drink water. This would be tantamount to suicide. If we died in large numbers, it could lead to a serious uprising on the outside. We never gave up hope, deep down inside, that if our situation grew that alarming, Arab leaders would finally stand up for us.

On day forty-three, the Israelis made some concessions. They promised to make improvements in the clinic and kitchen and allowed a television and radio in each cell. They agreed that our families could bring us two pounds of sweets on both *Eids* every year.* *Mlukhiyyeh, za'atar,* and olive oil could be delivered by Palestinian institutes. Our families were also permitted to bring us dark blue or brown sweat suits to sleep in. The Israelis didn't want us to have too much color. However, our most important demand, to be considered prisoners of war, was categorically rejected.

We celebrated our victory with soup. I was proud of our achievements—but as I savored my cup of lukewarm soup, feeling the ecstasy of it sliding down my throat into my empty, shrunken belly, I was truly celebrating being able to eat again.

We had other ways to resist.

---

*Muslim holidays, after Ramadan and after the Haj.

A new rule had been implemented: we had to be strip-searched before seeing our families on visiting day. This, we could endure. What we would not tolerate was the addendum that our mothers and sisters be strip-searched as well.

Each new policy was tested first on one prison and then implemented throughout the prison system. Asqalan was the guinea pig this time.

We requested that the Israelis terminate the new policy and resume the less intrusive frisking, as before.

They refused.

We held large meetings, deliberating about how to respond. We agreed on two unified acts: first, we would no longer meet our families, so that these visits would not be the source of our sisters' humiliation. Second, when the guards came to count us, we would not stand. If they would not cooperate with our request to treat our families with dignity, we would not respect their roll call. They could count us while we lay in bed.

On September 10, we began the action. The guards were angry and nervous that the resistance would spread to the other prisons. They took away the clothes, televisions, and radios that we had earned in our hunger strike. Worst of all, they confiscated our pens, paper, and books. Our books were our souls. The guards understood that without our books and pens and paper, we would be like a balloon with too much pressure. We'd explode in their faces.

September 11, they brought reinforcements—thirty soldiers in each section with tens more waiting in the courtyard, equipped with gas bombs, gas guns—and gas masks.

Two guards roughly pushed open the door to the cell, flanked by several soldiers. Their gas guns were at the ready.

"Count!" they called.

We did not move.

"You're not going to stand?"

"You made a new rule, so we made a new rule. Rule for rule. Count us as we are."

They shot the gas guns repeatedly into the closed cell, spraying white powder all over us. My skin instantly burned so badly I wanted to tear it off with my hands. They threw two gas bombs inside. My eyes stung severely from one, and I was gasping and choking from the other. Thick batons came down bluntly on our backs, arms, legs, and shoulders. One glanced off my head. The pain barely registered as I frantically gulped for air. I was suffocating.

People were shouting all around me. "Help! Help!"

"We have sick people here! We will die!"

"Where are you, Khomeini? Where are you, Saddam? Do something! Your people are getting killed by the occupation and you're busy fighting each other!"

The window opened to the courtyard, but there was no relief there. The courtyard also had been bombed heavily with gas. We turned on the water tap full force, desperately trying to suck in some oxygen from the flow of water.

After several minutes, the soldiers threw oxygen bombs in the cell, clearing the worst of the gas. I gulped the air, but the oxygen bombs did nothing for my blazing skin.

Abu Wahid handed me a gas bomb canister. "Look at what it says," he told me. I still could not open my burning, watering eyes. "Not to be used in closed spaces," he read aloud, and "Made in the USA."

Three times that day the guards kicked open the door to each cell. "So? Are you going to stand now?"

Our answer never wavered. We would rather die than break a decision we had made as a group.

"No. Count us as we are."

The gassing was repeated each time. Prisoners with asthma needed to be hospitalized. Sixteen arms and hands were broken.

They placed us under complete lockdown in our cells for an entire week. The prison was like dynamite; one little spark and it would explode. But we did not want the guards to detect our anger and sorrow. We organized ourselves more than ever, holding extended meetings in our circles. We passed hours singing. We even shouted jokes from cell to cell, to demonstrate that we were not broken. It helped conceal the extent of our frustration. No matter what actions we took, we could not do enough to change our reality. I despised feeling powerless.

The Israelis transferred those they considered the "warm heads" to Nafha. They could never comprehend that decisions this big were not undertaken by a small group of leaders, but were decided upon collectively by us all.

At last they agreed to end the strip-search policy. We stood once more at roll call. Our radio, TV, and, most important, our books were returned.

There were moments when the solidarity between us cracked. The case of Ahmad became prison legend. Ahmad was from a very wealthy family in Jerusalem. He had become a favorite target of the guards and was beaten frequently. He had been in prison three years and was still struggling to adjust.

Prison can do strange things to people's minds. Ahmad saw a huge cock-roach crawling on the wall one day. He trapped it, made a bed for it in a little box, and was entirely devoted to it. Ahmad always made sure to get a small bag of seeds at the canteen to grind up for his little friend.

One day, he couldn't find the seeds. He stood up in the middle of his cell. "Who ate my bug's seeds?" he demanded with agitation. Everyone exchanged glances with each other, smiling. Yusuf laughed aloud. Ahmad erupted in fury. "You took them!" He lunged at Yusuf, knocking him over and kicking him forcefully in the head.

The laughter stopped abruptly. Yusuf, unconscious and bleeding, was taken to the hospital in Ramle, where he remained for more than two weeks. A special committee was appointed to investigate the incident and recom-mend action. The verdict was given: Ahmad's foot must be broken as punish-ment for kicking Yusuf in the head. Three prisoners brought a toilet seat out to the courtyard, taking Ahmad to a corner. One slammed the toilet seat on Ahmad's foot with as much force as he could muster, smashing several bones. The other two were witnesses.

The story traveled like wildfire all over the prison system. We joked for months about "the crazy bug guy." But underneath the laughter, I was trou-bled. I understood that Ahmad had to be punished. He had broken our car-dinal rule by attacking a fellow prisoner. Our policies had to be enforced if we were to retain our standards of respect and brotherhood. But the special committee didn't seem to acknowledge Ahmad's psychological state when devising the consequence. The extremity of prison life for someone who had grown up with so much privilege, the abuse from the Israelis—this had skewed something inside him, and his connection to that cockroach was very deep and very real.

It was 1985. I was lying on my bed, lost in a book. Suddenly I heard yelling emanating from the cell at the end of the corridor. A few moments later, whoops of joy from a closer cell. The news traveled fast, thanks to our sec-tion's "journalist," equipped with cart and broom as he moved down the cor-ridor, informing us. Prisoner exchange, just as Asim had predicted! An officer was moving from cell to cell, carrying a list. Six Israeli soldiers cap-tured in Lebanon were being released in exchange for 1,000 Palestinian pris-oners. Everyone on the list should gather his belongings and be ready to be released.

We sat waiting, tension flowing through our central nervous systems.

Riyyad Malabi caught my eye. "Maybe today will be your lucky day, Sami!" he said.

The Malabi brothers were heroes in the prison, the stuff that myths were made of. After the Israeli occupation forces had destroyed their home in Shu'afat, they were caught with a stash of weapons intended to destroy the Knesset.* But here in my cell, Riyyad was not Rambo-sized as I had imagined. He was quiet and polite, preferring to read rather than socialize.

I tried to dampen my hopes, reminding myself that the opportunity would more likely be given to people with much longer sentences to serve.

The officer arrived at our cell.

"Three people," the officer said. "Riyyad Malabi. Abu Wahid. Sami Al Jundi." A shock shot through me like a bolt of lightning. Five years of my life saved! The ten of us in the cell hugged each other as one body, jumping up and down and shouting. Riyyad, Abu Wahid, and I grabbed our clothes and quickly said goodbye to our cell mates, giving them our remaining pens, paper, and shampoo. We deliriously headed to the courtyard. I was almost happier for Riyyad and Abu Wahid than for myself. Abu Wahid was sixty years old and had already been in prison for fifteen years, Riyyad had been locked up for eleven—and both of them had been sentenced for life.

The courtyard was buzzing with excitement as we joined one hundred others. I hugged each new friend I encountered, wondering out loud how it would feel to walk freely in the Old City again, eat with my family, start my new life. Riyyad was dancing with pure joy. We heard a voice from the loudspeaker.

"There's been some changes. If your name is called, return to your cell."

A deathly silence fell over the courtyard. Names started to be read over the loudspeaker, one by one.

Riyyad was standing next to me, shifting his weight slowly from foot to foot. When his name was called, he froze like a mummy. The blood drained from his face. I was so crushed watching him that I almost missed my own name.

Riyyad and I headed back to our cell slowly, silently. As we approached the door, Riyyad turned to me.

"Don't lose your hope, Sami." He embraced me like I was his little brother. What could I possibly say back to him? I would be released in five years. But when would the door open for Riyyad again? I just held him tightly.

*Israeli Parliament building.

Our cell mates had been having a party in honor of our freedom. The guard unlocked our cell and swung the door open. They took one look at our faces and immediately abandoned the bread with margarine and chocolate.

"What happened? What's wrong?"

"They sent some of us back."

They stared at us blankly, waiting for some further explanation. We had none. It was not until a few days later that we learned what had happened. At the last moment, the Israeli government refused to release twenty-seven prisoners from our list—those they deemed too dangerous. A difficult negotiation ensued. A different list was made. I learned later that Abbas was on that second list and was released. I comforted myself imagining that my sacrifice led directly to Abbas's freedom.

But none of that was known yet. Standing there in the cell, no one knew what to say or do. All eyes were still on Riyyad and me. Riyyad picked up a piece of bread, margarine, and chocolate, shrugged, and took a bite. He handed it to me.

I took my own bite of "cake" and attempted a smile. "I guess prison has more to teach me about life."

CHAPTER SEVEN

꩜

AFTER 1985, WHEN MANY of the old prisoners had been released in the prisoner exchange, it was time for me to take my place as an "old prisoner."

I served on the elections committee. We held elections twice annually, distributing a ballot with the names of all five hundred prisoners. Everyone chose twenty-one names. The twenty-one elected served as the wider council for the prison. They voted internally for fifteen to serve on the smaller council. From the fifteen, it was narrowed down again to five—the steering committee for the entire prison. From the steering committee, an overall prison leader was selected while the others each chaired a committee: education, security, intra-prisoner affairs, and liaison with the Israelis. The only points of contact with the Israelis were through chosen representatives. The steering committee member dealt with them if the issue concerned the entire prison. Each section had a liaison to address the guards for matters pertaining to the section and each cell had a liaison for issues in the cell.

In 1986, I was elected to Asqalan's smaller council. I was proud that so many people trusted me to keep our system strong and pure. I took my responsibility as something holy. Fellow Jerusalemites came to me with requests to work in the kitchen. I would not promise them this patronage—these were decisions for the steering committee to make. I could only submit their names—and I did not automatically do that. If the request came from someone who needed to focus on studying, I told him that it was not yet his time to work.

I served on the education committee with excitement, organizing the courses and conducting the exams. In Asqalan, unlike Beer Al-Sabe', we had four levels of organized courses, and members of the education committee had to have successfully completed them all. I had placed out of levels 1 and

2 upon arrival in Asqalan. I had already covered that material in Beer Al-Sabe's new prisoner course: the history of Arab countries, Fatah, and the Palestinian struggle, as well as Jewish and Israeli history and world revolutions. I was placed in level 3 in Asqalan, focusing on economics and ancient history. I quickly advanced to level 4, where I studied philosophy and literature. Only twenty of us had passed all four levels. I was as honored to be part of this elite group as I was to serve on the committee itself.

We held large weekly meetings in the courtyard for all the movements of the PLO. Though our shared identity as political prisoners was more powerful than any specific ideology, strong differences were revealed during these sessions. The biggest gulf was between members of the religious groups, such as the Muslim Brotherhood, and the secular, nationalist parties, such as Fatah and PFLP. But between the secular groups, we had our own chasms. PFLP accused our leaders of being no different than the other leaders of the Arab world. We refused to consider this possibility—our leaders were not royal, privileged elite! Our leaders were revolutionaries, *fedayeen*! They were living in the same harsh conditions, we argued back, as the refugees in the camps.

In 1986, I was chosen to facilitate the large meetings. It was flattering to be asked, but the task was not easy. All of the movements sitting around the circle must be heard and respected. I had to walk between words, linking opinions and ideas. A careless comment on my part could spark a heated discussion. There were those who were eagerly waiting for me to slip up so they could pounce on my mistake. I had to monitor under-the-table jabs from the Democratic Front toward PFLP and vice versa. But we had worked together across party lines to build a well-organized prison system and we had to maintain it, even during times of internal political tension. I often brought up PLO agreements that all the factions had signed, or provided examples from other revolutions: Vietnam, Cuba, the Bolsheviks. Historical lessons were important for us to reflect on—and it was harder to refute something that happened years ago in Russia.

The old prisoners were invaluable in these meetings. They were warm and respectful to everyone. The positive tone they established influenced the younger prisoners. They helped me facilitate.

"We're all fighting for justice for our people, aren't we?" Abdel Fatah said as an argument threatened to escalate. There were murmurs of agreement and nodding heads. "There's space for all the colors in the resistance."

When discussion focused on occupation, we raised our voices so the guards standing around the perimeter of the courtyard could hear.

"Every occupation in this land came to an end!" Abu Sadeq said extra loudly. "The Romans, the Turks, the British—they all ended up in the rubbish bin of history!" he concluded with a flourish of his hand.

There was often a gap between me and the next man in the circle during these meetings. "Why doesn't anyone like to sit next to me when I facilitate?" I complained to my younger brother Azzam, who had been moved to Asqalan.

"You don't know why?" I shook my head as Azzam grinned. "Sami, you always hit the leg of whoever is next to you when you're trying to emphasize a point!"

I returned the smile. "Well, you're my brother. You have to sit next to me then!"

The subject of the next meeting was negotiations with Israel. I had written an essay to start us off, posing the central question: should we negotiate? I argued yes. We needed to work with the Arab countries to develop a shared political platform and solve the conflict through negotiations.

The discussion had the potential to be stormy. PFLP members might accuse Fatah of selling our homeland to Arab governments and giving up historic Palestine, while Fatah members would retort that we had contributed to the struggle more than any other party. I needed to structure the meeting carefully. I asked everyone who had a comment to raise his hand. Hands shot up immediately. I went around the circle.

Asim spoke first, bringing up Ho Chi Minh, who had simultaneously negotiated with the French while fighting. "When he returned from negotiations, people threw rotten eggs at him, calling him a traitor," Asim pointed out. "But now the capital is named after him."

"Lenin was weak when he negotiated with the Germans," Abu Abdallah reminded everyone, adjusting his neck brace. "But he knew if he made concessions, he could buy time to become stronger and reconquer those areas. Abu Ammar* is doing the right thing. We are not surrendering!"

A young prisoner argued against the idea. "There's no compromise in Islam," he said. "When the Prophet sent his messenger to Persia, he didn't negotiate. He just sent the message—if you accept Islam, you will live in peace."

"Ah, however," my former teacher Diab countered, "this same Prophet made an agreement with the king of Ethiopia in order to protect his people when they were weak! And what about Salah el Din? When he liberated

*Yasser Arafat's nom de guerre. Arafat was a founder of Fatah and was chairman of the PLO.

Jerusalem from the Romans, he promised to let the Christians stay and to protect their holy sites. He even permitted the Jews to come back after the Christians had kicked them out! There is absolutely a place for compromise and peace agreements in Islam!"

I managed to conclude the meeting by emphasizing the points we shared. Our sense of solidarity was still intact, perhaps even strengthened. I drew a deep breath of relief as everyone got up and walked away, chatting pleasantly with one another across movement lines. But Azzam left the circle ruefully rubbing his sore thigh.

"*Wallah,* Sami. I swear, my leg is numb!" he groaned.

My proudest moment occurred when the education committee asked me to teach the new prisoners' course. I spent weeks feverishly preparing for my new role. I tried to remember everything my old teachers, Abdel Fatah and Diab, had done. I wanted to approach the course exactly as they had.

We spent the first weeks reviewing the ninety-page Fatah manual in exhaustive detail. The thin booklet was chock-full of notes about the conduct expected from Fatah members—the rules of engagement when fighting, the courteous behavior required toward civilians, the treatment of fellow Fatah brothers. I expanded on each note with quotes from speeches by Abu Jihad* and Abu Ammar, or with information from other books that I had spent hours poring over the night before, to ensure I was drawing on a large and accurate base of information. I made eye contact with each new prisoner as I spoke, and smiled encouragingly when asking questions, as Diab and Abdel Fatah had. We often spent an entire three-hour meeting discussing just one bullet point from the manual.

I felt uneasy teaching the ideology of the Fatah movement. The curriculum did not acknowledge the changes that had occurred since I had been a new prisoner. The PLO was now based in Tunisia and Yemen, not south Lebanon. Fatah was not the same organization it had been. For the first time, the Fatah leaders had begun to speak about a peace process—there were even rumors that under-the-table negotiations with Israel were taking place. But inside the prison walls, we were still teaching that change was created only through armed struggle.

I wanted to teach my students about Gandhi. I was drawn to the idea of "White Revolution," the phrase we used for Gandhi's tactics against the

---

*Abu Jihad (Khalid al-Wazir) was a founder and leading commander of Fatah.

British occupation of India. I wanted them to read about the Hindu man who came to Gandhi, blood still staining his hands from having murdered a Muslim child. Gandhi instructed the man to find a Muslim orphan of the same age and raise him, providing him with a father's love and an Islamic education for twenty years. I had contemplated the anecdote for months when I had first encountered it. How easy it was to destroy a soul—the baby had been murdered in a matter of moments—and how much time, effort, and love was required to build a soul. But Gandhi was not part of the Fatah curriculum.

Even more upsetting was what was happening among our Fatah leaders. Our commanders, who I had once believed were pure as snow, were now tainted with corruption. In 1983, there had been an internal split within the movement, with the breakaway group calling for an end to the corruption. Infighting and violence between the groups broke out in 1985. I felt hypocritical teaching Fatah ideals to new prisoners when our representatives were betraying those very values. We taught about Fatah's democratic principles, yet movement elections had not been held since 1979. The new prisoners often raised questions about these inconsistencies. No matter how thoroughly I had prepared for our meetings, I had no satisfactory answers for them.

Several of my students did not pass the exam at the end of the course. I knew that it was not a reflection on me as a teacher. There had been significant changes since my days as a new prisoner. The hunger strike had brought a transistor radio and television to each cell—and even though their usage was limited, it still cut into reading time. More crucial, after the big prisoner exchange of 1985, the ratio between new and old prisoners had shifted dramatically. Our community elders had been lost. The prison committees were growing weaker. Our mission became much harder.

In addition, five of the new prisoners in my course had dropped out of school as young children and could not read or write past a first-grade level. I set up a basic literacy course for them. I enjoyed teaching them the reading and writing of the Arabic language. Compared to the mixed feelings I had about teaching Fatah ideology, Arabic was unblemished beauty.

Yusuf was eighteen years old and was from my neighborhood in the Old City. He could not stop smiling as he fiddled with his notebook and pencil on the first day of the course, waiting for our first literacy lesson to begin. I had some first-grade primers. We began with the letter *alif*. Within three months, the five young prisoners could read aloud from fourth-grade books and write simple sentences. In six months, they were at a high school reading level. My students now had access to anything they wanted to learn about; the entire world was open to them! We in prison had achieved something for these young men that teachers in the school had failed to do. I imaged a day when Yusuf was free, back in the Old City, and helping his children with homework. I beamed at the image. I had given Yusuf the gift of his own language.

IN THE YEARS FOLLOWING the 1982 Israel-Lebanon war, thousands of prisoners had been released in prisoner exchanges. Thousands more were transferred. All West Bankers in Asqalan were sent to Juneid prison in Nablus. More than three hundred youth from Gaza prison, most of them eighteen or nineteen years old, were sent to Asqalan in their place, now composing the vast majority of our total population. The conditions that the new prisoners had experienced in Gaza prison had been much harsher. The Gaza prison was completely run by the military. Torture during interrogations was more severe. The cells were overcrowded. The system of organization and education was much weaker. There was more violence inside the prison—both from the Israeli soldiers and between the prisoners.

There had been no system of democracy in Gaza prison. Large groups of friends from the same area would simply take control. Most of the new Gazan prisoners had been part of the same Fatah groups, either in the refugee camps of Jabalia in the north of Gaza Strip or Khan Younis in the south. They trusted only each other. During prison elections, the new Gazans voted exclusively for themselves. The newcomers quickly took control.

In the courtyard, a new arrival from Jabalia camp introduced himself to me. "Originally, I had a five-year sentence," he told me conversationally. "But I suspected that my friend in prison with me was a collaborator, so I killed him. Now I have a life sentence." An intense chill ran up my spine.

The Gazans were immediately suspicious of Jerusalemites, partially because of Section Eleven. Forty-five prisoners from Jerusalem were awaiting their trials in Section Eleven. They were permitted to wear civilian clothing and have weekly visits from their families. The Jabalia and Khan Younis youth had not experienced similar treatment in their Gazan prison. They presumed that the Section Eleven prisoners must be providing the Israelis with information in exchange for these benefits. The Gazans, who greatly outnumbered the Jerusalemites, were now in control of the Fatah security committee. It was always the security committee that ensured we knew how to respond to the Israeli guards during counting, hunger strikes, etc. It was also the security committee that handled all allegations of collaboration.

They began investigating the Section Eleven Jerusalemites. Esam Hashimi from Shu'afat refugee camp had arrived in Asqalan just one month earlier. He was nineteen years old and was short and somewhat frail. The security committee accused him of being a collaborator. In the middle of the night, two Gazans strangled him.

"We killed your dog. Come and take him," one of them spat to the guard who arrived for the morning count. The guards pumped tear gas into the room, interrogated the murderers, and put them in solitary confinement. What else could be done? They were already serving a life sentence.

I started shaking when I heard the news, passed by the corridor cleaner in hushed whispers. I thought about Esam's mother, then about my own mother. If they did this to Esam, they could do this to any of us. They spread rumors that Esam had been not only a collaborator, but a homosexual as well. A poisonous wind had arrived in the prison.

Those accused of collaboration lost their right to vote. More and more prisoners from Jerusalem were charged, allowing the Khan Younis and Jabalia groups to consolidate their grip on power. The Gazans smugly published the names of "confessed collaborators" in the security records and distributed them throughout the entire prison system. The names leaked to the outside world as well. The men would be forever branded. I asked myself continually why the Gazans were behaving this way, but I never arrived at a reasonable answer. All I knew was that it had to do with wanting control and the desire to exercise authority over others.

My cell mate Adnan had asked the guards to change his section to one not controlled by Fatah so he would be safe from the Gazans. The Gazans had gotten word of his request and decided that he must be a collaborator. The attack happened in my cell. I tried not to watch, keeping my eyes trained carefully on the open page of my book, but I could not escape the sounds. Curses and insults; threats to stab him with knives crudely fashioned out of spoons; kicks followed by moans of pain. I winced with each strike. How could I possibly help him? If I tried to intervene, I would be next. The following day, Adnan's body was yellow, green, and dark purple. His eyes were barely slits in a face that was swollen beyond recognition. I could not bring myself to look at or speak to him.

I slowly shut myself down and built my own internal world. In the courtyard, I was reluctant to shake anyone's hand or even return a greeting of

"*Sabah el khair,* Sami!" If someone saw me conversing with a prisoner who was under investigation, maybe I too would be accused. I monitored my every movement. I forced myself not to glance up during count, or even scratch my leg. Making eye contact with a guard could get you labeled a collaborator. I brooded constantly about the days when we shared the same hopes and dreams, the same suffering and spirituality. How could we have let the sacred trust and solidarity between us be shattered?

Forty-three Jerusalemites in Asqalan prison were charged with collaboration. More beatings followed. The guards did not know or did not care. I was sick to my stomach day and night. With each new accusation, my anxiety and misery grew. Everything was in chaos—and it was all taking place under the umbrella of Fatah security.

Old prisoners wrote articles for the prison magazine about how something inside us was broken, how we had now become birds whose wings had been clipped. The most courageous of them posed the question: doesn't targeting innocent, good people just serve the Israeli agenda? Movement leaders from outside sent letters via capsules, expressing their shame and grief at what was happening on the inside. Abu Ammar himself sent messages, advising the hotheaded, arrogant young prisoners to listen to those with experience and to rebuild the hope and the trust. But the poison continued.

Nizar sought me out in the courtyard one sunny afternoon.

"Hey, Sami! I was in the hospital in Ramle yesterday and I saw someone who knew you!"

"Really? Who?"

"Abed. He told me the story about what happened in Al Makassed hospital after you were injured . . ."

I tried to hide my alarm. "Did he?" I answered vaguely. Maybe Abed had only told Nizar that I had asked him to throw the stuff in my room down the well. Maybe Abed had not mentioned that, while still under the influence of the chloroform, I had given Eyeglasses his name, leading to him being subsequently arrested and interrogated for fifteen days before being released. My fear turned into panic over the following days. Of course Abed would have told Nizar that part of the story. And now, maybe Nizar would report his conversation with Abed to the security committee. My shameful breach would be discovered. My panic became paranoia. The security committee believed I was a collaborator. The Gazans were sharpening those spoons into knives with the express purpose of stabbing me. When they whispered in the corner of the cell or the courtyard, they were plotting against me. They came to kill me every night in my dreams. I stopped sleeping.

I took my brother Azzam aside one afternoon in the courtyard.

"Azzam, I can't stay here."

"Don't leave, Sami, please," Azzam pleaded with me. "Then for sure they'll say you're a collaborator!"

"What they say is their business. My safety is my business."

I faked severe stomach cramps the next morning and, en route to the clinic, told the guard that I feared for my life. Within a week, I was transferred to Kfar Yona, a prison for people with special problems. Some really were collaborators. Others did not want to be associated with any particular movement. Some, such as the high-ranking PLO official Faisal Husseini, were there because the Israelis did not want him mixing with other prisoners. And others were exactly like me.

I was safe again. The nightmares stopped. Within days, Azzam joined me. After I left Asqalan, he also told an officer he no longer felt safe. All of the youth from the Old City whom Azzam had been arrested with had been accused of collaboration. Likely it was only a matter of time for Azzam as well. Also, my little brother preferred to be with me.

Everyone in Kfar Yona stored his problem tightly inside his own heart. But the other prisoners grew to trust me.

"Believe me, Sami, I did nothing. I am clean." After what I had witnessed this last year in Asqalan, I could believe them.

I saw a few I had known from Beer Al-Sabe' or Asqalan.

"*Ya* Sami, we never expected to see you here!"

I shrugged my shoulders. "Me neither, but what can you do? This is life."

There were Jewish Israeli political prisoners in Kfar Yona. Yaacov Ben-Efrat and Assaf Adiv were from Tel Aviv. They were members in *Derekh Hanitzotz*,* an Israeli Marxist movement with close connections to the Democratic Front for the Liberation of Palestine. They were serving several years in prison for the connection to the DFLP, as it was considered a terrorist organization by the Israelis. I was curious about Yaacov and Assaf. I already knew that there were Israelis who were struggling to end the occupation. Mordechai Vanunu, who had leaked information in 1986 about Israel's nuclear weapons program, was with us in Asqalan—but held in solitary confinement. Our only contact with him was to call out "*Boker tov*,** Vanunu!" as we passed his cell on our way to the courtyard.

*Hebrew for "Path of the Spark."

**Hebrew for "Good morning."

I sought out opportunities to converse with Yaacov and Assaf, to learn more about these Israelis who cared about Palestinians, about our reality, about the truth. They did more than just care; they were actively working for our freedom. They believed that all means to achieve a two-state solution—including the use of violent struggle—were legitimate. Our political discourse was exciting and dynamic—they were Jewish, I was Muslim; they were Israeli, I was Palestinian. And yet we were clinging strongly to the same basic ideal: we refused to live under occupation or to be occupiers.

"Why are you in Kfar Yona, Sami?" Yaacov asked me in the early weeks of our friendship. Cautiously at first, I told them the pieces of my story I felt comfortable revealing. But as we became closer, Assaf and Yaacov gained my full trust. I did not feel safe opening up to the other Palestinian prisoners, knowing that they may soon be back in the regular prison system, possibly spreading my tale to others. There was no such risk in confiding in my new Israeli friends.

We spent most of our day in the corridors, socializing with each other. Shabtai, however, was under lockdown in his room. Shabtai was a Russian Jew serving ten years for collaborating with the Soviet Union against Israel. Shabtai and I played chess together for hours. I held the chessboard up to the window of his cell. He stretched his hand through the bars to move the pieces. Shabtai prided himself on his prowess in chess and I was his partner of choice. I had gotten a lot better since my early years in Beer Al-Sabe'—in fact, in 1986, I had won the chess tournament in Asqalan. Shabtai and I were evenly matched. Our games were often intense, and the loser sometimes flew into a rage. Once or twice, the chess pieces went flying through the corridor as one of us slammed the raised board in anger. But soon after, we would be joking again.

"Good thing you're locked inside that room, *ya* Shabtai, or I would have hit you for sure!"

Being Shabtai's friend and chess partner had its advantages. Shabtai was a person of means and influence. He had his ways of acquiring special food or other contraband, which he shared with me. Shabtai once arranged for an officer's son to get a good job in South Africa in exchange for visits from prostitutes. The officer was discovered and was discharged immediately. I laughed when I heard the news. All prisoners dream of being kicked out of the prison—but the officers typically don't share that fantasy.

We could chat with the guards in Kfar Yona, unlike in the regular prison system, where all communication had to go through liaisons. If a guard had decent coffee from outside, he often offered us some, or slipped us dried sage or fresh mint for our tea. I was reminded of the early days in Jalameh, passing hours with Bisan.

The guards were two people in one: twenty-four hours inside with the prisoners and then twenty-four hours outside with their families. If you added up their time, some of them served even longer than we did. "We are the same as you," a guard named Ro'e commented to me as we drank coffee together. "I've been here for twenty years. Okay, our situations are different—but still—I am inside the prison."

Interacting with someone who just that morning had been outside was an exciting contact to the world beyond the walls. I pumped Ro'e for information: What was life like outside? How did people behave? What had changed in the past seven years?

The lives of the guards were connected to ours. This was why soldiers were brought in to beat us when conflict erupted, Ro'e confided, rather than the guards doing it themselves. The guards were too embedded in the prison. They would continue to be with us after the flare-up was over.

On the nineteenth day of our big hunger strike, I had seen a guard cry. I had filed the incident away in my memory, but now in Kfar Yona, I reflected on it in more depth. The guards were people, no different from us. Sitting and drinking coffee with Ro'e, it was not so difficult to see his humanity.

IN 1988, I RECEIVED a message from the old prisoners in Asqalan: "Brother Sami, we know you. We need your help. Come and put your hand back with the people."

Messages such as this had been sent before, but I still had not felt safe. But now, the most extreme members of the Khan Younis and Jabalia groups had been transferred to Nafha prison. Asqalan was flooded by *shabab* from Jerusalem, scores of whom were arrested after the outbreak of the Intifada,* including my little brother Mazin. Prisoners who had been released were re-arrested. Other old prisoners had been transferred back to Asqalan from other prisons. When elections were held again, the old prisoners had regained their authority. They had slowly been able to build influence with the

*Literally "shaking off," used to mean "uprising." The Intifada, a popular revolt in the West Bank and Gaza against Israeli occupation, started in December 1987 when an Israeli truck collided with vans carrying Palestinian workers, killing four at Gaza's Erez crossing.

remaining Khan Younis and Jabalia youth. They brought Asqalan prison back under control and restored the old system. Esam was exonerated posthumously. It did little to comfort his family, I was sure, but I breathed deeply when I heard the news.

Yaacov and Assaf both encouraged me to return. "You can do more good there," they told me. "Your brothers will understand why you left and will forgive you."

As my prison sentence neared its end, I knew in my gut that I had to confront my problem. Otherwise, rumors would always circulate about me: Sami didn't feel safe with his Fatah brothers; Sami abandoned the movement. I wanted to be able to look my brothers directly in the eye and say to them, "Here's Sami. I am with you." Plus, Azzam had been released shortly after arriving in Kfar Yona. I wanted to be with my little brother Mazin.

I told the Israelis that I wanted to go back to Asqalan. Because they had removed me from Asqalan for my own protection, they were willing to let me return if I signed a statement asserting that I took responsibility for anything that might happen to me. Nerves churned in my stomach as I sat on the metal bench of the prison truck, my wrists and ankles in cuffs. What exactly would I be returning to? I had crossed a very clear red line in telling the Israelis that I was not safe. I might be beaten harshly. Even worse, I could be snubbed, ignored, considered a traitor, outside the circle of trust.

I told the security committee my full story as soon as I arrived back in Asqalan. The security head held a small stick.

"Give me your hand, Sami." I did. He rapped my hand lightly fifteen times. I waited for him to continue, but the stick had already been put away.

"You've had your punishment now. The old chapter is closed. Now go be with the brothers."

I stood for a moment as relief flooded over me. Then I quickly joined the others in the courtyard. Yusuf, my former student, saw me first. "*Ya* Sami!" He ran to me and wrapped me in a bear hug. "If you've returned, then things really must be back to normal!" For days, old friends constantly approached me, shaking my hand, patting me on the back. "We're glad to see you, Sami."

It was good to be back.

The new Gazans were now part of the reestablished program, studying in the courses. I could tell that some of them felt ashamed. Even so, I could not trust them. I did not confront any of them about the dark and ugly things that had transpired. What if they got back in the circle of control? I was invited to serve on the security committee. I refused. I was willing to take part only in the education and publication committees.

In the final week of 1989, a scrap of paper was slipped into my hand in the courtyard. I unfolded it back in my cell. "Brother Sami, we want you to write this year's article for the Fatah movement." I read the note twice to make sure I understood it correctly. This was the most important piece of writing produced by Fatah in the entire prison system. The essay would be read by all prisoners in every prison on January 1, the anniversary of the Palestinian revolution and the birth of the Fatah party. The author of the annual article was selected with great care by the upper leadership of the movement. I now had not the slightest doubt that my relationship with Fatah was fully repaired and restored.

Most meetings now revolved around the Intifada. In refugee camps, villages, and towns all over the Occupied Territories, Palestinians were protesting home demolitions, deportations, detentions—all examples of repressive Israeli occupation. I was proud of my people, mass numbers of them engaged in large-scale civil disobedience: refusal to pay taxes; general strikes; boycotts. I was proud of the stones they threw. Each rock carried a clear and simple message: we refuse to live under occupation; we demand freedom. The stones were a form of White Revolution in my eyes. I could count on one hand the number of Israeli soldiers or settlers who were victims of stones. At first we thought the uprising would last only a few weeks but more and more people joined in. As the numbers swelled, the Intifada became increasingly organized.

The Intifada gave us hope. We wanted to be out on the street taking part in the demonstrations. We sent messages of solidarity and support to our people, hiding the papers in capsules under our tongues and passing them through the mesh net to our families on visiting days. Some of the messages contained advice, such as suggesting that neighborhoods organize underground classes to serve as a substitute for our regular schools that the Israelis had closed. We read statements from lead organizers and debated their strategies. I hoped that we would not repeat our mistakes from the past: in 1936, Palestinians had risen up against the British Mandate but stopped the revolt when some of our leaders assured us that we would receive our independence. The promises had been empty. This Intifada should not stop until the occupation ended.

Years earlier, I had read a book about military strategy written by British military historian and general Basil Liddell Hart. One quote came back to me: "It is more potent, as well as more economical, to disarm the enemy than to attempt his destruction by hard fighting." As youth all over the Occupied Territories threw stones, I reflected on the statement. Armed combat is not the only way to disarm your enemy. Our youth with stones were facing guns and gas and rubber bullets from the Israelis. But it was impossible for the army to use tanks and F-16 fighter jets against the stones. And when the international media showed images of a powerful, well-equipped army pointing guns at kids with stones, it became clear to all the world who the real victims were.

It was September 13, 1990. Ten years to the day that Badawi, Abbas, and I had been making the bomb.

"Sami Al Jundi. Be ready!" the loudspeaker announced in Hebrew, followed by the single word "*shikhrur.*"

Release.

My heart pounding, I collected my belongings.

The guard led me to the officer on duty. The officer took me to the gate that opened to the world outside. Just as he was about to unlock it, he casually consulted a slip of paper on his clipboard.

"You have a three hundred–shekel fine on your record," he told me. "You have to pay it before you can leave."

"Three hundred shekels? For what?"

The fine was from a week before my arrest, when I had been caught smoking in the cinema. Israeli law forbade smoking in the cinema, and therefore, we always lit up when we went to see a film. I had received a twenty-shekel ticket but was locked up before I could pay it. Over the past decade, the fine had multiplied.

"If you don't pay," the officer sneered at me, speaking with a Russian accent, "I can take you back inside for another month." He waved his hand toward the cells. "Back with the prisoners."

Anger swelled inside me. He was trying to break me. He could take me—if I did not pay—back with the prisoners. As if this were a horrible threat. Clearly he didn't understand that these prisoners were my brothers.

I stood up straight and looked him squarely in the eye. "Please bring me back inside."

"What?"

"I prefer not to pay the fine. After ten years, one more month is no big deal."

The officer sputtered in surprise. "Your family is outside! I'm sure they can give you the money."

I was deliberately calm. "Of course they can. But it's a good opportunity to spend another month with my brothers."

I flew back to my cell with exhilaration. No one could believe that I had returned voluntarily. I was the star of the prison. Everyone came to hug me. Our souls seemed to take flight. We felt stronger than the prison itself. They called me a hero. I knew that I was not.

I did not return for that extra month in order to give fortitude to the brothers; I did it because the officer wanted to break my spirit. But when I saw the joy in their eyes, I realized that I had done something enormous. To a prisoner, the day of release is the brightest day in his life. By choosing to remain in prison, I had challenged that. Being here is worthwhile too, my action confirmed. The hour of sunlight together in the courtyard each day was enough. Freedom could start in our minds.

That day, no one was dreaming about his liberty. Everyone was imagining the day he would hear his name over the loudspeaker followed by the Hebrew word *shikhrur* and would tell the officers, "You know, I'd rather stay here. Getting released is not as important to me as my brothers are."

I was the only prisoner to ever receive two freedom parties in one month. Asqalan prison had an odd tradition with freedom parties. There were songs, jokes, and speeches, as in all the other prisons. But in Asqalan, you could expect to get eggs smashed on your head and to be covered with olive oil, margarine, *za'atar*.

"You'll be clean soon enough!" everyone would joke, as they showered you with eggs and rubbed spices in your face and hair.

The prisoners saved more than sixty eggs for my second freedom; more eggs for one party than in the history of Asqalan prison. My brothers lined up, each one smearing me with something precious that they had managed to squirrel away. Eggs dripped down my face. Black pepper, *za'atar*, and every other spice under the sun combined in my stinging eyes. Yolk was up my nose, olive oil dripped down my neck, and margarine smothered my hair. It took me a full hour in the shower to scrub myself. I needed to shampoo my hair three times.

I had never felt so wonderful and so clean. And I mean before the shower.

CHAPTER EIGHT

꩜

MY SECOND RELEASE was days away. But my excitement was tempered by the tragic news that broke on October 8, 1990. The corridor cleaner moved from cell to cell repeating the same horrific sentence: "Massacre in Al Aqsa Mosque."

My heart was racing as we tuned the transistor radio. A Jewish extremist group known as the Temple Mount Faithful had led a march to place the foundation stone for the Third Temple on Haram Al Sharif.* The leader of the group had announced that the Arab-Islamic occupation of the temple area must end and that the Jews must renew their ties to the sacred area.

Thousands of Palestinians had gathered inside Al Aqsa to protect it. Muslim worshippers began pelting stones at Jews praying at the Western Wall. Israelis responded by unleashing their full arsenal directly into the compound of the mosque: gas bombs, helicopter gunships, and thirty-five continuous minutes of automatic machine-gun fire. The attack was not from security forces alone; Israeli settlers were shooting alongside the army and police.

Twenty-three Palestinians were mowed down in the death trap. The dead included a sixty-year-old woman from Tamra, a northern village inside the Green Line. Worshippers from Bethlehem and Ramallah. Seven people from the Old City. Hundreds more were wounded. Panic shot through me. Was my family okay? The newscaster did not give names.

By midafternoon we knew the identities of those who had been killed. Badawi and Abbas's cousin Burham had been a five-year-old kid when I last

---

*Arabic for "the Noble Sanctuary"; the compound includes the Dome of the Rock and the Al Aqsa Mosque. Jews call it the Temple Mount and believe it to be the site of the First and Second Temples.

saw him. Now, at fifteen years old, he was the youngest victim of the massacre. A former cell mate's father was also slain. Another victim's father was
from Deir Yassin, like mine. But none of my brothers had been killed. My
mom's name was not listed. My panic subsided.

October 12, 1990. Early in the morning, from over the loudspeaker: "Sami Al
Jundi!" followed by "*shikhrur!*"

I hugged my cell mates goodbye.

"Promise us," Abu Wahid said. "Promise us that you won't forget about
your brothers inside. That you will talk about us always."

My heart beat quickly as the same Russian guard walked me to the small
gate at the side of the prison. He opened it.

"Do you have anything on that sheet that needs to be taken care of?"

He glanced down at his clipboard. "No, everything is okay. You can go and
meet your family now!"

"Check again. I want to be certain that my entire case is closed."

He waved his arms toward the open gate. "Go on. You're done! Congratulations! Just don't do anything to get yourself back in here!"

I strode two large steps outside the prison and then stopped. The gate
locked behind me with a distinctive click. It was strangely quiet. No sounds
of breathing or coughing or rustling of book pages. The early morning sunshine was bright and the air smelled fresh and clean. I threw my arms wide
open and filled my lungs with as much freedom as they could hold.

My family would be waiting at the parking lot, 150 feet away. My walk
turned into a run until I reached a small, old, red Fiat parked alone in the
middle of the gravel lot. A black plastic bag was tied to the antenna.

I knocked on the car window, peering inside. My father, Samir, and Azzam
quickly opened the door, climbing out to greet me with huge bear hugs and
tousles of my hair.

My father touched my eyes with his fingertips. They were callused from
an additional decade of making brooms.

"My son. I'm sorry. I did not come to you enough while you were in
prison," he said. "But I'm here now, to take you home."

I took his hands in mine, moving them away from my face. I did not want
him to feel the moisture in my eyes.

Samir got in the driver's seat with my father sitting next to him. I slid into
the backseat next to Azzam.

"Why is there a black bag on the antenna?" I asked.

"Black flags are everywhere in Palestine," Samir answered. I was so happy to see my father and brothers that I had almost forgotten about the massacre.

"*Ya Allah*," Azzam said, punching me in the ribs. "You have bad luck. Of all the sad days to get out of prison . . ."

"What a party you would have had last month!" Samir added. "An entire busload of people from the Old City was waiting here to greet you!"

Samir pulled onto the main road. I gripped the door handle. "Samir! You're driving too fast! Slow down, please!"

Samir laughed. "Sami, this old piece of junk isn't capable of speeding! We're going less than fifty miles an hour!"

Fifty miles an hour felt like riding in a missile. Still gripping the door handle, I rolled the window down in order to savor the view. Green leafy trees, rocks speckled with sunlight . . . the world was much more beautiful than I had remembered.

"This is Latrun," Azzam announced as we approached a big intersection. Latrun. I had been there on a class picnic in fourth grade. The Latrun in my memory held no relationship with the junction we were now passing. I had to create a clean file in my brain to store new information about every place we passed.

An army jeep was blocking the road. Two soldiers waved for us to pull over. One soldier approached. I held my breath for a moment. What were soldiers on the outside like now?

"Why do you have a black plastic bag on your car?" the soldier asked, leaning into the window.

Samir answered without hesitation, "Because we're in mourning about what happened at Al Aqsa."

"You have to take this off."

"We can't," Samir said. "We have yellow license plates* and we're about to drive through a Palestinian village. If we don't have the black bag, we'll get stones thrown at us."

The soldier fingered the bag for a moment. "Take it off the car."

Azzam jumped out, pulled the bag off the antenna, and shoved it in his pocket. "Happy?" he asked the soldier as he hopped back in the car. The soldier motioned for us to pass.

A half-mile later, Samir pulled over again. Azzam jumped back out of the car and refastened the black bag to the antenna.

---

*Israeli cars had yellow license plates, as opposed to blue West Bank plates. As Israel annexed East Jerusalem in 1967, East Jerusalem licenses plates are yellow as well.

Samir pulled over a third time as we neared Ramallah. My father handed me a sack. "Here, Sami, go and change into these."

I looked inside. There were jeans, sneakers, and a colorful button-down shirt. Civilian clothes! I went behind a grove of small trees by the side of the road and took off my prison pants, pulling on the crisp, new denims. I slowly buttoned the purple, black, and yellow shirt. Here I was, dressed in nice clothes, like any normal, regular person. I stuffed my prison clothes into the bag. I did not want to see them ever again.

I got back into the car and we continued to Jerusalem. "What's this place?" We were passing a small town composed of red-tiled roofs.

"Givat Ze'ev. It wasn't built yet when you were arrested." A new settlement.

We entered East Jerusalem, driving on the road leading to French Hill.* "And this neighborhood?"

"Ramot." Another settlement.

As our little Fiat approached the Old City, the signs of grief were everywhere. All the shops were closed. Black flags waved from every rooftop. I had not stepped out of Asqalan prison into a new, beautiful life after all. I had stepped into sorrow and despair. Samir took me directly to the home of a *shaheed*. I pushed away my fantasy of a hero's welcome. Being celebrated and meeting girls—this was trivial next to our collective tragedy. I was just another mourner, a part of my people, with one joint soul.

Late that afternoon, Samir took me to Al Makassed to donate blood for the wounded. The last time I had been at the hospital, it was my own blood spilling.

"He just got out of prison today, after ten years," Samir told the nurse, as we registered our names.

"Really?" She gave me a cup of juice before anyone else. "You don't have to give your blood on your release day!"

I shrugged. "Why shouldn't I? I'm no different from anyone else."

They took only one unit of blood from me, rather than the two units they were taking from everyone else. "You just returned home. One unit's enough!" the nurse said, handing me another cup of juice.

Finally, Samir took me home. My mother had arrived just minutes before from visiting the mothers of the martyrs. She recognized the sound of my footsteps in the courtyard. Before I could say a word, she flew out of her chair and threw her arms around me, pulling me close. Her tears wet my

---

*A neighborhood in northeast Jerusalem.

cheeks as she rubbed her face against mine. "*Ya habibi, ya* Sami, you came home." I felt as if I were eight years old again.

That evening, visitors arrived to greet the released prisoner. They pumped Samir's hand vigorously when he answered the door. "Good luck in your new life, my son!"

"Not me!" Samir pointed at me, sitting on the couch. "Him!"

"You?" The visitors looked me up and down, shaking their heads, while I grinned and nodded. "Ten years? Impossible. You're still a baby!"

My father was sipping coffee at 6:30 the next morning, the only one awake. I sat next to him and poured some into a *finjan*,* taking a small sip and swishing it in my mouth before swallowing. Ahhh . . . thick, dark, sweet coffee. I could drink as much of it as I liked now.

"We organized buses to go north to Tamra today," my father told me. "We must pay our respects to the families of Tamra's two martyrs. You should come."

An hour later, I was boarding one of the four buses filled with residents of the Old City, many of them relatives of the martyrs, for the three-hour drive to Tamra.

Someone popped in a cassette and soon the bus was filled with songs describing the green, verdant hills and valleys of Palestine. Everyone else sang along, but it was my first time hearing these songs. The bus passed through numerous Palestinian villages inside '48,** as beautiful as the songs conveyed.

"This is Ara," Azzam told me as we drove past one village. "And this is Um El Fahm," Riyyad said as we passed another.

The relatives of the martyrs began to consult with each other as we neared Tamra. Burham Kashour's brother leaned over to my father and Samir and asked them a question. Samir slid out of his seat and tapped me on the shoulder.

"Sami, they want you to give the speech on our behalf in Tamra."

"Shouldn't the brother or the father of a *shaheed* speak?"

"They're proud to have a newly released prisoner represent us."

"I'd be honored, of course."

The buses pulled into an open square in the middle of Tamra. We were immediately absorbed into the crowd, exchanging condolences.

*The small cup used to drink Turkish coffee.

**Inside Israel's 1948 borders; inside the Green Line.

More than two hundred people crowded into a tent that had been set up on the field of the school. A leader from the village council stood in the middle of the circle and welcomed the Jerusalemites. He introduced me. I joined him at the front of the circle.

I looked around the crowd, Palestinians from Jerusalem mixing and merging with Palestinians from Tamra. Palestinians from the Occupied Territories often viewed Palestinians from inside* as less deserving of respect. I felt a surge of warmth to see us united like this. The Intifada was bringing us together as one family.

"My name is Sami Al Jundi. I'm here to grieve with you in these dark days. I was asked to represent all of us from Jerusalem, not because I know how to talk particularly well, but because I gave ten years of my life for my people and my homeland; I was just released yesterday. But my sacrifice is nothing next to the souls of your martyred relatives. And although we are mourning, we are also proud to stand here with you, our brothers and sisters from inside '48. It should not take a terrible tragedy like this to remind us that we are one people, sharing the same grief and spilling the same blood. We must remember all who gave their lives to pave the way for the Palestinian people to live with full dignity. If we respect their blood and their sacrifice, we must continue to strive with that same dignity for our freedom. In the end, our people will be free in our homeland. Allah *Yerhamhum*,"** I concluded. "Those who fell are with Allah now. May Allah bless them and all of us."

On the bus ride back to Jerusalem, passing now familiar villages and towns and roads, I wondered: how many days would I have to mourn before it would be acceptable to meet girls?

~☽☾~

ABBAS CAME TO VISIT ME with Badawi's brother, Zakaria.

"Sami! Welcome home!"

"Thanks!"

"I was supposed to get five years more than you, but it worked out the other way around."

I was glad Abbas had not had to endure the full fifteen years he had been sentenced. His heart had never fully recovered from the shrapnel that had

---

*Inside '48, or inside the Green Line.

**Plural for "*Allah yerhamo*," Arabic for "God have mercy on them."

punctured it. He was weak and frail. He seemed duller than I had remembered, as if his inner light had dimmed. Would he expect us to go back to how we had been before? I did not intend to. I wanted a good relationship with Abbas, but I did not want my future connected to his. From now on, I would make my own decisions, not influenced by anyone else. Abbas was friendly but did not seem any more eager than me to rekindle what was.

I woke up at 6 every morning and lay in bed, eyes still closed, waiting for guards to enter my bedroom and call out, "Count!" My stomach rumbled whenever it was mealtime in prison. I watched people coming and going freely in the Old City. Did any of them appreciate that they were drinking and eating whatever they wanted, whenever they wanted it? Were any of them able to feel with the brothers who were still locked in tiny cells?

At first, I could not get enough of large groups of people, children playing, women talking, people walking on the streets, laughing, joking. Now it was beginning to wear on me. In every house there were children shouting, TV sets blaring. Where could I find some quiet and privacy? In our small cells, if two of us were talking, our voices had been so low that the other six could not hear. But outside, there was no respect for solitude. People jabbered loudly in the middle of the street. I overheard their private business whether I wanted to or not.

I missed the meetings, all of us gathered in a circle to talk about books and ideas. Samir had books in his house. I began to spend more and more time there, reading.

"How are our people in prison doing?" everyone asked me. I remembered my promise to Abu Wahid and started to answer fully. But soon I realized that no one cared about the details. We had always nursed so much hope that our people outside struggled on our behalf, but this, I was slowly discovering, was true in rhetoric only. The only ones who truly cared were their family and close friends.

And my mother.

Early Friday morning, my mother started to leave the house.

"Where are you going?" I asked her.

"It's visiting day!"

I remembered the disorientation my mother had experienced with her brain tumor and was concerned. "But *Yamma*, I'm home, I'm free!"

My mother patted my cheek gently. "Yes, my son, you got your freedom, but I have other sons in the prison."

"Who?" I had been the last of the Al Jundi brothers to be released.

"Prisoners from Lebanon. Their own mothers cannot come. I've been visiting them for years."

A few days later, my mom prepared to leave the house again.

"It's not Friday, *Yamma,* there are no prisoners to visit."

"I know, but on Sundays I visit elderly, infirm people in the Old City."

The next evening she was getting herself ready yet again. "Off to support the old people, *Yamma?*"

"No, Sami, I'm going to my Hebrew course."

"Why are you studying Hebrew?"

"I have to understand what the soldiers are saying when the other women and I protect the kids from being arrested during demonstrations."

I shook my head in amazement. I had thought that my best teachers were fellow prisoners like Abdel Fatah. My mother had to be added to that list.

I was quick to learn: money was essential on the outside. I was ashamed to take pocket money from my father. I needed a source of income. The brothers in prison had assured me that all the national institutes would open their doors for me as a former prisoner.

I went optimistically to the offices of *Al Sha'b* newspaper in East Jerusalem. I chatted with the other employees as I sat in the reception area, one from Qalqilia, another from Jenin. After half an hour, the director was ready to meet me.

I walked into his office. We shook hands. "How can I help you?" he asked, inviting me to take a seat.

"I'm looking for a job. I can do anything—clean the offices, work as a typist. But my ten years of experience writing for the prison magazine could qualify me even as an editor." It was my way to subtly inform him.

The director jumped up, looking startled. "The police station is right next to our office! Israeli security is crawling all over! You will be constantly checked and questioned on your way to and from work. I'm very sorry, but I cannot give you a job, knowing that it will put you at such risk."

I stood up calmly as he showed me to the door. "Thank you anyway. I hope you are equally concerned about the safety of your employees from Qalqilia and Jenin. Their way back home must be just as dangerous as mine, as I live a mere three-minute walk from your office. Thank you again, sir, for your time."

I left the office.

I tried not to be discouraged as I walked back to Samir's house. A pretty young woman was sitting and chatting with Samir and his wife, Sabah, when I entered.

"Hello. I'm Sami," I said to her.

"I know. My mother and I visited you in your home last week. My name is Fadia."

"Oh, that's right! I remember!" I did, vaguely. Azzam had told me that Fadia was engaged to be married, so I had not seen much point in paying attention to her.

"How did it go at *Al Sha'b?*" Samir asked. I recounted the story, demonstrating the director's reaction. Samir, Sabah, and Fadia laughed.

"So what will you do now?" Fadia wanted to know.

"I have no idea. I always dreamt of being a doctor, but it's too late for medical school."

"Have you thought about becoming a nurse?" Fadia asked me. She was smart, this one.

The next day, I went to register at the nursing program at Al Makassed. My application was not accepted. I was twenty-eight years—too old, the director of the program told me.

"But," the director continued, "you should talk to the head of the workers' union. They're currently hiring janitors."

I found the head of the union.

"So you were a prisoner," he said cautiously. "Which movement?"

"Fatah."

Before I knew it, I was being ushered out the door. "There are no job openings right now, but maybe in the future. Make sure you leave your telephone number."

I smiled at him before exiting. "Thank you for taking the time to meet me. I hope all is well with you and your comrades in the Communist Party."

There was plenty of activity in Jerusalem to occupy my time. The Intifada was still in full swing. I could finally be a part of the collective uprising. I did not want to be an organizer. I just wanted to participate with my people. Tens of thousands had been arrested, injured, or killed. Schools and universities had been closed by the Israelis for months at a time. Entire neighborhoods and villages had endured raids, curfews, closures, and other forms of repression. It could not be for nothing.

I was especially eager to support the ongoing strikes. In prison I had extensively studied the 1936 Palestinian general strike. It had been organized by grassroots committees and then spread. The general strike had protested the British policy of allowing Jewish immigration and increasing land sales, and it was a call for independence. Our strikes were calling for an end to occupation and for independence. All commerce in Palestinian cities shut down after 1 p.m. This impacted tourism—which, in turn, affected the Israeli economy. This was far more effective than sneaking off to Nablus to search for a soccer ball stuffed with dirt. And no one died in a premature explosion. This was the kind of resistance I wanted to take part in.

At night, Fatah activists in the Old City met up with Bilal, the leader of our group. We plastered posters of *shuhada* on shop doors. We gave packets of flyers to kids to distribute in the *souq*, informing everyone about the next day's strike or demonstration. During confrontations with soldiers, I threw a few stones from Damascus Gate and then quickly ran away. I had no intention of getting arrested again.

It took me time to recognize the changes in Jerusalem. There were no longer as many coffee shops in the Old City for people to socialize in. All the cinemas in East Jerusalem had closed. After dark, the roads were deserted. Religion had started to seep more into people's lives. Many in the Old City had always been devout Muslims, but Islam as an authority in society was unfamiliar to me. Part of the draw had to do with the hardships of the Intifada, which had led people to seek comfort in religion. Also, the Islamic movement Hamas* had been established three years earlier and was beginning to gain a strong foothold in Gaza and some parts of the West Bank. There were international influences as well: people were inspired by the 1979 Islamic Revolution in Iran and the recent ouster of the Soviets by the *mujahideen*** in Afghanistan. As the Soviet Union and communism started to break apart, Islam was filling the void. But that did not entirely explain the shift toward religion. I began to suspect that religion was becoming more about status and prestige than true devotion to Allah. Neighbors who had never prayed before were now walking around as if they were sheikhs. They tried to persuade others to become religious. Samira's husband dropped by regularly.

"*Ahlan*, Sami. I'm on my way to Al Aqsa to pray. Would you like to come?"

"Maybe someday soon," I always answered politely. "I'm not ready yet."

*Acronym for Islamic Resistance Movement, founded in 1987.

**Resistance fighters in Afghanistan who rebelled against the Soviet-backed Afghan government.

ASIDE FROM PECKING SANAA on the cheek more than ten years ago, I had never touched a woman. Now in my late twenties, I wanted to marry every pretty girl I saw.

A friend of my mother's came to visit the newly released prisoner. She brought her twenty-year-old daughter, Hind. Hind was tall and her body curvy and voluptuous. Her skin was milky white and her eyes were green. I felt stirrings of excitement that I had never experienced before.

I turned to my mother the moment they left. "We have to ask her family if she will marry me!"

The next day, my sister Hanadi went to her family's house to deliver a message from my father: we would like to come to their house and ask about Hind. Hanadi returned an hour later.

"Well?" I almost pounced on my little sister when she walked into the courtyard. "What did they say?"

Hanadi grinned. "What do you think they said? It would be a pleasure to have you in their house and they hope you will find the answer that you are looking for . . ."

My father and I went to Hind's home the very next day, with Samir and Sabah. We sat with Hind's parents and brothers, making small talk.

"So, what can we do for you?" Hind's father asked at last. At that moment, Hind came out with a tray of coffee, as was customary. Immediately my stomach started doing flip-flops.

My father took his coffee cup and sipped it. "We are here because my son Sami would like to marry Hind."

Hind's father nodded thoughtfully. "We have known your family for a long time, Abu Samir. It would be our pleasure for our families to be united through Hind and Sami. But Hind must also agree."*

I was almost shaking with excitement when Hind and I sat in a smaller salon to talk privately. Her makeup made her green eyes brighter than emeralds. Her curves were calling to me from her short, snug dress.

"I'd like to get married as soon as possible," I said.

"That sounds nice." Hind smiled. She was so sweet I wanted to taste her. "What kind of home do you have in mind?"

"A beautiful home! Here in the Old City, with nice furniture and a lot of books. But not too many children."

---

*Though marriages were arranged by families, most often the young man and woman involved traditionally gave or refused their consent to a match. Often, marriages were arranged by families at the request of the young people themselves.

"Sami, there's one thing that's important to me. I'm in my second year of university studying sociology and I want to complete my degree."

"No problem at all! I think it's great that you will continue to study. If you want to work after finishing your degree, that would be fine with me also!"

The smile spread across her entire face. "Then we can marry."

I wanted to hug her, or more, but our families were in the next room.

Hind and I joined them, each of us trying to hide our coy smiles, both of us failing miserably.

"It looks like the young people agree," Hind's father said. "Come back in a week, Abu Samir, and we will give you our final answer."

Two days later I dropped by Hind's house for an unannounced visit.

"Sami!" she said, standing up from her lunch in surprise. Her hair was not done. Instead of the formfitting dress, she had on a large house robe. She didn't look sexy or voluptuous at all. She looked rather dumpy. "It's nice to see you!" A clump of green *mlukhiyyeh* clung to her front tooth.

I found my father at the Arab Blind Organization. "*Yaba*, I changed my mind. I don't want to marry Hind."

"Why not, Sami?"

I was embarrassed to admit how shallow I was. "I don't want my wife to study," I lied.

Hanadi passed the news to her family. Two days later, Hind found me in the shop Samir owned in the Old City. Her green eyes were flashing with anger. "Why did you call it off? I want to know the real reason."

"I don't want my wife in university," I insisted.

"I don't believe you, Sami. There's a different reason."

Her eyes penetrated mine. How could I say that I no longer found her attractive? I lowered my gaze, ashamed. I knew my behavior constituted a form of violence. "You're better than me, Hind," I stammered. "You have your whole future ahead of you." She stormed out of Samir's shop before I managed to mutter, "I'm sorry."

A week later, entering Samir's house, I spotted a beautiful, graceful young woman on the neighboring rooftop, hanging laundry to dry. I stared at her until she met my eyes. She smiled flirtatiously. Embarrassed, I ducked into the house. Sabah was cooking lunch. "Who is the girl next door?" I asked.

"Oh, you must mean Maram! Why do you ask?"

"I want to marry her."

Sabah smiled. "They're a very good family. We can ask them."

The next day, Samir and I went to their house with my parents. We sat with her father, waiting for Maram to bring the coffee. Her father spoke first.

"I never considered allowing my daughter to marry a former prisoner. Prisoners are chickens in a pen. But you seem like a fine young man. And I know your family well."

Maram brought out the coffee. But—she was not the girl I had spotted on the rooftop! This must be the laundry hanger's elder sister! Maram was bony and awkward. I did not know what to do. I didn't want to cause Maram pain or embarrassment. I announced to the room that I had changed my mind.

"Why, Sami?" both families asked as a chorus.

I addressed Maram's father, faking indignation. "What you said about prisoners, sir. Those prisoners are my brothers!"

I returned to Samir's house dejected, and found Fadia there playing cards with Sabah. "You want to play, Sami?" Sabah asked me.

"Sure." I sat down. Sabah went into the kitchen to make tea and Fadia dealt me a hand.

"Something's wrong." It was a statement more than a question.

I poured out my engagement woes to Fadia. She listened sympathetically. "You shouldn't just settle for the first girl you see," Fadia said. "We have to find someone really special for you to marry."

Fadia dropped by a few days later as we were watching the news. Before long, Samir, Fadia, Sabah, Azzam, and I were all playing cards. Fadia was laughing and smoking like one of the *shabab*. She was fantastic.

"I have some ideas for you, Sami," she said after the card game, and began listing different girls from the neighborhood. But I had learned my lesson from my first two hasty engagements—I had to be more cautious. Meanwhile, Fadia and I played cards together several times a week, talking more and more. I liked talking to Fadia. And because she was already engaged, it removed any pressure.

Samir helped me find a part-time job in a private school inside Haram Al Sharif. I cleaned the classrooms and the bathrooms, and made tea and coffee. I took my work seriously. Education should take place in a clean and sanitary environment. I made an effort to brew the best pots of tea possible so that the staff would feel well cared for and that would be reflected in how they taught the kids. I loved watching the children, how they talked, how they played, seeing the future in their eyes.

Money was still a problem—the job paid very little. Samir offered to let me help a few mornings a week in his shop. I took pleasure in twisting the silver and semiprecious stones into bracelets, earrings, and necklaces for Western tourists. I especially enjoyed talking to customers. I picked up some simple phrases in English, but it wasn't enough. I registered for an English course at the British Council. With every lesson, I strived to practice my new vocabulary with customers.

With the Intifada still ongoing, the shop was closed every afternoon. I used the opportunity to show my new friends around the Old City, bestowing on them the famous Palestinian hospitality. I often took them to meet families of *shuhada*. I wanted the foreigners I befriended to return to their countries of origin and describe what they had witnessed. I wanted them to understand the price that we paid from the occupation.

My brothers and I were driving back to the Old City after playing soccer on the French Hill. Samir turned the red Fiat onto Salah el Din Street. It was afternoon, so the strike was in effect. Metal gates were padlocked over the storefronts.

Three border policemen stopped the car just as Samir was backing into an empty spot near the post office.

"What do they want?" Azzam muttered under his breath.

They opened the doors of the car, pulled us out, and threw us against the wall of the post office.

"Were you in prison?" they barked as we handed them our ID cards. We all nodded, exchanging silent glances with each other.

"How long?" one policeman asked.

"Four years," Mazin answered.

"Two and a half years," from Samir.

"Five years." Azzam.

"Ten," I told them, careful not to specify "years."

They began to beat my brothers, slapping them, kicking them, punching them. They brushed me aside.

"This one here?" one policeman said scornfully. "He was in prison only ten months, probably just chucked a stone or two."

I imagined how I would gloat to my brothers later that night that I, the Al Jundi brother who had served the most time, got off scot-free as they were abused. But out of the corner of my eye, I noticed a police officer rifling through our IDs and talking on his walkie-talkie.

The soldier with the walkie-talkie approached us. "Who the fuck is Sami?"

I was standing alone near the wall.

"I am."

"Ten, you motherfucker? You told us ten?"

"It wasn't a lie." I tried not to smirk. Nothing makes police angrier than being mocked.

The men stopped tormenting Mazin, Samir, and Azzam and turned all their attention on me. The ID checker used his walkie-talkie to call for reinforcement. In four separate cars they arrived: special forces, army, border police, and regular police. What an honor! I required four different kinds of Israeli security to beat me!

The border police demonstrated for the regular police.

"Punch him like this," one said, delivering a blow with his fist to my stomach. I doubled over with a groan.

"No, like this," said another, who kicked me hard on the side. I dropped to the ground.

"And when he's down, you can really get him . . ." the first one said again, as they began kicking me and pummeling me with their clubs. Blows and boots landed everywhere—my back, my shoulder, my stomach and chest.

Three of them dragged me up the six wide stone steps of the post office. A fourth one kicked me. I rolled down the stairs, my hip hitting the middle step. I landed hard on my shoulder and grunted in pain. A group of them lifted me off the ground and heaved me up to the top of the steps. I landed with a crunch. The others kicked me down again. And again.

I'm still here, I said to myself with gritted teeth as two soldiers grabbed me by my arms and legs and swung me back and forth, tossing me up the stairs again.

I tumbled a fourth time down the stone steps. The police and soldiers roughly grabbed me from under my arms and dragged me to a tree growing next to the sidewalk. Through the blood streaming down my face, I caught a glimpse of my brothers. Samir and Mazin were holding Azzam back, knowing what would await him if he tried to come to my defense. I knew they could not help me. Nobody could protect me.

One soldier twisted my arms behind my back. A policeman grabbed the back of my hair and slammed my face into the tree.

"Cry!" he shouted at me.

I couldn't speak. All I could do was shake my head no.

"Cry, dammit!" he repeated in a voice choked with rage, smashing my face into the tree again. "Just fucking cry and we'll leave you alone!"

But I was stronger than the entire entourage of Israeli security. They could not make me cry.

Finally they pushed me toward my brothers. I stumbled and fell.

"Get him out of here," they told Samir. "We don't want to see any of you around here again." They piled into their cars and jeeps and peeled away.

Mazin and Samir gently helped me stand up.

"Are you okay, Sami?" Samir asked.

Blood was gushing from my head and nose, covering me. I smiled. "You bastards are so lucky I was there to save you from getting beaten!" Mazin rolled his eyes.

"You had to say 'ten,' you smartass?" Azzam teased me as they helped me limp home through Herod's Gate.

I took a warm shower and gingerly rinsed off the blood. Every inch of my body was throbbing. I swallowed a handful of aspirin and crawled into bed to sleep off the hurt.

The next morning, I woke up from a sharp spasm shooting through my torso. Each breath I took brought a new dagger of pain. I dragged myself to the bathroom and looked in the mirror. My face was gashed and swollen and my nose was totally misshapen. I was covered with bruises.

"How is Mr. Ten doing this morning?" Azzam chided me when I hobbled into the main room where my family was eating breakfast.

I started to laugh, but fireworks of agony exploded inside me. I held my side and moaned.

Samir stood up and grabbed his car keys off of the TV stand. "*Yallah*, I'm taking you to the hospital."

The X-rays revealed that I had a fractured arm and several broken ribs. The doctors had to stitch my face back together. My nose was broken. I was covered in bandages. But my self-respect had never been stronger. They had not made me cry. I grinned to myself each time I thought of the incident.

⁂

PLAYING CARDS AND TALKING with Fadia became part of my routine. She began to spill out her own engagement problems. Her fiancé was in prison for drug use. She did not want to have anything to do with him anymore.

"We should get engaged, Fadia!" I blurted out one day. "You're suffering from your engagement and I'm suffering from not having anyone to marry. So why not marry each other?"

She didn't respond at first. Then she said quietly, "You know, Sami, when you were in prison, each time I heard your name mentioned by your brothers, a jolt went through me. I could never explain why. When I first laid eyes on you, my hands were shaking so hard I couldn't hold my tea glass. 'This is the one I want to marry!' I thought to myself. But I never imagined you felt the same . . ."

We started laying out plans right then and there—we would live with my parents initially. Only one or two children, we both agreed, and of course she would continue the computer course she was taking. Once she officially broke her engagement, I went with my parents to her family. Fadia's father had passed away when she was fourteen. Her uncle told us he would give us an answer within a week. I did not see Fadia for seven long days. When we returned to her family's house a week later, they agreed. Fadia and I were engaged. We set May 17, 1991, as the date of our wedding.

Fadia's and my wedding was shaping up to be a party like the Old City had not seen for years. Music had not been permitted in weddings since the start of the Intifada. But because I had just emerged from a decade in prison, my wedding was considered an exception. Music and dancing! That alone would be reason enough to bring out the entire neighborhood in droves!

I was fattened like a sheep the entire week before the wedding. "Eat more, Sami!" my mother coaxed me all week.

"You have to eat good so you can perform well on the big night," Azzam said, elbowing me.

The day before the wedding, Riyyad and Mazin took me to Ramallah to buy my wedding suit. The next morning, Samir and Azzam woke me early and took me to the barber.

"My little brother Sami is getting married today!" Samir said, pushing me down on the swiveling chair. "Give him the wedding treatment!"

"*Elf mabruk,** Sami!" the barber said as he wet my hair and began to cut and style it, using an extra dollop of gel for good measure. "I heard there will be music at your wedding party!" He shaved me with a straight edge and patted my face and neck with lotion and cologne.

Back at Samir's house, dressed in my new, shiny black suit with my gelled hair and smooth, perfumed cheeks, I stared at myself in the mirror. A stranger stared back. I felt like an impostor, as if I were posing as an elegant gentleman. The suit was itchy and restricting. I felt as if I was back in prison in these clothes. Samir knocked on the door.

"*Yallah,* Sami, we have to go!" My brothers took me to my parents' house, where friends, relatives, and neighbors had already started to gather to partake in a huge feast.

*Arabic for "A thousand congratulations!"

A neighbor took me aside. "Now listen to me, Sami," he told me. "As soon as you are alone with Fadia, you have to crack her open." He made a motion like breaking a stick. "Otherwise, she'll think you're weak!"

"Make sure you're gentle with her," a cousin coached me five minutes later, putting his arm around my neck. "She will be scared and it will hurt her. If you are gentle now, she'll reward you for it later!"

"Are you a lion or a hyena, Sami?" a classmate of Samir's asked me next, pinning me by my shoulders to the wall. "Don't be a hyena. You know what a lion does. You have to wring the cat's neck!"

Aunt Fatmeh also took me aside. "Sami, if Fadia puts her foot into the bedroom before you, you must step on it hard."

I was baffled. "Why, Aunt Fatmeh?"

"You must show her that you are the man!" Aunt Fatmeh must have seen the panic on my face because she laughed and stroked my arm. "Don't worry, *ya habibi*. Don't you think your bride is also collecting advice from all the women?"

Was sex so difficult that it required all these tutorials? I thought it would be something natural, something amazing! What if I didn't do it right? I needed time to sort through all the instructions. Maybe tomorrow or the next night I would be ready to lie with Fadia, but there was no way I could do it tonight! I did not know nearly enough!

My father patted me on the shoulder just before we left the home.

"Sami, don't worry about this nonsense everyone is telling you. You'll be fine."

His words did little to calm me down.

The entire group walked through the Old City to Fadia's house, snow-balling as we proceeded, the way demonstrations did. Samir, my father, and I entered Fadia's home. Coffee was brought out. We were not allowed to touch it yet.

"With your permission, we have arrived to take our daughter," my father said.

"*Twakkaloo 'ala* Allah,"* Fadia's uncle replied. We drank the coffee. Fadia's brothers brought her out. Her uncle took her hand and gave it to my father.

"You can walk with your bride, Sami," my father said to me.

---

*An Arabic expression often used to confirm a deal, literally meaning "Rely on God."

I looked at Fadia. Though she was covered in a brown *abaya*,* I could see some of her dress sticking out from underneath. The gown was white as snow.

The army of supporters outside was already singing and celebrating. I took hold of Fadia's arm.

"Hello, Fadia," I said softly.

I did not have to see her face to know she was glowing. "*Ahlan*, Sami," she replied.

Her brother took hold of her other arm. We walked out of her house. To my surprise, a scrawny black horse greeted us as soon as we emerged from her alleyway. Azzam was standing right next to it. "No room for a car, Sami," he said, laughing. "So you'll go on horseback!"

The horse and I eyed each other suspiciously. It was so skinny I could count its ribs. This horse was expected to carry me? Before I could protest, my brothers and the neighborhood *shabab* hoisted me up onto its bare back. The crowd closed in around the poor horse, laughing and clapping, and slapping its hindquarters to make it go. It lurched ahead, with me grabbing onto its mane for balance. The revelers crowded around us so tightly that they practically carried me up the steps, horse and all. The beast suddenly gained confidence, shaking its head forcefully. Everyone moved back to give it some space. But the slick suit material was slipping right off the horse, no matter how tightly I clung to its mane. The *shabab* jumped back in, catching me just in time and pushing me back up.

"Sami fell from the horse!" Azzam announced to laughter and cheers.

I swatted at my younger brother good-naturedly. "If you had found a proper horse with a saddle and reins, I'd show you what real riding looked like!" They all knew I had never been on a horse.

The *shabab* were singing and dancing around the horse as we slowly progressed to my parents' house. Finally, a wedding people could celebrate, after four long, dark years! We reached the narrow alleyway. No horse, no matter how malnourished, would be able to squeeze through. But the *shabab* were determined that I would be carried until the very end. They lifted me off the horse and right onto the shoulders of one large, brawny youth who continued down the alley, leaping and singing, with me riding his shoulders with no more grace than I had been riding the horse.

*A traditional Arabic or Islamic overgarment or cloak for women.

The courtyard was overflowing with guests. Young boys crowded onto the wall separating our house from the neighbors', kicking their legs, clapping, and singing. The roof was packed with people as well.

Fadia and her entourage of women arrived moments after I did. I followed them upstairs into my mother's room. All the furniture had been removed to convert the room into a small party hall with a wooden platform holding chairs for Fadia and me. Fadia and I sat on our raised chairs. A cassette was blaring. I was the only man among a hundred women. I knew I should not be gaping. But who knew if I would ever get an opportunity like this again? Fadia shot me a sharp glare. I tried to look away, but where could I rest my eyes? Women filled every inch of the room! Did Fadia expect me to stare at the ceiling? I gazed instead at Fadia. In her white bridal gown and expertly applied makeup and hair, Fadia was the most beautiful woman in the room.

My ten-year-old brother, Majdi, pushed his way into the room and weaved his way toward the platform. "Sami! All the men outside are waiting to congratulate you!" I reluctantly followed him into the courtyard to shake hands with the men, accepting envelopes stuffed with cash.

When I finally made it back upstairs, the dancing had grown even more frenetic. Aunt Fatmeh was a dynamo in the center of everyone, lighting a fire underneath each and every woman. I danced with my mom, with Aunt Fatmeh, with Fadia.

At 10 p.m., the tape player was turned off. We could not take too much advantage of the exception we had been given. The guests began to leave, emptying our courtyard. It was time for Fadia and me to enter our new bedroom for the first time, the room that formerly belonged to Riyyad. Only Aunt Fatmeh and Fadia's aunt, Um Ibrahim, remained.

Aunt Fatmeh patted me on the arm. "Sami, we will be sitting here until morning. Anytime you want to *eat,* just tell us you are *hungry* and we are waiting to serve you." I stared at her blankly. "You know, Sami, to *eat!*" Aunt Fatmeh handed me a box in which to place the sheet that Fadia and I would lie on as we consummated our marriage. "When you are *hungry,* just come bring this to me."

I was surprised. I knew a bloody sheet on the wedding night was traditionally taken as confirmation of the bride's virginity, but I had assumed that this tradition had ended long ago. I did not want to disrespect an ancient custom. "Okay, Aunt Fatmeh."

Fadia and I sat on the edge of the bed, talking shyly about the evening. "Did you see me almost fall off the horse?" We both laughed. After a few minutes, we changed to our nightclothes and lay facing each other in the bed. The afternoon's advice began crowding back into my head. I tried to push it out, and imagine instead a calm, blue sea. Just as I laid my hand on Fadia's shoulder, there was a loud rapping on the door, followed by Aunt Fatmeh's shrill voice, "Are you hungry, Sami?"

"No, thank you, Aunt Fatmeh, I'm not hungry!"

Fadia and I tried to muffle our giggles. Ten minutes later, Aunt Fatmeh urged me once again, "Sami, are you sure you're not hungry?"

"No, Aunt Fatmeh, not yet!"

Finally, three or four knocks later, I was able to answer, "Yes, Aunt Fatmeh, I am hungry!" Aunt Fatmeh opened the door. I handed her the box with a stained bedsheet inside. Aunt Fatmeh's celebratory ululations pierced the silent night. Fadia's aunt went immediately to report the news to Fadia's mother. Aunt Fatmeh began to close the door.

"Wait, Aunt Fatmeh," I half-whispered. "I really am hungry! Is there any food left over?"

Aunt Fatmeh's grin grew wide enough for me to see her gold tooth. "Look under the bed, *ya* Sami."

Curious, I pulled a tray out from under the bed and uncovered it. It was piled with warm *qedrah*.* Fadia and I sat on the floor and, smiling at each other with relief, we ate.

꧁꧂

FADIA BECAME PREGNANT a few months later. I was both excited and terri-fied. I was still just discovering life myself. How could I guide a child through the world?

At 1 o'clock on a February morning, Fadia woke me up. She was in her seventh month. "Sami, I'm having contractions."

"The baby's not coming for two more months. Go back to sleep," I re-sponded groggily. I rolled over and returned to sleep myself.

My mother shook me awake just before dawn. "Fadia's water broke. She's having the baby!" I woke up, disoriented.

"What? Are you sure?"

"Yes, I'm sure! She's been up all night crying in pain." My mother shook me with more force than she ever had. "What kind of husband are you to be sleeping at a time like this? Take Fadia to the hospital!"

---

*A Palestinian specialty made of rice, meat, and chickpeas, prepared often at large gatherings. *Qedrah* originated in Gaza, according to some, in Hebron according to others.

I sprang into immediate action, calling Fadia's mother to meet us at Herod's Gate. Step by step, I helped Fadia walk through the bitter cold to the gate.

"Take us to Al Makassed!" I shouted to the first taxi driver I saw. He saw Fadia's condition and sped there directly. I jumped out to warn the hospital while Fadia's mother helped Fadia out of the cab. But before they got far, I was gently pushing them back in. "No room in the hospital," I said grimly. "Quickly, to Augusta Victoria!" Augusta Victoria was the refugee hospital. I was not sure whether my UNRWA card was with me, but no matter. They would help us. We reached Augusta Victoria five minutes later, but when they learned that Fadia was only in her seventh month, they also turned us away. "We don't have an incubator here!" the head doctor said firmly. "Go to an Israeli hospital. You are a Jerusalem resident. You'll be covered by Israeli insurance!"

Snow started falling as we reached Bikur Cholim's hospital doors in West Jerusalem. The doctors immediately took Fadia to the delivery room and ushered her mother and me out. I paced the waiting room nervously. What kind of baby would come out after only seven months in the uterus? What if something happened while Fadia was trying to deliver?

It was afternoon and the ground was covered in snow by the time the doctor came out. "You have a baby boy. Would you like to see him?"

"Of course!"

The doctor led Um Fadia and me down the hall. He turned to us. "He weighs less than four pounds," the doctor said gently. "His lungs are not fully formed yet. We're not sure if he will make it. We're going to do everything we can." He opened the door and pointed to a glass box. The baby inside looked like a tiny, bloody kitten, eyes still closed. This was my son?

"God help this baby," Um Fadia murmured under her breath.

I stared at the puny, red, wrinkled creature. *He is not a bloody little cat,* I tried to convince myself. *He is a tiny little mule. Stubborn and tough. He will cling onto life.* But looking at him, I could not imagine how this little thing could possibly survive.

I went to the delivery room where Fadia lay crying in the bed. I sat next to her. "Did you see him?"

"I can't bear to look at him! I'm praying for him. It's all I can do."

The following day, Fadia and I had to choose a name for the baby's birth certificate.

"Let's name him Saber," I suggested, holding Fadia's hand. This was my father's name, meaning "patience."

Fadia wrinkled her nose. "Saber is an old-fashioned name. You've said before that you like the name Nasser. Let's name him Nasser."

Nasser means "the one who helps achieve victory." I nodded slowly. "Okay. Nasser."

The doctor led me to the incubator where Nasser lay. "His life is still hanging by a thread," he warned me.

An agonizing pain pierced my heart when I saw the feeding tube connected to his teeny, red foot. *If he dies,* I prayed, *please don't let him suffer more. He has already suffered so much in his first twenty-four hours.*

After two days, it seemed that my prediction had been right: Nasser was a stubborn little mule. Fadia brought herself to look at him. She smiled at Nasser through swollen eyes. "We have a little boy," she whispered incredulously. "A tiny little red baby boy."

Each day our baby boy grew a little bigger and stronger inside the incubator. Winter melted and spring began to bloom. On the thirty-sixth day, they told us that Nasser's size and weight were stable. His internal organs had completed their development. We could hold him for the first time. We could take him home.

I had never held a newborn before. Though Nasser was much stronger and sturdier than the bloody little kitten I had first laid eyes on, I was scared that the very pressure of my hands might hurt his skinny, small body. I stared into his eyes. "Your suffering is over now, little man," I said to him softly. "You are going to grow up to be big and strong." I never realized I could feel this kind of connection to another human being. This baby in my arms, the baby we almost lost, was a part of Fadia and of me.

We bundled Nasser in blankets to take him home. We proudly walked into the courtyard carrying him. He was still very small. Azzam looked at the bundle of blankets in Fadia's arms. "Where's the baby?" he asked. "Where's Nasser?"

Fadia struggled to care for the needy little guy. I was still terrified that I would break or hurt him when I held him. Fadia's mother and siblings stepped in, showing her how to feed and change the baby, and showering Nasser with love and attention. I adored my baby boy but older children were more interesting to me, I realized quickly; they cried less and could walk and talk.

I had a wife and a baby to support now. My salary at the schools was not enough. I found a job in the produce section of a large supermarket in West

Jerusalem. I tried to keep my prison record secret, but many of my fellow Palestinian workers knew my story. After three months, the Israeli manager called me into his office.

"We have to let you go."

"Why? Has my work not been satisfactory?"

"No, no, you've been fine. But we're making some financial cuts and we're letting the newest workers go first."

Arguing would change nothing. I walked out of the supermarket, passing a worker who had started his job a month after me. But that worker had not spent a decade in prison. Apparently ten years was not punishment enough.

I got on a bus heading straight to City Center. Twenty minutes later, I found myself standing outside the café where I had worked in 1980. I had avoided the restaurant since my release. I finally mustered the courage to enter.

A stranger was behind the counter, making sandwiches. He returned my greeting.

"Do Morris and Reuven still own this place?" I asked tentatively. "Does Galit still work here?" I felt ridiculous asking about Galit. Why would she still be cleaning tables and slicing tomatoes after thirteen years?

The man chopping cucumbers paused for a moment. "Hey!" he called to his coworker in the back. "Those guys from Argentina, do you know where they are?"

"They sold this joint years ago. Maybe they went back to Argentina."

I left, disappointed, wishing I had some way to let Galit, Morris, and Reuven know that I wished them well. That I had always wished them well.

My father sat me down a few weeks later. "Sami, I'm buying you a Ford Transit. Drivers can make good money. You can pay me back from your earnings over time."

Two days later, my father and I walked to the parking lot off Salah El Din Street. There was a beautiful sky-blue, ten-passenger 1990 Ford Transit. He must have been saving up from the day I had been released. I choked over my words when I tried to thank him.

He waved his hand. "Forget it, Sami. Just do something good for your life, for Nasser's future."

The next day, I signed up with the Red Crescent to transport families once a month to visit their relatives in prison. I knew exactly what those visits were like on the prisoners' side of the mesh net—now I was experiencing it from the perspective of the families. The families loved me. I could tell them what life was really like for their loved ones. I represented hope that their sons and brothers would be outside someday soon.

I registered with a taxi office in East Jerusalem. At first, I drove on small trips within Jerusalem. Before long, they gave me my first steady assignment: driving a group of ten construction workers from their homes in Halhoul to their jobs in Asqalan and Isdud.

My father woke Fadia and me up at 4 every morning. Half-asleep, I slipped out of bed, washed my face, and shaved. Fadia made coffee, which I sipped hurriedly as I tied on my boots and grabbed my Transit keys and ID. As Fadia and my father began to pray, I left the house and walked toward Herod's Gate. The predawn air smelled clean. The cats that ruled the Old City at night and guarded its secrets saw me and sensed that their hour of sovereignty was drawing to an end.

The road to Halhoul was empty. The air, which would soon be brutally hot, ran in currents like rivers, fresh and cool. The workers were always waiting for me under the light of the village mosque.

I passed Zakariyya every day but entered only once. The road also passed near Asqalan prison. I always accelerated; I had no desire to linger there.

CHAPTER NINE

I STOPPED TO BUY FALAFEL next to Al Hakawati Theatre in Jerusalem, where I was about to attend a *dabkeh** performance. "Aren't you Sami Al Jundi?" asked a young man behind me in line.

"Yes," I said. He looked familiar, but I was not sure where from.

"My name is Hussam. We were in a few Fatah meetings together. I did some time in Nablus prison. Not as much as you, but a few years."

"Are you going to the performance?"

"No, I work right here." He pointed to a building next to Al Hakawati.

"What's that place?" I didn't see any sign.

"It's the Palestinian Center for the Study of Nonviolence."

"Nonviolence—you mean like Gandhi's White Revolution?"

Hussam smiled. "Yes, something like that. Right now we're strategizing nonviolent ways to resist settlement expansion. You want to come in and take a look around?"

I did—but the *dabkeh* was about to begin. We made plans to meet at the center the next morning.

I told Azzam and Mazin about my appointment as we drank tea late that night. They laughed.

"You're advocating nonviolence now, Sami?" Mazin said. "You, a fighter with the Fatah movement? Come on!"

I tried to defend myself. "Well, Hussam is there and he's also from Fatah. And they're working against settlements. So they're doing something good for our people!"

---

*A traditional Palestinian dance, often performed at weddings.

Azzam filled his cup. "You know what they're doing against the settlements? They plant olive trees on our stolen land! You call that resistance?" He snorted. "Forget about them, Sami."

But I was a free man, and I wanted to decide for myself. The next morning, I walked briskly to the Palestinian Center for the Study of Nonviolence.

Hussam was waiting for me outside. "*Sabah el khair,* Sami!" We walked inside the building and up four flights of stairs. Hussam opened a door and we entered a reception area filled with books. "Sami, I want you to meet Lucy Nusseibeh, our director. Lucy, this is Sami Al Jundi, with the Fatah movement."

Lucy Nusseibeh was tall, glamorous, and blond, and her Arabic had just the slightest trace of a British accent. "You are welcome here, Sami."

Over coffee, Hussam filled me in on the history of the Palestinian Center for the Study of Nonviolence. The center had been founded by Mubarak Awad in 1985. Israel had deported Awad in 1988; he now lived in Washington, D.C. Hussam handed me a booklet from the library shelf. "This is Mubarak's blueprint for direct-action nonviolent resistance against the occupation," he told me.

I read the booklet in bed that night. In order to prevent the army or settlers from taking over land, chain yourselves to one another across the road so army jeeps cannot pass through, Awad wrote, or plant olive trees on the land to create "facts on the ground," the way settlers did with their caravans and outposts. Encourage people to buy Palestinian-made products rather than feeding the Israeli economy. Throw flowers, not stones, at soldiers at demonstrations. Force them to see our humanity. And for those who would call you a coward, remind them that nonviolence does not protect you from the violence of your oppressor. But be stronger than your opponent—do not respond to their violence with your own. The purpose of demonstrating is to communicate to the world: the occupation must end and there must be equal rights for both peoples living in this land. The message will be stronger if it is delivered using nonviolent methods.

The more I read, the more excited I became. Here was a vocabulary to articulate the thoughts and ideas that had percolated in my mind while in prison! Much of the information I had absorbed from the hundreds of books I had read was stored in forgotten corners of my brain. But now, lying in bed next to Fadia, I felt those hidden corners opening. I had encountered all these ideas before, in the writings of ancient Greek philosophers, in Russian literature. Reading about Gandhi and the years it takes to build a soul. I wanted to revisit everything I had read and grappled with during my decade in prison through the prism of nonviolence. Nonviolence was not simply an absence of violence. It could be a way of life.

I went back to the center the next day, and the days and weeks that followed.

On September 13, 1993, Israelis and Palestinians signed the Oslo Accords on the White House lawn. My family and I watched the historic event together on television.

"At last!" My father exhaled slowly as Yasser Arafat and Yitzhak Rabin* shook hands and Bill Clinton smiled in the background. "We will finally be at peace."

I jumped up and dashed out onto the street.

I found Bilal, the leader of my Fatah group, passing out flyers just outside Herod's Gate. He smiled broadly as he handed me an enormous stack.

"*Yallah,* Sami. Hand these out everywhere. But not under cover, like before. No more Intifada! We can operate in the light!"

"The Intifada succeeded!" the paper read. "Our prisoners will soon be released. The PLO will return home. The strike is finished. Put flags on your cars and in your homes. The *shuhada* who were killed, your sons and brothers who were injured or imprisoned, led to this victory! *Mabruk!*"**

I ran through the narrow cobblestone streets of the Old City, pressing a flyer into the hand of every person I saw. I bumped into Azzam outside our house. "Come help me!" I called to him. He ducked inside and grabbed Mazin, Riyyad, and Sa'ed to assist as well.

Everyone took the flyers joyfully, sprinkling us with candies. Shop doors were opened wide and music poured out from the *souq*. People on the street were singing and dancing. Abu Jalal waved his cane wildly in the air. "*Mabruk!*" people called out to each other as we weaved our way through them to distribute more flyers.

I arrived at Damascus Gate and handed the flyer to an old shopkeeper right under the ramparts. He clenched the flyer in his fist and thrust it into the air. "We're free! Our suffering is over! Long live Palestine and a bright future!"

Bloodshed marred that bright future early on. On February 25, 1994, Baruch Goldstein, an American-Israeli who lived in Kiryat Arba, an extreme ideological settlement near Hebron, walked into the Ibrahimi Mosque and

*Prime minister of Israel and chairman of the Labor Party.

**Arabic for "congratulations."

opened fire, gunning down twenty-nine Muslim worshippers and injuring dozens more.

Enraged demonstrations erupted immediately. I was working as a guard for the school I used to clean and could hear the distant sounds of the chanting and gas bombs being shot. A policeman with an Uzi machine gun stood fifty feet from me, next to one of the gates of Haram Al Sharif.

I spotted Abu Ahmad's seventeen-year-old son, Majdi. He had been a toddler when his father and I worked together at the cabinet factory in Deir Yassin; on our morning bus rides, Abu Ahmad used to tell me stories about the mischief Majdi had gotten into the night before.

Majdi was wrapping his face in a *kuffiyeh*, preparing himself to join in the demonstration and throw stones. The policeman aimed his gun. Before I could shout out a warning, deafening cracks filled the air. Majdi fell to the ground. The policeman disappeared. *Shabab* came out of nowhere, arriving at Majdi's fallen body as quickly as I did. There were four bullet holes in his chest. The *shabab* and I carried Majdi to Abu Ahmad's house. Word had arrived just moments before we did. Abu Ahmad was pale as a ghost as we lay his son's body at his feet. He collapsed to his knees, weeping inconsolably. "He was my smartest son," Abu Ahmad managed to say between sobs. "My best boy."

Despite the violence, the peace process continued. The Gaza-Jericho Agreement was signed on May 4, 1994, allowing for the return of the leadership of the PLO, which had been considered essentially a government in exile for twenty years. The newly formed Palestinian Authority would begin its administrative rule in Gaza and Jericho.

As the Authority and 7,000 Palestinian police crossed the Allenby Bridge from Jordan into Jericho, thousands celebrated their return in the streets outside the Old City. Fadia, two-year-old Nasser, and I squeezed onto the steps of Damascus Gate and exchanged joyful congratulations with all who passed by, including the large number of Israeli soldiers stationed outside the Old City.

Bilal and two other Fatah friends bounded down the steps, with large Palestinian flags tucked under their arms. They headed into Damascus Gate. I knew what they were up to.

"I'll be right back," I said to Fadia and dashed inside the gate. I climbed up on the ramparts and met them at the top.

"Sami, take this!" Bilal handed me one of the ten-foot flags. Crouching down, so as not to show our faces, we swung the huge flags over the side of the ramparts, spreading our arms as wide as we could. The first Palestinian flags to legally hang from the walls of the Old City of Jerusalem since 1967— and we had unfurled them! Clapping, cheering, and whistling rose up from the throng below. We grinned at each other. Teenage boys started jumping up on the ramparts.

"Please! Let us hold the flags!" they begged.

They deserved their chance as well. I handed my flag to one boy and scrambled down from the ramparts. Fadia and Nasser were waiting where I had left them.

"Did you see that?" I poked Fadia's arm with excitement. "Did you see those flags that your husband hung?" Fadia had. Everybody had. I grabbed Fadia by the elbow and began to push through the crowd toward my Transit. "*Yallah,* Fadia. We're going to Jericho! We have to welcome our Authority!"

I could smell independence for the first time in my life. I was bursting with pride and joy.

The line of cars, decorated with olive branches and flags, stretched all seventeen miles from Jericho to Jerusalem. We got out of the cars and celebrated on the side of the road.

"Our brothers returned!" a neighbor called to me as I hoisted Nasser onto my shoulders.

"There will be justice for everyone now!" I shouted back.

Our dream of a Palestinian state was turning into a reality before our eyes. Finally we would be able to show the world what Palestinians could achieve!

Israeli soldiers were guarding the entrance to Jericho. We greeted them with smiles, putting flowers and olive branches inside the barrels of their guns. They smiled back. One soldier removed the flower from his gun and poked the stem through the buttonhole of his uniform's pocket. He was about the same age as I had been when I was arrested.

"We hope things will be better for everybody," he said, shaking my hand.

We finally entered Jericho. Fadia and I greeted the Palestinian police— actual Palestinian police! With uniforms and matching gloves and Kalashnikovs! I was nearly jumping out of my skin with euphoria. We stopped the car to pose for pictures with every policeman we saw, enveloping them in jubilant bear hugs after each photo. We were all wiping away tears.

"Welcome home, *habibna.** Welcome home."

*Arabic for "our beloved."

The next morning, I walked past a newsstand on Salah el Din Street. A newspaper caught my eye. There, on the front page, was a photo of Palestinian flags draped over Damascus Gate.

It was really over. Freedom had come. We would be able to speak freely without fear. The violence would end. I smiled, seeing my beautiful city under my flag. Many flags would follow, I knew, but I had hung the first.

⁂

FADIA MADE IT CLEAR that she wanted a sibling for Nasser. Nasser was enough, in my opinion; I could still recall the trauma of his early days. But Fadia wore me down. Nine months later, I held my newly born daughter, Asala, for the first time. As I looked down on her in my arms, she stared right back at me, challenging me from the first moment. I could not imagine why I had ever resisted.

However, with Nasser climbing into everything and a newborn in the house, my longed-for space to read and reflect diminished even more. To Fadia's dismay, I began to spend more and more time at the Center for Nonviolence.

Lucy was taking a coffee break one afternoon. I shared with her my difficulty finding a decent job, now with two children to feed. The next day she approached me, smiling. "Sami, would you like to work part-time with us?"

"Doing what?"

"A variety of things: driving, helping organize activities. Whatever is needed."

"I'd love to!"

Hussam draped his arm around me that afternoon. "I've got my Fatah brother on the inside now!" I was uncomfortable. Hussam wanted me at the center because I was with Fatah, like him. That was no different than the workers' union in Al Makassed only hiring fellow Communist Party members. Hussam was my friend, and now my colleague, but I began to sense that working at the center was a job for him, rather than something he was passionate about.

I was reading at the center when a man with a shaved head, wearing a saffron robe, and carrying a drum walked in.

Hussam jumped up to greet him. "Good to see you, Herokushi! Sami, I want you to meet Herokushi. Herokushi is a Buddhist monk from Japan."

I had met several Japanese tourists in the Old City, but never a Japanese Buddhist monk. In his youth, Herokushi had no intention of becoming a monk, he told me as we drank tea. He had been a hooligan back in Japan, using women for sex, constantly high or drunk. He sank lower and lower until eventually he reached rock-bottom. He realized that he needed to get himself under control and make up for the hurt he had caused his family and friends. He was drawn to Buddhism and eventually became a monk. Tattoos were not permitted for Buddhist monks—his had to be scraped off by a knife. He rolled up his sleeve and showed me the scars on his arms.

Herokushi explained the principles and teachings of Buddhism to me, and I offered information about the conflict—as well as rides home in my Transit. He was the unofficial ambassador for his temple in Japan, and he regarded supporting a nonviolent struggle for equality and justice as part of his mission. Herokushi chain-smoked as we talked, each in our broken English, about how to best support the Oslo process. We occasionally went out for a beer in the evenings. Neither smoking nor drinking was permitted for Buddhist monks, but those transgressions were tolerated in Herokushi's case. He enjoyed the "bad boy" reputation he had in his temple.

Herokushi walked into the center one cold day. He had an idea. A march to show support for Oslo, starting in Jenin in the north West Bank all the way south to Hebron, nearly one hundred miles!

"Imagine," he said, "walking through dozens of villages, towns, and refugee camps, how many people will be reached by our message!" Herokushi was ready to walk from Jerusalem to Japan if it would have an impact. His commitment and enthusiasm were contagious. Lucy and Hussam asked me to help organize the march.

I solidified the route quickly, arranging with locals where we would stay each night. The participants gathered at the center two weeks later. In addition to Herokushi, there was a professor from Austria and one from Germany, a female Dutch Buddhist monk, two other British Buddhist monks, two more women from Japan, and two Americans, one of whom was a religious Jew. It bothered me that I was the only Palestinian participating. I had contacted many Palestinian NGOs and institutes, but most of the people I had talked to laughed at the idea. As we rode to Jenin, I pledged to myself that I would serve all of the participants with the same dedication they were bringing to this march.

We staged a big parade throughout Jenin late that afternoon. The monks beat their large drums with wooden sticks. All of us chanted the Japanese Buddhist mantra the monks had taught us on the Transit: "*Nam Myoho Renge Kyo!*"

A police colonel in Jenin had invited us to spend the night in his training camp, converted from its former use as an Israeli prison. We rose at 6 a.m. and ate the breakfast the colonel had organized for us. It was a beautiful day. The lush green farmland and the distant mountains of Nazareth were visible in the sunrise. The colonel lined his officers up. We marched between the rows of police, beating the drums and chanting while the policemen clapped and chanted with us, and we were on our way.

We marched through village after village that morning, people gathering at the side of the road to clap with us as we chanted and drummed. Kids trailed after us, laughing and imitating our chanting. I explained our mission to the onlookers, so we would be regarded as more than an entertaining spectacle. People in cars waved to us. The same buses and cabs passed us repeatedly, the drivers honking and calling out words of support. The drivers told their passengers about us. They were our only media.

The road climbed up, up, gradually but steadily for twelve miles, until we reached Silat al-Dhaher, a large, sleepy village that hugged the mountain. This was the highest point of our climb. Silat al-Dhaher was covered with olive, fig, pomegranate, and apricot trees. Children picked fruit straight from the trees, dashing to the side of the road to offer it to us. The village mosque, famous in all of Palestine for its long minaret, called to us. There was not a cloud in the afternoon sky. We gazed over the valleys of orchards and fields and could see the Mediterranean and the coast: Hadera, Netanya, Tel Aviv. Old women met us with trays of soft drinks and a restaurant owner gave us falafel. We still had hours to walk that day, but after Silat al-Dhaher, the winding road sloped gently down.

I fantasized about my soft, cozy bed as we neared Sabastiyah, our destination for the night. We had been marching for ten hours. But my fatigue melted away when Sabastiyah's hillside of ancient ruins came into view. The ruins dated back 10,000 years and represented a cross-section of every culture that had lived on this land, from Canaan to Byzantine. The stones were bathed in the golden light of the setting sun, transforming the archaeological ruins into a majestic work of art. The smell of fresh earth filled my nostrils, mixed with the aroma of lemons and jasmine from the surrounding trees and plants. There were olive trees everywhere.

Dozens of people from modern-day Sabastiyah met us on the road outside the village, cheering and clapping as we approached. Hundreds more received us in a big meeting room, where a large dinner had been prepared. The room was quivering with silent anticipation, as men and women of all ages waited for us to talk.

"Our march is to support your peaceful struggle for freedom," the German professor explained as I translated. "The Oslo Accords were signed because of your suffering and sacrifice during the Intifada and now you are on the road toward independence, a democratic government, and the full end of occupation! The fruit of Oslo needs our support so it can be harvested!"

The words were absorbed by the residents of Sabastiyah like dry, parched earth receiving a long-awaited downpour.

After dinner we held communal prayers for all the faiths that were present: Muslim, Buddhist, Jewish, and Christian, reading prayers for peace found in each faith's holy books. We gave a necklace made of 1,000 origami doves to the village council. Herokushi showed the children how to make their own. They fashioned hundreds of the peace bird with bright, colorful thin paper that we had carried, Herokushi bundling them together to start a new necklace.

We slept in homes on mats and blankets. As soon as I lay my aching body down, I fell into a deep sleep.

Nearly the entire village assembled at the main square at 7 a.m. to see us off with waves and cheers. Dozens of the villagers walked several kilometers with us. They blanketed us with respect as deep as Sabastiyah was old.

We headed toward Nablus on a pleasant, winding side road that climbed past orchards, fields, and small villages. A few kilometers before we reconnected with the main road, we passed an intimidating chain-link fence topped with barbed wire. It was imposing, ugly, and entirely out of place in these lovely hills dotted with inviting villages. Inside the fence were large concrete blocks and towers. This was Dan Shomron, a combined Israeli settlement and army base. Any Palestinian arrested in the vicinity was brought to Dan Shomron and from here, transferred to prison. Dan Shomron was feared in this area the way children are terrified of monsters.

"*Nam Myoho Renge Kyo!*" we shouted even louder, the monks beating their drums with an extra reserve of strength. We wanted to be heard by the settlers and soldiers who caused so much fear and then hid behind fortified fences. We wanted them to know that the time for peace had come.

We continued marching, plied with food and drink by every village we passed. I was eager to reach Nablus. Imagine the size and momentum our peace march would gather once we reached the big city! But as we entered Nablus, passing huge mansions nestled into the hillsides, we felt like strangers. The few people who had gathered by the side of the road weren't clapping or cheering. They were looking at us as if we were crazy. Some of them jeered at us outright. "What are these idiots doing?" one man commented to his wife as we passed.

I had spoken to many Nabulsis* while planning the march. Those with the mansions on the hills had said they did not have space to accommodate us. Finally, I had reached out to contacts in Balata refugee camp, on the southern outskirts of Nablus. They had agreed enthusiastically to host us.

We turned off the main, wide street into Balata. Here, the roads were narrow and dirty. The homes were small and overcrowded. There was not a single tree. I could smell the poverty and touch the festering anger in the camp.

There was a feast for us inside the home of Hussam Khader's family.** Everyone surrounded us eagerly, the children making colorful origami doves and the youth and adults talking to us with excitement about the new Palestinian Authority and the peace process.

The people in Balata gave us a warm send-off the next morning, as we marched and chanted, *"Nam Myoho Renge Kyo!"* But as soon as we reached the main Nablus–Ramallah road adjacent to the camp, we felt alone again. I now understood why we were spurned in the city and welcomed in the refugee camp. It was not the mansion dwellers who had participated in our struggle. Their children had not been imprisoned, injured, or killed during the Intifada. Their homes had not been demolished as a form of collective punishment. It was youth from impoverished refugee camps like Balata who had paid the price to bring Oslo. I had never touched the divisions between village and city, city and refugee camp, elite and poor, as I was doing now.

We walked directly into the early morning sun, hugged by its warmth and glow. We passed old men and women in traditional Palestinian dress riding on donkeys, carrying sheep cheese to sell in Nablus. The area was famous for its cheese because of the plentiful verdant grass on which to graze the sheep. The road leading to Huwwara village was surrounded by fields planted with golden corn and rippling wheat. An army base rose from the middle of the fields. I pointed to it. "Someday soon, that army base will be gone and the wheat and corn will cover all this area!" I said to the Dutch Buddhist monk.

High on a distant hill, we could see the red rooftops of Elon Moreh. It was while protesting the construction of Elon Moreh that Mahmoud Al Kurd, the BodyBuilding Champion of the West Bank, had been killed. I tried not to

*People from Nablus.

**Hussam Khader was a lead organizer in Balata at the beginning of the Intifada. He was deported by the Israeli army to south Lebanon in 1988.

look at it. Instead, I focused on the hilly fields and the farmers and shepherds who paused to wave at us. The road climbed up, up, up to Turmus'aya village, on the top of a high hill, surrounded by ancient, beautiful olive trees.

There was another big dinner for us in Turmus'aya. Speeches were made by community leaders about their hope to achieve freedom and peace. The villagers treated us as if we were that hope, dropping on them from the sky. By the end of the evening, we had hundreds of new, brightly colored doves to add to the necklace.

The next day, we walked to Ramallah. In the villages and refugee camps on the outskirts of the city, we were greeted graciously. In Ramallah, we were treated with mockery, if we were noticed at all. This time, however, we were expecting it.

From Ramallah, we walked to Jerusalem. Faisal Husseini, the Palestinian Authority minister for Jerusalem affairs, greeted us personally outside the Orient House.* "It's wonderful that you came all this way for the sake of justice and peace for the Palestinian people," he said to a small crowd. "We hope in the future, people can come and walk all over this land without any fear." We proudly presented to Husseini the necklace of 1,000 origami doves made by children from Sabastiyah, Balata camp, and Turmus'aya.

From Jerusalem, we continued southeast. The weather had been beautiful until now, but as we walked through Abu Dis, a cold rain pelted us. When we reached the top of Wadi Nar,** the rain mixed with snow. We sang to keep our spirits high as we walked slowly and carefully through the slush-covered road, the monks beating the drums to keep us stepping in unison. The smell of wet grass rose up to greet us from the sides of the steep road, which wound like a snake down to Wadi Nar and back up the other side to Beit Sahour. Sun peeked out from the clouds, through the intermittent rain and snow.

We were greeted again with celebrations in Bethlehem. The road from Bethlehem to Hebron was lined with villages and refugee camps—Dheisheh, Arroub, Halhoul. We were received warmly at all of them. The Hebron mountains were high, and the cold was biting. We arrived in Hebron in the late afternoon and held a press conference and a parade on the steps of the Ibrahimi Mosque, where the Goldstein massacre had occurred. Israeli soldiers watched us drum and chant from a small distance, their arms draped

*The PLO headquarters in Jerusalem.
**Arabic for "Fire Valley."

arrogantly over their M16s. Though our march was celebrating an approaching era of freedom, democracy, and peace, most of the West Bank and Gaza
were still under Israeli military control. The occupation was not over yet.

I came to the center a few days before Christmas. A group of volunteers was
getting ready to leave with Hussam.

"What's going on?" I asked.

"We're on our way to Dheisheh camp. The last Israeli jeeps just pulled out.
They're tearing down the fence. You want to come?"

The main Jerusalem–Hebron road passed directly by Dheisheh refugee
camp and was used regularly by Israeli soldiers and settlers. Youth from
Dheisheh had often pelted army vehicles or settlers' cars with stones and, occasionally, Molotov cocktails. The Israeli military had responded first by
blockading entrances to the camp and then by erecting a twelve-foot-high,
thick metal fence. By 1987, the entire length of Dheisheh camp, a full kilo-
meter, had been cordoned off from the main road. There was only one gate
in the fence, a turnstile controlled by soldiers.

I had first seen the fence while visiting my family from Zakariyya just
weeks after my release from prison. The sight of it had filled me with anger
and sadness. The entire refugee camp had been made into a prison.

Of course I wanted to help tear down the fence.

We arrived at Dheisheh and joined the growing crowd. Based on the array
of languages I was hearing, internationals from many countries had joined
us. To my surprise and delight, there were Hebrew-speakers as well. A few
shabab from the camp grasped the thick chain links and began to rattle them
tentatively. The fence swayed just a bit.

"If soldiers see us, they'll shoot us for sure," one middle-age woman muttered. A few others within earshot glanced around furtively as if they didn't
truly believe that the army was no longer inside Bethlehem.

A tall, muscular Italian woman stepped out of the group, grabbed hold of
the fence, and shook it forcefully. "Shake! Shake! Shake!" she shouted, each
word accompanied by a powerful thrust of her arms. The fence began to
sway violently. The *shabab* from the camp looked at each other in disbelief.
A foreigner was taking the first bold step? And a woman at that! We jumped
to the fence as if a fire had been lit under us and began shaking it with all
our collective might, shouting, "*Allahu Akbar!*" at the top of our lungs. We
were tearing down the very infrastructure of occupation! I caught the eyes
of people I knew from Zakariyya and smiled. I was proud to be here, to be a

part of the Adawi family from Zakariyya. I was proud to be a part of opening the way for residents of Dheisheh to taste their freedom. Within ten minutes, our section of the abominable cage came crashing down. Only the turnstile remained. The crowd lurched toward the gate to rip it out of the earth as well, but a member of the camp's organizing committee stepped in front of it.

"The turnstile remains," he said, "as a reminder."

CHAPTER TEN

⟪⟫

I EXPECTED THE FLEDGLING AUTHORITY to call meetings with all those who had been the grassroots organizers during the Intifada, those who had carried the streets. A few were invited to join the new Palestinian security apparatus, but most were ignored. We knew money was pouring into the Authority from the European Union and rich Arab countries, but we saw very little evidence of it being used to help the people. Some of those who had come from Tunisia, however, seemed to have the resources to build themselves grand mansions. The Authority was still very young, I told myself when these concerns of corruption arose. We needed to have patience.

Asim, my cell mate from Beer Al-Sabe', began working with the Authority. I met him for coffee one morning in Ramallah. Getting there was not as easy as it had been. I used to drive directly from Jerusalem to Ramallah without stopping. Now there were two new checkpoints I had to pass. Why were Israeli blockades being added when the West Bank and Gaza were supposed to be transitioning into an independent Palestinian state? The new checkpoints were often nowhere near the Green Line, but deep inside the West Bank. Traveling to, from, and within the West Bank began to grow more difficult.

"Sami, I have good news," Asim told me when I arrived. "There's a job waiting for you working with the police!"

I was vaguely interested. "What kind of job?"

It was to interrogate people arrested for criminal acts.

I had too much experience with interrogation already. Today I might be asked to interrogate criminals, but tomorrow I could be required to interrogate people arrested for political reasons. No matter how you looked at it, it was an ugly practice.

"No thanks. I'll stay a civilian."

"Sami, come and meet Peter Weinberger," Hussam called to me as I entered the center one day. Peter and I shook hands. "He's an American studying at Hebrew University for his spring semester of college. He's going to volunteer with us while he's here."

Peter and Hussam continued to talk as I made myself a cup of coffee. I glanced over at them now and then, trying to size up this youthful new member of our team. Peter had unruly blond hair and his brown eyes seemed earnest as Hussam told him about our activities. It was not until he stood up that I saw how short he was.

"I've got to get home now," Peter said in English. "I'll come by tomorrow after class."

"Do you want a ride home?" I asked Peter in my still-limited English. I did not understand his response.

"Do you speak Hebrew?" Peter asked me, and when I nodded yes, he switched to Hebrew. "Thanks for the offer, but it would be completely out of your way."

"I don't mind at all. It would be my pleasure."

We got in my Transit. "Where did you learn Hebrew, Peter?"

"I spent a few summers traveling in Israel through the American Zionist Federation. I learned some Hebrew there, volunteering on a kibbutz. And now I'm studying Hebrew in university."

"So you're Jewish?"

"Yes." Peter gave me a sideways glance. "Is that a problem?"

"No, of course not! But I'm curious: how did spending summers with the American Zionist Federation lead you to working with us at the Palestinian Center for the Study of Nonviolence?"

Peter's voice was quiet and slow, as if he were evaluating each word. "As a kid, my Jewish identity was really connected to Israel. When I was a teenager, I read some books by Kahane. They appealed to me."

I interrupted in shock. "Kahane? Are you a Kach supporter?" Meir Kahane was the ultranationalist American-Israeli rabbi who founded Kach, an extreme right-wing Israeli political party, now illegal. Kach endorsed the idea of a "Greater Israel" and called for the ethnic cleansing of Palestinians from the West Bank and Gaza. Baruch Goldstein, the perpetrator of the Ibrahimi Mosque massacre, had been a Kach supporter.

"I don't support Kach any longer! I never really did . . . I only flirted with the ideology. Look, I was an awkward, scared, angry kid in high school. Militant Zionism spoke to my feelings of isolation. But I realized pretty soon that Kahane is all based in anger, and that wasn't what I was looking for. By the time I made my second trip, my political views had already shifted to the left, though I still had a romanticized view of Israel and Zionism."

We spent the rest of the drive talking about what Peter knew about Zionism—both the Kahane extreme ideology and more mainstream expressions.

Over the next weeks, Peter rode with me often. I would drive him home via meandering, dilapidated West Bank roads.

"Why are these roads so crappy?" Peter asked me once.

"They're from before 1967," I told him. "The only new roads in the West Bank are for settlers."

We joked and laughed constantly on those rides. Peter was a goofy kid of twenty and I was still making up for lost time. I spent many evenings drinking beer at restaurants with Hussam, Peter, and other internationals who passed through the center.

Fadia was angry that I was out so much. "Why do you spend all your time with foreigners?" she demanded. "The kids and I need you at home."

"Why don't you come with me and meet my friends?"

Fadia shook her head disapprovingly. "You know I won't go places where beer is served. Especially not if you're drinking it!"

I knew I was not the husband that Fadia deserved. I loved her as much as ever, but we were different in so many ways. I was not willing to curtail my freedom for anyone's sake. I realized I was being selfish, but I continued to spend time with Peter and my other new friends.

I introduced Peter to the famous Arabic oud player, Marcel Khalife. He popped in cassettes of reggae greats, translating their Jamaican English to Hebrew. I fell in love with Peter Tosh.

We talked about women.

"The girls love you, Sami," Peter remarked ruefully one day. "They don't even give me a second look. I'm too short."

I tried to reassure him that girls liked him, too. But he got embarrassed and blushed often when talking to girls. Not that it really mattered, he always insisted. He had a girlfriend back home to whom he was resolved to stay faithful.

"I hate my ears," he said one day out of the blue. "Sami, do you think people can tell that I'm Jewish from my ears?"

Peter winked and we both burst out laughing. It was impossible not to be fond of Peter.

Late one night, on the way back to Jerusalem from a village south of Hebron, I realized that we had never finished the conversation we had started
that first ride.

"So what is it exactly that made you come here, Peter?"

As always, Peter thought carefully before speaking. "If there's something
that I don't know, then I need to learn about it. There's a lot I don't know
about the Palestinian reality. So I came here to learn."

I pressed him further. "But how did you go from an interest in Kach to
even wondering about our situation?"

"I read a poem."

I was amazed. "A poem inspired you to understand our side of the story?
Which poem?"

"It's by Mahmoud Darwish. It's called 'Identity Card' in English."

Identity was not yet in my English lexicon. "Can you tell me some lines of
the poem in Hebrew?"

"It began something like . . . *Katav, katav, ani aravi . . .*"

That was all I needed to hear. I jumped in and recited the entire poem in its
original Arabic, "Write down! I am an Arab," until the last of the six stanzas:

> *Write down, then,*
> *at the top of Page One:*
> *I do not hate*
> *and I do not steal.*
> *Starve me,*
> *and I will eat my assailant's flesh.*
> *Beware of my hunger*
> *and of my anger.*

Peter was silent for a moment when I finished. "It's a very powerful poem,"
he finally said quietly. "I wanted to understand the subtext behind this
poem."

Peter told me that after encountering the Darwish poem, he began a
search that led him to the D.C.-based NGO Nonviolence International,
founded by the same peace activist who had founded our center, Mubarak
Awad.

"I was intrigued by the idea of a nonviolent Palestinian movement," Peter
said. "I realized—maybe there's more to this other narrative than I was willing to accept. So when I decided to spend a semester in Jerusalem, I wanted
to get involved with your center. There's a lot to experience here that I can't
learn from an office in D.C."

From that moment, I made it my personal mission to show Peter all the aspects of the conflict that he had never had the opportunity to witness. I took him around the Old City and all over the West Bank. I pointed out sites of religious, historical, and political significance. I shared with him my personal connection to many of the places. What conclusions he drew would be up to him.

"You see this settlement?" I pointed to a cluster of red rooftops nestled atop a nearby hillside. "It was expanded after Oslo was signed." Fifteen minutes later, along the same curvy road, "This one too—built after Oslo."

"Why do you keep pointing out the settlement construction after Oslo?" Peter always asked me a lot of questions.

I tried to measure my words the way Peter measured his. "Oslo was supposed to pave the way for a two-state solution. But instead, it seems to be paving more and more settlements, eating up the land that should be for our state."

It was not just Israel that was to blame, I explained to Peter, but our own leadership as well. The Authority was now doing Israel's dirty work for them, detaining those whom Israel demanded. Palestinians with high-level positions were benefiting from the further entrenchment of the occupation. Companies owned by Authority officials sold cement to Israel to build new settlement housing units.

Peter was fascinated by the reading I had done in prison.

"What was the most influential book you read?" Peter asked me one afternoon as we were stuck in traffic. It was difficult to isolate just one.

"A book about two Persian philosophers, Mani and Mazdak," I finally answered. "Mani lived around the year 250. He spoke about a conflict in every human between the soul—which represents light, good—and the earthly body, which is dark, evil. Though Mani acknowledged that every human being had both, the light and the dark did not mix, like oil and water. According to Mani, it was easy to differentiate good from bad.

"Mazdak came around 250 years later. Mazdak agreed with Mani that humans have both a dark side and a light side. But they don't coexist separately, like oil and water; they're mixed together like water and wine. You can't distinguish them easily. It is only through our actions that we can hope to free our light. Our responsibility is to behave in ways that will help us find our light. We have to serve the light."

Peter chewed on that for a few minutes. "Do you believe in that?"

"I do," I answered. "But our job is bigger than serving our own light."

"How so?"

"Everyone else has light and darkness inside them. Even the darkest heart always has some small point of light. We have to help them find their light also. And then it will grow. This is the essence of nonviolence. Not to fight the person, but to fight the darkness in his heart. The only way to do this is through growing his light."

"What about soldiers? What about settlers?"

"I try not to hate the settlers—I hate what they're doing," I told him. "Burning our farms, uprooting our trees, taking our land . . . it's their actions we have to work against. Same thing with soldiers. Or with Palestinians who use violence. The only way to change their behavior is if we're willing to talk to each other. To build respect for each other as human beings."

"Some of the settlers I've met . . . I can see the hatred in their eyes. How can you talk to someone who hates you so much?"

"They were educated to hate. Did you know that one small settlement uses enough water for ten Palestinian villages?" Peter shook his head mutely. "Most settlers don't know that either. They get an extreme education. They're being taught to hate Palestinians. This whole region needs to undergo reeducation."

Peter looked at me in disbelief. "You learned all this in prison?"

"I first read about Mani and Mazdak in prison. But it's only been since I discovered the Center for Nonviolence that I started to understand what it meant."

Peter Weinberger made me hopeful. Here was a Jewish-American young man who had started out immersing himself in Zionist ideology who was now actively working for peace with justice. I wished that I could take credit for Peter's transformation, but the credit belonged to Peter only. He came on his own to Mubarak Awad and then to us because he wanted to discover the reality for himself. Peter had found his own light.

Lucy had a new task for me. "Sami, there are seven professors here from Norway and Sweden. They want to understand the settlement expansion. I want you to show them what's going on."

I greeted the professors the next morning and led them to my Ford Transit.

"Let's start in the Bethlehem area," I told them. I wanted them to see an expansion of a settlement, still under construction. There were no homes yet on the newly expropriated land, just a few caravans perched on the hilltops. I guided the Transit up a narrow dirt road hugging the side of the steep hill so they could get an up-close look.

We saw a young man on the top of the hill operating an enormous bull-dozer. I guessed he was about nineteen years old. A second one, even younger, was standing guard with an Uzi machine gun.

"What's that bulldozer doing?" a professor asked. "Does that belong to the IDF?"

"This isn't an army bulldozer. It belongs to the settlers. It's smoothing over the land where the trees were cut, to flatten it for more containers." I pointed at the pile of olive trees and Mediterranean medlars lying on their sides, their roots exposed. "You see that? This used to be the village's trees."

Just then the teenage guard spotted us. He waved the Uzi wildly, scream-ing, "Get the hell out of here!" The armed teenager shouted something to the bulldozer driver, cocked the gun, and pointed it at the Transit. The bulldozer began to advance on us quickly, the youth still training his Uzi directly at our heads. The bulldozer made no signs of stopping. There was no time to turn around.

"Back up, Sami, quickly!" one of the Swedish professors yelled, but I was already gunning the Transit down the edge of the steep hill in reverse as fast as I possibly could, the bulldozer advancing even faster, until its shovel was less than six feet from my face. The professors in the car were screaming. Halfway down the hill, the bulldozer stopped chasing us. I safely navigated the rest of the dirt road in reverse, turning around when we got to the bot-tom and driving away as fast as I could accelerate.

It was only when we were back on the main Bethlehem–Jerusalem road that the pounding of my heart subsided. That bulldozer could have easily flipped my Transit over the side of the hill into the valley below. What if I had gotten those professors killed?

"Take us straight back to Jerusalem, Sami, please," one of the professors said, his face ashen.

The other professors sat silently, their eyes as huge as those of a beaver.

"How was it?" Lucy asked us as we entered the center half an hour later.

"Well," said a Swede, "we now know the meaning of 'settlers,' that's for sure!"

"Thank God for Sami," another said, patting me on the back. "He saved our lives."

We got a call from a group of Israelis from Peace Now. Settlers from Shiloh had spent the entire night cutting down 3,000 olive trees belonging to the village Turmus'aya. The villagers had discovered the trees in the morning.

The Israelis wanted to respond. "What do you think if together we raise money for the village to purchase new olive trees?" they asked me. I thought it was a fantastic idea. The people of Turmus'aya would feel supported and would know that some Israelis were against settler behavior. Most important, they would be able to replant new trees. Within a week, we had raised the money that we needed. Lucy contacted the village council in Turmus'aya to set up a visit. Five Israelis from Peace Now met me at the center and we drove there together.

The village council had prepared lunch for us, thanking us for coming. The food was delicious, but the atmosphere was heavy, like a home that had lost a *shaheed*.

After there was nothing but thick black mud left in our *fanajeen*,* Bassem, the head of the village council, finally asked, "Now what can we do for you?"

One of the Israelis spoke for the group. "When settlers behave in these despicable ways, it also hurts Israelis who are committed to peace. We came today because we want to stand in solidarity with you. We came also because we want to help you buy and plant new olive trees." She placed a large envelope in front of Bassem.

Bassem looked at the envelope, scratching his chin. Finally he said, "The only one who can accept this gift is Abu Kassab. Abu Kassab is the oldest man in Turmus'aya. He has spent his entire life tending his trees. He knows these trees like nobody else. He is sitting on the land now. We will respect whatever he decides."

Bassem led us toward the olive tree groves on the mountain behind the village. Shiloh was visible as we walked, its red roofs perched on the next hilltop.

We rounded a corner. I stopped in my tracks. A soft moan escaped the lips of the Israeli woman next to me. "Those bastards," she cursed under her breath.

The Deir Yassin massacre was in front of me. Trunks and branches were strewn everywhere, like torsos, arms, and legs. Three thousand young trees, old trees, trees in the prime of their lives. Three thousand murdered olive trees.

Bassem pointed to an old man sitting under one remaining olive tree at the edge of the destruction. "This is Abu Kassab," he told us. "You can offer him your gift."

---

*Plural of *finjan*, the small cup used to drink Turkish coffee.

We approached Abu Kassab tentatively. His head was covered with a white *kuffiyeh* and he wore the traditional *qumbaz* closed with a wide belt. The creases in his face were as deep as if they had been plowed by a tractor. The old man sat hunched over on a small rock, staring blankly where his orchard had been.

"*Assalamu 'alaikum,* Grandfather," I said hesitantly.

Only then did Abu Kassab look up, noticing our presence. "*Wa 'alaikum Assalaam,*" he said to return my greeting, pushing himself to a standing position with the help of his walking stick. He began talking in Arabic, pausing so I could translate his words into Hebrew. "My father and I planted many of these trees. Others were planted by my grandfather or great-grandfather. I have a story about every single one." He hobbled to a large gnarled tree, lying on its side. "This tree had my grandfather's name. It was planted by my great-grandfather in honor of his son's birth." Abu Kassab tapped another tree gently with his stick. "This one was for me, when I was born." Abu Kassab shuffled a few steps and bent down, touching the trunk of another smaller tree. "This tree carried the name of my youngest son. I planted it myself the day he was born." He stroked the bark of his son's tree as tears made their way down his weathered face, finding their path through the furrows and creases.

"*Ya haj,* there is hope to plant olive trees here again. We would like to offer you funds for 3,000 new trees. We would like to help you plant them on your land."

Abu Kassab seemed not to have heard. "I hope you have been treated well here, my son. Did you and your friends have lunch? Were you served coffee?"

"Yes, *ya haj,* everyone has been very kind to us."

"Good. I'm glad to hear that." The old man paused, his fingers pressing a rubbery green leaf. "Now, please, keep your money. I cannot accept this gift."

"But why? You can use this to plant new trees . . ."

"We can plant trees again with our own money. Our problem is not money." Abu Kassab carefully lowered himself back onto the rock. "The Israelis who are with you . . . please thank them for me, my son. Please tell them . . . this is not something personal."

We understood it was time for us to leave. Bassem and the villagers guided us back to the Transit, leaving Abu Kassab alone with the remains of his trees.

I THOUGHT ABOUT ABU KASSAB for days. The old man in Turmus'aya had put his humanity, homeland, and self-respect above money. Lessons like that could not be learned in school. Nasser was almost four years old and Asala was a toddler. It was not too early to begin to educate them about their homeland, their people, and their identity. I began to take them all over the Old City, showing them the holy places, telling them stories about the larger history and my personal history. I took them to the Jewish Quarter and showed them where my old house used to be. I took them in my Transit to Hebron, Jericho, Ramallah. I drove past Deir Yassin and Zakariyya with them, pointing out their grandparents' villages. I was worried about their future, growing up in the middle of the conflict. But at least I could prepare them by making sure they knew who they were and where they came from.

I was thrilled about the upcoming elections. January 1996 would be the first opportunity in history for the Palestinian people to select our own government! After the elections, the Palestinian Authority would be a legitimate, democratically elected government.

The Center for Nonviolence established a Democracy Center to hold lectures and panel discussions throughout the West Bank. We offered opportunities to hear from the parliamentary candidates and to participate in discussions about the institutions of democracy or the role of women in a democratic society. But, like our march through the West Bank, the meetings in cities were poorly attended. The events in villages and refugee camps were filled with people eager to learn. By helping to educate on the issues around our new democracy, I was doing something enormous for my people.

But the prospects for our bright future continued to grow bleaker as checkpoints and settlements mushroomed and violence continued unabated. Negotiations with Israel had led only to a harshening of occupation and a hardening of anti–peace process sentiment. The voices of extremism on both sides were gaining strength. The November 4, 1995, murder of Israeli Prime Minister Yitzhak Rabin by an Israeli Jew revealed the deep hatred taking root among Israelis. Movements like PFLP and Hamas railed against Oslo at every opportunity, and they were finding a widening audience, even at our town hall meetings.

"The elections grow out of the Oslo Accords, and Oslo is nothing but a ruse to let the Zionists take over our homeland!" a Hamas activist stood up and shouted.

Fatah supporters argued back staunchly, "You have to trust Abu Ammar! We'll get our homeland with the 1967 borders, we'll get East Jerusalem, our refugees will return . . ."

"You're lying to your own people! Besides, democracy does not grow out of Islam! We need *shari'a** law!"

Not all meetings went like that. We brought female Palestinian activists to Doma, the most isolated village I had ever been to. From the twisty, tiny mountain road that led to Doma, I could see the Jordan Valley with the lush green ribbon indicating the river, and the mountains of Jordan beyond. The village was very small and impeccably clean. There was not even a cigarette butt on the road. Teachers from the school greeted us and led us to a small room next to the auditorium to serve us refreshments. Everything was silent as we ate the snacks and drank soft drinks. "I hope a few people will show up," I whispered to one of the activists as we got ready to enter the silent lecture hall.

The teacher opened the door to the hall. The auditorium was entirely packed with men and women who had been sitting there the entire time, waiting silently. When we entered, they stood up and began clapping for the speakers. The female activists began their presentations about the significance of women's participation in the upcoming elections. I wished I could sit among the villagers rather than in the front with the presenters. I would have been proud to be one of them. The people of Doma listened attentively and, after the presentation, dozens of hands were raised with thought-provoking questions and comments. What kind of instruction about democracy or nonviolence could we offer these people? They had a much deeper lesson to offer us, about true respect and engagement. The presenters and I were humbled.

January 20, 1996, was election day. Fadia and I left our home early that morning to cast our votes at the boys' school in A-Ram, on the outskirts of Jerusalem. We were still under Israeli military control; the power of the Palestinian Legislative Council (PLC) would be severely curtailed. But I smiled as I cast my ballot. We were taking the first step on a long road.

I knew many of the newly elected Parliament members from prison and from my work at the center. I received a call one day. "Sami, we need to bring

*The canonical law of Islam.

delegates from Gaza to Ramallah for Council meetings from time to time. Can you help us?"

Helping our new democracy get on its feet—this was cleaner than inter- rogating criminals, as Asim had originally offered me. I agreed immediately.

My tasks would include shuttling Legislative Council members back and forth from Gaza to Ramallah and serving as an administrative assistant at the Council sessions themselves, arranging logistics for hotels and meeting venues. I reported to my first day of work eagerly. But after several weeks, I began to dread the Council sessions. There was rhetoric about brotherhood and equality, but the hierarchy was clear: I was the lowest on the totem pole. If the members of Parliament treated me as a lowly driver, then how much did they really care about ordinary Palestinian people?

I was also disillusioned with what I observed inside the sessions. Political parties, including my own, were voting as blocs, unconditionally supporting anything that was raised by a fellow party member. What kind of burgeon- ing, vibrant, democratic process was that? I quit after two months.

⁂

MURIEL AND ISABELLE, both Jews originally from France, came frequently to the center to have coffee with Hussam and me. Isabelle was a puppeteer and learned about us while participating at a workshop at Al Hakawati The- atre. I had met Israelis from Peace Now during demonstrations and direct actions. But that was different than our getting to know each other person- ally. I did not feel like a Palestinian talking to Israelis. I was Sami, talking to Isabelle and Muriel. It felt good. Muriel and Isabelle were also excited by our growing friendship.

"Let's take this a step further!" Muriel declared one day. "Let's start a real group dialogue. Saturday night, I invite you to my apartment. My friends have never spoken face-to-face with a Palestinian. All they know is what they see on the news. They would be thrilled to have the chance to meet you and talk to you."

Hussam and I exchanged a quick glance. "Let Sami and I talk it over," Hus- sam said. "We'll let you know tomorrow."

Hussam and I deliberated. Going to an Israeli's home to talk with her friends—would this be "normalization"? Fatah strongly discouraged any ac- tions or relationships that reinforced the stranglehold status quo of the oc- cupation. Social relations with Israelis were viewed as exactly that. On the other hand, there was no problem partnering with Israelis who were working against the occupation. And how else would more and more Israelis be convinced to join our struggle if they did not know us and understand our situation?

"Let's give it a try for a meeting or two," I finally suggested. "We can see if this is something serious, or if it's just about having fun."

That Saturday evening, Hussam and I drove to Muriel's home in West Jerusalem. We climbed the stairs to her third-floor apartment slowly, careful not to talk to each other in Arabic. We had heard that this was an extreme neighborhood.

Muriel was waiting for us at the door.

"Welcome, Hussam, Sami! We're so glad you came!" Isabelle was standing next to Muriel and, sensing our hesitation, she pulled us into the room and offered us drinks and snacks. Muriel had arranged chairs in a circle. Other guests trickled in. In addition to five of Muriel's Israeli friends, there were two other Palestinians whom Isabelle had met through her connection with Al Hakawati.

We sat awkwardly for a moment until Muriel suggested we introduce ourselves around the circle. She began.

"My name is Muriel, I'm French-Israeli, and this is my apartment. I'm a psychologist and am very interested in art and theatre."

Isabelle went next, introducing herself as a secular French Jew who was passionate about her work in puppetry and children's theatre.

The man sitting to my right went next. "My name is Edgar. I'm an Algerian French Jew, and an *oleh hadash*.* I work with an NGO to help former prisoners acclimate again to society."

It was my turn. "Funny you mention your work with former prisoners," I began, turning to Edgar, "because I spent ten years in prison! But I'm sure that your organization was not designed to reacclimate me." Some of the Israelis in the group laughed nervously. I felt it was important to mention having been a political prisoner, but I did not say what I had been arrested for. "My name is Sami, and I work for the Palestinian Center for the Study of Nonviolence."

Some of the Israelis in the group mentioned having served in the army or continuing to do reserve duty. I felt strangely at ease with that—they had been soldiers, fighting my people, and I had been a fighter also, ready to kill soldiers.

*Hebrew term used to mean "new immigrant."

The conversation only touched lightly on political content. We needed to establish a basis before delving into the hard issues. Edgar volunteered to host another meeting two weeks later in his home in Ein Kerem.

"What did you think?" Hussam asked me as I drove him home late that night.

"It was a good meeting," I said, crossing the checkpoint from Jerusalem to Hussam's village. "Not bad." Hussam agreed.

I did not tell Hussam the full truth—that from the moment I had stepped into Muriel's apartment with Israelis and Palestinians ready to sit together and really talk as equal human beings, I had felt, for the first time in my life, as if I had come home.

Our biweekly meetings soon became weekly. My mind raced for hours after each one: our lives in this land were inextricably connected to each other, whether we liked it or not. The only solution was one addressing all of our needs. There was no other way.

I was excited each week as Saturday approached.

"What's the use of those meetings?" my brothers asked me with a trace of scorn.

I tried to explain that in our unique community I found a kind of peace, both within the group and within myself. When I walked into each meeting, I had partners thinking with me on how to create a better reality. I knew I was doing something for Nasser's and Asala's futures.

I was not able to convince Riyyad at all. Mazin and Azzam remained skeptical. Samir came to a few meetings but then stopped. Fadia thought I was just wasting my time.

I tried to persuade my friends to join me. "Violence brings nothing but more blood and more hatred."

"But Sami, you were a freedom fighter!"

"That's right. Our leaders gave us slogans—and little people like us were used as pawns for those slogans. I'm not prepared to die for a Palestine that stretches from the river to the sea. I'm prepared to talk, as a human being, with other human beings."

The discussions ended with my friends shaking their heads and saying, "We hope you succeed, *ya* Sami. *Insha'allah.*"* But there was no optimism in the sentiment.

---

*Arabic for "God willing."

After six months, our group expanded to more than twenty people. The political discourse was surprisingly easy. The Israelis who participated were self-identified left-wing peace activists. All of us shared the basic starting point that Palestinians had the right to our own country and Israelis had the right to live in safety. Though I found myself educating the Israelis on the finer points of our situation, there was already strong agreement that the occupation needed to end immediately and that settlements and checkpoints were disastrous obstacles to peace.

We shared preconceptions we had held about "the other side." I told the story of looking for Floppy Hat's tail when he came to issue identity cards for my family after the 1967 war. Arieh, an Israeli sitting across the circle from me, laughed out loud. "We heard the same rumor on the other side of the Green Line about Arabs having tails!" he said.

We discussed the faltering Oslo Accords. Political hard-liner Binyamin Netanyahu had been elected as the Israeli prime minister, and his opposition to the Oslo Accords was no secret. Extremists on both sides were doing their best to sabotage the peace process. A new tactic adopted by Islamic Jihad* and Hamas was on the rise—suicide bombings. The first suicide bombing had occurred in April 1993, a few months before the signing of Oslo. In 1994 and 1995 combined, sixty-four people were killed in suicide attacks inside Israel. On February 25, 2006, the #18 bus line in Jerusalem was bombed, killing twenty-six. Hamas claimed responsibility. On March 3, the same bus line was bombed again, killing nineteen.

Muriel had heard the explosion on February 25, she told us at our next meeting. "They're terrorists!" she said, shaking with anger. "Bloodthirsty murderers who have been brainwashed to kill Jews!"

I struggled with my own deeply mixed feelings.

When bus #18 blew up, I had been watching the news at the coffee shop inside Herod's Gate. Eight dead, the newscaster told us initially. In ten minutes it was up to eleven.

"How many now?" someone passing on the street called to us inside.

"Fifteen and still rising!" a friend yelled back.

People cheered when the numbers climbed like they were points in a soccer match. I was ashamed to be sitting with friends who were celebrating. But I could not be fully against the bombings either. We had no air force or army. What other tools did we have to pressure Israel? My Israeli friends did

---

*A Palestinian resistance movement fighting for Palestinian sovereignty and a potential Islamic state. *Jihad* in this sense refers to military struggle.

not hear the sounds of their army's M16s or Uzis killing us during demonstrations in Gaza and Jerusalem. They heard only the explosions from the bombings. Of course the Palestinian street felt satisfied when a bus was bombed! Palestinians wanted Israelis to know the same pain they felt—blood for blood.

On March 4, the Dizengoff shopping center in the heart of Tel Aviv was attacked by a suicide bomber, killing thirteen. One of the dead was a girl celebrating her fifteenth birthday. Sitting at home with my mother, I watched the grisly scene unfold on the news.

"All those children. All those mothers," my mom said, tears trickling down her cheeks.

The news showed hundreds of angry Israelis outside the rubble of Dizengoff, holding signs reading, "NO PEACE! WE WANT WAR!"

My mother's tears stayed with me the next day as I sat with my friends in the coffee shop, talking about the bombing. Blowing yourself up in the middle of children . . . it served only the interests of the extremists. How could we tell the world with moral legitimacy that the Israelis were killing innocent people if we did the same thing? The bombings projected an image to the Western media of Palestinians as terrorists. The suicide attacks garnered sympathy for Israel all over the world and gave Israel an excuse for its continued violence and repression against us. Bombings hardened Israelis against us and against peace. It did nothing but damage our own cause.

My friends looked at me as if I were crazy, told me I was soft, and changed the subject.

The weekly meetings kept my hope and sense of inner peace kindled. Every time I saw a new face in Muriel's apartment, that hope grew a little more. Despite the descent into pessimism and bloodshed, we still nurtured new voices.

We spent hours talking about Jerusalem. We had many dreams for our shared city: establishing a joint Palestinian-Israeli youth group; starting a peace café. Our problem was always funding.

Ghadyaan Qaimari, an oud player, hosted a meeting in his home in Abu Dis, a Palestinian town just bordering Jerusalem. A new checkpoint now separated Abu Dis from Jerusalem; Ghadyaan could no longer reach the meetings at Muriel's or Edgar's homes. I drove the Israeli group members to Ghadyaan's house.

Ghadyaan's elderly mother embraced each one of us at the door and brought us fruit juice. Ghadyaan spoke about how the new checkpoint affected their lives. Family members had to quit their jobs in Jerusalem because they could no longer get to work. Ghadyaan could no longer reach Al Aqsa to pray. But most difficult was his mother's situation. She was ill. What used to be a five-minute drive to Al Makassed for her treatment had turned into an onerous process of army permissions and checkpoints.

The Israelis took all this in quietly as we sat in Ghadyaan's beautiful garden, eating special cakes his mother had prepared and drinking tea with fresh mint. We were only fifteen minutes away from Muriel's apartment, but for them it was an entirely different world.

Yoel was new to our group. I occasionally saw him at demonstrations against home demolitions in East Jerusalem or protesting closures of the Gaza Strip. Yoel and I went to El Khadr village together to plant olive trees when its land was being expropriated in order to expand the settlement Efrat. Soldiers blocked our way.

"This is a closed military area," one soldier said. "You have to leave."

I could not argue with him without risking imprisonment. But Yoel's status as an Israeli Jew was more privileged. He confronted the soldiers directly.

"Closed military zone? This is the West Bank, not your land! You should be back in Israel, not serving this extreme government!"

The soldiers were only nineteen or twenty years old. They shuffled their feet and muttered, "We're just following orders."

Yoel and I attended a seminar about religion and peace. Twenty-five Palestinians and Israelis from different NGOs sat around a big table. Someone from an NGO in Ramallah recognized me. "Aren't you Sami the driver?" he asked in a manner that made me feel five inches tall. Introductions began before I could respond. First, a Palestinian woman with a law degree. Next, a Palestinian professor at Birzeit University. Third, an Israeli with a PhD in conflict resolution. It was Yoel's turn. He stood up.

"My name is Yoel Weinberg," he said. "And sitting next to me is Sami Al Jundi. I will introduce myself and then I will introduce Sami." I raised my eyebrows in surprise. "I am originally from America. I have a master's in economics from the Hebrew University. And Sami here"—Yoel put his hand on my shoulder—"Sami has a master's in human relations. And his master's is worth much more than mine, because he received it in Ashkelon* prison."

I blushed at Yoel's words, but I needed to set the record straight. "I don't really have a master's," I told everyone at the table.

*The Israeli city built on what was al-Majdal/Asqalan before 1948.

Yoel sat back down next to me. "What you have, Sami, is more than a master's degree." He turned back to the rest of the group. "Believe me, everyone. This man has more than a master's."

One morning in 1997, Lucy requested that all the staff meet at the center. Funding was drying up and the Israeli government was fining us for taxes they claimed we owed. They were using this leverage to shut us down. We had one month to wrap up our activities. After that, the Palestinian Center for the Study of Nonviolence would be closed.

~

NOVEMBER 15, 1997. It was our annual Independence Day, in recognition of the Palestinian National Council's declaration of an independent state of Palestine in Algiers on November 15, 1988. I placed a small Palestinian flag on the hood of my car and drove to Ramallah to join in the festivities. Kids would be on the streets with flags, vendors would be selling falafel, shawarma,* and cold drinks. Families on the sides of the roads would be grilling meat. Patriotic music would be playing from all the shops on the streets. I arrived early, planning to stroll around and soak up the atmosphere of the festive day.

My Transit was stopped in traffic near Al Manara.** A Palestinian policeman with a crisply ironed uniform leaned slightly into my open window.

"Get out!" he barked. He was young with a sunburned face and blue eyes. I could tell from his accent that he was not from Ramallah. I pulled the car to the side of the circle and stepped out, waiting for him to explain what he needed.

He poked me roughly in the chest. "You should be ashamed of yourself, driving a car with yellow plates in the middle of Ramallah on this national day for Palestinians! Give me your license and identity card."

I handed him my ID, encased in blue plastic like all Israeli-issued ID cards.

"Blue ID? Yellow plates? You're Israeli!" he shouted. A curious crowd began to gather. "Ya kalb!*** Israelis like you are trying to stain our beautiful day?"

---

*A Middle Eastern specialty made with meat grilled on a spit, eaten on pita bread. Similar to the Greek gyro.

**A roundabout in the center of downtown Ramallah; literally means "the lighthouse."

***Arabic for "you dog," used as an insult.

I remained calm. I only needed to explain logically. "I'm Palestinian like everyone here. Jerusalem Palestinians were given blue Israeli IDs and yellow plates because Israel won't concede that East Jerusalem is part of the West Bank. It's a political maneuver on their part. You need to know about this."

The police officer got angrier. "Oh, so now you're a political scientist? You're trying to educate me?" He thrust his face so close to mine that flecks of his spit landed on my nose. The number of onlookers grew.

I took a deep breath to make sure my voice remained even. "No, I'm not a political scientist. I just want you to understand this point about Palestinians from Jerusalem . . ."

"Still lecturing!" He held my identity card up over his head and shouted to the crowd, pointing at me with his other hand, "Israeli! Israeli!"

My nerves were frazzled. My voice finally rose. "I'm as Palestinian as you! And even if Israelis did come to Ramallah to celebrate the day with you, you should respect them!"

His fist flew at my face, hitting my left eye squarely. I stumbled backward in shock. Before I could summon a response, two unfamiliar men pushed their way forward from the now-giant crowd. They leapt at the police officer and punched him in the nose. The policeman fell to the ground while the men disappeared into the crowd as quickly as they had emerged.

The officer got back on his feet, cursing. He covered his nose with his fingers, but blood was streaming through, staining his hands and his clothes. Two other policemen arrived.

I looked around frantically, seeing if I could escape, but even if I could, he had all my identity papers.

"Are you all right?" one of the newly arrived officers asked his colleague.

He took his hands away from his nose to point at me. I saw immediately that his nose was broken. "He's Israeli and his friends attacked me!"

The police arrested me on the spot. One officer took me away in his car and another followed driving mine.

We entered the police station. I tried to peek inside the opened doors to the offices to see if there was anyone I recognized, but none of the faces in the station were familiar.

A lieutenant wearing civilian clothes sat at the desk. "So, Adel, what happened?"

I restrained an impulse to laugh. The policeman's name was Adel! Arabic for "justice." My throbbing, swelling eye was a contradiction to his very name. Adel told the lieutenant that I had physically assaulted him alongside the two men.

The lieutenant turned to me next. "Who are your friends?"

"I have no idea who those guys were. I came to Ramallah by myself."

"We need names!"

"How can I tell you their names? I've never met them before! I guess they didn't like what they were seeing . . ."

The lieutenant stared at me harshly for a moment, drumming his fingers on the table. "Tamer! Take him downstairs!"

The policeman he called Tamer grabbed me roughly by my arm and dragged me down the steps. He shoved me into a three-square-foot cell. Before Oslo, this had been an Israeli police station. The tiny cell must have been used to confine prisoners as a form of punishment. The second policeman, whom they called Ziad, followed Tamer. They began shoving and punching me. I locked my arms tightly at my sides so that I would not impulsively strike back.

"Go ahead, hit me as much as you like, no problem. It won't be the first time. The Israelis have beaten me many times."

Cursing me, they left the suffocating cell, locking the door behind them, but returned after several long minutes.

"So you're not going to tell us the names of your friends?"

"I already told you what happened. Adel is not speaking the truth."

Ziad and Tamer shoved me a few more times and left again, only to return in five minutes. This continued for an hour. Then they took me back up to the lieutenant. What was I doing in Ramallah? he asked me harshly. Who were those friends? I did not mention my prison record. I wanted to know how he dealt with any ordinary person. I wondered: if I had taken the job offered to me by Asim, would I be in the lieutenant's place? I thanked God that I was not the one sitting behind that desk.

The lieutenant turned to Tamer and Ziad. "Take him back downstairs," he directed them. "Help him talk about who his friends were."

They led me down, putting me in a larger cell this time.

"Put your hands against the wall," Tamer told me. "And stand on one foot."

I had done this many times before; when Israeli police stopped us during the Intifada they routinely made us stand on one leg with our hands against a wall. The two men began to shove and punch me again, harder this time. The abuse continued for nearly an hour.

Then Ziad grabbed my hair and banged my head into the wall forcefully.

I flashed back to 1991, when Israeli police and soldiers had beaten me on Salah el Din Street. They had similarly slammed my head into the tree and screamed at me to cry. I had not cried.

Now, as my head smashed into the wall again, I caught a glimpse of Ziad's arm from the corner of my eye. A Palestinian flag was stitched onto the sleeve of his uniform.

The men forcing me to place my hands on the wall and stand on one foot as they beat me were not Israeli soldiers or police. I was staring at the same flag stitched onto Ziad's arm that I had hung over the Old City walls the day the Authority had returned to Jericho. These were Palestinian police. These men were supposed to be my brothers. I felt as if suddenly I had lost my entire family. I broke down into sobs.

"Stop crying!" Ziad ordered.

I could not stop. I had not realized that a person could contain so many tears.

"When *il Wahsh,* the colonel, comes, he'll give you something to cry about, *ya kalb!*"

The colonel was on his way! I managed to control my sobbing and wiped my eyes with my sleeve. Someone with the rank of colonel would surely be intelligent and rational. He would bring some measure of reason and justice to the whole mess. I did not give much thought to the fact that Tamer had referred to the colonel as "the Beast."

The lieutenant came down after another hour. "*Il Wahsh* is ready to see him now." Ziad and Tamer grabbed my arms and half-carried me up the stairs.

I stumbled across the threshold of the colonel's office as Tamer and Ziad pushed me inside. "*Assalamu 'alaikum,*" I managed to say.

The office was big. The colonel sat on a leather chair behind a solid desk made of dark brown, polished wood. He had bulging eyes, unkempt hair, and a large moustache. The top three buttons of his shirt were open, with black and white chest hairs plainly visible. He reminded me of a wolf.

The colonel stood up. "This is the *kalb* who attacked Adel? Turn him in to the Israelis! They know how to deal with dogs like him!"

The Oslo Accords stipulated that if an Israeli attacked Palestinian security forces, the attacker would be handed over to the Israelis.

"I prefer to solve this problem here, inside the home."

Il Wahsh raised his voice. "A dog like you will tell us how to handle things?!"

"Before you send me to the Israelis, please let me tell you what happened."

"Adel already told me. You broke his nose, *ya kalb!* Take him to the Israelis now!"

"If you turn me over to the Israelis, I'll tell them yes, I did it," I said, struggling to control my rising fury. "I don't want to show the Israelis that Palestinian police are dishonest. I don't want them to know the reality of our justice. So I'll confess. But it will be a lie."

"Outside!" *il Wahsh* snarled. "Get this animal out of my face!"

Tamer pushed me into the police car and drove to the outskirts of Ramallah, followed by Ziad and Adel in my car. Seething, I promised myself that I would take this up with people I knew at the PLC.

When Tamer yanked me out of the backseat of the car, I realized we were at the Palestinian side of the DCO.* The Israeli and Palestinian DCOs were housed in the same compound and worked cooperatively on security in Ramallah. Tamer and Ziad needed to turn me in to the Palestinian DCO. The Palestinian DCO would then hand me over to the Israeli DCO.

We walked inside a small office. A clean and kempt older man was sitting behind a desk.

"*Assalamu 'alaikum.* Can I help you?" He had only two stars on his uniform, I noticed. A lesser rank than *il Wahsh*, but he struck me as far more dignified.

"*Wa 'alaikum assalaam,* Abu Tayseer. Yes, I think you can. *Il Wahsh* wants you to turn this one over to the Israelis—he punched our police officer here." Tamer shoved me in the direction of the lieutenant while tossing his head toward Adel.

Abu Tayseer looked back and forth from Adel to me. "I can take their testimonies. Go back to your station; leave the two of them with me."

I was led to a small, empty room where I waited for fifteen long minutes while Abu Tayseer spoke to Adel. A policeman entered. I stiffened, unsure of what to expect.

"Abu Tayseer wants to talk to you."

The policeman led me back into the small office.

"Please, sit down." Abu Tayseer indicated a seat across from his metal desk. I sat hesitantly. The lieutenant looked at me for a long moment, while I tried not to tap my toe nervously. Finally he spoke. "Look, my son, we want to know the truth about what happened."

I told Abu Tayseer the entire story. I still did not mention my time in prison. By now it had become a point of principle.

Abu Tayseer was quiet for a moment when I finished. Finally he said, "*Ya* Allah, what do I do with this? I heard one account from Adel and a different one from you." He stroked his chin. "I'm not the one who can rectify this. Only Abu Abed can do that."

*District Coordinating Office.

"Abu Abed?"

"He's the colonel at this DCO. He's at the Independence Day celebration now but will be coming back soon."

Abu Tayseer brought me to a room with four young cadets. They had a break during their shift and were watching an Egyptian movie on TV.

"This is Sami Al Jundi," Abu Tayseer told them. "He is here as your guest."

They poured me a cup of thick, sweet coffee. With shaking hands, I lit the cigarette they offered me and took a long drag, though I had not smoked for years.

"How did you get that black eye?" one asked.

I told them what happened.

"I know the cops at that station," another said, rolling his eyes. "I don't trust them at all."

"It's all villagers there," the third added scornfully. "Not educated."

They were from Khan Younis, Gaza, they told me.

"Khan Younis? Do you know Talal Abu Tayir or Asim Al Tawil?"

"Of course! How do you know them?"

"From prison."

"You were in prison?"

"Ten years—Beer Al-Sabe' and Asqalan."

"You were in prison for ten years and this is how you were treated?" The young men from Gaza looked at each other in disbelief.

"Please, keep it between us."

"Why should you keep that a secret?"

"Because my prison record shouldn't matter in this case!"

"We need to go and kick their asses!"

"No, don't! I'm already in enough trouble!"

"Okay, okay. Don't worry, Sami. Colonel Abu Abed will never hand you over to the Israelis—I'm sure of it."

I wanted to believe them, but I could not stop shaking. They plied me with cigarettes and tea for the next two hours. Close to 9 p.m. someone entered with a message:

"The colonel arrived."

Five minutes later: "He's ready to see you."

The four policemen took me to the colonel's office. The room was smaller and more humble than the office of *il Wahsh*. There was a desk and a table placed together at a right angle, forming a *T*. Abu Abed stood up when we arrived and shook my hand. He was heavyset, with dark skin. Most of his hair was covered under a beret, but what I could see was beginning to go gray. His clothes had the combined look of a gentleman arriving from a party and the discipline of a soldier; all the buttons were fastened, and he smartly wore a brightly colored scarf.

"Hello, brother Sami."

Brother? I eyed my four new Gazan friends suspiciously. Had one of them slipped the information that I had been a prisoner with the Fatah movement?

Adel was in the room as well. He refused to meet my eye. Abu Abed returned to his chair and asked us to sit next to each other. Abu Abed offered me a cigarette. I noticed that Adel had one as well.

"Mr. Adel." Abu Abed cleared his throat and started slowly. "Exactly what happened today near Al Manara?"

Adel cleared his throat as well and began. After he had politely inquired why I had a blue ID card, I had shouted at him and then, unprovoked, had assaulted him. The other two men, Adel asserted, had leapt out of my car to punch him. And my black eye? His hand accidentally hit me while he was defending himself.

"And he refuses to tell us who his friends are," Adel concluded.

Adel sat down. "Anything else you want to add?" the colonel asked.

"Only that *il Wahsh* told us to bring him here and that you are supposed to turn him in to the Israelis."

"Is that all?"

"Yes, sir."

Abu Abed looked at me. "Brother Sami Al Jundi, tell us what happened exactly?"

I told the story. "I swear on the Qur'an, on holy books for all religions, this is the truth," I concluded.

Adel jumped up. "He can't swear on the Qur'an! He's Israeli—you can see it on his ID! And he . . . he . . ."

"*Uskut!*" the colonel commanded him sharply. "He did not interrupt you. I asked you if you were finished, you said yes, and that's it!"

Adel turned bright red and sat back down.

Abu Abed smiled. "Friends, I will not allow Sami Al Jundi to swear his story is true," he announced to the room.

Adel looked up hopefully. My heart began to sink.

Abu Abed continued, "I will not allow Sami to swear it because I will swear in his place. Sami, you don't know the people who punched Adel. And I say this not because Sami worked for the Palestinian Legislative Council. I say this not because Sami was in prison for ten years. No. I say this because two men came up to the mayor of Ramallah while I was sitting next to him during the celebration. One of them, Ramzi, is the mayor's bodyguard. 'Something happened near Al Manara,' Ramzi told his boss. 'A policeman was mistreating someone from Jerusalem. We know who this guy is from when he worked with the Parliament. The cop called him Israeli and punched him. We couldn't just see that and do nothing. So we went after the policeman. I think we broke his nose.' The mayor told Ramzi, 'Next time something like that happens, break his head.'"

Abu Abed took a long sip of water. "Now Adel, do you still want to turn Sami over to the Israelis?"

Adel dropped his head. He did not answer. Abu Abed continued, a bit more gently, "Young man, you have to learn about your people in Jerusalem. You have to learn how to treat people. Tell *il Wahsh* I said that. Now, I want you to kiss Sami's head." Adel looked up in surprise. "Go on. Kiss his head."

Adel kissed me on the head and muttered an apology.

"Never mind," I told him. I truly meant it. I did not want to see Adel ashamed and broken. I just wanted him to know the truth—Palestinians from Jerusalem are no less than Palestinians from anywhere else.

The colonel turned to me. "My son. Keep what happened to yourself. We're a new Authority. We clearly have a lot to improve upon. We're sorry about what happened. But now we'd like to invite you to eat with us."

I thanked him but declined. "It's late. My family expected me home hours ago. I'm sure they're very worried."

The four policemen from Gaza hugged me and shook my hand. "You see, brother, everything worked out. We told you it would. God is great."

"So maybe you can do us one favor, if you're willing," Abu Abed said as he shook my hand goodbye. "You will pass Abu Tayseer's house on your way home to Jerusalem. Can you give him a ride?"

"With pleasure." My ID and keys were returned to me. I glanced at my watch. It was just after 10 p.m. I had been stopped in Al Manara a bit before noon.

Abu Tayseer offered me another cigarette as we waited at a line of cars at the checkpoint. I took it, letting out a small laugh.

"Please, share the joke."

"I stopped smoking during my ten years in Israeli prison. But now, after ten hours in Palestinian prison"—I lit the cigarette and inhaled deeply— "It seems that I've started again."

Late that night, safe in my bed with Fadia, I remembered the jubilant day in Jericho when we had greeted the returning Authority with hugs. We had made the sacrifice to bring them here. The Intifada and the years of resistance leading up to it were what led to Oslo—there would have been no Palestinian Authority or police at all without our struggle. The police should have been hugging and thanking us that day, not the other way around. We had believed that we were witnessing a dream becoming reality. But in reality, it remained only a dream. Real independence was farther away than ever.

I will never celebrate Independence Day again, I pledged to myself. What independence would I be celebrating? The one that the Israelis did not yet permit us? Or the one I had just experienced a taste of with the Palestinian Authority?

CHAPTER ELEVEN

꧁꧂

SUMMER 1996. I WAS AT the Jerusalem Hotel celebrating Muriel's birthday. I piled my plate with a colorful variety of food at the open buffet. A young man stood behind me in line. He had glasses, an earring, and a ponytail.

"How are you?" He greeted me in Hebrew with a slight American accent. "My name is Ned Lazarus."

I returned his greeting in Hebrew.

"Are you a new immigrant?" he asked, recognizing that I spoke Hebrew with an accent as well.

I laughed. "Not quite. I'm an old, old immigrant. But the government still hasn't managed to absorb me."

"Oh, you're Palestinian, not Israeli! I'm really sorry. That was a stupid thing to say . . ."

"No problem, Ned."

Our plates filled with food and a Taybeh beer in each of our hands, we went to find two empty spaces at a table.

"So what are you doing in Jerusalem?" I asked him.

"Have you heard of Seeds of Peace?" I had not. Ned told me it was a summer camp in Maine that brought Arab and Israeli teenagers together. It had been founded by a Jewish-American journalist named John Wallach in 1993. That first summer there had been forty-five Israeli, Palestinian, and Egyptian boys at the camp. In 1994, it was a larger number of participants, both boys and girls, and other Arab countries began to send small delegations as well. Selected by their ministries of education, the youth lived together at the camp, engaged in joint activities such as sports, art, drama. Most important, they had facilitated dialogue on a daily basis to discuss the conflict. Ned had been a counselor at the camp. I was immediately interested in learning more.

"Do the kids continue to work together when they come home?"

"So far, not really."

I took a sip of my beer. "It sounds to me like a man with one foot."

"What do you mean?"

"A man cannot walk with just one foot—he needs both feet in order to step forward. The conflict and suffering is here, not in Maine. So it's here where they must create change. The kids have to continue meeting once they return home."

"I agree! That's actually why I'm here. I'm going to organize meetings between the Seeds and establish a newspaper that they can write together."

I loved that Ned referred to the kids as "Seeds," as if they were the physical embodiment of what needed to take root and grow. I liked how earnest and serious this young man was.

Before the end of my second beer, Ned asked, "You want to drive with me from time to time, helping bring Israeli and Palestinian kids together?"

It sounded like an enormous challenge—and an incredible opportunity to make real change.

A week later, my cell phone rang.

"Hi, Sami. This is Ned. Are you free tomorrow?"

"I can make myself free. What do you need?"

"The kids started writing for the first edition of the *Olive Branch* newspaper. I have to go to Hebron and Bethlehem to pick up their articles and photographs. Could you take me?"

"Sure. What time?"

Ned and I spent the first of many days together in my Transit, driving all over the West Bank and Israel to meet with Seeds and their families and to bring the kids to activities. He told me about his background. As a Jewish American, he had grown up with a strong connection to Israel. His Hebrew was excellent and he was familiar and comfortable with Israeli society. But Ned would also be entering Palestinian homes. I explained customs and rituals to him as we drove. Ned quickly absorbed everything I taught him. His strong respect for Palestinian tradition was evident, whether in homes, shops, or on the street. I began to educate him further about the broader situation in the Occupied Territories: the political movements, the economic situation, the differences between city, village, and refugee camp. I grilled Ned extensively about Seeds of Peace. I wanted to understand every small detail about how the organization functioned. We told each other stories about our families and our lives. We spoke in Hebrew, as Ned knew only a few words of Arabic, but he was eager to learn the language. He pieced together the Arabic alphabet from road signs until he could read Arabic fluently.

During one eight-hour drive, taking kids from Jerusalem to their homes in Eilat and back, Ned and I stopped by the Dead Sea late at night to make coffee. Ned stretched out his legs as I lit the small camping stove and poured bottled water into my *ibreiq*.* We listened to the gentle lapping of the large, salty lake on the desert rocks.

"You know what we should call your Transit?" Ned asked as I stirred heaping teaspoons of sugar and black coffee into the boiling water. "Al Buraq."

I contemplated Ned's suggestion as I poured the sweet, thick coffee into *fanajin*** and handed one to Ned. Al Buraq was the winged horselike creature that, according to the Qur'an, traveled in a single night from Mecca to Jerusalem and back with the Prophet Muhammad on his back.*** I took a sip of the coffee, savoring the rich flavor as I sat next to my colleague under the stars at the lowest point on earth. Al Buraq was exactly the right name for my Ford Transit.

September 1997. We were in Al Buraq when Ned's cell phone rang. It was Ro'e Cohen. Ro'e was a thirteen-year-old Israeli Seed from Ashdod.‡ He had returned from the camp a few weeks before and had just started the ninth grade.

"My classmates don't believe me, Ned!" I heard the spillover of Ro'e's voice. "They don't believe that I lived with Palestinians!"

"What did you tell them?" Ned asked.

"I told them that they would see for themselves—that I would invite some of my Palestinian friends to school to talk to them." There was a pause. "Can I do that, Ned?"

Ned spoke to Ro'e at length—how would it work, what were his goals, did he have his teacher's support? Ned and I talked it over for hours. Would

---

*Tin coffeepot with a long handle, to be placed directly over a stove, used for making Turkish coffee.

**Plural of *finjan*: a small cup in which Arabic or Turkish coffee is served.

***The Western Wall is also referred to as Al-Buraq Wall in Islam, referring to the Prophet Muhammad's journey.

‡Ashdod was built in 1956 approximately four and a half miles northwest of Isdud, a Palestinian town that was depopulated during the 1948 war. Palestinians still commonly refer to Ashdod as Isdud.

anyone at the school create problems for us? Would there be demonstrations against us? We decided it was important to try. Ro'e invited several of his Palestinian friends and other Israeli Seeds from Ashdod to participate. I reassured the worried Palestinian parents. "It will be entirely safe. Arafat himself supports Seeds of Peace," I reminded one concerned mother in Jericho.

The day of the presentation arrived. I picked Ned up at 6:30 a.m. We picked up Adham, a fifteen-year-old boy from Beit Sahour, near Bethlehem. We drove to Jericho to get Shurouq and to Nablus to pick up Aboud, both of them sixteen years old. We continued to Ashdod, singing along to "Aicha" by the Algerian singer Cheb Khaled. We picked up Ro'e, a little guy with bleached-blond hair and freckles sprinkled across his nose. I could not help but smile watching his excitement. I pulled into the parking lot. Shurouq, Adham, and Aboud, laughing and joking just moments before, were a bit subdued as we entered the front door. It was their first time in an Israeli school.

Ro'e led us down the corridor to his classroom. It was silent as we walked in and took our places in the front of the room. I tried to assess the looks coming from Ro'e's classmates. Curiosity? Hostility?

Ro'e's teacher introduced the guests from Seeds of Peace. "It took a lot of courage for these young Palestinian students to come here today," she said to the class. "I expect you to treat them with respect." She turned the floor over to us.

"What are we supposed to say?" Shurouq whispered to me. I had no idea. This was the first time we had ever done this.

But Ro'e, the star of the day, took the lead. "I wanted you to meet some of my friends," he said to his classmates, his brown eyes earnest. He introduced the other Seeds.

One by one, they shared the preconceptions they had held about "the other side" before going to camp. They spoke about how sleeping in the same cabins, eating side by side, and discussing every aspect of the conflict impacted their perspectives.

"I lay awake the whole first night of camp," Aboud told the group. "I was scared the Israeli kid in the bed next to me would try and kill me."

"I know it sounds weird, but it took me a while to realize the Palestinian girls in my cabin were the same as me," said Shirly, an Israeli Seed from Ashdod. "I mean, I never really stopped to wonder before if Palestinians go to the bathroom!"

The room erupted in laughter and everyone relaxed. Ro'e's classmates were invited to ask questions. Several hands shot up.

"What do you do in your free time?" a tall blond girl asked Shurouq.

I was taken off-guard. I thought all their questions would center on the conflict.

"Listen to music, hang out with my friends, watch TV," answered Shurouq. "Same as you."

"The reason you want your refugees to come back is so that you can push us into the sea!" a freckled red-haired boy in the back shouted out.

"I'm a refugee myself. All my life I've dreamt of returning to Haifa," Aboud responded, not the least bit ruffled by the outburst. "But my dreams don't involve pushing anyone into the sea. We're all human beings. We can find a way to live together."

"Do your friends and family give you a hard time for meeting together?"

"Of course!" Shurouq, Palestinian, and Dana, Israeli, answered simultaneously, looked at each other, and laughed. Shurouq continued. "But I'm proud of myself. When my friends ask me why I talk to Israelis, I tell them, 'I'm representing you, my homeland, my people.'"

The class period was ending. Most of Ro'e's classmates clambered for the door. But a few of them lingered in the front of the room. They made a point of shaking hands with Aboud, Adham, and Shurouq.

"It was really amazing to hear from you," one girl said.

"I hope you'll come back again," added the freckled boy with the red hair.

Ned and I had not planned for an evaluation, but once we were alone in the classroom, it happened automatically.

"This question about the right of return," Aboud said thoughtfully. "I have to research this more before the next presentation so I can give a better answer."

Adham swatted Shirly with a rolled-up piece of paper. "You didn't think that Palestinians went to the bathroom?"

We drove back to Ro'e's house for a lunch that his mother had prepared and then to the nearby beach. Aboud, Adham, and Shurouq had not seen the sea for years. The kids swam and splashed in the warm Mediterranean and made a human pyramid on the sand, happy to be at the beach and exhilarated about what they had just accomplished. As the afternoon grew later, we began the long route home, dropping Adham in Beit Sahour, Shurouq in Jericho, and Aboud in Nablus.

On the final stretch back from Nablus, Ned and I reflected on the day's events.

"That was pretty great," Ned said.

"Yeah."

I popped my Cheb Khaled cassette into the tape player and cranked up the volume. As I navigated the empty, dark road back home, I was bursting with hope.

Ned called me the following afternoon. "What are you doing on Thursday, Sami? You able to drive?"

I told Ned that I was supposed to show some people from Denmark around for *Shabibeh*,* but five minutes later I called him back. "I can come with you, Ned."

"What about the people from Denmark?"

"Never mind that. Whenever you need someone, just call me. When I work with Seeds of Peace, my soul is speaking."

⁂

THE SEEDS SPREAD THE WORD about Ro'e's presentation via e-mail and phone. Soon, Ned was receiving e-mails and phone calls from other Israeli and Palestinian Seeds asking us to help them organize presentations in their schools. We ate platefuls of hummus together thinking it through. How could we reach the maximum number of students? Would all Israeli schools be as welcoming as Ro'e's had been? Would Palestinian schools be receptive to us as well?

Sara, who lived in Hebron, invited Noa Epstein from outside Jerusalem to speak to her school. The principal brought us directly to Sara's class when we arrived. "We have an Israeli visitor," she announced.

Noa introduced herself to the class. She shared her experiences with Seeds of Peace and her vision for a future of Israelis and Palestinians living without occupation or violence.

One boy came up to me after her presentation. "If I had known in advance that there was an Israeli coming to the class, I would have left," he said. "Two months ago, settlers killed my uncle. All Israelis were settlers and soldiers to me. I didn't know that there are Israelis like this girl." He paused for a moment. "She's just like us."

Noa had planted a seed of peace in this boy's mind. I hoped that it would have a chance to grow.

Ned called me one afternoon. "You've met Yaron Avni from Ashkelon, right?" I had. Yaron was dark haired, funny, and spit out words quicker than my

---

*The pro-Fatah youth movement.

brain could digest them. "He invited us to his family's *Pesach seder**
tomorrow night. Are you up for it?"

I had never been inside an Israeli family's home. Until Seeds of Peace, the
only Israelis I had known were left-wing peace activists, like Muriel and Yoel.
I looked forward to the opportunity to interact with a family from the heart
of Israeli society. Fadia was never happy when work was going to keep me
away from her and the children, but she knew I was excited. My parents were
happy as long as I was involved in anything that would not lead me to being
hurt or imprisoned again. I did not mention to my brothers or sisters where
I was going as I left the Old City to pick up Ned.

Yaron's parents welcomed us at the door of the small apartment and
showed us in. There must have been fifty people crowded around the twelve-
foot-long table! They squeezed over to make room for us. I slid into a chair
next to Ned and looked at all the faces: Yaron's siblings, cousins, parents,
aunts, uncles, grandparents. Yaron's grandparents were from Morocco and
spoke Hebrew peppered with Arabic. Three generations of Israelis at the
same table! It reminded me of *iftar* meals at Ramadan with my entire family.

Small booklets were passed around the table.

"It's a *Hagaddah*," Ned told me.

I flipped through mine. It looked like a children's book, telling the Pesach
story with pictures and songs. I was surprised when Yaron's grandfather
started chanting aloud from it. The booklets were not holiday souvenirs as I
had assumed; they were part of an important ceremony connected to Jewish
ritual! We tasted items on the table according to the instructions of the
Hagaddah—matzah, bitter herbs. I tried to pay attention to everything: what
foods we were supposed to eat and when, why we were dipping hard-boiled
eggs into bowls of salty water. I knew from the Qur'an that Moses and the
Jews had been lost in Sinai, but hearing the *Hagaddah* read aloud by Yaron's
family gave me new details and a different perspective.

It was difficult to hear the whole story because gossip, laughter, and conversation rose louder and louder. Nobody seemed to mind that Yaron's grandfather was still in the midst of chanting the *Hagaddah* and he certainly appeared
undisturbed by the chatter of voices and the clatter of dishes being carried
back and forth from the kitchen. The Moroccan-Israeli food was delicious.

Yaron's father was a supporter of Likud, the largest right-wing Israeli political party. My conversation with him was intense, but it was passionate,

---

*Ritualized meal on the first two nights of the Jewish holiday Pesach, or Passover.

open, and warm. Our voices were raised, but that was mostly because there was so much competing noise. Nobody took anything personally or got upset. There was no uncomfortable silence. In fact, there was no silence at all. At the end of the meal, Yaron's entire family sang with the *Hagaddah* once again while banging on the table. They were wonderful.

Yesterday I had been in a West Jerusalem supermarket. When I had answered my cell phone in Arabic, the other shoppers stared at me as if I were suspicious. The day before, a nineteen-year-old soldier had demanded to see my ID in a manner that communicated that he had the power and I was barely tolerated. Those incidents did not connect to my emotions sitting around the Pesach table with multiple generations of Yaron's family. I felt safe, welcome, and wanted.

I needed to bring as many Palestinian Seeds as possible to Israeli homes. If I had had this opportunity at their age, how different might the rest of my life have been?

Filmmaker Mark Landsman had taught a group of Seeds how to use video cameras at the camp in Maine and they were now filming a year of their life back home. Bushra, a Palestinian member of the video team from Al Arroub refugee camp, invited Sivan, an Israeli member of the team from Nahariyah, to her home. Sivan's parents were afraid to let her go. But they were happy to welcome Bushra in their home—in fact, Sivan invited the entire video team one Shabbat.

I spoke directly to Bushra's father, Abu Tareq, about bringing his daughter with us to spend the night at Sivan's. Abu Tareq looked me directly in the eye. "Sami, we're giving you our trust. You're from Zakariyya like many in Arroub camp. Take care of Bushra like your own daughter."

I was not surprised that Bushra's parents were less fearful than Sivan's. Palestinians had more experience in Israeli society. We had been working as laborers in their cities for years. Most Israelis had never entered a Palestinian city or refugee camp unless it was as a soldier, with a gun. It was this inequality that I believed caused them shame when they were invited as guests. And shame often translates into fear.

Mark Landsman, Ned, and I started driving early in the morning, picking up the members of the video team from towns, cities, and checkpoints all over Israel and the Occupied Territories. We reached Sivan's house late in the afternoon. The kids talked and laughed together, while Sivan's parents, Ned, Mark, and I chatted pleasantly. In the evening, Sivan's mother led prayers over the Shabbat candles and we ate a huge meal. Everyone shared stories until late at night.

I was developing extensive experience visiting the homes of Israelis, but it was the first time in my life that I had slept in one. I lay in bed wrestling with strange new feelings. Who from my friends would believe that Sami, a prisoner from the Fatah movement, was sleeping in the home of Israeli Jews? An old proverb came to my mind: *Eat in a Jewish home but sleep in a Christian one.* The logic about eating was based on the similarity between Jewish and Muslim dietary laws. Why sleep in a Christian home? Because Jews might kill us in the middle of the night. Now, the adage seemed ludicrous. Whom exactly should I worry about killing me? Sivan's father, who had just offered me coffee? Or her mother, who had put fresh sheets on the bed and a clean towel for me in the bathroom?

Ned's cell phone rang a few days later. "Ned! They agreed!" I heard Sivan's breathless voice on the other end. "My parents said I can visit Bushra!"

"That's great! What changed their minds?"

"Meeting Bushra herself. And because it would be rude not to accept Bushra's invitation after she came to my house."

Sivan's parents called Ned and me multiple times, seeking reassurance. Were stones ever thrown on the roads we would be using? Were we sure there were no extremists inside the camp who would try to hurt Sivan? Did we promise to be by their daughter's side every moment?

Fadia and I had two children of our own and a third on the way; I could relate to how they were feeling. I reassured them that the road to the camp was safe. We had been to Al Arroub many times; we knew the camp, Bushra's home, and her family. We would not let Sivan out of our sight.

Sivan herself was not afraid at all. She had spent hours with Ned and me in Al Buraq going to different activities. She had lived with Bushra for three weeks at camp. But I was the one who had promised Sivan's parents that I would protect her no matter what, and that pledge was sacred. Yes, the situation was quiet. Yes, I had checked with Abu Tareq many times over the past week, including that morning, that the camp was calm. I was 99.99 percent sure that everything would be fine. But the .01 percent possibility that something could go wrong terrified me. Approaching the military tower at the entrance to Al Arroub camp, I was all eyes and ears, a soldier inside my head.

Bushra's mother, Um Tareq, opened the door of the house as I was parking Al Buraq. Before Sivan had both feet on the ground, Um Tareq had wrapped her in a strong embrace. Bushra hugged her next, kissing her repeatedly on both cheeks as if Sivan was a long-lost relative.

Sivan presented Um Tareq with a gift. "This is from my mother," she said, as Bushra helped translate. Um Tareq hugged Sivan again, even tighter.

Bushra showed Sivan around the house and then sat her down in the salon where her younger sister, Rasha, plied us with nuts and fruit juice as Um Tareq finished cooking. We were very hungry, but lunch was worth the wait—rice with minced meat, chicken, green beans, and bowls of spicy olives and warm pita bread.

After lunch, Abu Tareq took out the family photo album, showing Sivan photographs of Bushra and her brother and sister growing up. Bushra took out her Seeds of Peace photo album and the girls reminisced, laughing about good-looking male counselors and silly evening activities. I watched them with amazement. They made it look completely normal, as if friendships like this happened every day. I wished it came so easily for me.

We drank sweet tea with sage as the afternoon grew late. I saw Um Tareq slip some money and whisper instructions to Bushra's twelve-year-old brother, Tareq, who immediately dashed out the door.

Just as we were preparing to leave, Tareq came running back, breathing hard, and handed his mother a box wrapped in pink paper with a bow. Um Tareq presented the box to Sivan. "Please give this gift to your mother from me," she said. "And tell her we hope to welcome her in our home."

We set off in Al Buraq for the four-hour drive back to Nahariyah. I glanced at Sivan in the rearview mirror. Her face shone with the warmth and love she had absorbed from Bushra's family.

Friendships spread from the Seeds themselves to their families. Bushra was also close friends with Noa. Um and Abu Tareq invited Noa's entire family to visit them often in Al Arroub.

No matter what, we had to keep doing this.

⁓

NED AND I WERE BUYING office supplies in East Jerusalem. An older man entered the stationery shop. I exchanged greetings with him.

"Who is this one?" he asked me, raising his eyebrows toward where Ned was browsing notebooks.

"He's my colleague in Seeds of Peace," I replied. "Ned's from America."

The old man snorted. "I have no use for foreigners. But at least he's not a Jew." Words began to tumble out of the old man's mouth. "You can't trust the

Jews! They've deceived everyone in historical memory." From the corner of my eye, I saw Ned standing very still. "The Jews will burn your house down, take your homeland, and kill you! Hitler was right about them!" I felt as if the old man had just stabbed me with a knife.

"How can you say such hateful things? How do you ever hope to have peace here?" I angrily answered.

"Peace? Where is the peace?!"

"I found peace with him," I said, pointing to Ned. I purchased the supplies and got Ned out of there before the tirade could continue.

"How much of that did you understand?" I asked Ned.

"Enough," he answered grimly. We walked down the street to eat at Ikermawi's.

"There has to be a way to reach people like that," I said, dipping a piece of warm pita into hummus.

Ned took a bite of falafel. "If you substitute the word *Jew* with *Arab,* you can hear that old man's speech practically word for word from Jews," he said. "I wonder if he realizes that."

Ned and I made a pact, sealed by hummus and falafel. Every activity we organized would have at its core the mission to uproot the hatred and bigotry gripping both our peoples. It was one thing to resist people's actions; I would never back down on my stance against occupation, settlements, and land and water expropriation. It was another thing to be against other human beings.

In 1998, the peace process was continuing to falter. Frustration among Palestinians was growing. I was sitting at Al Hakawati for a meeting with *Shabibeh.* We were discussing the use of nonviolence.

"It's helpful when developing connections with internationals," said my friend Ra'ed. "It's easier for foreigners and even Israelis to support us."

I tried to push them another step. "There's more to nonviolence than resistance. Yes, there is occupation and brutality. That is the truth. But it's not the whole truth. There is also beauty in Israeli society. When you discover the beauty, you can make real connections. It is only when we each recognize the equal humanity of the other that we are willing to stand up for each other's rights alongside our own." I described the activities that I had been organizing with Ned and the blossoming relationships between the kids.

The room became icy.

"I support nonviolence," someone finally said. "But not what Sami is doing. That's normalization."* He said the word with scorn.

The next day, Ned and I were walking on Salah el Din Street. Ra'ed was getting out of his car with two friends.

"*Habibna,* how are you?" I shook hands with Ra'ed.

"*Hada* Sami Al Jundi." Ra'ed introduced me to his friends. "*Malek al tatbiyyeh.*" He grinned at me.

I forced myself to smile back. "I'm only doing what Abu Ammar agreed to," I said and walked away.

"What was that all about?" Ned asked.

"He said, 'This is Sami Al Jundi, King of Normalization.'"

"Was he joking?" Ned asked incredulously.

"Yes. But a joke can say a lot."

I tried not to let Ned see it, but Ra'ed's comment had hurt me. At the next *Shabibeh* meeting, I was greeted with a distinct aloofness. More and more friends began to grow distant and cold. When I had worked for the Center for Nonviolence, my friends had called me naive or soft. Now, I overheard them calling me a traitor. I no longer felt welcome in Fatah meetings.

I was losing my place inside my own society, my status inside my movement. Was Seeds of Peace worth the price? I bumped into an old cell mate in Ramallah. He avoided eye contact and scarcely returned my greeting. I could not take the growing isolation any more. *Khalas,* I said to myself. I will end my connection to Seeds of Peace. I'll fulfill the driving that I already promised Ned and then I'll walk away.

The next day, we had a large school presentation in the Israeli coastal city Herzliya. One girl in the audience stood up during the question-and-answer period. "We liberated Jerusalem in 1967—it's our capital!" she said angrily to the Palestinian Seeds. "Why can't you just accept that?" Other kids around her started to cheer. The atmosphere became slightly hostile. Ned looked worried.

A Palestinian Seed hesitantly stepped forward to answer, when Inbal (Bala) Shacked, an Israeli Seed with a loud laugh, tough demeanor, and a stomach full of fire, grabbed the microphone. "First of all, I don't like how you asked that question, like you're attacking the Palestinians who are in

---

*Normalization is the concept of normalizing relations with Israel both politically and culturally. It has a negative connotation among most Palestinians and Arabs, with the belief that one should not normalize relations while still living under conditions of occupation and inequality.

this room," Bala began. "It's not fair to put them on the defensive like this. They wouldn't be standing here right now if they didn't want to make peace. Second, you should know this about me: I'm right-wing, my family votes for Likud, and I live in a settlement. And third, let me tell you something—thousands of Palestinians live in Jerusalem. It is the heart of their religious, social, and cultural life. Are you saying that they don't have the right to call it their capital? My Palestinian friends believe Jerusalem is their capital. And even though I consider Jerusalem my capital, I understand their feelings."

I was in shock. I had heard Bala arguing that student's same point with Palestinian Seeds many times. But when her Palestinian friends were put in the corner, her instinct was to defend them. Not only that—Bala proved that she had developed an understanding and respect for what we think and feel. And this from a girl who was a self-proclaimed right-wing settler!

I had a hard enough time trying to discuss these issues with small groups of colleagues and friends. Did I have the courage to make a statement that had the potential to be so explosive in front of two hundred of my peers, like Bala had done?

Someday I would have the strength to speak loudly in front of a crowd: We are not alone in this land. There are others here, with children as innocent as ours.

Bala was my answer to whether all the agony Seeds of Peace was causing me was worth it. I could not walk away.

Every single time I saw the kids together, I felt a deep sense of satisfaction. I wanted to share it with my closest circle—my family. We needed more drivers. Who could I trust to drive our kids? My brothers. Mazin started driving with us, then Azzam. Soon I asked Riyyad and Sa'ed.

Riyyad was willing to drive, but he made it clear that he was suspicious of Seeds of Peace. "They're using you, Sami," he said to me.

Fadia said the same thing. They were not talking about Ned. Ned had been to my home many times. He was the first person outside of the family to hold Yazan, my new baby son. All the family loved Ned. It was the leadership of the organization they did not trust.

"Where do the donations come from?" Riyyad challenged me. "Who serves on the board of directors?"

"Americans."

"Jewish Americans? Arab Americans?"

"Well . . . mostly Jewish," I had to admit.

"You see? Seeds of Peace is serving a Zionist agenda! I bet some of the people who give money to Seeds of Peace make even larger donations to support the Israeli military!"

I could neither refute nor substantiate Riyyad's claims. I did not personally know the Seeds of Peace donors.

After a while, Riyyad refused to drive anymore. "I'm not going to feed my family with dirty money," he said.

My mother could never understand why Seeds of Peace caused such conflict inside the family. "Sami's work is nice," she said time and again. "It's dealing with children, with families, with humanity."

"They're brainwashing those kids, *Yamma*," Riyyad replied angrily. "They're brainwashing Sami."

My father had his own critiques. "Why do they only bring rich kids to the camp? How many youth from the Old City or from refugee camps participate?"

"There are kids from refugee camps!" I protested, citing Bushra from Al Arroub as an example. But he had a point and I knew it. Speaking English was a requirement for the selection process, and most of the kids with adequate English skills came from the elite sector of society. Given the level of English in the public schools in East Jerusalem, it was unlikely that my own children would be able to participate in Seeds of Peace. Yes, every summer there was a handful of kids from camps or villages. But they felt the gulf between themselves and the more economically privileged members of their delegation. Most of them dropped out of the program shortly after camp. Seeds like Bushra were the exception.

Mazin and Azzam drove initially only to earn money. But over time, they too felt the magic of being with the kids. They began to spend nearly as many hours on the road with the Seeds as I did. Yael, an Israeli from Jerusalem, called me the morning of every activity.

"Hi, Sami! Do you know who is picking me up today? Can you send Azzam?"

Azzam and Mazin were now part of the Seeds of Peace family. Nothing made me happier.

Ned and I were running ourselves ragged.

"Sami, the New York office finally agreed to hire someone else," Ned said after returning from camp in the summer of 1998.

"Who?"

"Roy Sharone."

I did not like the sound of it. Who was this guy, sharing his family name with Ariel Sharon?* Was he some kind of spy, sent from the Israeli Ministry of Education?

I knew only what Ned told me—Roy was twenty-two years old, had been born in Israel but lived most of his life in America, and had been an incredibly enthusiastic counselor at camp. I trusted Ned, but I was still skeptical. Would this Roy really understand what we were trying to do here? Would he fit in with our program?

Roy came to Jerusalem and moved into Ned's apartment. At first, this tall, wild-haired, loud guy drove me crazy. Everything Roy was asked to do, he planned down to the smallest, most minute details. But I grew to appreciate how meticulous Roy was. More important, he had the energy of three people. And most crucial of all, he believed in our mission with his heart and soul. Within weeks, Roy became like my little brother.

With Roy on board and my brothers driving, we doubled our number of school presentations, workshops, and home visits, organizing it all from Ned and Roy's apartment and Al Buraq.

﷽

WE TOOK A GROUP OF Israeli and Palestinian Seeds to Jordan. They did presentations at the schools of the Jordanian Seeds and visited the ancient ruins of Jerash, Petra, and the incredible sandstone valley of Wadi Rum. The highlight of any trip to Wadi Rum is a jeep ride in the desert. I negotiated a price with the owner of the jeeps.

"Fifteen dinars each," he said.

"That's too much. Eight dinars."

His counter-offer was thirteen. We settled on eleven.

A half-dozen jeeps materialized out of nowhere driven by Bedouin teenagers who looked younger than the Seeds. Ned, Roy, and I each climbed into a jeep with seven or eight of our kids. The jeeps took off. We roared over the silky red sand, which parted like water, closing again behind the vehicle. The Seeds were shrieking with joy. Golden and pink rocks bathing directly in the late afternoon glow flew by. The cloudless sky was a brilliant blue.

---

*Ariel Sharon was Israel's foreign minister in 1998, and he was the defense minister during the 1982 Lebanon War. An Israeli government commission determined to hold him personally responsible for the massacres in Sabra and Shatila refugee camps. He was also considered one of the most enthusiastic political supporters of the Israeli settlement movement.

My driver stopped his jeep and we all tumbled out, brushing sand off of our hair and clothes. The desert was flat and the horizon was far. "This is the border with Saudi Arabia," he told the Seeds.

"There's no wall or fence or anything?" one of the Israelis asked, unsure whether to be excited or scared.

"No, just the desert. We cross all the time—we have relatives just a few kilometers from here."

"Take us to Saudi Arabia!" some of the kids pleaded with him.

The young driver laughed. "I can't. We could be arrested for taking tourists."

The kids scrambled on the golden rocks for a few minutes, taking pictures, and then piled back into the jeeps, shouting and singing as if the world belonged to them.

On the way back to Wadi Rum, Roy's jeep pulled up from behind. "Suckers!" Roy shouted as his car roared past ours. The Seeds in his jeep turned around to face us, making the victory sign. It was all the encouragement the kids in my jeep needed.

"*Yallah*, faster!"

"We can pass this guy, come on!"

The Seeds egged their drivers on until a full-fledged race was on.

The kids arrived at the parking lot in Wadi Rum collapsing with laughter. There was a large Bedouin tent next to the parking lot. Ned, Roy, and I consulted with each other briefly. Everyone could get one drink each before boarding the bus for the long drive back to Amman.

Noa approached me, her turquoise eyes glistening with tears. "Sami," she said, trying to control the trembling in her voice. "I can't find my wallet. It was with me before the jeep ride. I had British pounds, U.S. dollars, Israeli shekels, and Jordanian dinars . . ."

"Wow, what an international wallet!" I tried to make her smile, but it backfired. The tears began to overflow. "Come on, let's go find the jeeps."

The currencies added up to hundreds of dollars, she explained as we walked. Many relatives had given her money to bring them back something special from Jordan.

We saw no jeeps anywhere on Wadi Rum's single road. Night was beginning to fall.

"What if it was stolen? Should we tell the police?" she asked.

"If we get the police involved, it will shame the community," I explained to her. "There's a more respectful way to try and find it . . ."

An old man drove past us in a white jeep. I waved and he stopped the car. I told him the story quickly, mentioning that Noa was Israeli. In Bedouin tradition, even an enemy is respected if she or he is a visitor.

"Get in the car," he said. "I know one of the drivers. I'll take you to his home."

Noa and I climbed in the jeep and sat next to the man. Seeing Noa's distress, he tried to reassure her. "Don't worry, young lady. If the wallet is in the car, you will find it."

"But what if it fell out during the ride?"

The man did not answer; he did not have to. He drove us to a tent. Many people were gathered around a mat outside, eating their big meal of the week.

"*Assalamu 'alaikum*," I said, and told the story of Noa's wallet.

The father of the family patted the mat next to him. "Before anything, you must sit and join us for dinner."

"It would be a great honor to eat with you, sir, but we must hurry. There are dozens of people waiting for us and we have to drive to Amman tonight. Please, can we quickly check the car?"

The father took us to inspect the jeep. "Was this the one you were riding?"

"I have no idea," Noa answered. "The jeeps all look the same."

The man called his fourteen- and sixteen-year-old sons over. "Were one of them your driver?"

Turning red, Noa shrugged again. "I'm . . . I'm not sure."

"Go with them to all the jeeps and don't come back until you find her wallet," the father instructed the boys.

"Get into my car," the old man said. "If you start a good deed, you should finish it."

We went from one driver's home to another's—tents or small cinderblock houses with iron sheet roofs—with nothing but empty desert separating them.

We arrived at the home of the seventh and last driver. The driver had taken the jeep to his cousin's house. Away we sped through the desert to the cousin's house. The uncle told us that the boys had gone with the jeep to a friend's house.

Noa began to cry again. "Sami, let's go back. The whole group is waiting for us."

"Don't give up hope!" I hated seeing Noa so upset.

We saw the final jeep parked in front of the friend's house. The boys jumped out of the car and ran toward it. Seconds later one of them started singing, "We found the wallet! We found the wallet!" while the second boy held it up over his head, dancing.

They handed Noa the wallet, with every shekel, dollar, pound, and dinar inside. We drove back to the boys' homes, the atmosphere in the jeep nearly as festive as it had been during the afternoon desert ride.

"Sami, we have to give them a gift. Whatever you think is right, take it from my wallet."

I opened Noa's wallet and pulled out twenty Jordanian dinars. But the youth refused.

"Just hours ago we were negotiating the price of the jeep tour—now you're refusing the money?"

The boys climbed out of the jeep. "That was different. That was work. But if we took money for helping you, we would be ashamed of ourselves." They shook our hands with finality. "Have a safe trip back to Amman."

The old man drove us back to the coffee shop tent. I offered him forty dinars. He laughed. "Do you think after those kids refused *baksheesh** that I would take it?"

He smiled to Noa and in Noa's return smile, tears sprang into her eyes again.

Ned strode over to me. "Sami, the kids are collecting money to help Noa make up for what she lost."

I grinned. "Not necessary! We found the wallet!"

The Seeds gathered around and we told the whole story, including how the boys and the old man refused to accept even a small token of our appreciation. All the kids were jumping on Noa and hugging her. The owner of the coffee shop was caught up in the moment as well.

"One free drink for everyone!" he proclaimed. "I'm no less generous than those young drivers!"

We all finally piled back into the ancient, creaking bus for the long ride back to Amman. The kids were talking with animation and singing camp songs. I stared out the window and thought about the old man and the boys who spent over an hour trying to track down the missing wallet. Noa, an Israeli in Jordan, had been treated with the highest level of respect from the traditions of Bedouin culture.

I reflected on Noa's tears. The first time she had cried because she lost her money. The second time she had cried because she lost hope. But in the end

---

*Arabic for "tip," sometimes interchangeable with "bribe."

she cried because she realized how wrong she had been to think that one of the drivers might steal her wallet.

I contemplated the Seeds pooling their money to help Noa recover some of what she had lost. They had responded to Noa's situation as if they were all members of the same family. The restaurant owner had as well. We were all connected, the Palestinian, Israeli, and Jordanian Seeds, Ned, Roy, the Bedouin drivers, the restaurant owner, and me.

Worn out from the hours of desert wind and sun, the kids dropped off to sleep. The bus was dark and silent as it climbed the snaking, mountainous road. There was a Seeds of Peace Frisbee next to me on the seat. I picked it up and ran my finger around the edge of the disk. Circles. It was all about circles. When we see ourselves only in the circle of our national groups, Palestinians think only about the needs of Palestinians, and Israelis think only about the needs of Israelis. But we can break our small circle and link ourselves with the circle of human beings. No one exemplified this better than these teenagers.

Holding tightly to the Frisbee, I drifted off to sleep.

JANUARY 1999. Tim Wilson, the director of the Seeds of Peace camp in Maine, came to visit. I was excited to meet the man I heard the Seeds talk about with reverence and respect. Tim was an older, large, African-American man who had been the director of summer camps for years. At the end of the trip, Tim dictated a memo that Ned typed, saying it was as important for Seeds of Peace to invest resources equally in the region, where the Seeds lived their entire lives, as it was to invest in the camp.

A new building was under construction in French Hill, a neighborhood in northeast Jerusalem.

"Wouldn't it be perfect to rent a room or two there?" Ned commented each time we passed it.

"Maybe the owner is some wealthy, peace-loving philanthropist!" Roy chimed in. "Maybe he'll donate space."

John Wallach, the founder of Seeds of Peace, and board member Alan Ginsburg came to Jerusalem. John had long-term vision and a childlike mannerism, smiling and talking about his dreams with a youthful innocence. John's and Alan's enthusiasm for our work was evident.

"You don't need an office," Alan commented after he observed a school presentation. "You need a center—a big place to hold all your activities. Why don't you scout out a place?"

The building in French Hill immediately jumped to mind. It was nearly completed. We stopped by. A friendly, energetic man answered my knock with a large smile and greeted me in Arabic.

"Do you own the building?" I asked.

He laughed. "No, I clean the building. My name is Issa."

"Can we look inside?" Ned asked.

"Why not?" The owner was a Palestinian man named Abu Firas, Issa told us as he showed us around. Perfect! French Hill was in occupied East Jerusalem. If the building had Israeli owners, it would be regarded as a settlement. But, as the building was Palestinian-owned, it was acceptable for the Palestinian kids, and as it was located in one of the few mixed neighborhoods in Jerusalem, it felt safe to the Israeli kids. We tracked Abu Firas down. He was willing to rent the building to us. Issa would stay on and work with us.

It was June 1999. Ned, John, and I sat with Abu Firas and our lawyers in a coffee shop. John picked up the pen to sign the long-term lease, then paused for a moment. He turned to me.

"Sami, before I sign, I want to ask you one question. Do you promise me that this center will always be full? You will continue to bring Palestinians and Israelis together to work toward peace with the same spirit and energy I see now?"

I struggled to find the right words. "John—for the sake of our children, Israelis, Palestinians—for the future generations—I promise you that we will continue to do the impossible. We will always bring Palestinians and Israelis together at our center."

John opened the pen as if he were waking from a deep sleep. "If you guarantee this, Sami, then I feel confident about signing."

John signed the contract. The Seeds of Peace Center for Coexistence was born.

The grand opening of the Center would be October 26, 1999. We had a massive amount of work to do to coordinate the opening and to be ready to launch activities from our new base of operations. We needed once again to expand our team. Adam Shapiro, who had close-cropped hair and a will of steel, was sent from the New York office to be the new director of the Center. Falestin Shehadeh and Jared Fishman, who had been camp counselors the previous two summers, joined our team as well. Falestin was tall, slender, and soft-spoken; Fishman was bearded, energetic, and made everyone laugh. With a fortified staff, we feverishly started preparations.

The morning of October 26, I woke up at 6:30 and jumped out of bed. Fadia brought me coffee. "Are you excited for the big day?" she asked.

"I just hope everything goes okay." I threw on my green Seeds of Peace T-shirt with the logo across the front—an outline of three figures casting a shadow of olive branches. This was the same shirt that the kids wore every day at camp. It symbolized their shared identity as Seeds.

I was at the Center by 7 a.m. By 7:30, my cell phone started ringing non-stop: kids from Gaza wanting to know what time they should be at Erez,* kids from Bethlehem wanting to know which of my brothers was picking them up, kids from Egypt and Jordan who were hosted by the families of Israeli and Palestinian Seeds asking if they could come to the Center, bus drivers calling to confirm their routes.

We had hired a caterer to make a huge barbecue in the Center's garden and had procured a water truck. We had rented a small stage, sound system, and hundreds of chairs. People started arriving at 2 p.m.: one bus from Haifa, another from Tel Aviv, one from Nablus and Ramallah, two vans from Hebron and Bethlehem. By 2:30, the Center grounds were packed with Israeli and Palestinian delegation leaders, parents, and politicians. Yossi Sarid, the Israeli minister of education, was there and so was Naeem Abu Hummus, the Palestinian minister of education. Jordanian, American, and Egyptian ambassadors showed up. Faisal Husseini, the political leader of East Jerusalem for the PLO, and Ehud Olmert, the Israeli mayor of Jerusalem, were both there. American donors and board members had flown in for the occasion. And in the midst of the VIPs were hundreds of our most important young guests from Gaza, Petach Tikvah, Nablus, Afula, Haifa, East Jerusalem, West Jerusalem, Tel Aviv, Tulkarem, Arabeh, Amman, Cairo, all of them wearing their green Seeds of Peace T-shirts. People were everywhere, inside the Center, in the yard, in the parking lot, spilling out into the empty lot next to the Center. It was amazing. It was overwhelming.

The Center staff was going a hundred miles an hour, checking that everyone had what he or she needed, that everything was secure and safe. Though the ministers had security with them, the best security was that everyone was there together: Israelis, Palestinians, Egyptians, Jordanians, Jews, Christians, Muslims—even a Buddhist! Herokushi entered with his saffron robe and encouraging smile.

The chairs filled quickly and guests sat on the wall and in the field behind the wall, and stood in the back. I tried to do a quick estimate of the numbers.

*The main checkpoint/border separating Gaza from Israel.

There must have been close to eight hundred people! John Wallach initiated the ceremony. The U.S., Egyptian, and Jordanian ambassadors spoke, as well as Yossi Sarid and Naeem Abu Hummus.

The speeches from the politicians ended. John turned the stage over to one Seed from each delegation to talk. Next, Noa Epstein and Rasha Hammo sang a duet in Hebrew and Arabic that they had sung together many times before—at camp and at other special activities—"A Time for Peace." Then the Seeds stood up, all of them in their green T-shirts, and sang the Seeds of Peace anthem as John raised the Seeds of Peace flag.

By 10 p.m., the kids had all been transported home. The stage, speakers, and rented chairs had been trucked up and carted away. The garbage had been bagged and thrown in the dumpster. Issa and I sat on the balcony with a cigarette and a cup of tea, looking at our beautiful green Seeds of Peace flag fluttering briskly in the breeze. It was a new era for Seeds of Peace. It was a new era for all the Middle East.

❧

FOR THE FIRST TIME IN MY LIFE, I had my own office. I hung a picture of Yasser Arafat being presented with the Seeds of Peace pin, which he had since worn proudly on the lapel of his jacket. I tacked up a huge road map so I could always help drivers navigate the small roads and bypass any "flying checkpoints" that might crop up. I hung photos of the Seeds kids and of Nasser, Asala, and Yazan lined up like the figures on the Seeds of Peace T-shirt. I hung a Seeds of Peace Frisbee, as a reminder about the circles. I sat back behind my big desk and surveyed my office. *Sami, don't let this desk get in the way between you and the kids,* I cautioned myself. Offices represent bureaucracy, and bureaucracy is poison, even in an organization like Seeds of Peace. We made a staff policy: our office doors would always be open. The entire Center was for the Seeds.

Dialogue groups began the very next week. There was the next Jordan trip to plan, followed by the annual winter workshop at Kibbutz Yahel in the Negev Desert. We worked constantly and were always exhausted. The pace was too draining for Falestin. She quit after a few months. Huwaida Arraf, a young woman who was much tougher than her slight frame would suggest, was hired to replace her, giving us new energy and ideas. The rest of us approached burnout occasionally as well, but each time we brought Israeli and Palestinian youth to our Center, our human-being circle grew larger—and that gave us an enormous burst of energy, enough to keep us working until midnight and to return to the Center early the next morning. Our Center was bursting with life and vibrancy. I knew in my gut that we were on the right path.

I was going to the Seeds of Peace camp, as a Palestinian delegation leader. It was my first trip to America and to the camp.

Members of my delegation came to me at the camp when they had problems or concerns.

"I don't want to sleep in the same room with Israelis!" one boy insisted.

"Ibrahim, you knew from the start that the cabins are mixed, Israelis and Palestinians together. Everybody is a human being here."

Rana from Jenin was crying. "I want to go home!" she wailed when I asked her what was wrong.

"Why?"

"The facilitators give the Israeli kids more time to talk! They won't let me say anything!"

It was hard to know whether this kind of discrimination was real or whether it was a perception that both sides shared; I had heard Israeli kids make the same complaint.

"Express yourself clearly and strongly with whatever time you're given, Rana," I coached her. "Become friends with the Israelis in your group—but never give up your own thoughts or beliefs."

I got calls from parents when we came home.

"What happened to my daughter at that camp?"

I was alarmed. "What do you mean?"

"The girl I sent you was interested only in talking to her friends and in shopping. But now she is doing research about water, about settlements. She's reading books about the *Nakba!* She says she wants to be more prepared for the dialogue groups you're planning at the Center!"

At camp, the Seeds entered the dialogue room from the art shack or the canoe. At the Center, they came from their homes. The Israeli kids might have taken a bus—afraid of it exploding. The Palestinian kids may have been harassed at a checkpoint. The youth from Gaza might not have gotten permission to cross Erez and the Israeli Seeds sitting alone in the circle would have to deal with the implications that their army prevented their fellow members of a peace organization from coming to meet them. The reality, in all of its complexities, was brought into the circle in Jerusalem much more than in Maine.

The winter workshop at Kibbutz Yahel was our biggest activity of the year. Activities at Yahel were similar to those at camp, including sports and art. We brought the kids to the incredible sand dunes of the Negev Desert, which they rolled down, screaming and laughing. They continued their intensive dialogue in a beautiful, relaxed atmosphere. The annual winter workshop at Yahel became a treasured tradition.

My best moments with the kids were not at the camp or the Center or even at Yahel. They were in Al Buraq. The rides were always lively—the Seeds laughing with each other, debating with each other, learning from one another, with Peter Tosh or Cheb Khaled playing in the background. But even in Al Buraq, there were reminders of our reality. Mazin and I sat in the Transit waiting for the kids to cross from Erez. The sun was setting, casting pink and yellow light over the southern landscape.

Mazin looked at the sunset and then turned his gaze to the monstrous military installation that Erez had become, fortified with concrete blocks, barbed wire, and sniper towers. "Beautiful country," Mazin said mournfully. "Fucking people."

It would have been easy to run in circles just to keep up with the growing number of activities, but we needed to develop a comprehensive programming strategy. I began to conceive of our program as having five stages:

The first stage was the selection and preparation of the delegations for camp, which the ministries of education were responsible for. Camp was the second stage. The third stage was the follow-up program after camp: continued dialogue, home visits, school presentations.

When the Seeds graduated from high school, the fourth, most sensitive, critical stage began. The majority of Israeli Seeds were entering the army for their mandatory military service and the majority of Palestinian Seeds were entering university. How should we, as a peace organization, prepare them for this next stage? How should we help them deal with the dilemmas they would face?

The issue of Israeli Seeds becoming soldiers was thorny. In some units, Israelis were forbidden to interact with Palestinians. Other Israeli Seeds could not reconcile being a soldier with being a part of Seeds of Peace and lost contact with us. But many of the Israeli soldiers wanted to stay involved with Seeds of Peace. This was equally complex. The nineteen-year-old Palestinian Seeds were in university, carrying pens. The nineteen-year-old Israeli Seeds were in the military, carrying M16s. How can someone serving in the army be an ambassador for peace? How could Palestinian students be expected to sit at a table with Israeli soldiers? Would the leadership of Seeds of Peace welcome the participation of Palestinian Seeds who had joined a militant re-sistance group? I suspected not. It was inherently unbalanced.

At the same time, I understood that most Israeli youth did not feel they had any choice but to serve. Indeed, many of them served proudly. Since birth, their society had prepared them to be good soldiers. The entire ideol-ogy of the Israeli state was built on its military. Would it be serving our goal to refuse to let Israeli Seeds participate because their government forced them to be soldiers? It was especially important in this stage to keep the rela-tionships between the Seeds alive, to make sure the Israelis understood how their participation in the army affected their Palestinian friends.

"What will happen if you're guarding a checkpoint that I'm crossing?" the Palestinian Seeds wanted to know when the issue came up in dialogue groups.

"Wouldn't you prefer that I be at the checkpoint, knowing I will treat people with respect, rather than someone who might be abusive?" the Israelis often retorted.

For the Israelis, the primary concern was often how their power at the checkpoint was used. For the Palestinians, it was the structural violence in-herent in having to cross a checkpoint under the control of armed soldiers who regarded them as the enemy.

The fifth stage was for the graduates. What could Seeds of Peace offer our adult members, those who had completed university and/or the army? The vast majority of our participants were still under twenty years of age. But as the years marched on, our "kids" were growing up. We would have to address this soon.

The year 2000 began in a flurry. We took the Israeli and Palestinian kids back to Jordan and to Egypt. Our activities expanded to include families and friends of Seeds. Our connection with the families and the communities grew stronger. Parents knew if their kids were with us, they were being taken care of. "I'm not pro-Israeli and I'm not pro-Palestinian," Ned often said. "I'm pro-kid."

Jen Marlowe, who had been a counselor at the camp, joined our team in June 2000. After a long day of leading art or drama projects at the Center, she would drive north to spend the night with Slava and her family in Afula and then spend the next night in Silat al-Dhaher near Jenin with Asmaa and her family. It was clear that she loved the kids, loved our mission, and loved our work.

Al Buraq was getting too old and worn-down for the amount of driving I was doing. I gave it to one of my brothers and Alan Ginsburg provided the funding for a newer, white Seeds of Peace Ford Transit, which we named "Daddy G" in his honor.

Azzam and Mazin began working nearly full-time. They joined us regularly when we drank Taybeh beer at Askadenia, the East Jerusalem restaurant that became the staff hangout. Adam and Fishman invited the staff to their apartment for dinner one night. Azzam propped his feet up on their leather couch.

"Azzam, will you take your feet off my couch?" Adam said.

Azzam gave Adam his famous one-cocked-eyebrow expression. "What? Your ass is better than my feet?"

We all burst into laughter. Their huge hearts, combined with Azzam's acerbic wit, made Azzam and Mazin brothers to all the staff.

A few days before our summer Jordan trip, we received two pieces of bad news. The first was that John Wallach had been diagnosed with an aggressive form of lung cancer. The second was that the Camp David summit to resolve the final status issues of the Oslo Accords had failed. I was shocked about John but not surprised about Camp David. The agreement that Arafat had been pushed to sign was not acceptable to me or any other Palestinian. But the collapse of Camp David gave extremists on both sides new license to spew their rhetoric. The drumbeat of war was gaining strength. I hoped progress could be made before it grew any louder.

Our Jordan trip that summer coincided with the Jerash music and cultural festival. Musicians from all over the Arab world were performing at the ancient Roman amphitheatre in Jerash. We could take the kids to see Ehab Tawfik, a famous Egyptian singer!

The security guards carved out a special place for our entire group, right on the floor of the amphitheatre, close enough to touch Ehab Tawfik on the stage. The reserved section was filled with green T-shirts. People pointed at us, whispering, "Who are they? Are they going to perform, too?"

We were putting forty-five Israeli youth with 9,000 Arabs from all over the Arab world. I paced around the perimeter of our special section, reminding the kids to speak only English. There was no need to broadcast that we had Israelis in our midst.

The concert began. Ehab Tawfik took the stage. The music and the excitement penetrated the entire crowd. Our kids started to clap and dance. Ehab Tawfik leaned over the stage between songs and asked us, "Who are you? What's up with those T-shirts?"

Slava threw a Seeds of Peace T-shirt onto the stage. It landed at Tawfik's feet.

"We're Seeds of Peace!" Slava shouted back. "I'm from Israel!"

My heart stopped. I felt as if Slava's words were amplified to all 9,000 people from every country in the Arab world.

Tawfik straightened up. He kissed the tips of his fingers and then flicked his fingertips over us, as if the kisses could sprinkle down on us.

"Let's welcome the peace group!" he announced into his microphone. "Come on, everybody, clap for peace!" The crowd started clapping and chanting, "*Salaam, salaam, salaam!*"*

My heart began to beat again. The crowd of 9,000 had embraced our small group. The magic of the music and the word *peace*, said by the right person at the right time, brought everyone into the human-being circle that night. I hoped that the satellite channels, especially in Israel, had broadcast that moment. I wanted Israelis to see 9,000 Arabs from all over the Arab world—loving music, clapping for peace, and warmly enveloping us.

Summer 2000 ended with a huge talent show, hosted by Tal, a Jewish Israeli Seed, and Aseel Asleh, from Arabeh village in the Galilee. Aseel was a natural choice to host the talent show; he was one of the most dynamic, friendly, engaging kids I had ever met. A Palestinian from inside Israel, he used his knowledge of Israeli society and Hebrew language, along with his strong identity and pride as a Palestinian Muslim Arab (not to mention his ability to quote the lyrics of Tupac Shakur), to create a web of friendships that connected Seeds from every delegation, nationality, and religion. Everyone was drawn to Aseel, especially when he smiled. Aseel's smile could light up a room. I had spent long hours with Aseel in Al Buraq, driving between the Center and his village. We talked about his plans to study in university and his love of music and computers. Aseel taught me how to use the computer in my office.

Hundreds of Seeds poured in for the talent show. It was the largest gathering since the opening of the Center. Aseel always had the energy of twenty kids packed into his one sturdy seventeen-year-old body, but during the talent show he was a dynamo, one moment coaching a performer in the corner, the next moment doing a silly routine on stage with Tal to introduce the next act. Ned pulled him aside and whispered something in his ear. Grinning, Aseel leapt up on stage. "Hey, Seeds of Peace!" he shouted into the microphone.

*Arabic for "Peace, peace, peace!"

It was the start of the Seeds of Peace cheer. The sea of green T-shirts stood up, shouting in unison, "Hey!" back to Aseel.

I smiled broadly as I watched the Seeds cheering and clapping, led by Aseel. It was Aseel in all his glory.

It was Seeds of Peace in all our glory.

CHAPTER TWELVE

✿

THURSDAY, SEPTEMBER 28, 2000. I was at the Center, organizing transportation for a meeting. I called home to see if Sa'ed was available to drive. My mother answered.

"Sami, Ariel Sharon is on Haram Al Sharif. One thousand soldiers and police are with him!"

It had been announced earlier in the week that Sharon would pay a visit to Haram Al Sharif to emphasize Israeli control of the holy site. It was an incendiary political act in the wake of the failed Camp David summit and an effort to directly challenge Israeli Prime Minister Ehud Barak. Sharon, the former general and defense minister who spearheaded the 1982 invasion of Lebanon and championed settlement-building in the West Bank and Gaza, was now the chair of the Likud Party and leader of the opposition. He would be the number one beneficiary of a renewal of hostilities.

"*Shabab* are filling the compound to protect the mosque," my mother said, anxiety in her voice.

Fishman and I drove to the Old City. East Jerusalem was electric with tension as I walked toward Herod's Gate. Police and soldiers were everywhere, some of them on horseback. I had not seen the Old City so militarized in years. Sharon had already left but demonstrations were just getting under way. Fishman and I went up on Haram Al Sharif together. People were crying and calling out, "*Wen asalaam?*"* Fishman wanted to take pictures. I told him it would be a bad idea. We did not stay long.

Friday, September 29. The protests in Jerusalem intensified. One Palestinian killed in the Old City, the news reported early that day . . . A few hours later

---

*Arabic for "Where is the peace?"

it was three . . . Soon it was five. A knot in the pit of my stomach grew tighter with each death. Tires were burning around the city, sending thick black smoke into the air. Several roads were closed.

Saturday, September 30. The demonstrations had spread. Kids all over the West Bank and Gaza were throwing stones at armed soldiers. But now, with a Palestinian police force, there were Palestinians with guns as well. Whenever Palestinian police or gunmen shot a few rounds at the soldiers, it gave the army license to fire live ammunition at unarmed twelve- and thirteen-year-old boys.

I sat on the balcony, smoking a cigarette, trying to momentarily escape the relentless stream of worsening news.

Ned opened the door to the balcony. He looked a little gray. "Twelve-year-old boy killed in Gaza," he said. "French TV caught it on film. Horrible." Ned slumped into a chair next to me. "Everything is collapsing."

Ned, Roy, Huwaida, Fishman, Larry Malm (a former Seeds counselor and yearlong volunteer), and I had an emergency staff meeting at the Center. Adam and Jen were back in the United States; they would be returning in a few days.

"Is this going to blow over?" Fishman asked.

"Yes, sure. It will only last three more days," I answered.

"I hope it ends in three days," Fishman responded. "If not, it won't stop for three years."

We talked for hours about how we, as Seeds of Peace, should respond to the escalating violence. Ned left the room frequently to check the news.

"Let's start calling the kids," Roy said. "They need to hear from us." We divided up years of camp and geographic areas, holed ourselves up in our offices, and began making calls.

I was hit by a tidal wave of grief, anger, and fear as I called Seed after Seed from Ramallah, Nablus, Tulkarem, Gaza. When Enas from Gaza City heard my voice on the other end of the phone, she burst into tears. For ten solid minutes I did nothing but listen to her weep. When she was finally able to speak, the words tumbled out in such a rush that I could barely understand her.

Sunday, October 1. Two Israeli security forces were killed, one by a Palestinian colleague on a joint patrol and the second in gun battles around Kabr Yusuf* in Nablus. By day's end, the total number of Palestinians killed in the

---

*Arabic for "Joseph's tomb."

West Bank and Gaza rose to twenty-three, eight of them children, and two of them shot by helicopter gunship fire. Dina from Nablus was huddled in the corner of her bedroom, shaking in terror, when I reached her. Helicopters were hovering above her house, shooting. Her thirteen-year-old neighbor had been killed as he stood on his balcony. She was convinced that soldiers were going to burst into her house at any moment and kill her and her family. This was looking less and less like an *intifada* and more and more like a unilateral war.

Greater numbers of Palestinians took to the streets en masse, angrily shouting against this brutal use of lethal force. Protests erupted in many Palestinian towns and villages inside Israel as well. The news reported roads being blocked off in the north of Israel and live ammunition being used on Palestinian citizens of Israel. Three Palestinians from inside '48 had been killed.

My phone rang. It was my nineteen-year-old brother, Majdi. "Everyone in the Old City is demonstrating against this bloodshed. Where are you? We need every voice, *yallah!*"

"I'm at the Seeds of Peace Center. I have to work," I said. It was a lie. I had no work. I just sat, listening to the deteriorating events on the news and calling Seeds to check on their well-being. I could not admit the real truth: Seeds of Peace staff members were not permitted to take part in demonstrations; it would compromise our ability to be trusted by kids and families on both sides. I felt self-disgust every time I picked up the phone to find out what was happening in the Old City. I should not have been calling; I should have been in the streets, with my people.

Monday, October 2. I sat on the balcony at the Center with Roy, smoking and drinking coffee. I had not slept much the night before. I had not shaved. The news was growing grimmer by the moment. A group of Israeli Seeds was in the corner office writing a letter to Israeli Prime Minister Ehud Barak and Palestinian Authority President Yasser Arafat, demanding a cessation of the excessive violence and a renewal of negotiations. Larry stepped out onto the balcony. He was white as a sheet. He stood for a moment in silence as Roy and I stared at him, dreading to ask what had happened.

"Aseel was shot in the neck. He's at the hospital in Nahariyah."

I must not have heard right. Aseel Asleh? Shot? There must be some mistake. Roy jumped up. "We're going to the hospital." Nahariyah was a three-hour drive from Jerusalem, but that did not matter. Aseel had been shot; we had to go there and be with him and his family.

Ned grabbed his cell phone. "Let me call his sister to see if she knows any more details."

I went to get the Transit keys from my desk. When I got back to the kitchen, Ned was just hanging up the phone.

"Nardin said the roads to Nahariyah are blocked and that we'll never get to the hospital," Ned reported.

Roy was impatient. "Doesn't matter. We have to try to get there."

Larry tried to be the voice of reason. "Maybe we should wait a few hours to see if the roads clear up—and hopefully then we'll know more about Aseel's condition?"

Fishman was usually the first to crack a joke, but now he was sitting with his head in his hands.

We debated, argued, tried to contact Nardin again to no avail, and finally decided that road blockages or not, we had to try to reach Aseel. We got into the Transit and I started to drive. Just as I was approaching the exit of Jerusalem, Larry called Aseel's house again to see if there was any update.

He hung up the phone moments later, his hands shaking and his voice trembling. "No need to go to Nahariyah."

No one said a word. I turned the Transit around and drove back to the Center. It was only after we were inside, on the second-floor balcony, that we began to cry. I silently rolled cigarettes and offered them to my colleagues. Everyone took one and lit up through their tears, even though most of them did not smoke. *Ya* Allah. Just yesterday, it seemed, I was driving Aseel and Slava home through the Jordan Valley, both of them laughing and trying to spot sheep in the desert mountains. Just yesterday, it seemed, Aseel and Slava were discussing borders and whether they were necessary. Aseel thought they were not. Aseel believed that all the world should be open.

"They killed Aseel," Roy said quietly, in a monotone voice, over and over. "They killed Aseel."

This Intifada was not going to stop after three days. I had been wrong. This was the end of everything.

Somehow we all got to our homes that night. Somehow we drifted off to a few hours of fitful sleep.

Stunned Seeds and foreign journalists streamed into the Center the next day. The Seeds decorated the main room with candles and flowers and photographs of Aseel. We walked around the Center shaking our heads and holding each other in silence. Ned ordered pizza to feed the kids and arranged rides home for them with my brothers. But he was moving and talking as if he were in a trance.

We called Aseel's friends, those who had not yet heard. We still did not know what had happened. All we knew was that he had been shot in the neck by Israeli police and pronounced dead at the hospital.

Rana from Jenin broke down when I told her. "What's the use of talking to Israelis? I don't believe in peace! How can there be peace if they killed Aseel?" she sobbed.

Adam returned that afternoon. Adam and I lowered the green Seeds of Peace flag to half-mast. We hung six huge black sheets from the Center roof in every direction—a sign of mourning in the Muslim tradition—Aseel's faith.

Ned pulled me into his office and shut the door, something we almost never did at the Center.

"I just spoke to Hadara," Ned said, his voice constricted.

Hadara was the representative from the Israeli Ministry of Education who selected and prepared the Israeli delegations. She had never liked Aseel, it seemed to me. Though he had gone to camp as a member of the Israeli delegation, Aseel always spoke loudly and clearly about his identity and history as a Palestinian. He talked about the racism and discrimination that his community faced inside Israel. My guess was that Hadara did not appreciate that.

"What did she say?"

Ned could barely look up. "She said, 'It is a catastrophe.' I said, 'Yes, it is a catastrophe.' She said, 'It's a catastrophe for the organization.' I said, 'Yes, it's a catastrophe for all of us.' She said, 'It's a catastrophe for the organization that this boy, who was educated in this organization, was out there throwing stones.'"

"What is she talking about? We know Aseel! That's not Aseel!"

"I know. I said, 'We have no idea what happened there. No one knows anything about throwing stones.'"

"What did Hadara say?"

"She said, 'There are pictures from the police—Aseel was throwing stones.'"

The Center was in crisis-control mode. The phone was ringing off the hook with Seeds who had heard about Aseel and wanted to know details. Ned and Adam were talking to John Wallach and Bobbie Gottschalk* in the States, trying to determine how Seeds of Peace should respond. A steady stream of

*Cofounder and vice president of Seeds of Peace.

Seeds were coming in and out of the Center, wanting to offer their help, wanting to grieve with us and with each other. In the midst of the chaos, a middle-age man stormed inside the Center.

"Can I help you?" I asked him.

"Why is your building covered in black flags?" he shouted.

"One of the kids from our program was killed," I told him. "Aseel Asleh from Arabeh. We're in mourning for him. Is there a problem?"

"Yes, there is! When Israelis die, you don't put up black flags. There are widows and war veterans in this neighborhood, but you didn't put up black flags for them! But when Palestinians die, you put up black flags? If you don't remove them, I'm going to the French Hill council!"

Before I could respond, Iddo Felsenthal, a seventeen-year-old Israeli Seed, interjected. His normally level voice was raised. "It has nothing to do with whether he was Israeli or Palestinian! Someone from our organization was killed, a member of our family!"

The man sensed that Iddo's and my tempers were both rising. His tone became more conciliatory. "Okay, okay, I understand. But do you really need so many black flags? Your entire building is covered in black."

Adam, Ned, and I talked it over when he left. We did not want to antagonize the neighbors or create more conflict. We would keep one big flag in each corner of the building. That would still communicate our grief. The others we would remove.

Ned left messages with Aseel's family but was not able to get through.

Nardin, Aseel's twenty-year-old sister, called Ned the next day. "Where are you?" she asked. "We need you here." Ned, Huwaida, and I immediately left for Arabeh with several Seeds who were at the Center to mourn. We did not say much during the three-hour drive. We pulled into the driveway of Aseel's home, where I had dropped him off so many times before. A large sign in front of the driveway read, THE MARTYRED HERO ASEEL HASSAN ASLEH. There were black flags and Palestinian flags everywhere. The house was overflowing. Delegations from Arab parties of the Knesset were there. There were colleagues and friends of Um Aseel, a teacher, and Abu Aseel, who owned a small market and was active in the community. Aseel's classmates were there. There were scores of people from Arabeh and neighboring villages who had not known Aseel personally. The killing of Aseel and other Palestinians from inside '48 was a tragedy for all the community.*

---

*Twelve Palestinian citizens of Israel were killed in the first eight days of October 2000 by Israeli security forces, and one man from Gaza was also killed inside Israel—thirteen total.

Nardin came and took us inside. She was wearing one of Aseel's green Seeds of Peace shirts. So was Aseel's fourteen-year-old sister, Siwar. Um Aseel burst into sobs when she saw us in our green shirts. "Tell them the truth about Aseel! Don't let them lie about him!" She hugged me—a desperate, clinging hug. "This is Sami, who brought Aseel to the States for his third summer at camp. He always brought Aseel back home safely."

"We are all your children here, Um Aseel. Our hearts are broken with yours." What else could I say? I kissed her hand.

Um Aseel clutched at my T-shirt. "The T-shirt, the green Seeds of Peace T-shirt. Aseel was wearing it when they killed him!" she sobbed. My heart skipped a beat. Aseel was killed wearing the Seeds of Peace T-shirt?

I went to the men's tent and sat in silence, sipping bitter coffee. How could we support Aseel's family? We had to be here with them as much as possible, every day if they needed us. We had to be strong for Aseel's friends from Seeds of Peace who were in such shock and pain. But who would support us? The Center staff was Aseel's second family. Who could we turn to?

Ned, Huwaida, and I returned to Arabeh the next day. Aseel's family took us to the cemetery. Ten-year-old Bara'a prayed in front of his brother's grave, palms up in supplication, red-eyed. He then went to Nardin's side and buried his face in her sweatshirt.

Nardin took us to the spot where Aseel had been killed. It was off the main road leading from Arabeh to Karmiel. Aseel had gone to the demonstration without informing anyone, Nardin told us. When his mother and father learned he was there, they went to bring him home. There were police on the road—Nardin pointed out the spot—and the demonstrators were in the valley below, near the olive grove. Um and Abu Aseel stood on a mound of dirt trying to locate their son. The green Seeds of Peace T-shirt made him easy to spot. Aseel stood on the opposite side of the road from the center of the demonstration. Um Aseel called his cell phone, but it was shut off. Suddenly three police climbed over the guardrail and charged toward Aseel. Aseel turned to run into the olive grove, with the policemen chasing him. One of the police struck him with his rifle butt on his back, just below his neck. Aseel stumbled and fell. The olive trees obstructed Um and Abu Aseel's view of their son. They heard a shot ring out. The police walked out of the olive grove. "You can come and get him now," Abu Aseel heard a policeman say. After that, Nardin told us, her father fainted. The other demonstrators managed to get Aseel into a car, which got held up by soldiers at a checkpoint, before he was switched to an ambulance, which got held up at another checkpoint, before he reached a hospital over an hour and a half later. He was pronounced dead on arrival. Abu Aseel and Nardin saw his body before burying him in the village cemetery. His back and shoulders were covered in bruises. The fatal bullet, a doctor in the hospital had surmised, was shot point-blank to his neck. Nardin led us to the tree under which Aseel had been executed. I crouched down, gathering small stones, stained with Aseel's blood. Aseel was buried in his Seeds of Peace T-shirt, Nardin told us, soaked in the same blood.

Ned sat with Abu Aseel alone, in Aseel's room, to write down every detail of the story. It was there that he asked him the difficult question that we would all be asked repeatedly in the weeks to come—not because anything would justify the killing, but because we had to be able to answer clearly and truthfully. Abu Aseel looked Ned straight in the eye and answered his question. Aseel had not thrown a single stone.

We made the six-hour round-trip drive from Jerusalem to Arabeh the next day, and the day after that, each time bringing different groups of Aseel's Jewish and Palestinian friends, placing flowers and lighting candles at his grave, drinking bitter coffee with his family. We returned home at 2 a.m., went to sleep, woke up, and began the drive again. Even so, we could not bring all the Seeds who wanted to come. The West Bank and Gaza were still in flames; there was no way to get those Seeds inside the Green Line.

At home late at night, physically and emotionally exhausted, I held the small stones with Aseel's dried blood on the palm of my hand. I had known other *shuhada*. But this was the first time that the *shaheed* was a child whose hopes and dreams my colleagues and I had helped to nurture, whose potential for the future we had taken pride in. A piece of our heart had been ripped out. They did not just kill Aseel. They killed his dreams. They killed our dreams.

꧁

TED KOPPEL ORGANIZED a town hall meeting in Jerusalem, to be broadcast for an episode of *Nightline*, and asked us to bring youth from Seeds of Peace to sit in the studio audience. We brought several Seeds, including Moran, an Israeli girl from Rishon LeZion who was Aseel's friend and had been to his home both before and after his death. Koppel interviewed a panel of Israeli and Palestinian politicians, including former Palestinian Authority Higher Education Minister Dr. Hanan Ashrawi, Palestinian negotiator Saeb Erekat, Arab Knesset Member Azmi Bishara, Israeli Jerusalem Mayor Ehud Olmert, Knesset Deputy Speaker Naomi Chazan, and Israeli Deputy Defense Minister Ephraim Sneh. During the question period, Moran asked the deputy minister why lethal force had been used against her friend, who was an Israeli citizen. Sneh responded that security forces had to respond to threats against their lives.

Undaunted, Moran spoke up again. "My friend was seventeen years old. I don't think he was a threat to anyone. Why was he shot?"

Following the broadcast, there was an outcry from within Israel that an Israeli had dared to be critical of her country's security forces on international television during this time of crisis. Moran was now getting death threats calling her a traitor.

The Seeds wrote messages filled with rage and despair on Seedsnet, the Seeds of Peace daily Internet forum that Aseel had helped create. Seeds from Ramallah, Nablus, and Khan Younis wrote about the deaths of uncles and friends. Louay, from Rafah, Gaza, wrote about his home being destroyed. His family was given ten minutes to get out with whatever possessions they could carry. Hilly, an Israeli Seed from Arad, wrote that she had spoken up in class about the deaths of innocent Palestinians. A classmate screamed that she had become "Arafat's whore." She was not sure if she could continue speaking out. Danny, an Israeli Seed from Upper Nazareth, wrote about cowering on the floor as Arab and Jewish mobs rioted outside, throwing stones. He heard sounds of gunfire outside his window. The streets in his neighborhood were blocked and the sky above him was covered with black smoke clouds. Finally I wrote my own message.

Life here has turned upside down; there is war in the Middle East. Everybody is afraid. Last night no one slept well, including me.

In the Old City of Jerusalem, people were afraid because they thought the settlers would come to make trouble in Palestinian homes. In Gilo, no one slept well because they feared shooting, and they felt the loud rumble of the tanks. On the other side, in Beit Jala, no one slept because the tanks were bombing their homes.

Three Israeli mothers didn't sleep well, because they were thinking about their sons kidnapped by Hizbullah. Dozens of Palestinian mothers were not sleeping well because they have lost their sons. Many people did not sleep because they were in the hospital. A lot of religious people, Jews and Muslims, did not sleep well because they were thinking about Joseph's Tomb and Tiberias Mosque, both destroyed by mobs this week.

Many people in Palestinian villages did not sleep because the settlers went to make trouble there. Many settlers didn't sleep because Palestinian groups are shooting at their settlements. Azmi Bishara, the Palestinian-Israeli member of Knesset, did not sleep because 300 Israeli kids threw stones at his house, then 300 Palestinian kids threw stones at the Israeli kids, and then they all threw stones at each other. The family of an Israeli taxi driver from Rishon LeZion didn't sleep because he was killed when Arab-Israelis threw stones at his car. The family of a Palestinian man in Bidea, the same night, maybe the same time, did not sleep because he was killed by settlers.

A Palestinian group didn't sleep because they were shooting at an Israeli bus in the Gaza Strip. And Israeli units in the army did not sleep because they were busy destroying two big buildings in Gaza.

Ned did not fall asleep until 6 in the morning because all night he was thinking about this situation. In the Arab governments, no one slept, because they were thinking about demonstrations in the Arab capitals, and how they can take the people's anger far away.

We would like to sleep. We hope the leaders will make a quiet situation for us in the Middle East. If they don't sit together now, they must sit together tomorrow, or after tomorrow, or after one month. They must do it quickly. We want to sleep. We want to sleep. We want to sleep.

Peaceful sleep was not in our near future. On October 12, two Israeli soldiers were lynched by a mob in the Ramallah police station, the same one where I had been detained. An Italian television crew caught it on film, including a Palestinian man triumphantly displaying his blood-soaked hands to the crowd below. I was disgusted by the act and terrified of what the response would be. The army sealed off all Palestinian cities. A few hours later, the police station and Sawt al-Falestin* radio station in Ramallah were attacked by helicopter gunship, and buildings near Arafat's headquarters in Gaza were bombed.

Jen was supposed to return to the region the next day. John told her to wait in the United States. But a week later, Jen called me from the airport to see if I could pick her up.

"I thought John told you to wait in the States," I said to Jen as she got into the Transit. "Are you trying to get yourself fired?"

"I have to be here with the kids," she said with a hard edge in her voice that I had not heard before. "Seeds of Peace can fire me if they want to. I have to be here."

---

*Arabic for "Voice of Palestine."

INITIALLY ONLY THE FOREIGN PRESS covered what happened to Aseel. In the Israeli press, his murder warranted only a name and a statistic. But a week later, a journalist named Naava from *Ma'ariv*, a mainstream Israeli newspaper, contacted Ned. She wanted to go to Aseel's home.

I drove while Ned used the time in the Transit to tell Naava as much about Aseel as he could squeeze into the three-hour ride. Naava was polite, but I could tell from her comments and questions the story she intended to write—that Seeds of Peace must have failed if one of its star participants had attacked the police and gotten himself killed.

We got to Arabeh and Naava met Nardin and Abu and Um Aseel. She went to the grove where Aseel was killed. Naava was not at all prepared for what she heard and saw; the story of how Aseel was killed, the eloquence, intelligence, and pride of Aseel's family. On the way home, she called her editors, her friends, and her family, to tell them about the incredible people she had just met. When she got back to her office, she broke the real story in the Israeli press. It was the first humanizing story about any of the Palestinian victims from inside Israel. Aseel's story broke through when nothing else could.

A few weeks later, we learned that one of Israel's main television channels was doing a report on Aseel. It was airing the next Friday night. I went to Ned and Roy's apartment to watch it with them.

"If Hadara was right that the police have photos of Aseel throwing stones, this is where they will come out," Ned said, clearly worried.

The segment began. Abu Aseel took journalist Itai Engel to the olive grove where Aseel was killed and told the entire story. It was followed by an interview with the district police commander. Ned stiffened when the interview began.

Engel asked the police commander what exactly happened in Arabeh. Looking nervous, the police commander muttered something about having run out of nonlethal crowd-dispersal mechanisms.

"So then you go to live ammunition?" Engel asked.

The police commander stuttered a nonresponse.

"Why was Aseel Asleh killed?" Engel pressed.

The commander looked down and finally said, "I don't know."

The segment ended. Ned fell to the floor, weeping. Roy had to pick him up.

There were no incriminating photos, no evidence against Aseel. There was no explanation for the murder of our friend.

My worry for my own children increased. Nasser was nine years old, Asala was six, and Yazan was now two. All I ever wanted was to create a better future for them. I was sad and frustrated, knowing that I could not protect them from suffering. All I could do was create other, positive opportunities for them, to counterbalance the violence and pain they were witness to. I took them to the same club in the Old City that I had played in as a boy, helping them get involved in sports activities and *dabkeh* classes.

We organized meetings with the Seeds in as many cities as we could, so we could support them and they could support each other. Many Palestinian Seeds asked why Seeds of Peace was not protesting the killings. Some of Aseel's Jewish Israeli friends wanted to stage a demonstration about what had happened to Aseel. The Center staff was equally desperate to pursue some kind of meaningful action. We created a book for Aseel's memory, but it was not enough. Ned and Adam had a series of very difficult conversations with John Wallach. John refused to make a statement of condemnation about Aseel's killing. A statement calling for an investigation, yes. Condemnation, no. Seeds of Peace as an organization had to remain apolitical, John insisted. The Seeds could do what they wanted as individuals, but not through the organization. Though Ned and Adam had gotten Aseel's story out to the media, we were unable to lead our kids in publicly condemning his murder.

A spate of bloody bombings began inside Israel. The first was a car bomb on November 2, near the Mahane Yehuda market in West Jerusalem. Larry had been just blocks away and returned to the Center completely unglued. I had no more ambivalence about the bombings, as I had once had; I hated all the killings. I no longer distinguished between "my kids" and "their kids." They were all our kids. Targeted assassinations of Palestinians resumed a week later, almost always killing civilians who were in the vicinity.

I was sitting behind my desk one afternoon, unshaven, playing Internet chess, when Amit called. Amit was a Seed from the Jerusalem neighborhood of Gilo, considered a settlement by Palestinians, as it was in East Jerusalem. Gunmen from Beit Jala, a town bordering Bethlehem, had been shooting at Gilo for weeks now.

"I'm safe enough," Amit replied to my asking if she was okay. "But I can hear Beit Jala being bombarded right now. I'm worried about Najib. Can you call him and make sure he's okay?" Najib was from Beit Jala. He and Amit had been at camp together the previous summer.

"Why don't you call him, Amit? I'm sure Najib would appreciate hearing from you."

Amit hesitated. "I can't bring myself to call him. I don't know why. I just can't. But please make sure he's okay. Tell him that I worry about him and I only hope things will get better very soon—for both of us."

I called Najib. "I can hear the shooting around me," he said. "My three-year-old brother can't stop crying." We hung up just as tank shells were landing around his home.

Huwaida, Jen, and I went to Beit Jala the next day to see Najib and to survey the massive destruction. Najib, fifteen years old, had always been gregarious, funny, and lively. But when he greeted us, his eyes were hollow.

Najib told us that the tank shelling had continued until 4 a.m. Then helicopter gunship fire began. The father of Najib's girlfriend, a doctor, had been assisting the injured when he was shot from a helicopter. Najib had been one of the first people on the scene, collecting pieces of his girlfriend's father so that he could be buried.

"I've been throwing up all day," he told us.

Huwaida had brought presents for Najib's little brother. She handed them to Najib. He thanked us but seemed puzzled, as if he could not comprehend what possible purpose Play-Doh, stickers, and alphabet blocks had.

We were scared on New Year's Eve. Binyamin Kahane, the son of Kach founder Meir Kahane, had been ambushed in his car and killed by Palestinian gunmen near the Israeli settlement Ofra. Gangs of right-wing settler youth were on the rampage in the West Bank and East Jerusalem seeking vengeance for the murder. The Center staff went to Ned's apartment to drink, watch a soccer game on TV, and try to forget about the fact that the New Year was beginning with displays of hatred and violence. My colleagues' apartment offered a view of southern Jerusalem all the way to Bethlehem. Larry, Roy, and Ned had spent evenings sitting on their porch counting missiles falling out of helicopters onto Beit Jala.

We heard the sound of explosions.

"Shit," Fishman said. "They're bombing Beit Jala again."

Silently we filed out onto the balcony to see what was happening. We were confused for a moment at the display of colorful lights and patterns that sizzled through the air.

Fireworks. It was midnight.

"Happy New Year," Jen said.

We continued to talk every day to kids in crisis, helping them deal with conflicted emotions. We organized dialogue groups for Palestinian and Jewish kids inside Israel. Fishman spearheaded a new edition of the *Olive Branch*, where our Seeds were given an outlet to write about what they were going through. Though we did as much as we could under the deteriorating circumstances, depression settled in at a deeper level. Ned was moving, talking, even thinking in slow motion. Roy, who had always been so enthusiastic about everything, in constant communication with everyone, began leaving his cell phone in the car or not answering it. Fishman, our staff comedian, was overwhelmed with fear, stress, and uncertainty. His newest running joke was a reminder that he would be leaving us for law school in May. "May *Salamah!*" Fishman announced at every staff meeting, a pun on *Mah salamah*, Arabic for "goodbye." Huwaida, though more active than ever, was getting pulled in the direction of organizing nonviolent demonstrations against the occupation, outside of her capacity with Seeds of Peace. Only Adam and Jen seemed to function with full energy. They had been in the States during that first horrific week when the madness had exploded around us. Perhaps they were not as traumatized as everyone else.

Adam, Huwaida, and I went to a coffee shop in downtown Ramallah to meet with a group of twenty older Palestinian Seeds. The Seeds were angry. This was not the time, they insisted, for Palestinians and Israelis to be talking about peace. Not when the Israeli army was killing scores of Palestinians, most of them unarmed civilians. How could we meet with Israelis who are— or who soon will be—in the army? I understood their fury, but I tried to present a different logic: the violence made our work even more urgent. If Israelis do not understand that our humanity and blood are equally valuable to theirs, then we will never be safe.

The group of older Seeds dismissed my words. They began drafting a statement to the Palestinian Ministry of Education, asking the ministry not to send a delegation to camp. I was dismayed. "You don't represent all the Palestinian Seeds!" I pointed out to them. "You cannot take this responsibility on behalf of the entire Palestinian delegation!" They continued writing the letter.

A few weeks later, I received a fax from the Palestinian Ministry of Education. It was concise. The Ministry of Education would not send a Palestinian delegation to Seeds of Peace camp that summer. Thirty-eight schools had been partially damaged or destroyed throughout the Occupied Territories. The Ministry of Education office in Ramallah itself had been bombed.

Many families in Khan Younis and Rafah were now homeless and were sleeping in the schools. They had to focus on getting their education system functioning again.

My heart sank as I read the fax. I called John Wallach right away. The Israeli Ministry of Education, he told me, was also refusing to send a delegation. *Well,* I said to myself as I hung up the phone, *at least both the Israeli and the Palestinian ministries of education are being equally shortsighted. The situation may not be balanced, but their stupidity is.*

The Center staff had long, difficult conversations about whether we thought Seeds of Peace should circumvent the decisions of the ministries of education and send Israeli and Palestinian kids to camp that summer. Adam and Huwaida were against it. Even in better days, it had been difficult for our kids to befriend the other side and painful for them to return home and be called "traitor," "Arab/Jew lover," or worse. Adam thought it would be irresponsible to put the kids in that situation under these circumstances, especially without the support of their governments. How could we ask kids from the West Bank and Gaza to shed their emotional defenses, Huwaida asked the rest of the staff, when they needed those defenses to cope with everything blowing up around them? Ned and I wanted kids to go to camp. Now more than ever, they needed to taste the possibility of peace. But we did not think it was wise to organize a delegation without ministry support. We debated passionately. What was best for the organization? More important, what was best for the kids? In the end, most of the Center staff agreed that we should not send Palestinian and Israeli kids to camp. Adam communicated our majority staff opinion to John Wallach. John dismissed it out of hand. He was determined for Seeds of Peace to go ahead with camp no matter what. He used whatever leverage he could. Lindsay Miller, a vice president of Seeds of Peace and wife of Aaron Miller (the third-highest U.S. diplomat working on Arab-Israeli negotiations), was dispatched to meet with high-level Palestinian officials to persuade them to send a delegation, while John tried to convince Hadara from the States. In the end, the mayor of Haifa, Amran Mitzna, agreed to send a delegation of kids from Haifa. Two-thirds of the Haifa delegation would be Jewish and one-third Arab. Though Arafat gave his support for a delegation, the Palestinian Ministry of Education refused to organize it. There would be no Palestinian delegation.

On the one hand, I was proud that kids from Haifa would be, in essence, representing Palestinians. These kids were the products of a system of injustice and discrimination that began in 1948, nearly twenty years before the occupation of the West Bank and Gaza Strip. No one knew the Israelis like they did. But kids from Haifa did not have personal experience of the occupation and violence in the West Bank and Gaza. How could they fully represent the Palestinian issue? And how could we hold camp without a Palestinian delegation, as if they didn't matter? Wasn't the entire idea of Seeds of Peace camp to bring Israeli and Palestinian youth together? Or was it to demonstrate to American donors that Seeds of Peace would march on, even during the Intifada, even without a Palestinian delegation? I thought about the photographers and journalists who constantly flocked to the camp. Were they there to help our youth get their message out to the world? Or, I wondered for the first time, were the kids being used for the purpose of the cameras?

As May approached and violence escalated, Fishman made his "May *Salamah*" jokes with more frequency. Larry had been holding it together until the Or Commission began. The Commission was the Israeli government's investigation of the October killings of the thirteen Palestinians inside Israel, Aseel included. When it became obvious that the policeman who pulled the trigger would not be held accountable, Larry's anger and bitterness began to rise in him like bile. Though he was at the Center as a yearlong volunteer only, I had been hoping he would choose to stay. It was clear now that he would not.

But I was stunned when Roy told me he would also be leaving with Larry and Fishman.

"Why, Roy?" I almost pleaded with him to change his mind. Roy had been with us for three years.

"I love the kids, I love you guys like brothers and sisters, and I will always be proud of what we did together. But the situation is too fucking depressing. It's suffocating me."

"Roy, we can still do something. We have to keep trying . . . "

"There's another reason, Sami," Roy explained. Roy had dual Israeli and American citizenship. He had so far managed to be in Jerusalem nearly three years without being called up to serve in the military except for two weeks of basic training the previous fall, most of which he spent cleaning toilets in the barracks. But that luck was running out. If Roy stayed, he would have to serve in the IDF for several months.

"There's not a snowball's chance in hell I'm going to do that, especially not now," Roy said. "You know me, Sami . . . I'm a lover, not a fighter."

Fishman left in May and Roy followed soon after. Twelve others could not fill the hole that my brothers left, in the Center and in my life.

Now it was just Ned, Jen, Adam, Huwaida, and me to carry the load. And Ned had continually grown slower and sadder, as if he was carrying all the despair, exhaustion, and responsibility of the conflict on his back. He caught the flu at the end of March and could not seem to bounce back. He spent all of April on his living room couch. I took him twice to visit doctors, the only times he left his house. The doctors checked for mononucleosis, then for something with his thyroid. Perhaps deep grief and watching the destruction of your life's work was carried in the thyroid.

Huwaida and Adam also had one foot out the door. Their focus had turned away from dialogue and had moved toward strategizing about how to nonviolently resist the new levels of brutality that the army was inflicting on Palestinians. With others, they founded the International Solidarity Movement.* They asked me several times if I wanted to work with them. I did. I was proud of what they were doing. But to go in the direction they were heading would mean leaving Seeds of Peace.

"I support you," I told them. "And I'll help you however I can. But I'm staying with Seeds of Peace."

Seeds of Peace, despite the dark days, still represented hope. Even with his energy gone, Ned was staying. Jen was there. We could still make a change.

Adam and Huwaida came to me for help not long afterward. They explained their idea: they wanted to get kids all over East Jerusalem to simultaneously release 5,000 balloons in the colors of the Palestinian flag.

"I'd be proud to help," I told them.

I filled five Ford Transits with Al Jundi kids. Each Transit was stuffed with balloons. The Transits went to different locations: Damascus Gate; Mount of Olives; Salah el Din Street. At the exact same moment, the kids released the balloons, briefly covering all of East Jerusalem under the Palestinian flag. I watched my daughter Asala's little face radiate as her balloons drifted higher and higher in the sky. Adam and Huwaida were teaching our kids how to be strong, how to take action. This was exactly the kind of activities Seeds of Peace should be endorsing.

But instead, the leadership of Seeds of Peace distanced themselves from Adam and Huwaida, especially when the International Solidarity Movement

---

*A movement of Palestinians, Israelis, and internationals committed to resisting the Israeli occupation using nonviolent methods and principles.

came under harsh criticism from the Israeli press and government. Adam and Huwaida were leading Palestinians, Israelis, and internationals in jointly and nonviolently fighting oppression and aggression. Wasn't this one of the best ways to support the possibility of peace? Why would Seeds of Peace not embrace that? Claiming that Seeds of Peace was nonpolitical did not hold up. Conflict and its resolution are inherently political. Desmond Tutu, the South African archbishop, once said, "If you are neutral in situations of injustice, you have chosen the side of the oppressor." Riyyad's warnings came echoing back to me . . . Seeds of Peace is a Zionist organization. I shook those thoughts away. I knew what Ned, Jen, and I did day-to-day and I knew what motivated us. It was not driven by what was beneficial to one side or the other. It was motivated by love for our kids, all our kids.

⁓⁓⁓

CAMP BEGAN IN JUNE 2001, with a delegation of Jewish and Arab kids from Haifa meeting with kids from Jordan and Egypt. In the middle of the summer, the Palestinian ambassador to the UN started asking why there was not a Palestinian presence at Seeds of Peace. Saeb Erekat, the chief negotiator for the Palestinian Authority, made it clear that he wanted there to be a Palestinian delegation at camp the following summer, even if it was organized outside the Ministry of Education.

While camp was in session, Adam and I helped Israeli and Palestinian Seeds organize and lead separate workshops on courageous topics that they chose. The Israelis' workshop questioned military service. The Palestinians' workshop examined nonviolent resistance. We knew the themes were controversial, but we also knew this was what the youth wanted. Adam was willing to stand up to John and others in the organization who would disapprove. These were the last workshops I organized with Adam before he left Seeds of Peace.

Mike Wallach and Jethro Berkman, both former counselors at the camp with long and deep connections to Seeds of Peace, joined Ned, Jen, and me at the Center in the fall of 2001. Ned had taken time off over the summer and his energy had returned. We had new, enthusiastic kids from Haifa who were eager to jump into activities we planned for them. We held meetings with the Palestinian kids throughout the West Bank and Gaza. Palestinian and Jewish kids from inside Israel began school presentations again, "Bring a Friend" events, and home visits on holidays. The Haifa Seeds took the lead in organizing a Seeds of Peace booth in a Jewish-Arab community center's multifaith holiday festival in Haifa. We still could not bring the Seeds from the West Bank and Gaza together with the Seeds from Israel. But we did what we could, when we could, where we could. We even brought Noa's family to visit Bushra's in Al Arroub refugee camp from time to time.

I passed by Jen's office one day in December. She was looking at a card and shaking her head in dismay.

"What is that?"

She handed me the card. There was a photo on the front of a large family—grandparents, parents, and kids. They looked American, they were on a beach, and they were wearing olive green IDF T-shirts. HAPPY HOLIDAYS was printed across the front of the card.

"It's Fred's holiday card."

I waited for the punch line. Fred's holiday card? Fred was the president of the Seeds of Peace board of directors. How could he be sending out holiday cards of his family in Israeli army T-shirts?

Jen was seething. "There's more." She told me about a letter she had seen. It was addressed to Fred's personal contacts, asking them to support Seeds of Peace in these difficult days. According to the president of the board's letter, the reason Seeds of Peace should be supported was that an Arab teenager who became friends with Israelis would not become a terrorist and blow Israelis up.

I left Jen's office, disgusted.

I was driving with Jen when her cell phone rang. It was Bala, who had spoken out so forcefully at the presentation in Herzliya. Bala had just seen a *60 Minutes* segment about Seeds of Peace. The three Palestinian Seeds Morley Safer had interviewed—Rasha, Jawad, and Dina—had all been close friends of Bala's.

"Did you see the piece?" Bala asked Jen. Jen had. I had not, but I had heard that Rasha and Dina had stated that they did not want to be in contact with their friends from "the other side" and that Rasha had said she would not recommend someone joining Seeds of Peace because she did not want their hearts to be broken as hers was.

"I haven't spoken to Rasha or Dina in a year and a half," Bala said. "When I saw the show, I picked up my phone and called Rasha. I just wanted to hear her voice. But it was an old number. I didn't get through."

"Do you want me to give you the new number?" Jen asked Bala.

"No. I'm not supposed to talk to Palestinians right now anyway because of my job in the army. And besides . . . " She paused. "Rasha said on TV that she doesn't want to talk to Israelis." Bala hesitated. "Will you give them a message from me?

"Sure."

"Tell Jawad and Rasha and Dina that I say hi and that they look really great. Dina looked so beautiful, studying in America, wow. Tell them . . . " There was silence.

"Bala, are you there? Did I lose you?"

We heard the sobbing from the other end of the cell connection.

"Tell them they look great and I hope they are doing okay and to stay safe and . . ." Bala could not continue. She hung up the phone.

January 2002. We organized a seminar in Ramallah for the Palestinian Seeds. We began the seminar by going to *al-Muqata'ah,** where Arafat had been virtually imprisoned since the middle of December. Abu Ammar met with us for half an hour, answering questions from the Seeds.

"I still wear my Seeds of Peace pin," he said at the end of the gathering, showing it on his lapel, next to his pin of the Palestinian flag.

Before the seminar, Mike and Jen had traveled all over Israel recording video messages and questions from Israeli Seeds. That night, the Palestinian Seeds watched the video. In small groups afterward, they processed their feelings about whether their friendships with the Israeli Seeds were real, and whether those relationships meant anything in these times. Most of them were not ready to talk to the Israeli Seeds; others said that despite everything, they saw no way other than dialogue. Many of the Israelis on the video had expressed their concern about the safety of the Palestinian Seeds and sorrow about the situation. I was surprised at how much that meant to some of the Palestinian Seeds. Ten of the Palestinian Seeds made video messages back to the Israelis, trying to describe what they had been living through and why it was impossible for them to have gone to camp or to come to the Center.

"Hold on, guys. Don't give up hope. Peace is our only chance," Anan from Jericho told his Israeli counterparts over video.

Khaled, a sweet, goofy kid from Nablus, wanted to say hi to Matan, an Israeli boy who had been in his bunk. "I hope you are safe, Matan. I just don't want any other Seeds to get hurt," Khaled said in his message.

*Arafat's compound.

But while the seminar progressed, horror was happening all around us. A Palestinian gunman broke into a Bat Mitzvah party in Hadera and killed six people. A Palestinian boy in the group Ned and I were facilitating received an urgent call in the middle of the discussion. His friend had been badly beaten at a checkpoint and was hospitalized. As we hung out late into the night, tanks encircled Arafat's compound, where we had been just hours before. In the morning, Samir Rantissi* talked to the group about how Seeds could be media advocates. As he spoke, the Sawt al-Falestin radio and TV station was blown up in downtown Ramallah and fighter jets demolished the police station in Tulkarem. But yet, a girl named Jamilah wanted to close the seminar by singing the Seeds of Peace song.

"How did I, a Jewish American, get here? In Ramallah, encircled by tanks, with all of you?" Ned addressed the group as we were wrapping up. "Because of the power you have had on me with your stories, your lives, who you are. Maybe telling your stories and influencing how a handful of people think won't end the conflict. But it does do something very powerful. Powerful enough to have brought us all here."

I was worried about getting everyone home safely. Nearly every West Bank city had been invaded during the course of the seminar. I talked to friends all over to assess the situation. It was still the lull before the real storm. We had to move quickly.

"The tanks are quiet for the time being," I told the kids. "You can even go and touch them with your hand." I realized that this might be taken as advice. "But don't do that!" I added dryly.

I tried not to show my anxiety as Azzam, Mazin, and I loaded up the Transits. I ran through all the possible points of friction in my mind. Who was killed in recent days, where, and by whom? Where were the tanks and where were they moving? Which roads had had ambushes lately? Which checkpoints were easier at which entrance to which city?

I drove the Nablus kids home myself, dropping them off at Huwwara checkpoint and pulling over to make sure they crossed safely. I remained there a few minutes longer, staring at the field with the army base in its middle. This was the same field I had marched past with Herokushi. At the time, I had predicted that the corn and wheat would eventually take over the field and that the army base would disappear. I had not imagined that tanks would be planted all over the field, replacing the corn and wheat altogether.

*Assistant to Yasser Abed Rabbo, Palestinian Authority minister of culture and information.

MARCH 3, 2002. Israeli tanks, F-16s, and helicopter gunships attacked Beth-lehem. Jen and I headed to Bethlehem after the army pulled out. Najib and Fadi, another Seed from Beit Jala, agreed to show us the damage, with Jen filming to show the Israeli seeds. We started the video tour on the main street in Bethlehem, where a police station had been totally destroyed by F-16s. The neighboring Red Crescent clinic and several shops were demol-ished as well. Najib's face, body, and voice showed his distress.

"Fadi and I are here to show you some stuff that we faced in the past month," Najib began. "As we all know, Gilo has been shot at, and I feel really sorry for that. But the main thing I feel sorry for is Bethlehem. It's the place where Jesus was born. I feel like I'm walking in Afghanistan, not in the holy land. If they consider this a war on the Palestinian Authority, okay, hit the Palestinian Authority, but what do the innocent people have to do with that?" Najib indicated the man behind him, shoveling the bro-ken glass and rubble off the sidewalk in front of his demolished shop. "Israelis that we met at camp, that I played with all the time and talked with and shared the same table and slept in the same room, are going to be soldiers and are going to do these things to us . . . this was really hard for me when I realized this . . . "

Najib and Fadi took us to one of many homes in Dheisheh camp that had been reduced to a mound of concrete rubble and twisted metal. The tent that the family was now sleeping in was next to their demolished home.

"This is the house of refugees from 1948. And the same thing happened in 2002," Fadi said softly. "They don't know what to do about it, you know?" Fadi fell silent for a moment. "I am sure that they will rebuild the camp."

Our last stop was Bethlehem University, where several classrooms had been destroyed by direct missile fire.

"I'm supposed to study here next year," Najib told the Israeli Seeds as Jen filmed the holes in the walls, the smashed windows, the seats covered with rubble, and the dangling ceiling tiles and lights, ready to crash down at any moment. "What do you expect? How am I going to face it? How can I study here if these things continue?"

Fadi wrapped up his thoughts. "The last thing I want to say to every-body . . . try to feel with us, what happened to us and . . . " He struggled to find his next words. "Okay. That's it. Try to feel with us. Thank you."

We played the video to a group of Israeli Seeds a few evenings later. There was a collective gasp in the room when the camera panned from Fadi's and Najib's faces to the rubble of the police station. "Oh my God," muttered Julia from Beit Shemesh.

"It's so much harder to watch Najib and Fadi show me the destruction of Bethlehem than it is watching it on the news," said Rita from Afula to a circle of nodding heads. "I know Fadi and Najib. I trust them."

Najib's comment about becoming soldiers triggered a long discussion about the army: whether to serve; what were the consequences of refusing to serve; whether it was possible to make changes from within the system; how to feel about protecting your country when you know of the abuses suffered at the hands of soldiers from your friends on the other side. The issue of the army was difficult for Israeli Seeds in a time of relative peace. It was excruciating for many of them now. A growing number of Israeli Seeds, many of them friends of Aseel's, became conscientious objectors and refused to serve in the army.

March 27. A Palestinian suicide bomber attacked a hotel in Netanya in the middle of a Pesach seder, killing twenty-nine and injuring scores more.

March 29. The IDF began the reoccupation of large swaths of the West Bank, bringing in its wake the bloodiest weeks since the beginning of the Intifada.

Mike, Jen, and I were trying to talk about other things as we ate lunch at a Chinese restaurant in West Jerusalem. We heard a thudded boom. Another suicide bombing.

At the Center the next morning, I checked the Al Jazeera Web site. "Israeli troops surround Arafat's compound in Ramallah," the ticker read when I logged on. No surprise. Every time Ramallah was invaded, tanks surrounded the compound. A moment later a new headline popped up. "Israeli troops enter al-Muqata'ah." What? This was something new—troops were actually trying to take over the compound? Gun battles around Arafat's headquarters were raging. Arafat's own life was being threatened.

The fighting around al-Muqata'ah continued to grow fiercer. We went to Ned and Mike's apartment that night to watch the news. The reports coming in were grim and scary. My cell phone rang. It was Fadia, wondering when I would be home. I went into the kitchen to talk while the rest of the staff remained glued to the TV.

Mike entered the kitchen. "Tel Aviv," was all he said.

I understood immediately. "How many dead?"

"Don't know. Just happened."

I joined my colleagues in watching the grisly footage of yet another suicide attack. Cell phones were blocked—we were unable to reach our kids in Tel Aviv to check on their welfare.

We watched the multiple horrors on TV, alternating between CNN, BBC, and local Israeli and Arabic stations, piecing together the details of the bombing in Tel Aviv, the worsening siege of al-Muqata'ah, and reports of summary executions of five Palestinian militants by the IDF.

Another drama began to unfold on Jen's cell phone. A text message from sixteen-year-old As'ad. As'ad lived in El Bireh, near Ramallah. As'ad often needed to talk, at length. When his three-year-old cousin with a breathing problem had been killed from tear-gas inhalation a year before, Fishman had been in contact with him on a daily basis. But even for As'ad, this text message seemed desperate.

"Jen, remember how I told you that the Israeli army had already done everything they possibly could?" he wrote. "I was wrong. Now they took over the local TV station and are playing porn!"

Jen wrote back, "What? You're kidding, aren't you?"

He was not. Ned confirmed he had seen it mentioned briefly on an Israeli news site.

Around midnight, back in our news coma, Jen's phone beeped again. Another text message from As'ad. Jen showed it to me in horror.

"Please, it's not funny. I'm sitting here, fully dressed, waiting for them to come and take me. They've already taken my cousins."

I knew what As'ad was talking about—all over Ramallah young men and boys between the ages of fourteen and thirty were routinely being rounded up and arrested. Stories from roundups a few weeks before had included all the detainees being blindfolded, hands tied behind their backs, and numbers written on their forearms until a member of Knesset who was a Holocaust survivor spoke out harshly about the numbers.

Ned and Jen started a furious bout of text messaging with As'ad, trying somehow to give him the strength to endure all that he might have to.

I tried to write something he could hold on to as well. But I could not get the image out of my head of As'ad, sitting on his bed fully dressed in the middle of the night, waiting for soldiers to come and take him.

Things were no brighter when the sun came up the next morning. Moments after I learned that As'ad had not been taken during the night, I got a text message from Ned. It was brief.

"Soldiers searching Bashir's house."

Bashir began with Seeds of Peace the same year Seeds of Peace itself began—1993. Bashir, now twenty-two years old with a recently completed degree in civil engineering, had been on the lawn of the White House along with the rest of the pioneer Seeds during the historic handshake between Rabin and Arafat, with the promise for a future that now was nothing but rubble.

We had decisions to make at the Center about our upcoming week. We were scheduled to hold a Coexistence Marathon for the Haifa Seeds—the exciting weekend-long culmination of ten weeks of dialogue groups. We decided to cancel. The situation was too unstable. We did not realize how wise this was until a few hours later, when Mike came into my office with his next one-word utterance.

"Haifa."

Fifteen people killed. We called the Haifa Seeds and then went out to the balcony to smoke cigarettes.

"I never get used to the sick feeling in my stomach," Jethro said. "I never know what to say when you get someone's mother on the line and I ask if her daughter is okay, and she's crying because she doesn't know the answer."

How much longer could our luck hold out before another of the losses was from our family? Tanks were back in Qalqilyah, Ramallah, and Nablus and were poised for an even larger operation. I ground out my cigarette and we went inside to start calling the Palestinian kids. I knew we would hear shooting in the background and terror in their voices.

Ned's cell phone rang as I drove Mike and him home late that night. It was Sivan, the Israeli Seed who had once visited Bushra in Al Arroub refugee camp. I could hear her tears from the other end of the line. "Ned, *ani lo y'cholah od*," was all she said.

"What does that mean?" asked Mike, who did not speak Hebrew, after Ned hung up.

I translated for Mike. "I can't anymore."

The leadership of the organization evacuated the American staff while the violence raged. My colleagues returned at the end of April. While they were gone, 248 Palestinians and 53 Israelis had been killed. A portion of Jenin refugee camp had been flattened. There were a lot of Seeds who needed our support. And we had to turn our attention to camp.

In September I contacted Sari Nusseibeh's office. Nusseibeh was the president of Al-Quds* University and, since the death of Faisal Husseini a few months earlier, was now the PLO's representative in Jerusalem. His wife, Lucy, had been my boss at the Center for Nonviolence. I broached the idea of

*The Arabic name for Jerusalem.

organizing a delegation of Palestinian kids from Jerusalem under his umbrella. He agreed.

The kids who came to the interviews all studied in private schools in Jerusalem. Many of them were the children of Nusseibeh's friends or colleagues. They had grown up with privilege; they were not directly suffering from the occupation as much as youth from the West Bank or poorer neighborhoods in Jerusalem were. With a few exceptions, they were not interested in politics. I called John, expressing my concern that these kids would not be able to adequately represent our issues and reality. But John was most concerned with having a Palestinian delegation in the summer of 2002, no matter the quality. The Israeli Ministry of Education had received harsh criticism from the Israeli press for not sending a delegation in 2001. They also decided to send a delegation in 2002.

Every summer a small number of Seeds were selected by the Center staff to return to camp as "Peer Supports," to give guidance and support to the younger campers. Returning to camp was the dream of every participant. The meeting to select the Peer Supports lasted a full day. We notified the kids and dealt with the fallout of those who were angry or disappointed that they were not chosen.

Jen came to the next week's staff meeting with a look of disbelief. She had just gotten off the phone with Hadara. There were two Haifa Seeds whom the Ministry of Education was refusing to allow to return to camp: one Jewish girl and one Arab boy. The Arab boy, Haitham, had expressed Palestinian nationalist sentiments that were incompatible with an Israeli delegation, Hadara had said. And the Jewish girl, Shani? I could imagine the contempt in Hadara's voice as she told Jen, "She's more Palestinian than the Palestinians."

There was no way we would accept Hadara's decision. We had followed the procedures that had been established for years. The ministry selected the new campers based on its criteria; we selected the Peer Supports based on ours. From the moment the kids arrived at camp, we encouraged them to express their own opinions honestly. We assured them they would not be judged for their political points of view. But now, these Seeds were being penalized for exactly that. Trust was our most valuable asset. If we did not stand up for Shani and Haitham, we would lose all credibility.

Ned and Jen firmly and respectfully communicated all this to the Ministry of Education and to our supervisors in the United States. Hadara was adamant. The Seeds of Peace leadership was chiefly concerned about not antagonizing the Ministry of Education. John Wallach was losing his battle with cancer and, although still president of Seeds of Peace, was not able to steer the ship. Janet Wallach, his wife, had stepped in while her husband fought for his life.

Jen entered my office and sank into a chair across from my desk, holding a printout of an e-mail from Janet.

"What does it say?"

"That we don't have the right to tell the Israeli government who to select in their delegation." She shook her head. "They don't get it at all."

"What do you think will happen?"

"I don't know," Jen said, the hard edge in her voice returning. "But if Haitham and Shani are not allowed to return to camp, I'm quitting. I won't be a part of damaging kids."

The ministry also did not approve of the left-wing Israelis hired to cofacilitate the dialogue groups with Palestinian partners. Hadara insisted that a former Israeli delegation leader be hired as a facilitator. The upper management of Seeds of Peace conceded. A former representative of the Israeli government would now be sitting inside highly sensitive dialogue groups. The Ministry of Education had never hesitated to make demands in the past. But now, whether because of John's illness or the fear of losing the ministry's participation, Seeds of Peace was caving in to them more than ever.

Haitham's father was the deputy mayor of Haifa. He called a press conference to expose the Ministry of Education's decision and the politics behind it. The Ministry of Education backed down the day before the press conference. Haitham and Shani went to camp. Adam and Ned had already been on the ministry's blacklist. Hadara now added a new person—Jen.

The New York office began to send a succession of people to "run" the Center. First came Bill McLaughlin, a seventy-something former news correspondent at CBS and colleague of John Wallach's. Mister Bill had experience in the Middle East of the 1970s but absolutely no experience with conflict resolution or with youth. His main qualification, it seemed, was that he was neither Jewish nor Arab.

The one good decision Mister Bill made was hiring Reem as the administrative assistant, at my urging. Reem quickly became the glue that held everything together, doing thirty tasks in three languages simultaneously and managing to stay bright and cheerful all the time.

Mister Bill decided early on, it seemed to me, that the American staff were a bunch of pro-Palestinian left-wingers, and Jen the worst. Fortunately, Mister Bill showed up at the Center only a few hours a day. When he left for his home in the south of France that summer, he put me in charge of the Center, making a special point that there were not to be a lot of activities.

At times I agreed with Mister Bill that we should limit activities—the situation was bloodier than ever. But each time Seeds called us, wanting to organize a seminar or meeting, Jen was pushing the gas pedal and revving the engine. I was not going to be the one to stop her. Jen flew faster than a race car, planning and implementing activities with the Seeds, with me trying as best I could just to keep up.

Several Palestinian Seeds needed to cross the Allenby Bridge from Jericho to Jordan to fly from the Amman airport to their universities in the United States; Israel had closed Ben Gurion Airport to anyone from the West Bank or Gaza. It could take seven or eight hours to cross the Allenby Bridge, and on some days crossing was impossible. We needed a letter from the Palestinian DCO so our students could cross as VIPs, the only way to ensure that they would actually get across at all. Despite numerous calls and faxes, I had not obtained the letter. Without it, our kids would possibly miss their flights.

"Let's go to Jericho," Jen said. "Maybe we can find the people we need."

"Jen, it would be a waste of two or three hours. It's already Friday afternoon—there's probably no one in the office anymore. We have no chance."

"There's always a chance, *habibna*," Jen said, taking the Transit keys off my desk. "Maybe only 2 percent, but that's still a chance."

I loved that Jen felt as if we could surmount every obstacle in our path, but sometimes working with her was exhausting. I smiled at her patiently. "Two percent doesn't justify spending half our day chasing down a signature!"

"Sami, if we have even 2 percent, then we must try!" Jen walked out of my office with my Transit keys. I could not let her go to Jericho alone. I followed her, muttering under my breath.

We reached the checkpoint at the entrance of Jericho. The soldier checked my ID. "You have a blue ID. You can't enter," the soldier said to me. "And neither can the car, with yellow plates."

I started to turn the car around, but Jen was still talking to the soldier.

"Can internationals enter?"

"Yes, but . . ."

Jen did not wait to hear the rest. She was already getting out of the Transit. "Wait for me outside the checkpoint, Sami. I'll take a taxi to the DCO."

"Jen!" But she was already striding past the checkpoint down the street to the taxis.

I pulled into a small lot next to the checkpoint and began to wait, my frustration and irritation mounting. What could be taking Jen so long?

Finally Jen got into the Transit. Grinning, she handed me a piece of paper. It was a letter stating that our students would be on the VIP list the following morning.

"How did you get this, Jen?"

"Two percent, *habibna.* You only need 2 percent."

I laughed out loud as I guided the car back onto the road to climb up toward Jerusalem. "Your 2 percent, Jen . . . I will never doubt your 2 percent again."

John succumbed to his cancer that summer. I had not agreed with every decision John made, but I mourned when he died. John had been more than a boss, he had been an inspiration and a friend. I could not imagine anyone leading Seeds of Peace with the same vision, spirit, and energy that John had. His wife, Janet, became the interim president.

Ned organized a memorial service for John at the Center. Many people came to pay their respects, including Adam. Hadara apparently informed Janet of her displeasure that Adam had attended. Janet wrote Ned a harsh e-mail, stating that neither Adam nor Huwaida were permitted to enter the Center. I was shocked. Adam and Huwaida were personae non gratae at the Center? It was ludicrous. Seeds of Peace, an organization that was supposed to be about peaceful resolution to conflict, had blacklisted former key staff members for taking action—nonviolently—against occupation, the main root of the conflict. If Adam and Huwaida were blacklisted, who would be next?

Jen and I organized an overnight workshop in Haifa for Jewish and Palestinian Seeds from inside Israel. Two older Israeli Seeds, Bala and Danny, were helping to chaperone. I went to the Haifa train station to pick them up.

I looked out the car window for Bala and Danny as passengers filed out of the station. Two soldiers approached my car. I quickly averted my glance. But out of the corner of my eye, I saw they were smiling and waving to me. This was strange behavior for soldiers. I looked up—they were Bala and Danny! They had come directly from their army service in order to make the train. They got into my car.

"Good to see you, Sami!"

"Nice to see you both! But as soon as we get to the seminar, you have to change immediately into civilian clothes." They were Bala and Danny to me, with or without uniforms. But I knew that Seeds in army uniforms would be hurtful to some. Especially as Danny had his gun. "And you have got to keep that thing covered up!" I instructed Danny.

Danny and I shared a room that night. It was my first time sleeping in a room with a soldier, but I did not mind. I had known Danny since he was fifteen years old. I had taken him to and from his home multiple times and had chaperoned him on a trip to Jordan. I trusted Danny. I slept soundly.

When I woke up the next morning, Danny was already supervising the kids at breakfast. My bed felt a bit strange; why were my feet elevated? I got up, lifted the edge of the mattress, and dropped it in surprise. It was Danny's M16! *Ya* Allah! I lifted the mattress again to make sure I had seen right. I had. I had dreamt of holding a gun like this in my youth. But, I reminded myself, guns were made for one of two reasons: to shed blood or to create the fear of shedding blood. It was bad enough that I had been sleeping on a weapon that was used to enforce occupation. I did not want to touch it.

Danny was just returning from breakfast. I grabbed his arm and pulled him into the room, shutting the door.

"Danny, you crazy bastard! Get your gun from under my mattress! Don't you know your own army's rules? You're never allowed to leave your weapon with anyone, especially not a Palestinian! Do you know what your commanders would do to you if they ever found out, *ya zalameh?*"*

Danny just laughed. "Yeah, yeah, I know the rule, Sami. But you're like my brother and I know you will respect anything of mine the same as me."

For Danny to have left his gun under my mattress meant that he had enormous trust in me. Our connection was stronger than the M16. And it also told me that his heart and hands were clean. If he had ever injured anyone with that gun or used it while humiliating someone, he never would have felt safe leaving it with me.

"Okay, but Danny, please, cover that thing up and lock it away somewhere. Don't leave it with me again!"

We were informed that Mister Bill would not be returning to the Center. Jethro and Mike were leaving as well. Reuven and Suzan, an Israeli and Palestinian facilitator team from the camp, were brought on board to lead the Center. Reuven and Suzan were good friends, but they did not have the experience that Ned, Jen, and I had.

I had a difficult conversation with Janet. "We have years of experience at the Center. Just let us do what we know how to do."

Janet responded that Ned needed to move on. He had two months to train Reuven and Suzan and then would be stepping aside.

---

*Colloquial Palestinian equivalent to "man" or "dude."

I was stunned. This was how Seeds of Peace was thanking Ned for build-ing our program from scratch? Janet continued, speaking now about Jen. She recognized that Jen was needed for the program, but she was worried that Jen was another Huwaida.

Janet's decisions were put on hold in January 2003 when Aaron David Miller was hired as the new president of Seeds of Peace. Aaron had previ-ously worked in the U.S. State Department, as part of Bill Clinton's Middle East peace team. He had been an active participant in the Camp David summit. Aaron made several visits to the Center, trying to untangle the mess that the staff had become. He initially preferred continuity and com-promise, recognizing it was no small achievement that the veteran staff had kept the program alive and active during the past two years. Eventually Suzan decided to return full-time to her job as principal of a girls' school in East Jerusalem. The leadership team at the Center became Reuven as the administrative director, Jen and Ned as co–program directors, and me as Center supervisor. Ethan, a former American Seed turned counselor, and Marwan, a Palestinian from inside '48 who had been a facilitator at the camp, were also brought on board. There were advantages to a Palestinian delegation from East Jerusalem, I discovered. It was easy for the Palestinian youth to access the Center. Palestinians from Jerusalem met Israelis at the Center, in Haifa, and elsewhere for dialogue groups, joint holiday celebra-tions, school presentations, and workshops. We took the new Seeds to Kib-butz Yahel after a three-year hiatus. When we got out of the buses, I could not contain my joy. So much hope for the future had been born at Yahel over the years. It was not only in Maine that Palestinians and Israelis could live together as equal human beings, developing strong connections to one another. The Yahel workshop proved that it could happen right here, in the Middle East. Now that Yahel was back in our program, we could never, ever cancel it again. There were still huge gaps in our family without the Seeds from the West Bank and Gaza participating in joint activities. But we con-tinued to organize seminars with them in Ramallah and Jericho, trying to keep the flame alive.

With a letter of approval from Abu Ammar, I went directly to schools all over the West Bank to organize the 2003 Palestinian delegation. I was deter-mined to select as many kids as I could from refugee camps and areas that had been hardest hit in the conflict.

I was also in charge of the delegation's preparation. They needed to be ready to talk about water, settlements, refugees, and the Separation Wall* that was now being built. When sending a soldier to war, I told them, you must give him a weapon. Going to dialogue requires that you have a weapon as well—information. I encouraged the kids to talk from their personal experiences, whether of checkpoints or invasions. The more they could create warm and friendly relations with the Israelis, the more they would gain Israelis' support in our struggle for freedom.

In contrast, the Israeli Ministry of Education prepared the kids as if they were entering a battle that they had to win. I heard many stories from the Israeli Seeds about their preparation seminars. "If they bring up Jerusalem," certain delegation leaders coached them, "don't ever give in. You can never give up Jerusalem!"

By the spring of 2003, it looked like the internal crises in Seeds of Peace had passed. The program had endured and was truly beginning to rebound. Ned had fallen in love with Nahanni Rous, an American woman who came to volunteer at the Center that fall, and he began to contemplate life beyond Seeds of Peace. He told me before anyone else: he had decided to step down after the summer, on his own terms. "With you and Jen in charge, I know I'm leaving the Center in good hands," he said.

Ned had built close relationships with hundreds of Seeds over the seven years that had passed since we drank those first beers together at the Jerusalem Hotel. We knew they would want to say goodbye to the man who had been the linchpin of the home we had created together.

Jen and I sent out e-mails, asking who wanted to come to a surprise party for Ned. We had no idea how many would respond, especially among Seeds from the West Bank and Gaza, many of whom had not wanted to participate in activities that involved Israelis since the start of the Intifada. We had not tried to get travel permissions from the army in several years, and we doubted that it was possible. But when Ned entered the Center the day of his surprise party in May, two hundred Israeli and Palestinian Seeds from every city and town in Israel and Palestine greeted him by shouting,

---

*Construction on the barrier began in 2002. Israelis often refer to the barrier as the Security Fence to emphasize its intention to keep out suicide bombers; Palestinians usually refer to it as the Separation Wall or Apartheid Wall to emphasize its intention to enclose Palestinians. Much of its route cuts deep inside the West Bank, which has led to criticism that it was intended to be a land grab. The International Court of Justice used the term *wall* in its 2004 advisory opinion, which stated that its route was illegal and called for it to be removed.

"Surprise!" The packed hall erupted in song as a group of young Israeli and Palestinian men from Ned's bunk in the summer of 1995 paraded him on their shoulders, breaking spontaneously into "Aicha" by Cheb Khaled, reminding me of all the times that Ned and I had listened to it on the road with the Seeds. Rasha and Noa sang their beautiful Arabic and Hebrew duet, "A Time for Peace," their clear voices harmonizing together for the first time since the opening of the Center four years ago. The Al Jundi children were all there in white Seeds of Peace T-shirts. Noa's family came and so did Bushra's family, from Al Arroub refugee camp. Noa's and Bushra's parents had become friends through their daughters and spent the entire party together. Huwaida came. We did not care if she was supposed to be persona non grata. She would be welcome at the Center as long as we were there.

Jen stood on a chair, filming everything. We made eye contact from across the Center, packed with Israeli and Palestinian youth from all parts of our family, and smiled. We only needed a 2 percent chance. The dream was not dead. I was optimistic for the first time in years. The soul of Seeds of Peace had returned.

CHAPTER THIRTEEN

SUMMER 2003 WAS OUR MOST ACTIVE EVER. A tenuous *hudna** declared by Palestinian factions eased the violence and made it possible to do things we had not done for years. Hundreds of Seeds from the West Bank, Gaza, and all over Israel came together for seminars on the media, human rights, and Jerusalem. Among them were Seeds who had not seen each other—or for some Palestinians, had scarcely left their hometowns—for three years. We held workshops with friends of Seeds, widening our circle. We brought parents of Gaza Seeds to meet with parents of Israeli Seeds. We were doing the impossible with each waking moment.

In September 2003, Seeds of Peace held a large media conference in New York. The first session was about to begin. Aaron Miller, the Seeds of Peace president, pulled me aside and pointed out two women across the room. "Sami, who are they? Are they Israeli delegation leaders?"

The older woman was very tall and looked strong and sturdy, with large blue eyes, glasses, and a red face. The younger woman had wavy black hair and tanned skin. I knew most of the delegation leaders and I had not seen them before.

"I'm not sure," I told Aaron. "I can find out."

I walked over to the two women. "Hello! My name is Sami Al Jundi. I'm the supervisor of the Seeds of Peace Center in Jerusalem." I offered them my card.

The older woman, clearly in charge, took the card and looked at it disdainfully, it seemed to me. "My name is Yaffa. General Yaffa, they call me—I was a general in the army."

---

*Arabic for "temporary truce," or "cease-fire."

General Yaffa was a political appointee in the office of right-wing Likud Minister of Education Limor Livnat. The other woman, who introduced herself as Ronit, was also a political appointee in Livnat's office. Why were they here as delegation leaders? They were not teachers and had never accompanied the Israeli delegation to camp.

Yaffa, Ronit, and I found seats together as Christiane Amanpour from CNN spoke to the participants via live video feed about the role of media in politics, followed by a question-and-answer period.

When the session was over, Yaffa abruptly turned to her colleague. She said that the Israeli delegation was despicable and that the entire delegation would be leaving this shameful conference. I asked her what she was talking about. The questions, she told me, confirmed the bias there was in the organization.

"Everything was equal, Yaffa! Two Israelis asked questions and two Palestinians asked questions," I protested.

Yaffa gripped her purse stiffly and responded in a voice that seemed tinged with ice. No, she told me. All the questions had been Palestinian questions.

The Israeli Seeds had asked questions pertaining to Palestinian suffering. Hadara's comment to Jen, explaining why Shani would not be permitted to return to camp, flashed quickly through my mind: "She's more Palestinian than the Palestinians," Hadara had said.

"Yaffa, the kids are entitled to ask whatever they want," I said.

Yaffa shook her finger vehemently at me, informing me that the youth were here to represent the State of Israel. I tried to convince her that the Seeds represent themselves, their own opinions, but she was adamant. She was taking the delegation home.

I hurriedly found Aaron and told him what had just happened. Aaron nodded. "I had a bad feeling about her. Sami, ask Yaffa to meet with me over lunch."

With a smile, I approached Yaffa, who was still fuming in the conference room. "Yaffa, the president of Seeds of Peace asked if you would please talk with him at lunch about what happened."

Yaffa shrugged, agreeing to speak with Aaron, but warning me that it would not change her mind.

I organized a private table for Yaffa and Aaron. By the end of lunch, Yaffa had agreed that the Israeli delegation would stay. She had decided not to make a huge fuss out of a few days, she told me later. But she did not think Israelis of that age should mix with Palestinians. It was not good for Israel's ideology.

I suspected that Yaffa meant Israel's military ideology. The army was the backbone of the Israeli state. Israeli children were raised from birth to become soldiers. Anything that challenged that, such as young Israelis refusing to serve in the army, was considered a cause for alarm. In a flash of clarity, it occurred to me why Yaffa might be at the conference: to report back to the minister of education as to why approximately a dozen Israeli Seeds were refusing military service and even more were speaking out on behalf of Palestinian rights.

At the end of the conference, Aaron asked me what I thought about the Israeli Seeds who refuse to go into the army. His question reinforced my instincts that this was one of the Israeli ministry of education's central concerns, and that Yaffa had communicated this to Aaron at their lunch. I did not think it would be wise to tell Aaron that I thought those kids had made a very courageous and difficult decision and that I was proud of them. Instead, I told him that our goal was to build leaders. The truth was, an Israeli who did not serve in the army would never hold an important political post. But leadership was not only in the political realm. A leader could be a doctor in his or her clinic, a lawyer, a mother or father inside the family.

Aaron scratched his chin thoughtfully. There were several Israeli Seeds, he mentioned, who did not serve and who were studying in the States on scholarships that Seeds of Peace had helped them to procure. Maybe it would be prudent if in the future the organization only helped Israeli Seeds find scholarships if they have served in the army.

I was alarmed at the idea of Seeds of Peace making a policy like that. It was not our role to discourage military service, but it was certainly not our role to encourage it.

I returned to Jerusalem just a week before Fadia gave birth to our fourth child, a beautiful baby girl, whom we named Mera. At the Center, we were launching our yearlong program with a predominantly new program staff. The absence of a clear leadership structure caused confusion and frustration among the new staff. Aaron was calling himself the overall director of the Center, but he was based in Washington, D.C. And though Jen, Reuven, and I had job titles that signified responsibility, we lacked any real authority.

We held our first program meeting, to get to know one another and lay out the plans for the year. Jason, a tall young man with brown hair, was an American Seed turned counselor. Lana, who had curly hair and a wry sense of humor, had also been a counselor at the camp, and, with dual American-Egyptian citizenship, was well poised to develop a meaningful follow-up program with the Egyptian and Jordanian Seeds. Shachaf, soft-spoken but direct and earnest, had been an Israeli facilitator at the camp. Marwan had stayed on.

I should have been excited that we were launching a new year with a packed program, but instead I left the meeting feeling uneasy. This staff had a very different energy than our previous teams. I did not think they exhibited the same enthusiasm for working with the kids. I was not sure if they all shared the vision that Ned and I had developed and later staff had helped to nurture.

I was not the least bit reassured when Marwan brought up questions about his salary and vacation time and pushed for the staff to have time off on the holidays of each and every faith—which was often the best time for the kids to come to seminars. It seemed to me that Marwan wanted to squeeze as many benefits from the job as he could. I was also unsure about Jason, though I could not put my finger on why. But Jen had a lot of faith in him. Jason spoke both Hebrew and Arabic, understood camp from the perspective of a camper and a counselor, was smart, and seemed highly capable. Jen and Ned had lobbied Aaron to hire Jason, and they convinced me to give him a chance.

Marwan, Jason, and Lana were pushing heavily for graduate Seeds to be hired to lead programs and do other part-time jobs in the Center. I strongly objected. We would be opening up Pandora's box. There would inevitably be more Seeds who wanted to work for us than we were able to hire. It would lead to resentment and negative feelings. We were supposed to be preparing the youth to be leaders, I explained, bringing the belief of peace and coexistence into all facets of their societies. How could they be active as ambassadors in their own communities if they were only working internally, leading younger Seeds of Peace kids?

But Jen strongly supported the idea. "It's one of the goals we've been working for, Sami!" she countered.

The *hudna* had ended by late summer. Shootings, bombings, and invasions had resumed. The ominous construction of the Separation Wall was picking up pace. Travel permits from the army to bring kids from the West Bank and Gaza to meetings were once again difficult to obtain. It was a constant struggle to try to adjust to the ever-shifting reality. Jen and I often came into conflict about whether to go ahead with our scheduled activities. During peaks of violence, I thought it wiser and safer to cancel everything. Though always concerned about safety issues, Jen was determined that we do as much as we possibly could.

The negative vibe I had gotten at the initial program meeting grew stronger as the security situation deteriorated. Jason was especially vocal about his criticisms. It was as if he felt that the difficulty of our work was due to poor organization at the Center, rather than to the inherent overwhelming challenges of trying to bring youth from opposing sides of a conflict together during times of active hostilities. Jason had very clear ideas about how to make things function more smoothly, so that heroic efforts on the part of the staff would not be necessary. But it was exactly those heroic efforts that had always allowed us to do the impossible. Jen and I were for good, clear organization; in fact, Jen was highly organized. But we were against sacrificing the heart and soul of our program to bureaucratic efficiency.

Aaron sent Tim Wilson, the director of the camp, to spend a week at the Center, to meet with the Israeli and Palestinian ministries of education. Jen asked Jason to take Tim around. Jason's language skills would be helpful and he was now the Center's contact person with the Israeli Ministry of Education. Jason and Tim had a close relationship. Jen thought they would enjoy the time with each other.

Jen and I met at Askadinia toward the end of Tim's visit. "Did you notice that Tim seems to be repeating everything that Jason has been saying all fall?" I said. "It's as if Jason spent his time with Tim fashioning a pair of spectacles through which Tim now views everything at the Center."

Jen brushed off my concern. "Jason's a smart guy. He has some good ideas about how we can improve."

We held a Coexistence Marathon in December at *Neve Shalom-Wahat al-Salam*,* an Arab-Jewish village near Latrun that was founded on principles of coexistence. We went over the final details the evening before.

"It will be impossible to control the kids in that place," Lana predicted.

"I feel like we're in a boat that is sinking," Jason added.

Jen pointed out the positive aspects of the seminar. Yes, it would be chaotic—but that's because so many kids were signed up to come, which was wonderful. *Neve Shalom-Wahat al-Salam* was a special place in its own right. We had done many incredible workshops there in the past with a much smaller staff. It was hard work, but hard work had not been a problem for us. The workshops had all been great.

But despite Jen's attempts to increase morale, the mood was gloomy going into the weekend. I could not quite understand why.

---

*Hebrew and Arabic for "Oasis of Peace."

Seminars and workshops were usually an opportunity for staff to bond with the Seeds, but instead I saw staff members yelling at kids. Both Anan from Jericho and Orren from Netanya told me with disgust at different times during the seminar, "I've never been treated this way by Seeds of Peace staff before! I don't want to be here!"

Seed after Seed took me aside at different points of the event. "This isn't the Seeds of Peace we know," they said.

Tim joined us again at a midyear staff retreat in Aqaba, Jordan, in January 2004, bringing Leslie, the New York program director. Our goals were to evaluate what had gone well and what needed improvement during the first half of our program year, as we looked ahead to the second half.

The retreat started with a discussion about the Coexistence Marathon. Most of the new staff thought it had been a disastrous event. There was an undertone of accusation in the discussion. Jen took notes, not saying much.

"I feel uncomfortable that someone who usually talks a lot at our meetings is being quiet now," Lana said. "I wonder if the uncharacteristic silence is because there are staff members from the States here."

Jen spoke up. "I assume you're talking about me," she said. "I have a lot to say, and I will, throughout the retreat. I agree that there were problems during the marathon, but I also saw a lot of wonderful things happen. So for now, I thought it was most important for me to listen, to try to understand why everyone feels so negatively."

The atmosphere in Aqaba grew more toxic as complaints started piling up.

"I was almost shot three times," Jason said angrily. I knew the incidents he was referring to. There had been three times in the past months where Jason had felt in danger. I waited for Jen to set the record straight—that feeling unsafe, though a cause for concern, is not the same as almost being shot. She said nothing.

I pulled Jen aside at lunch. "Why are you letting them blame you like this for things that are not your fault?"

"It's obvious that Lana and Jason are really angry," Jen answered. "I don't understand why, but it seems to me they need to vent. Letting them get it all out might be more constructive than answering back."

After lunch, the conversation turned to our annual Yahel workshop. Most of the new staff wanted to cancel it.

They had a list of reasons.

"Vacations are different in Palestinian and Israeli schools, so no matter when we hold it, some kids will miss school. I refuse to have anything to do with an event that involves kids missing school!" Lana declared.

Marwan said it was imbalanced to bring kids from the West Bank and Gaza inside Israel when we were no longer able to bring the Israeli kids to Palestinian areas.

"That's no reason to cancel our programming!" I tried my best to stay cool and logical. "We have to keep doing what we can, when we can, where we can! If Palestinian kids agree to come and their families agree to send them, how can we deny them this opportunity? Aren't we still bringing them together in Maine? What kind of peace organization are we, if we block the way for those same kids to be together in Yahel?"

I argued vehemently, directing much of my frustration at Jen. Jen treasured Yahel—she should be supporting me! But Jen was asking everyone to voice his or her opinion, trying to determine what the majority of the staff thought we should do.

"This is a strategic mistake," I told Jen at the next break. I was furious with her. "The people who made this decision don't know the difficulties we faced building our program. They want to undermine it, Jen! You'll realize in the future that you made a huge mistake."

I repeated this prediction to everyone after the break. The new staff looked at me with condescending smiles. My anger took control of me. I raised my voice. I slammed my fist on the table. The staff voted. Yahel was canceled.

I mourned my former colleagues as I never had before. Where was Roy, or Jethro, or Fishman? Most of all, where was my original partner, my brother and friend, Ned? Seeds of Peace had been a way of life for us. We had worked because we believed this was the way to build hope for the future. What were these staff members working for?

I thought back to prison, when the new Gazans had taken control and nearly destroyed the beautiful, complex prison system that had been painstakingly built by the older prisoners. I felt like I was watching the same thing happen all over again.

AARON APPOINTED TIM to be the director of the Center. He would split his time between Jerusalem and Maine, where he was still the camp director. Tim did a good job of running the camp in Maine. But how much did he really understand about our situation here?

Tim called his first staff meeting. We sat around a table; Tim remained standing. The meeting was brief. "There's a new sheriff in town," Tim said. "Things are going to run differently around here." He did not specify how. He just looked at us as if surveying his dominion. "Not everyone sitting around this table is going to be here next year."

Jen came up to my office a few minutes later.

"What was that all about?" I asked her. "Tim is calling himself a sheriff?"

"Tim never got the respect he deserved in the organization," Jen said. "John always undercut him. Now Aaron has decided that Tim should be given carte blanche. Tim is going a bit overboard with this power trip, I think, compensating for the years that John did not allow him any real authority. It'll balance itself out over time."

February 2004. I was working on selecting the Palestinian delegation. This year we had partial support from the Palestinian Ministry of Education. We could recruit candidates in the schools.

I was interviewing prospective Seeds in a school in Ramallah. When the interviews were done, I stopped by the office to talk to the principal.

"She's talking to some visitors about Seeds of Peace right now," the secretary told me. "She said you should join them."

I walked into the office and found two young men talking to the principal. She introduced them. They were both PFLP leaders at Bir Zeit University. They were in her office to convince her not to allow her students to participate in Seeds of Peace. They used words like *brainwashing* and *normalization*. I tried to convey to the young men how important organizations like Seeds of Peace were for the Palestinian people, our kids, the future. But I knew it was a waste of time. PFLP ideology was critical of any relations with Israelis.

"Seeds of Peace is supported by the Palestinian Ministry of Education and Abu Ammar," I finally said.

"I understand," the more talkative young man responded, shaking my hand as they exited the office. "But you need to also understand," he directed his comment to both the principal and me, "we will do everything we can to stop Seeds of Peace."

Two weeks later, we held a two-day seminar for Palestinian Seeds at the Grand Park Hotel in Ramallah.

I noticed some of the Seeds congregating in the hotel's VIP room.

"What's going on?" I asked Khaled, a Seed from Ramallah I had known for eight years.

"Meeting for the old Seeds, who went to camp in 2000 or earlier," he answered.

Manar, an old Seed from Hebron, came up to me. "Sami, please, come into the meeting."

"The meeting is for the old Seeds—I was not invited."

"I'm inviting you. I don't feel good about this meeting . . . I'll feel better if you're there."

"Okay, sure." I entered with Manar just before the door closed to the VIP room. I saw Jen sitting on a table in the corner of the room. I took a seat near her.

Jason was leading the meeting with several of the old Seeds.

The first topic of discussion was the Palestinian delegation leaders and selection process. The Seeds were criticizing them harshly, but based on erroneous information. I was the only one in the room with direct experience in both the selection process and the functioning of the delegation leaders. I raised my hand and corrected the misinformation.

Jason asked me in a jovial tone why I was inside the meeting. I was a staff member, not an old Seed. Jason looked at one of the old Seeds, who then asked Jen and me to leave the meeting. The old Seeds needed to discuss things alone. Manar spoke up in protest. "We asked Sami to be here. We want him here!"

"Sami is a staff member!" The leaders of the meeting answered.

"Jason's a staff member, too!" I pointed out.

But Jason was also an old Seed, I was reminded, and therefore was entitled to be there.

If they were discussing issues affecting them as Palestinian Seeds, then Jason should not have been there; he had been an American Seed. Apparently the rules were bent to fit whomever those leading the meeting wanted in the room. Jen and I left and sat in the lobby, talking to the younger Seeds. I did not want anyone to detect how hurt I was. Seeds of Peace was an inclusive community, without divisions and hierarchies about who could participate in what discussion. This was foreign behavior in an organization that was supposed to educate about respect, tolerance, and dialogue.

Rajy, an old Seed from Ramallah, left the room talking on his cell phone. The caller waved to Rajy from across the lobby. Rajy went to greet him. I recognized Rajy's friend—it was the young leader of the PFLP from Bir Zeit University. I approached them.

"Hello, nice to see you again." I shook his hand.

The young man smiled at me, as if to say, *I told you we would do every-thing we could to stop Seeds of Peace.*

Rajy reentered the VIP room. Eventually, Jason left the room with a piece of paper in his hand. He went straight to Tim's hotel room with a few of the older Palestinian Seeds.

Other Seeds began to trickle out of the VIP room. Some of them seemed satisfied. Others looked disappointed.

Manar filled me in on the contents of the paper. It was a statement voicing disapproval of several aspects of Seeds of Peace, including our efforts at the Center to bring young Israeli and Palestinian Seeds together.

"I tried to argue against it," Manar said. "But they only wanted to hear their own voices."

I knew how difficult it would be for Manar or others to adamantly oppose such a statement. They would risk being accused of supporting normalization. I had a similar churning feeling in my stomach as in 2001, when the small group of older Seeds wrote a letter to the Ministry of Education, encouraging them not to send a delegation to camp. But the feeling was more ominous this time. Jason, an American with eight months of experience at the Center, had led the meeting where this statement had been drafted and I, a Palestinian with eight years of experience, had not been permitted inside the room.

The Sheriff called my cell phone minutes later. "I need to be picked up in half an hour. I have to go somewhere."

I called my brother Mazin and asked him to meet Tim outside the hotel.

Later that night, I asked Mazin where he had taken Tim. To the Israeli Ministry of Education office in Petach Tikvah, Mazin told me. He had seen several older Israeli Seeds there as he dropped Tim off, he reported. That was strange—if there had been a meeting planned by the Center staff, I should have known about it. I remembered Yaffa at the New York conference, stating that Israeli youth mixing with Palestinians was against their ideology. Jason was the Center's contact with Hadara. Was it possible that Jason had pushed the older Palestinian Seeds in a certain direction in order to satisfy the Is-raeli Ministry of Education's agenda? I imagined Tim entering a meeting with Hadara and a group of older Israeli Seeds and handing her the Palestin-ian Seeds' statement.

"It's not the Israelis who want to cancel binational programming," I imag-ined Hadara smoothly telling the Israeli Seeds. "It's the Palestinians who don't want to meet!"

If a conversation like that did take place, the Israeli Seeds would argue their individual opinions with clarity. They would not let themselves be used as puppets of another's agenda, as the older Palestinian Seeds had just unwittingly done.

The changes at the Center after that were rapid. Staff meetings started to feel like a tug-of-war: most of the staff pulling to cancel binational meetings, and me on the other side, tugging to preserve our program. Jen was in the middle, trying to serve as referee.

Younger Palestinian Seeds took their cue from the older ones. Palestinian Seeds from Jerusalem wrote a letter to the Israeli members of their dialogue group stating that they no longer wanted to meet with them.

The Sheriff was rarely in Jerusalem and when he was, his main focus seemed to be restoring Seeds of Peace's relationship with the Israeli Ministry of Education and developing connections with the Palestinian political elite.

March 2004. Jason had organized a meeting with a small number of older Israeli and Palestinian Seeds, to continue the discussion of where the organization should head. He had procured the travel permits from the IDF. Jen called me early in the morning.

"There's a full closure on the West Bank today," she told me. "I had forgotten that today was Purim." Closures on the West Bank were routine on Jewish holidays. There was a history of suicide bombings, especially on Purim. "I've been trying to call Jason to see what he thinks we should do, but his phone is shut off."

I checked the news. Israeli news sites indicated a high alert for an attack. I tried to reach Jason myself, without success, and called Jen back. "The permits are worthless if there's a closure," I said. "And there's a much higher chance of the Palestinian Seeds being harassed by soldiers or facing other problems on the road. I think we should cancel."

Jen agreed. Finally she was able to reach Jason to tell him our decision. She called me back. "Jason was really angry. He said he had received special travel permits that were valid during a closure. He refused to talk about it with me."

I was not sure what kind of travel permits were respected during a full closure, or how Jason had procured them, but they still would not prevent abuses at checkpoints. Ten minutes later, the Sheriff called from Maine, yelling. "J . . . some of the Seeds called me—not Jason!—and they are very upset. Why did you cancel the meeting?"

I explained Jen's and my concerns. Tim was furious. "Why didn't you call me? I should be the one making those decisions!"

"It's the middle of the night in Maine. I didn't want to wake you up! Jen and I are the ones here on the ground right now . . . We've been making this kind of call for years . . ."

"Tell the Seeds that the meeting will be rescheduled for when I am in town . . . and that this time, I will be inviting them personally!" Tim shouted.

I hung up the phone, confused and frustrated.

I often exploded in anger at staff meetings, sometimes toward everyone, other times specifically at Jen. I could hear the frustration in Jen's voice as she responded to my outbursts, but I did not care. I knew how committed Jen was to our work—how could she be giving in to the new staff?

One meeting ended with Jen and me shouting at each other. After the meeting, Jen came to my office.

"Sami, we have to figure this out," she said. "Fighting with you all the time is making it impossible for me to do my job."

We drank coffee and tried to talk through our problems. Jen had no intention of sacrificing the heart and soul of the program, she said. She was trying to help the Center make the transition to the Sheriff and the new staff's way of operating while preserving our spirit and essence. I understood the difficulty of her position, I told her, but every step we were taking was leading us down the wrong path. I could not sit by and watch that happen.

"So why do we argue with each other more than with anyone else?" Jen asked me.

"Probably because for both of us, getting the other's support is more important than getting anyone else's," I answered.

That afternoon, Marwan called out to me as I was walking past his office. I entered. The program staff was going to write a letter to Tim, Aaron Miller, and the board, he told me, saying that they did not want Jen to be the program director. They were all going to sign it.

I was stunned. Jason entered Marwan's office. He also tried to convince me to sign, telling me that things would improve if I did so and that I would have more power if Jen were gone.

I finally found my voice and answered, particularly to Jason. "You should support Jen more than anyone. It was Jen who advocated for you to be hired. If you bite Jen's hand today, whose hand will you bite tomorrow? Mine?"

Marwan reminded me that Jen and I were always fighting.

"Jen and I have many hard discussions, but I respect her fully. Her little finger works harder than all of you put together. If you think I'm going to sign that letter just because Jen and I yelled at each other this morning, then you haven't learned anything!"

I returned to my office, struggling over what to do. Should I tell Jen? She would be devastated if she knew that the program staff were plotting against her behind her back. But I had to warn her.

We sat on the balcony the next day to go over transportation details. I brushed the papers aside. "You have to be careful, Jen," I told her.

"What do you mean?"

"They want to kick you out. Marwan, Jason, Lana. They are trying to stage—" I made a topsy-turvy motion with my hands as I tried to remember the word in English—"a coup."

Jen laughed. "Come on, Sami, don't be ridiculous. They wouldn't do that!"

I was scared for Jen and for myself.

MY BROTHER AZZAM had been diagnosed two years before with diabetes. I had felt a special protectiveness toward Azzam since prison. But I could not protect him from the new illness that began to wreak havoc in his body, causing him aches and pains all over. Cancer, the doctors at Hadassah proclaimed after multiple tests. It had originated in his kidney but had spread. They would do all they could, but it was only a matter of time. Azzam was forty years old.

I began to spend all my free time with Azzam, either at the hospital or his home, where he sat on a couch covered with blankets, growing thinner and weaker. I tried not to burden my brother with my own troubles, but it was impossible to hide anything from Azzam. Beneath his quick, sarcastic wit, Azzam could, in a single, sharp sentence, cut right to the heart of any situation.

Out of the blue one day as we were watching our favorite movie, *The Good, the Bad, and the Ugly,* Azzam started talking about Marwan and Jason. They were not working for the benefit of the kids or the goals of Seeds of Peace, in his assessment. They had something else in mind.

Azzam had never warned me about anyone else. He had always considered the staff as family, same as I did. I never took Azzam's words lightly.

It was getting progressively harder to get month-long travel permits for Issa. "He was a bad hire," the Sheriff pronounced. Where was the loyalty, I wondered, to a man who for five years had been braving checkpoints to work with us, bringing cups of Arabic coffee to each of our offices multiple times every day?

The Sheriff instituted other new rules. No Palestinian without a travel permit would be allowed on the Center grounds. "We don't break the law," Tim announced. There was no discussion of which law he meant—the occupation law, the law that denied Palestinians access to their holy city of Jerusalem. Of course the Center had to worry about Israeli law—we operated in Israeli-controlled East Jerusalem. But we did not and should not police Palestinian Seeds who came to the Center on their own. The Sheriff was clear—any West Bank Seed at the Center without an IDF travel permit would have to leave, and any staff who transported them or permitted their presence would be fired. The conversation was closed.

A few days later Jen came to my office, ashamed. Zeina from Ramallah had managed to get into Jerusalem without a permit and came to the Center to work on a project she was leading. Jen had to ask Zeina to leave. "Zeina was outraged and had every right to be," Jen said sorrowfully. "It was disgusting that I had to ask her to leave the Center."

June 2004. The new staff had organized predominantly separate seminars and workshops for the summer program, including an Arab seminar in Amman for Palestinian, Egyptian, and Jordanian Seeds and an Israeli seminar in *Neve Shalom-Wahat al-Salam*. Several graduate Seeds were hired as summer interns.

Rana was a graduate Seed intern from the West Bank town of Beit Jala. We were not successful in procuring a travel permit for her. She would do the internship from home.

The first day of staff orientation was essential to creating the team that would be running the summer program. Jen called Tim in Maine. "Tim, I know your policy regarding permits, but please let me bring Rana to the Center tomorrow," she begged him. "I know I can get her through the Beit Jala checkpoint without any problem. It's vital that we have at least one day of staff orientation together so Rana can feel part of the team. Please make an exception."

Tim agreed. Jen picked Rana up in the morning and, by putting an Israeli newspaper on the dashboard of the car and cranking up the music on the IDF radio station, she and Rana sailed through the Beit Jala checkpoint without a problem.

Since the start of the Intifada, 2,500 homes in the Gaza Strip had been destroyed, nearly two-thirds of them in Rafah. Assassinations all over the Strip continued apace, with nearly half of the subsequent deaths being civilians. Invasions and killings occurred regularly. Seeds from Gaza wanted to come to the Center to tell their Israeli counterparts what they were living through, but there was a complete closure on the Strip.

Mahmoud from Gaza City called Jen. "Can you come with the video camera?" he asked. "We want to make a video message for the Israeli Seeds."

Jen agreed to film with the youth in Gaza the following day.

Four Gaza Seeds took Jen to film in Rafah. One boy, a friend of a Seed, stood on the rubble of what used to be his bedroom. "This is my house," he told the video camera. "I am an artist, but my colors and my pictures, all of them are destroyed . . ."

In Gaza City, the Seeds took Jen to the home of a family whose teenage son had been sitting on his front stoop when a missile struck a wanted man in a passing car. The boy had been killed as well.

At the end of the video, the Seeds from Gaza gave their own, direct messages to the Israeli Seeds.

"What we want from you guys is to feel about what's happening here . . . remember that you have Seeds, you have colleagues in Gaza, and they are suffering really," said Mahmoud. "I hope that everything's going to be better soon and to see you all."

"I want you to think deeply about what your government is doing against Palestinians," Ibrahim said to his Israeli colleagues. "And I'm sure you will prevent your government from doing more and more wild activities, because this will not lead to peace for you or for any Israeli citizens."

We showed the messages from the Gaza Seeds to more than fifty Israeli Seeds at the Israeli seminar the following week. The discussions after watching the video were difficult. Some of the Israeli Seeds were angry. But several of them approached me and told me they had ideas for video projects to communicate their reality to the Palestinian Seeds. Jen filmed a dozen responses.

The Sheriff called me from Maine the next day to ask me to get him a copy of the Gaza video. Apparently, Hadara was very upset that Jen had made a pro-Palestinian movie.

I did not bother wondering how Hadara had heard about the video nor did I protest her description of Gaza Seeds using video to communicate with Israeli Seeds as a pro-Palestinian movie. The frenzy of preparing the kids for the second session of camp overshadowed all else.

July 2004. Tim flew back to Jerusalem for three days between camp sessions.

That Friday night was Bushra's wedding, from Al Arroub camp. The Seeds of Peace table included many of Bushra's friends, most of the Center staff, including Ned, who had returned to Jerusalem for the occasion, and Noa Epstein and her mother, father, and sister. In his greeting to the hundreds of wedding guests, Abu Tareq included a special welcome to "the friends from Seeds of Peace."

All day Sunday I ran around frantically preparing the last details for camp. I had to be at Allenby Bridge with the Palestinian delegation early the next morning and would fly with them to Maine. I checked my e-mail late at night. There was a message from Tim. I read it quickly.

> Dear Seeds and Staff,
>
> I am concluding a quick visit to the Center . . . It is important that everyone realize we are on a new track and I intend to return with some new staff in September to help me with that. Some of the old staff will be moving on with their lives after devoting much time and effort during a difficult period. One of those will be Jen Marlowe, who will be leaving at the end of September . . .

I stopped reading in complete shock. Jen? Jen had quit? Did she raise her hands in surrender? Or did she no longer believe in our mission? And why had she not told me personally rather than making me read it on a staff e-mail? This was not the Jen I knew. I called her.

"*Habibna*," she answered the phone.

"Jen, I got the e-mail from Tim . . ."

"E-mail from Tim?"

"Saying that you're leaving us. Jen, I just saw you yesterday and you didn't say a word! When did you quit?"

"I didn't quit, Sami." I could hear in her voice that she had been crying.

"Jen . . ." I did not know what to say. "Why didn't you tell me?"

Jen was struggling unsuccessfully to keep her voice steady. "It just happened yesterday afternoon. Tim said he was starting a 'New Way' at the Center and that I belong to the 'Old Way,' Ned's way. He said I have a strong personality, which can be good at times and bad at times. He said he didn't need a program director anymore. He said he needed people out here who can run with the big dogs."

"Run with the big dogs? What is that supposed to mean?"

Jen half-laughed. "I have no idea, Sami."

"And the e-mail?"

"Hold on. I'm reading it right now." There was a pause for a moment. "I don't believe it."

"Jen?"

"Tim told me that I could decide how, what, and when to tell people. I hadn't decided any of that yet. I wanted to talk to you and Ned first. And then he sends this e-mail?"

I was aghast. "Jen, I'll be in the States tomorrow. I'll talk to Aaron. Don't give up!"

I found Aaron as soon as I arrived at camp. I worked hard to make sure my voice was calm and my logic rational as I explained that firing Jen was a disastrous mistake. She had warm and deep connections with dozens of Israeli and Palestinian families. She had the respect and trust of the Seeds and their parents. More than anyone else, she knew how to organize programs and activities. Not only that, the way she was being forced out would hurt the soul of the organization.

"I am not able to discuss personnel decisions," Aaron said.

Our work was about human emotions, I tried to explain to Aaron, building trust and connections, and developing moral imagination. We nurtured dreams. A peace organization could not operate like a corporation.

"Tim is the director of the Center. I gave him the authority to select his staff," was all Aaron would say.

I tried to discuss the decision with Tim later that afternoon, but I got nowhere. "If you want to make omelets, you have to break a few eggs," he said.

I walked away before I exploded in rage. We were not dealing with eggs, we were dealing with human beings. And we were not cooking omelets, we were trying to make peace.

Tim's and Aaron's inbox and voice mail were choked with messages of shock, outrage, and protest: from Palestinian and Israeli Seeds, parents, counselors at the camp, and many of Jen's and my former colleagues at the Center, demanding an explanation, imploring that the decision be reconsidered.

Tim refused to address any of the e-mails. Aaron repeated over and over that he would not discuss personnel decisions.

I had never imagined my beloved organization would treat its staff members this way, especially one who had dedicated years to making peace in the most difficult of circumstances.

Not all violence is physical.

On the way back from camp, the delegation was delayed crossing the Allenby Bridge. The bridge would be closing in half an hour and there were
hundreds of people ahead of us.

I got on the phone with contacts in the Authority, the Jordanian government, any of the kids' parents who had connections.

"We'll never cross, Sami. Let's just go get a hotel in Amman and try again
in the morning," the delegation leaders pleaded.

I had no money to put the delegation up in a hotel. "No, we still have
2 percent of hope!"

I continued making calls. A half hour came and went.

"The bridge is closed now. *Yallah*, Sami, back to Amman!"

Even the police at the bridge laughed at us. "There's no way you will cross
today. Why don't you just go to Amman?"

I finally got the call that I was waiting for. "Get your bags, everyone. We're
crossing!"

As we made our way through the passport and security checks, the delegation leaders shook their heads in amazement. "*Wallah*, Sami, we have
never seen anyone like you."

I grinned. "I told you we had 2 percent of hope. This is not my 2 percent.
This is Jen's 2 percent."

Back in Jerusalem, I met Jen in Askadinia for a beer. Jen filled me in on what
she had pieced together. Stories of supposed "mistakes" that she had made had
begun to trickle back to her from different Seeds. She deduced that Jason had
been feeding distortions about her to certain graduate Seeds and then encouraging them to call Tim to complain about her. A conversation with Zeina,
whom Jen had had to ask to leave the Center because she did not have a travel
permit, reinforced this. Jason had called Zeina the first day of the summer
staff's orientation to inform her that Jen had brought Rana to the Center without a permit, and to encourage Zeina to start an intifada against Jen.

"But it was Hadara who drove the final nail in the coffin," Jen said.

"Are you sure?"

Jen was fairly certain. An Israeli Seed had been in the Ministry of Education office. Hadara had told the Seed bluntly that she had gotten Jen fired.

"I suspect that Jason told Hadara about the video from the Gaza Seeds,"
Jen said. Jason was our point of contact with Hadara. "From what I understand, that was one of the main things used against me. And because Hadara
claims I encourage the Israeli kids not to go to the army."

If what Jen had surmised was true, it meant that Seeds of Peace was allowing the Israeli government to play a role in determining the organization's staff.

"I don't know what is most painful," Jen concluded. "That Jason has been turning Seeds against me, that I'm leaving the Center in his and Tim's hands, or that I'm leaving you to deal with this mess."

Noa and her family invited Bushra and her family to their home outside of Jerusalem to thank them for the hospitality shown to them at Bushra's wedding and countless other times in their home in Al Arroub. It was the last activity Jen and I did together. The day was simple. A delicious lunch. Coffee and stories and laughing and looking at pictures from the wedding. Over dessert, short speeches and toasts honored the new bride and groom, the families, and the unlikely friendship between them.

We had a goodbye dinner for Jen at Askadinia. Azzam came, though he was wracked with pain. The cancer had spread to his bones, liver, and stomach. He could barely sit up. Azzam insisted that I bring Jen to his apartment at 7:30 the following morning, on our way to the airport. Jen sat with Azzam on his balcony, having a cup of tea.

"So you are leaving today," Azzam said, in between fits of coughing.
"Yes."
"Yesterday was my last time out of the house," Azzam said. "It looks like we will be leaving together."

Jen would miss her flight if we did not get going. She tried to give Azzam a hug, but he pulled away from her in order to get a good look at his friend. "I hate your nose," he finally announced. "It is crooked. But I like your hair. Because it is unorganized." Jen burst into laughter through her tears and hugged Azzam one final time.

I took Jen to the airport and returned to the Center. For the first time since I had begun working with Seeds of Peace, I felt entirely alone.

⁓⁓⁓

THE SHERIFF CALLED a staff meeting. Surrounded by his "Big Dogs," he said it was time to launch the New Way. Bringing Israelis and Palestinians together was out. "Service learning" was in, led by older Seeds. The Sheriff described how he had successfully implemented a program of service learning decades ago in the Peace Corps in Thailand. This was the model he would implement here. Israeli Seeds would do community service in Israel, Palestinian Seeds in the West Bank and Gaza. Separate but equal.

There had been many long stretches since the start of the Intifada where we could not bring our family together. But that had always been out of situational necessity, and the staff regularly had tried to find creative solutions, whether via e-mail dialogue groups, video, or simply helping pass messages between Seeds. Now, it was our new philosophy terminating the joint meetings. How would separating our community of peacemakers lead to achieving peace? I could come to only one conclusion: there was a new agenda they wanted to fulfill, far from the soul of Seeds of Peace and from the hope we had always drawn from the eyes of our youth.

The Sheriff called me into his office the next day. "I am giving you a new title, Sami," he said. "You will now be the senior adviser to the director of the Center as well as Center supervisor." I almost laughed. What advice of mine had the Sheriff even considered so far? The fancy job title was to buy my silence. *Just take care of the physical plant and transportation,* was the not-so-subtle message. *Select the Palestinian delegation and keep your nose out of the program.*

Discussions between the Sheriff and his Big Dogs happened only behind closed doors. Our weekly staff meeting, to discuss, evaluate, argue, and decide, was terminated. I tried to turn myself into a mindless worker, just filling my place in a company, but I could not. I implored the Sheriff, "At least let me coordinate a media course for Palestinian and Israeli Seeds!"

"There's too much instability," the Sheriff said.

I tried to convince him to permit me organize dialogue groups for the Palestinian and Israeli kids who lived in Jerusalem. They would not be leaving their home city! No, he said. If we do this for Jerusalem kids, we would have to do this in all the cities. So rather than doing something positive for someone—we would do nothing for everyone. We had held a memorial service at the Center for Aseel every year since his death so his friends could remember him and tell new Seeds about whom Aseel had been in life and how he had been killed. When an Israeli friend of Aseel's asked Tim about organizing the memorial this year, Tim refused.

December 2004. Azzam was in the hospital. He was reduced to bones covered by leathery skin. He slept most of the time, but when he was awake, he was sharp as ever.

"Where does it hurt, Azzam?" Yael, the Israeli Seed who used to specially request Azzam to pick her up, had traveled for three hours to visit him from Nazareth.

"Shut up! Not your business!" Azzam gave Yael his famous cocked-eyebrow expression, his brown eyes sparkling for a moment before the pain dulled them again. I knew where it hurt. In his head, his arms, his stomach, his back. Everywhere.

I was sitting next to Azzam's bed. He stirred and asked me to bring his children. I brought Raed, Hiba, Abeer, and Yara to the hospital. He hugged and smiled at each one, trying to make them laugh.

"Go with your uncle now," he told them.

I took the kids home. Azzam's wife, Wafaa, remained by his side.

At 7 a.m., we got the call from the hospital. Azzam was gone.

I had lost my brother Roy, I had lost my brother Ned, and I had lost my sister Jen. And now I had lost my flesh-and-blood brother, Azzam. They had all, in different ways and for different reasons, left.

Calls and e-mails expressing condolence came pouring in. One call stood out: Slava, from Afula, who had thrown the Seeds of Peace T-shirt on the stage during the Ehab Tawfik concert in Jerash.

"Azzam is the reason I did not go to the army," she said. "He was driving me home one day and I was telling him how much I was struggling with my decision. He gave me his look—you know his look—and he said, 'What, one day at a checkpoint, you're going to stop and check me?' I realized right then—I could never stop and check Azzam. And any Palestinian crossing a checkpoint could be Azzam, or you, or Mazin. I could never stop and check anyone."

April 2005. Aaron Miller and a delegation from the board of directors came to visit the Center. They met first with the Sheriff and his Big Dogs. Then Reem and I had our opportunity to meet with Aaron, the board, and Tim.

The board members spoke at length about their support for moving from the Old Way to the New Way. I could barely contain myself. Our work day and night for years and years, with the kids, their families, school presentations, workshops, dialogue groups, home visits—all this was being discarded as the Old Way. My frustration was palpable.

"What exactly is your criticism of the new program?" Aaron finally asked me.

I described how I had first met Ned, telling him that Israelis and Palestinians meeting in Maine but not in the Middle East was like a man walking with one foot. I talked about the heady accomplishments of those early years, the world crashing down around us with the explosion of the second Intifada, and about gradually, carefully rebuilding our program in this new, much harsher reality. I explained why it was critical to continue on that path. We had been on a journey to the top, where people can be connected by respect and mutual care. We had almost reached the summit of the mountain before it all got destroyed. Tim's program was keeping our Center empty. It was depriving our organization of its soul.

I gave everyone a paper I had written about my vision for the strategy of Seeds of Peace. I had titled it "The Magic of the Dialogue and the Logic of the Philosophy." The document was more than twelve pages long. I had worked on it over time for years. The board members flipped through the pages like they were at a dentist's office casually perusing a fashion magazine.

"The kids have camp to do dialogue," one board member said. "Coming home is the time for them to be ambassadors in their communities!"

I shook my head. They still did not understand. "Three weeks at camp is not enough. They have only begun to scratch the surface of the conflict and its impact on each other's lives. When they work together back home, their knowledge becomes much deeper. Their relationships grow much stronger. And their commitment to work for peace is that much more firm. They need to visit each other's homes to feel this. They need to go to each other's schools to challenge the racism of their classmates. How can we send them to their communities to do service learning when their experience is still so little?"

Joe, the board president, held my paper up, pointing to one paragraph. "But, Sami, you wrote about community service here!"

I took a deep breath and continued. There was less than a 2 percent chance, but I had to try. "It is not a problem for service learning to be a part of the program. But it should not be the basis! There are over three hundred organizations doing service learning in this area! But I can count on one hand the number of organizations doing joint work with Palestinians and Is-raelis. So what is Tim doing? Adding one more organization to the three hundred? And the whole Middle East will lose a shining example of dialogue and nonviolence! If we look to the historical lesson from King Solomon, we will remember that the real mother refused to cut her son in half. The soul of Seeds of Peace—Israelis and Palestinians together—cannot be cut." By the end, I found myself begging. "Please, save Seeds of Peace. Save the program that John Wallach believed in. Help us continue to build the circle of human beings."

Aaron looked as if he were really pondering what I had said. "You make some good points, Sami. But we have to give Tim a chance to implement his new program."

I remembered the former board president's holiday card of his family in IDF T-shirts, and his fund-raising letter imploring his contacts to support Seeds of Peace because it stopped Arabs from becoming terrorists. There had always been board members whose understanding of "peace" meant just ending violence and hate against Israel without addressing the oppression of Palestinians. Perhaps the same board members wanted to grant the Israeli government veto power over our program.

"The staff is not Jewish," Tim announced to meetings of Palestinian parents and new Seeds, talking about camp in Maine. "That was in other years. It's not that way now." Did Tim, who frequently pointed out that he was African-American, not Arab or Jewish, think he was talking to Palestinians in a language we wanted to hear? Many of the parents looked as shocked by the comment as I felt.

"I want your children to learn to swim!" Tim said at the same meeting, describing the camp's location on a large lake. "Swimming is good. We call it 'lifetime.' It's a lifetime activity. Once you learn to swim, you always know how to swim."

One father spoke up. "I think most of them do swim!"

"Mmm . . . they get in the water, but . . . " Tim made a motion with his hand to indicate that their ability to truly swim was questionable.

The parents looked puzzled. Was there some hidden meaning in this man's words, or was he just talking nonsense?

The only time the Center was full was when American or European groups contacted us to do a presentation for them. In front of eagerly listening foreigners, Israeli and Palestinian Seeds described the vision they had and the work they did together to achieve it. The irony almost made me laugh. The Seeds were invariably talking to potential funders about a program that no longer existed.

There were a few small rays of light. Graduate Seeds who had taken part-time staff jobs were doing good work, leading local meetings and an occasional joint activity. Due to their dedication and persistence, a small memorial for Aseel was held at the Center in the fall of 2005. The parents' dialogue program that Jen had launched in her final year had continued unabated. And there was a committee of Israeli and Palestinian delegation leaders who organized a monthly Seeds Café open to members of the community. Tim, however, muttered under his breath about the Seeds Café and the parents' meetings.

Many Seeds and their parents saw what was happening. "It's awfully weird, this trend, perverse even," an older Israeli Seed said. "It appears that Tim's show is transparent to most of my delegation."

The mother of two Palestinian Seeds complained to me that the new staff was unorganized, uncooperative, apathetic, and just plain lazy. "Please, help the Center be as it once was," she pleaded.

After several e-mails to Bobbie Gottschalk, Aaron, and other colleagues in the States, sharing my alarm at the direction things were heading, Tim instituted another rule: all communication to the U.S. staff or board had to go through him.

The enlarged photographs on the walls of the Center used to provide me with joy. Each photo told a story, reflecting kids whose eyes were filled with hope. Now those eyes stared at me with accusation, reproaching me for having broken my promise to John. Photos of John himself were everywhere. I could scarcely bring myself to look at them.

My only refuge was my own small office. I sat there for hours, looking through the thousands of papers I had stored in my filing cabinet with details about each and every activity. I flipped through the dozens of photo albums and fingered the one hundred–plus videotapes that lined my bookshelves, documenting trips to Jordan and Egypt, Coexistence Marathons, school presentations, Palestinians and Israelis at *iftar* meals in Mohammed's house in Hebron, Purim at Shirly's in Ashdod, and Christmas with Meshleen in Haifa. The talent show where Aseel brought a crowd of two hundred Palestinian and Israeli Seeds to their feet by energetically shouting, "Hey, Seeds of Peace!" into the microphone. Years and years of working with these kids, watching them grow up, and welcoming new kids into our fold. How could I not have been deeply changed by them?

There was not a single photo or video from the past year and a half.

Older Seeds visited me in my office and surveyed our golden years on my walls, desk, and shelves. "In your office, I feel I'm back at the real Seeds of Peace," they sighed as they searched for themselves in an old photo from Yahel. "Why aren't there any activities anymore?"

I shrugged. "You'll have to ask Tim. He's the director."

Tim popped into my office frequently with requests. "Sami, please ask Mazin to take my wife to the supermarket." Or, "Sami, please ask Mazin to come to my home at 6:30 this evening to drive me to a restaurant."

Nothing was wrong with these requests, but where were the days where I was looking at four maps to coordinate transportation with five different vans, my mobile pressed against one ear and the land line on the other, in constant connection with the drivers, the staff, the kids, their parents?

Now I was reduced to coordinating the personal transportation for the Sheriff and his wife.

Tim called me one day, asking if Mazin could bring Saeb Erekat from Jericho to his home. He was having a party that night for important people: political figures and people from the U.S. Consulate.

I passed the request on to Mazin, but I was thinking about Ro'e, Bushra, Sivan, Aboud, Slava, Yaron, Najib. They used to be the important people.

Time dragged at the Center. Issa and I shared a long coffee every morning and I sent him home early almost every afternoon. With almost no activities, there was not much cleaning for Issa to do. I collected my salary like the rest of the staff. More irony: Seeds of Peace had begun to pay me better than ever before for doing next to nothing.

The only facet of my job with any meaning was selecting and preparing the Palestinian delegations. The Separation Wall was now complete in much of the West Bank. I went to Bethlehem to interview kids for camp. High slabs of concrete encircled the city. As I passed through the small opening in one slab of the wall, I shuddered involuntarily. WELCOME TO THE GHETTO, scrawled a piece of graffiti on the wall. The new Seeds of Peace policy, separating the members of our community from one another, was a mirror of the new reality.

༄༅

JANUARY 2006. Aaron Miller announced he was leaving. His three-year contract with Seeds of Peace had ended. It would not be renewed. Jason had also left. Tim would be stepping down from the Center in a few months as well. I was not sure why. Perhaps the organization had finally realized that the New Way had driven the program into the ground. I felt a small ray of hope. Maybe, just maybe, this meant I would be able to reconstitute the old program.

March 2007. Seeds of Peace replaced Aaron with a chief operations officer named Steven Flanders. Steven, a Canadian whose previous job was running a sports marketing company in the United States, seemed to have had no prior experience in organizations dealing with nonviolence, dialogue, the Arab-Israeli conflict, or youth. He met with us as a staff, talking about his "business plan" for the "company." John had had vision and inspiration. Aaron at least had understood the Middle East conflict. What was Steven bringing to the table?

Steven the Business Man returned a week later accompanied by another man. "This is Eyal," he said, introducing him. "Eyal worked as a human resources manager in several different companies in Tel Aviv. He will be the new director in the Middle East." Eyal went from office to office spending a few minutes with each one of us. He arrived at mine and sat in a chair opposite me. He knew nothing at all about Seeds of Peace, he told me, and had been informed that I was the man he needed to talk to. He could give me ten minutes to teach him.

"Ten years of activities all over the Middle East . . . building a huge program from scratch out of Ned's apartment and my Ford Transit . . . the philosophy and the goals behind it . . . our hopes, our dreams, what we understood from the eyes of the kids . . . do you think I can explain this in ten minutes?"

"Tell me as much as you can now, Sami."

I told him just the bare-bones history. Eyal nodded in all the right places. But I got the sense that he was there only to fill the ten minutes he had offered. I was not concerned that Eyal was Israeli, or that he had served as an officer in the IDF, as he mentioned to me. I was most bothered that he came from the business world. Steven, the new COO of the Seeds of Peace business, had chosen Eyal to run the Center as a branch of his corporation.

There began to be rumors of the possibility of closing the Center. Budget crisis, I was told. From what I could gather, Seeds of Peace was in deep debt. Tim and Aaron had enjoyed large salaries and likely Steven did as well. The organization had begun paying the rent for apartments for certain American staff in recent years. In the past, all staff had paid their own rent, from much more modest salaries, even when Roy and Ned's apartment had served as the Seeds of Peace office for three years. Shouldn't these excesses be dealt with before closing the doors to our Center?

May 2006. Abu Firas, the owner of our building, came by to notify us that new tenants would be moving in. I knew that closing the Center was under consideration. But I had assumed that my superiors would have the courtesy to let us know before we heard it from the landlord. Soon after, the Business Man and Eyal saw fit to tell us their plans. There would be an office in

Tel Aviv for the Israeli kids and one in Ramallah for the Palestinian kids. The Center would close in two months. I wrote an impassioned e-mail to my colleagues in the United States imploring them to keep a joint home for Seeds of Peace in Jerusalem and making one more plea to try to save our program. But it was a fait accompli.

I grew more nervous and agitated with each passing day. I lay in bed at night unable to sleep, feeling like my head would explode. I erupted in anger at Fadia and my kids at the slightest provocation. Once I threw a flowerpot across the room. Another time, I smashed my phone. I was ashamed after each outburst, but I could not control myself. Everything I had staked my life to build was collapsing on my head. By now, the poison was inside me.

End of June 2006. Ned and Jen were in town. Ned and I asked Eyal if we could hold a goodbye party at the Center for Seeds and staff for whom our home had meant so much. Eyal agreed. Ned sent out an e-mail announcing the event to several lists of Seeds. When Steven heard the plans, he canceled the event immediately. He commanded me to write an e-mail to everyone Ned had sent the invitation to, informing them that the gathering was canceled. I did not have a choice. I wrote the e-mail. He changed what I wrote, deleting certain sentences and adding others, and ordered me to send his version under my name. I tried to protest.

"Remember one thing, Sami," Steven said. "I pay your salary."

I exploded. "You don't pay me! This isn't your father's family business! I get my salary from the organization, just like you do! And you know what? You can fuck the salary! Respect is more important to me than a salary!"

My physical symptoms grew worse. My left side became numb and for periods of time I could not move the fingers on my left hand. The doctor said it was brought on by stress. I lay in bed stewing all night long. Seeds of Peace was a tainted organization. I felt unsafe. I began to have nightmares, similar to those in prison, when I imagined the new Gazans were after me with spoons sharpened into knives.

"Just quit, Sami. You've suffered enough!" Fadia begged me.

"Let them fire me," I answered. "At least then I'll get compensation."

But after the next night's anxiety attack, Fadia begged me again. "Forget the compensation. Your health is more important!"

The first-session kids were already at camp. I was putting the final touches on the preparation seminar for the second-session kids. I had a phone meeting with Tammy, director of the delegation leader program. She asked me details about the seminar. I explained the plans in depth. At the end of the conversation, Tammy told me that no one could fill my place.

The next day, the Business Man called me. "Sami, I don't want you to go to the preparation seminar. Somebody else will prepare the kids."

"Who?"

"Mai." Mai was a delegation leader. I assumed that Tammy took all the information from me and gave it to Mai to run the seminar.

I was featured in a documentary film called *Encounter Point*, which highlighted the efforts of grassroots Palestinian and Israeli peacemakers. Ned's wife, Nahanni, was one of the producers. When they had first approached me to appear in it, I worked for a vibrantly active peace organization. But by the time they began filming, I was spending most of my days in my office, playing Internet chess or writing poetry. What was there to film? I ended up playing a relatively minor role in the film. Even so, I was excited for the film's screening at the Jerusalem International Film Festival. Ned and Nahanni had personally invited all the Center staff to attend, including Eyal, and had purchased advance tickets for Issa, Mazin, and Reem. The film screened to a packed house, including hundreds of Israelis and Palestinians. But my brother and colleagues were not there. The Business Man and Eyal had Reem and Mazin moving office equipment from the Center to the new office in Tel Aviv until 8 that night. Issa was cleaning the new Tel Aviv office until 1 a.m.

The next day, Steven said he wanted to meet with us one by one. I sat in my office staring out the window listlessly, waiting for my turn.

There were three cars in the parking lot. A man exited from one car and began fiddling with the doorknob. Usually I would go immediately to find out what was going on. Instead, I just watched.

Eyal entered my office. "I need your key."

"Why?"

"We're changing the locks."

"I'm still the Center supervisor, Eyal. I need the new key."

"Okay, no problem. I'll give you the new key when the lock is finished being changed."

The locksmith departed. That left two other cars. One was for Eyal and Steven. There were two people inside the second car. I went on the balcony to take a closer look. They got out. They had guns. They were armed security guards from a private Israeli company. What were they doing here?

I did not have much time to wonder. I was called in for my meeting. Eyal and Steven both sat on one side of the desk; I sat on the other. The armed security guards were outside.

Steven began the meeting. "Sami, of course you're aware that we're closing the Center in Jerusalem. The board of directors therefore felt that your services were no longer needed." The Business Man paused for a moment. Then he continued, telling me that some of the board was not comfortable that a former prisoner was working at a high level on the staff.

I felt smaller than I ever had in my life. When the judge at my trial had announced, "Ten years," there was not even a trace of the smug self-satisfaction I thought I heard in Steven's voice. If I continued to sit with these people, I would shrink even more.

"Is there anything else you want from me?"

Eyal cleared his throat. "We need your telephone and the car keys."

"I would like to use the car to take my private things home."

"We can't let you do that. We need the keys now."

There were CDs and sunglasses in the car that belonged to me. I did not care. I dug the keys from my pocket and dropped them on the Business Man's desk. I walked out of the office, dug a few cardboard boxes out of the storage room, and began packing them with my personal items. Eyal entered my office and hovered, checking over every item I packed, with armed Israeli security guards lurking in the parking lot outside.

It had not been easy to create hope for teenagers and their families, connecting human beings to one another. Not easy at all. Gandhi knew. It takes years to build a soul. But it is so easy to destroy one.

Issa and Mazin were outside the Center waiting for me. They had been fired as well. When Issa saw me exit with my boxes, he began to weep. We dragged my boxes to the sidewalk. Steven and Eyal passed us as they pulled out of the Center in their car. The armed Israeli security guards followed them in their vehicle.

Mazin went to find a taxi. Issa and I lowered the Seeds of Peace flag and took it off the flagpole. The Seeds of Peace Center for Coexistence in Jerusalem was no more.

CHAPTER FOURTEEN

FADIA TOOK ONE LOOK AT ME WHEN I GOT HOME.

"They fired you, didn't they?" she asked.

I nodded mutely.

I had never felt more broken. But for the first night in months, I slept soundly. It was over. I should have walked out two years ago. The moment they fired Jen, they had fired me.

Fadia and Mazin told the rest of my family so I would not have to. My brother Riyyad and sister Hanadi said only, "Sorry about your news, Sami," when they saw me the next day, but their eyes said more. *We told you long ago this would happen,* their eyes said. *You always have to learn the hard way?*

My cell phone rang. It was a delegation leader from Jenin. He was en route to the Allenby Bridge, accompanying three kids I had selected from refugee camps in Jenin to Seeds of Peace camp in Maine when he heard that I had been fired. "Sami, it's your decision if these kids go or not," he said. "If you say it, we will all go back."

I was tempted to tell him to do that. Let Seeds of Peace see how they could manage without me and the relationships I had built! But how could I let those kids pay the price for my shattered pride?

"You send those kids to travel outside the country, to follow their dreams, to learn about other people, to represent the Palestinian people and the human face of the conflict," I told him. "I will never build my dreams on the ruins of other people's dreams."

Supportive phone calls and e-mails poured in, from Palestinian and Israeli Seeds, their families, delegation leaders.

"We can't believe they did this to you, Sami," I heard over and over.

Ned, Jen, and other former colleagues immediately launched a campaign on my behalf, exposing how Mazin, Issa, and I had been treated. They sent petitions to the board, signed by counselors and Seeds graduates, to pressure the organization to give us respect and legal compensation. In exchange for receiving my compensation, Eyal wanted me to sign a statement guaranteeing that I would not speak negatively about Seeds of Peace. Over two months of communicating through lawyers, receiving one humiliating reply after another from "the company," I grew tired of fighting. I signed the gag order.

I dreaded seeing former friends on the street. They would gloat that the organization I had defended to them so passionately had now turned and kicked me out like a dog. Let them laugh. "Yes, they fired me," I would answer them, "because I am not like them. I will not participate in their ugly game."

I had tried to guide Seeds of Peace so that the organization would be secure and respected. I had tried to bring Seeds of Peace to the center of the people. Instead, my involvement with Seeds of Peace had placed me outside the heart of my own people. And in the end, I was outside Seeds of Peace as well.

I fell deeper and deeper into depression. I stayed in bed until noon every day, playing the last two years in my head repeatedly.

In the past, I had asked my children Nasser, Asala, and Yazin to pose like the three silhouetted children on the Seeds of Peace T-shirt and photograph them. I had been so proud of the green shirts. Those photos of my children were tainted now. So were the T-shirts. I told Fadia to throw the shirts away. I did not want to see them ever again.

I went through the motion of registering with the employment bureau so that I could be on record as looking for work and get a tax break. When the clerk saw my prison record, he told me plainly, "I don't think anyone will give you a job." I did not care. I did not even try to find one. My family could survive on my compensation money for the time being.

I rarely shaved. I spent my evenings in coffee shops playing snooker, cards, and slot machines, drinking coffee or beer until late at night. I did not care about money. I did not care about anything.

Fadia tried to be supportive but as I continued to lose my compensation money in the coffee shops, she grew angry. My father sat me down and talked to me about how I was hurting my family. I knew Fadia had asked him to. I did not want to injure those I loved, but I could not bring myself to care about anything.

My sisters' husbands asked me, as they had asked me for the past sixteen years, if I wanted to accompany them to Al Aqsa Mosque. What did I have to lose? I began to pray. I fasted on Ramadan for the first time since I was a child. Fadia was delighted. But I was not praying or fasting out of any new-found devotion to Allah. I was trying only to stop the gambling and constant state of agitation that was causing me to lash out at my wife and children.

I tried to participate in actions and activities with other peace and justice or-ganizations but found myself left with a bitter taste inside my mouth each time. They all seemed to me now to be following U.S. or Israeli agendas. Their activities were for the sake of the media only. They were not working to build a large front to achieve real peace between human beings. They were only beautifying the face of the occupation. I gave up on all the peace organizations.

On Salah el Din Street, I passed the old man who had unleashed a torrent of vitriol on Ned and me at the stationery store so many years ago. "Ah, it's Sami from Seeds of Peace!" he said, and threw his arms up in the air in mock despair. "Tell me, Sami, where is the peace?"

"I don't work for Seeds of Peace anymore."

"No, no, Sami, you will always be Seeds of Peace." He threw his arms up again. "So tell me, where is the peace?"

I walked away.

My mother picked up on the depths of my despair more than anyone else. She told all the family about a dream she had had the night before.

"I was walking on a tightrope. If I could make it to the end, I would reach heaven. If I fell, I would fall to hell. I was walking very slowly, carefully plac-ing one foot after the next, trying not to lose my balance. Sami was skipping and running ahead of me on the rope. He kept looking behind him to en-courage and guide me. 'You're doing well, *Yamma!*' 'A little to the right, *Yamma,* that's good!' I was very pleased to see Sami moving so quickly and with so much confidence on the rope leading to heaven."

I took some comfort in my mother's dream—maybe in the end, I would find my way again.

In April 2007, a few months after my mother's dream, my extended family was sitting downstairs in the salon. My mother, usually so vibrant and talkative, suddenly seemed far away. She sat in silence as the conversation swirled around her.

"*Yamma*, are you okay?" Hanadi asked her.

"Yes, yes, I'm fine!" my mother reassured her.

"Would you like to go up to your bedroom and rest?" my sister pressed.

My mother grew irritated. "What are you talking about? I am in my bedroom!"

The family's chatter stopped immediately. "No, *Yamma*," Samir said. "We're sitting downstairs."

My mother continued to protest and then submitted, allowing Hanadi to help her up the steps to her bed.

We took my mother to Hadassah hospital the next day. They performed tests and delivered the news. It was another brain tumor, rooted even deeper than the first one had been. She would be given one radiation treatment every day for twenty days.

"There's no chance of it eradicating the tumor," the doctor told us. "But God willing, we can shrink it."

The phone rang off the hook at home. My mother received calls from her brothers Mustafa in Dheisheh camp and Mousa in Lebanon. She was continuously cheerful, to us and to the callers. A few days later, my mother became incontinent. We moved her to Hanadi's home so that my sister could help keep her clean and dry. The phone continued to ring nonstop until my mother lost her ability to talk. Even then, she smiled when she heard our voices or felt our presence.

By the time the radiation began, she was unconscious. One of her children was with her at all times to keep her covered, both with the white hospital blanket and with our love. I was sitting with her after the second treatment.

"There is no God but God," she murmured, as Muslims do when they have the sense that their death is imminent. I waited anxiously. My mother returned to her deep slumber, continuing to draw and release labored breaths.

They discontinued my mother's radiation. It was not slowing the growth of the tumor, the doctors said, and was only making her grow weaker.

My mother lay in her bed. I looked at her relaxed, peaceful face. It seemed as if she was in the middle of a conversation. Had she already made connection with souls from the other world? She moved her hands very, very slowly, touching her blanket, the edge of the bed. With each contact with something physical, a flash of this world darted across her face.

My daughter Asala and Azzam's and Riyyad's daughters came that night. I could feel the girls crying, though they shed no tears. My mother entered our world briefly and touched their hands. I watched intently. In those touches, my mother was giving something to her granddaughters. Whatever she gave them, it satisfied her. There was nothing left she needed to do. She smiled and slipped back to her other world.

The next day, the hospital called us to come and say goodbye. We filled the corridors: my father, my siblings, their husbands and wives, the grandchildren, and Mariam, my father's second wife. One by one, we went in to say goodbye.

It was my turn. My mother's body was still. Her mouth was partially open. As a student, she had told Dr. Allenby that she did not intend to leave her country and go to America. "The war is not over yet!" she had proclaimed. My mother had suffered so much throughout her life. Her personal war was finally over.

I kissed her on her forehead, her right cheek, and her left cheek. "May God cover you with his mercy," I whispered. "May God put you in heaven, where you belong with the other angels." It was customary to say these words over someone on the brink of death. I had said them before. But saying them to my mother was as if I was uttering them for the first time.

Her heart stopped beating at 2 p.m. We arranged immediately for an ambulance to come and take her to Al Makassed hospital so my sisters could perform the washing rituals. They doused her body alternately with very hot water and very cold water, the traditional method to ascertain that someone was truly deceased and not merely unconscious. They washed her body with special soap and sprinkled her with henna.

We took her to Al Aqsa Mosque as the sun was setting. Word had spread quickly and my mother was beloved. Hundreds of people prayed for her. The procession took us to the cemetery. Riyyad entered the grave to perform the last rites over my mother. On the other side of the grave lay her son, my brother Azzam.

On the third day of mourning, we went to Dheisheh refugee camp to grieve with my mother's family. My uncle Mustafa's house was filled with elderly people from Zakariyya. Old men were sitting on plastic chairs on the porch and driveway and the women were inside the house. The old women came outside when we arrived, crying. "They're here," the women said as they hugged and kissed us. "*Awlad* Yusra."*

---

*Arabic for "Yusra's children."

Uncle Mustafa sat on a chair, his eyes moist. "When she was sick thirty years ago, I came to the hospital every day to feed her," he said. "This time, the army would not give me permission to visit her for even one day. I could not say goodbye."

※

I STOPPED GOING TO THE MOSQUE. I did not want to rely on prayer to curb me of the dangerous habits I had fallen into. I had to control my behavior on my own. I returned to the coffee shops, but this time, not the ones with snooker and slot machines. Instead, I sat for hours every day at the coffee shop directly inside Damascus Gate, smoking, drinking coffee, and watching people come and go from the gate. Every person I saw reminded me of someone. A cell mate from prison. A refugee from Zakariyya in Dheisheh camp. A worker from Halhoul whom I had driven to Asqalan. A compact eighteen-year-old boy with a smile and a swagger that was so much like Badawi's.

When we were eighteen, Badawi, Abbas, and I had been debating which movement to join and how best to fight for Palestine. I thought about the three of us making the bomb in my bedroom. My heart started pounding and my palms grew sweaty, as if Israeli *shabak* and soldiers were about to drag me to the Russian Compound. I had not permitted my mind to wander back to my interrogation for years, but now, the memories started flashing in front of me, my heart becoming tight as if the torture had been yesterday, rather than twenty-seven years ago.

I had always emphasized to others that I had no regrets about prison. I had not lost a decade: I had taken an action I believed in, and prison was a place where I had read, developed, and grown as a person. I told people I was grateful to prison. If I had not gotten arrested, most likely I would have either killed or been killed.

But sitting at Damascus Gate, I had to admit to myself that I had lost. Prison brought me no fruit. In prison, we had always said we were opening the way for the next generation, but the Palestinian Authority closed that way and excluded us.

My decade in prison had had a similar trajectory to my decade with Seeds of Peace. The early years of both experiences had been full of discovery and excitement. But in both places, poison had entered, threatening to kill all that was beautiful. The old prisoners had triumphed over the poison in Asqalan. In Seeds of Peace, the opposite had happened. Ten years of prison had not damaged me as deeply as Seeds of Peace had.

And what had we really accomplished in Seeds of Peace? Even in those years when my colleagues and I had been soaring in our work—had there been any lasting impact?

I thought about the kids we had once worked with. I did see inspirational young adults like Noa, Slava, Bushra, and others who were deeply involved in work for peace and justice. But out of the hundreds of Israeli and Palestinian youth who came through our program—how many of them really became leaders for peace, beyond the rhetoric? How many of them participated in the nonviolent struggle happening against the Separation Wall at Budrus and Bil'in? How many of them were standing in solidarity with the families evicted from their homes in East Jerusalem? My suspicion was: not enough. Most of the Israeli kids went to the army and became part of the occupation. Most of the Palestinian kids went to university and focused on advancing their lives. Seeds who became doctors or engineers or lawyers without being engaged long-term in peace work were no different from anyone else in their society. Unless those young people jointly stood up against occupation and against violence, hand-in-hand pushing their leaders to make real change, the dialogue had been empty.

Where was Seeds of Peace now? Tim no longer worked for Seeds of Peace. The Business Man himself was let go just months after he fired me. From what I had heard, the board replaced him with a media and PR professional. She lasted less than six months. Service learning never really took off, but separate Seeds of Peace offices in Ramallah and Tel Aviv remained. Reem was eventually fired as well. The branches on the tree we had planted were withered and dry.

Ned, Jen, Roy, Fishman, and I—we had thought we could change the world. But like my decade in prison, we lost. I lost friends, I lost years of my life, and I lost my hope for a better future.

October 2007. I sat at the Damascus Gate Café, like I had every day for months. Damascus Gate was in a bustle, as always. I looked at the constant stream of faces. People entering or exiting the *souq*. Young men in jeans, their hair slicked back, hawking goods. Old women wearing threadbare dresses made from traditional Palestinian needlepoint selling sage and vegetables. Tourists talking with excitement in every language under the sun. Religious Jews going to the Western Wall to pray. It was a cacophony of noise and a crush of humanity.

I stared at the faces. Everyone was in motion, buying, selling, entering, exiting. Everyone except me. I sat at the same table every day, smoking and drinking coffee, waiting for something. A door to open. Anything that could revive my hope. Day after day, week after week, I sat, waiting, watching faces. Maybe there was something of a donkey in me: donkeys are well known for their patience. Maybe there was something of a camel in me: camels can go hungry and thirsty for weeks. I watched the faces.

A young woman buying a glass of juice reminded me of Noa Epstein for a moment. My mind wandered back to the day Jen and I had brought Bushra's family to Noa's home for lunch, Jen's final day of work for Seeds of Peace. In that one afternoon were the echoes of everything else I had done with Seeds of Peace: watching Palestinian and Israeli kids rolling down sand dunes at Yahel, screaming with laughter; seeing the youth engage in difficult, heart-wrenching discussions but refusing to walk away because it was too important; witnessing the kids speak out courageously in front of classmates and teachers, convincing them that the other side was every bit as human as they were and had the exact same rights and needs and fears; sharing the warmth and beauty of each other's homes, families, and holidays; standing by Aseel, his family, and each other in their and our hardest moments. Making sure, through dialogue or video or e-mails, that their stories were heard by those who would ordinarily not have any opportunity to hear them—and by making sure they were heard, knowing that they were changing someone, changing something.

Occupation did not end the day that Noa's and Bushra's families had lunch together. It did not stop the next person who was determined to carry out a bombing on a bus. It did not stand in the way of the tanks or shootings, stop the Separation Wall from being erected, or halt any of the other horrible attacks and injustices.

Even so, their relationship, what it stood for, and what it took to be built and maintained was nothing short of incredible. And no less wondrous was everything that afternoon reminded me of—everything that the Seeds, my colleagues, and I had accomplished together.

I had lost more than I could assess. But there were some things that no one could take away from me.

Khalas, I said to myself. How long can I sit on the sidelines, watching people, observing the flow of their movement, staring at the faces? All of them with work, family, school, all of them with children or mothers or fathers or grandchildren.

I am a part of these people.

Yallah, Sami, move. Stop being a poor example for your children, for everyone who sees you sitting here, day in and day out. The circle of blood is continuing; it is not acceptable for you to just sit and watch it.

Hundreds of faces. All of them in motion.

I ground out my cigarette and paid for my cup of coffee. There was still work to do.

I walked down the steps, into the stream of humanity, the din of the voices. Into the streets of the Old City of Jerusalem. I stepped back into the midst of my people.

Take Me to Al-Qastal

By Sami Al Jundi
Translated by Amal Eqeiq

There, in the cradle of yearning
Where the birds circle in cheerless skies
in the pine forests,
There rest the souls of the ancients
Did you ask the Swallow, my friend,
About Al-Qastal?

From a hill looking over Deir Yassin
Where love was first born
Thousands of years ago
Before the birth of Christ
Before the budding of jasmine
By the cradle of the goldfinch
Be sure to ask about Al-Qastal.

A deep valley
A mystifying magic and a nectar of secrets
A flock of pigeons and a nightingale
And the remains of a forgotten village and a cross
Ruins of a Babylonian minaret
There, where the moon is near
And our first concern is
Love and Al-Qastal.

Take me to Al-Qastal
Take me to the beautiful grave
Take me to my last home
And load me up with the tragedies of the Arabs
And all the fragrance of the ancestors
My home is the prettiest
My grave is the largest
My path is to Al-Qastal.

Sami and his family in their home in the Old City of Jerusalem in August 2010. Top, from left to right: Asala, Fadia, Sami, Nasser. Bottom, from left to right: Mera, Yazan. *Courtesy of Sami Al Jundi.*

ACKNOWLEDGMENTS

There are many people who were a part of this book, in so many different ways.

Carol Montgomery, Beth Martin Quittman, and Carol Grosman read and advised on early drafts of the book proposal.

George Greenfield and Moira Sullivan at CreativeWell went above and beyond their duty as literary agents to provide salient guidance on the development of the initial chapters.

Ronit Avni and Julia Bacha made sure we had whatever we asked for, be it access to peruse video footage or copies of *Encounter Point.* Nahanni Rous generously shared thoughts and concerns about the manuscript.

Ziad Abbas helped with research about the depopulation of Zakariyya and the wall around Dheisheh camp, and Sahar Francis assisted in research regarding prisoners in Israeli jails. Ibrahim Muhawi reviewed and edited translations of Sami's poems. John Asfour and Carolyn Forché generously gave permission to use their translations of Mahmoud Darwish's poems.

Wendy Pearlman endured endless, often ill-timed e-mails probing for background information or confirmation of facts.

Karam Dana reviewed the entire manuscript, offering crucial edits regarding the cultural, historical, political, social, and religious contexts in which this book is embedded.

Dorothy Zellner and Doreen Shapiro caught more misspelled words and misplaced commas than I care to admit! And much more than that, they provided constant support and insight.

Amal Eqeiq and Samer Al Saber did more than answer scores of questions, translate poetry, and edit dozens of footnotes (or shall we call them foodnotes?)—they all but held my hand during huge portions of the writing and editing.

Our wonderful editor, Ruth Baldwin, demonstrated not only excitement for the project but offered wise guidance every step of the way. Tamara Issak jumped on board with great enthusiasm in the eleventh hour, tying together dozens of loose ends. Sandra Beris guided us through the production process with grace and patience, and Antoinette Smith's level of attention to the smallest of details while copyediting was nothing short of amazing.

We are enormously grateful to each and every one of you.

There are those, of course, to whom "thanks" feel inadequate.

To the members of the OWMB: Roy Sharon, Adam Shapiro, Jared Fishman, Larry Malm, Huwaida Arraf, Jethro Berkman, Mike Wallach—we hope we have reflected here a bit of your experiences as well and that you will continue to "find the beauty." We will always feel proud of what we accomplished together.

To Ned Lazarus—Sami's original partner and our brother. So much of this would not have happened without you—in so many ways. We are both eternally grateful.

To Sami's flesh-and-blood brothers and sisters and Abu Samir—you supported Sami through good and bad, and along the way, took in all us stray Americans, treating us as nothing less than members of the Al Jundi family.

And finally, to Fadia. Sami's wife and Jen's sister. For teaching Jen how to make *waraq dawali*. And for putting up with Sami.

We thank you all.

Sami Al Jundi
Jen Marlowe

THE PRISON READING LIST
OF SAMI AL JUNDI

This is a partial list of the hundreds of books that Sami read during his ten years in Israeli prison.

100 Years of Solitude by Gabriel García Márquez

Aeneid by Virgil

Arab Nationalism Between the Reality of Separation and the Aspiration for Unity by Munir Shafiq

A Tale of Two Cities by Charles Dickens

Beware of Pity by Stefan Zweig

The Bread Vendor by Xavier de Montepin

Bridge of Sighs by Michel Zevaco

The Brothers Karamazov by Fyodor Dostoevsky

The Call of the Wild by Jack London

Confessions by Jean-Jacques Rosseau

Crime and Punishment by Fyodor Dostoevsky

Dawn of Islam by Ahmad Amin

Doctor Zhivago by Boris Pasternak

Fathers and Sons by Ivan Turgenev

Gone with the Wind by Margaret Mitchell

Grapes of Wrath by John Steinbeck

How the Steel Was Tempered by Nikolai Ostrovsky

Huckleberry Finn by Mark Twain

The Hungry Stones by Rabindranath Tagore

The Idiot by Fyodor Dostoevsky

The Iliad by Homer

Incoherence of the Incoherence by Ibn Rushd

The Incoherence of the Philosophers by Imam Ghazali

Letters from a Father to His Daughter by Jawaharlal Nehru

Martin Luther King Jr. speeches

The Mother by Maksim Gorky

New Testament

Notes from Underground by Fyodor Dostoevsky

The Odyssey by Homer

On War by General Carl von Clausewitz

The Palestinian Issue and the Political Projects for Resolution
    by Mahdi Abd Al-Hadi

Pedagogical Poem by Anton Makarenko

Prisoner of Zenda by Anthony Hope

Qur'an

The Sea Wolf by Jack London

The Social Contract by Jean-Jacques Rousseau

Sophie's World by Jostein Gardner

Spirit of the Laws by Baron de Montesquieu

Strategy: The Indirect Approach by Basil Liddell Hart

Thus Spake Zarathustra by Friedrich Nietzsche

Torah

War and Peace by Leo Tolstoy

White Fang by Jack London

GLOSSARY

꧁꧂

The first time a word, phrase, or term is encountered in the book, the explanation can be found in a footnote. If it is used more than once, this glossary is intended as a reminder of the definition.

Abu: Arabic for "Father." In Arabic, parents are usually called "Mother of" or "Father of" the firstborn son.

Abu Ammar: Yasser Arafat's nom de guerre. Arafat was a founder of Fatah and was chairman of the PLO.

Ahlan: Shorter, less formal version of *ahlah wa sahlan,* meaning "welcome."

Ahlan wa sahlan: "Welcome!" in Arabic.

Al Buraq: Winged horselike creature that, according to the Qur'an, traveled in a single night from Mecca to Jerusalem and back with the Prophet Muhammad on its back.

Al hamduli'llah: "Praise be to God."

Al Manara: A roundabout in the center of downtown Ramallah; literally means "the lighthouse."

Al-Muqata'ah: Arafat's compound.

Al-Quds: The Arabic name for Jerusalem.

Allah: Arabic for "God."

Allah yerhamo: "God have mercy on him"; said when someone has died. *Allah yerhamha* is the feminine equivalent and *Allah yerhamhum* is the plural.

Allahu Akbar! God is greater!

Ariel Sharon: Israel's defense minister during the 1982 Lebanon War. An Israeli government commission determined to hold Sharon personally responsible for the massacres in the Sabra and Shatila refugee camps. He was also considered one of the most enthusiastic political supporters of the Israeli settlement movement. In 1998, he became Israel's foreign minister. His September 28, 2000, visit to Haram al Sharif/Temple Mount sparked the Second Intifada. He was elected as the Prime Minister of Israel in February 2001.

Ashdod: Ashdod was built in 1956 approximately four and a half miles northwest of Isdud, a Palestinian town that was depopulated during the 1948 war. Palestinians still commonly refer to Ashdod as Isdud.

Ashkelon: The Israeli city built on what was al-Majdal/Asqalan before 1948.

Assalamu 'alaikum: Arabic greeting, meaning "Peace be upon you." Usually responded to with *Wa 'alaikum assalaam,* meaning: "And peace upon you!"

Collaborator: Term used to mean a Palestinian who secretly works with the Israeli military, often informing on other Palestinians.

Dabkeh: A traditional Palestinian dance, often performed at weddings.

Damascus Gate: One of the entrances/exits to the Old City.

DCO: District Coordinating Office.

Democratic Front: Democratic Front for the Liberation of Palestine (DFLP), a Marxist-Leninist movement in the PLO.

Eid: Muslim holiday, after Ramadan and after the Haj, which is the pilgrimage to Mecca, considered the fifth pillar of Islam.

Ein Jedi: Called Ein Gedi in Hebrew and English, a desert oasis next to the Dead Sea.

Erez: The main checkpoint/border separating Gaza from Israel.

Fatah: Largest movement in the PLO. Means "victory" and is also a reverse acronym for *Harakat al-Tahrir al-Watani al-Falestini,* Arabic for "Palestinian National Liberation Movement."

Fattaheen: Plural form of *fattah,* a traditional healer, fortune-teller, or someone who deals in black magic.

Fedayeen: Literally translated as "those who self-sacrifice," the term is used to mean "freedom fighters."

Finjan: The small cup used to drink Turkish coffee. Plural is *fanajeen.*

French Hill: A neighborhood in northeast Jerusalem.

Green Line: Refers to the 1949 armistice lines demarcating the border between Israel and the West Bank.

Habibi: Arabic for "my beloved" for a male; *habibti* is the female equivalent.

Habibna: Arabic for "our beloved."

Haj: Usually used to refer to someone who has completed the pilgrimage to Mecca. *Hajeh* (female) or *Haj* (male) can also be used to show respect to an elder.

Hamas: Acronym for the Arabic words for Islamic Resistance Movement, founded in 1987.

Haraam: Arabic for "forbidden" in a religious sense, used to mean "not right" or "have mercy."

Haram Al Sharif: Arabic for "the Noble Sanctuary"; the compound includes the Dome of the Rock and the Al Aqsa Mosque. Jews call it the Temple Mount and believe it to be the site of the First and Second Temples.

Harakat al-Tahrir al-Watani al-Falestini: Arabic for "Palestinian National Liberation Movement." The reverse acronym is Fatah, the largest movement in the PLO.

Herod's Gate: Another of the entrances/exits to the Old City.

Hudna: Arabic for "temporary truce," or "cease-fire."

Ibn Yusra: Son of Yusra. The plural is *Awlad Yusra*, children of Yusra.

IDF: Acronym for Israel Defense Forces; the Israeli military.

Iftar: The evening meal that breaks the daytime Ramadan fast.

Inside '48: Signifies Palestinians who live inside the 1948 borders of Israel, as distinguished from Palestinians living in the Occupied Territories. Roughly 20 percent of Israel's citizens are Palestinian. The community of Palestinians inside Israel are referred to by different names, often with political implications, including "Arabs of '48," "Arab-Israelis," "Palestinians inside Israel" (or simply "Palestinians inside"), and "Palestinian citizens of Israel."

Intifada: Literally "shaking off," used to mean "uprising." The First Intifada, a popular revolt in the West Bank and Gaza against Israeli occupation, started in December 1987 when an Israeli truck collided with vans carrying Palestinian workers, killing four at Gaza's Erez crossing. The Second Intifada was sparked by Ariel Sharon's September 28, 2000, visit to Haram Al Sahrif/Temple Mount.

Insha'allah: Arabic for "God willing."

Islamic Jihad: A Palestinian resistance movement fighting for Palestinian sovereignty and a potential Islamic state. Jihad in this sense refers to military struggle.

Khalas: Arabic for "enough" or "stop."

Knesset: Israeli Parliament.

Kuffiyeh: Traditional Arab headdress or scarf.

Meir Kahane: Ultranationalist American-Israeli rabbi who founded Kach, an extreme right-wing Israeli political party, now illegal.

Likud: A right-wing Israeli political party.

Lions' Gate: Another of the entrances/exits to the Old City.

Mabruk: Arabic for "congratulations."

Maqlubeh: Palestinian specialty made with chicken, rice, and fried vegetables such as cauliflower or eggplant; literally means "upside down" because of how it is served.

Maskeen: "Poor thing"; plural is *masakeen*.

Mlukhiyyeh: Mallow leaves, cooked often as a soup with a taste and consistency somewhere between okra and spinach.

Muhaqeq: Arabic for "interrogator." Refers to *shabak* officers involved in interrogation. Plural is *muhaqeqeen*.

Mukhtar: The head of a village or local community.

Nakba: "Catastrophe," used to describe the 1948 war and following displacement.

Narghile: Glass-based water pipe or hookah, also called *arghile*.

Neve Shalom-Wahat al-Salam: Hebrew and Arabic for "Oasis of Peace." A village, jointly established by Jewish and Palestinian Arab citizens of Israel, that is engaged in educational work for peace, equality, and understanding between the two peoples.

Normalization: The concept of normalizing relations with Israel both politically and culturally. It has a negative connotation among most Palestinians and Arabs, with the belief that one should not normalize relations while still living under conditions of occupation and inequality.

Orient House: The PLO headquarters in Jerusalem.

PFLP: The Popular Front for the Liberation of Palestine.

PLO: Palestine Liberation Organization, founded in 1964 and recognized in 1974 in Rabat as the sole legitimate representative of the Palestinian people. The PLO is made up of multiple factions.

Qumbaz: A traditional Palestinian robe worn by men.

Ramadan: The ninth month of the Muslim calendar. It is believed to be the month in which the initial verses of the Qur'an were revealed to the Prophet Muhammad. Observant Muslims fast from sunup to sundown during the holy Ramadan month.

Red Crescent: Part of the International Red Cross and Red Crescent Movement.

Sabah el khair: Arabic for "good morning."

Sahat al-tahqeeq: Arabic for "interrogation courtyard."

Salaam: Arabic for "Peace."

Sawt al-Falestin: Arabic for "Voice of Palestine," a radio station in Ramallah.

Sawt Ath-Thawra Al-Falestiniya: Arabic for "Voice of the Palestinian Revolution," a radio station broadcast in the '70s out of Baghdad.

Seder: Ritualized meal on the first two nights of the Jewish holiday *Pesach*, or Passover.

Separation Wall: Construction on the barrier began in 2002. Israelis often refer to the barrier as the Security Fence to emphasize its intention to keep out suicide bombers; Palestinians usually refer to it as the Separation Wall or Apartheid Wall to emphasize its intention to enclose Palestinians. Much of its route cuts deep inside the West Bank, which has led to criticism that it was intended to be a land grab. The International Court of Justice used the term *wall* in its 2004 advisory opinion, which stated that its route was illegal and called for it to be removed.

Shabab: Arabic for "youth," equivalent of the American "the guys."

Shabak: Hebrew acronym for *Sherut ha-Bitachon ha-Klali,* translated as "General Security Service," also known as "Shin Bet."

Shabibeh: The pro-Fatah youth movement.

Shaheed: "Martyr." The female is *shaheedah* and the plural is *shuhada.*

Shari'a: The canonical law of Islam.

Sheikh: Literally meaning "elder," is used to signify someone wise or a scholar of Islam.

Shikhrur: Hebrew for "release."

Shukran: Arabic for "thank you."

Sidi: Arabic for "Grandpa."

Souq: Arabic for "market."

Taboun: Flatbread.

Um: Arabic for "Mother." In Arabic, parents are usually called "Mother of" or "Father (Abu) of" the firstborn son.

UNRWA: United Nations Relief and Works Agency for Palestine Refugees. UNWRA provides assistance, protection, and advocacy for Palestine refugees in Jordan, Lebanon, Syria, and the occupied Palestinian territory.

Uskut: "Be quiet" or "Shut your mouth." The feminine equivalent is *Uskuti!*

Wadi Joz: A neighborhood of East Jerusalem, close to the Old City.

Wadi Nar: Arabic for "Fire Valley," a steep and twisty road that connects Abu Dis to Bethlehem.

Wallah: "By God."

Waraq dawali: Stuffed grape leaves.

Western Wall: A section of the retaining wall of the Temple Mount from the Second Temple period. The Western Wall is the most sacred site in Judaism. Often referred to as the Wailing Wall, because it is considered a site of mourning over the destruction of the Second Temple.

Ya Allah! Arabic for "My God!"

Ya kalb: Arabic for "you dog," used as an insult.

Ya zalameh: Colloquial Palestinian equivalent to "man" or "dude."

Yaba: Arabic for "Papa" or "Dad."

Yallah: "Let's go!" or "Come on!" in Arabic.

Yamma: Arabic for "Mom" or "Mama."

Yitzhak Rabin: Prime minister of Israel and chairman of the center-left Labor Party. Assassinated on November 4, 1995, by Yigal Amir, an Israeli Jew.

Za'atar: Dried, wild thyme.

Ziir: A large ceramic vase.